The Idiom of Drama

The Idiom of Drama

By THOMAS F. VAN LAAN

CORNELL UNIVERSITY PRESS

Ithaca and London

Standard Book Number 8014-0543-2

Library of Congress Catalog Card Number 72-87025

PRINTED IN THE UNITED STATES OF AMERICA
BY VAIL-BALLOU PRESS, INC.

For my wife

Preface

To be a poet means essentially to see, but mark well, to see in such a way that whatever is seen is perceived by the audience just as the poet saw it.

—Henrik Ibsen, "Speech to the Norwegian Students, September 10, 1874"

A play is the product of a creative mind viewing experience with the aid of a highly sensitive instrument, the potential dramatic form. The dramatist, in shaping his selected material into an organized whole, exploits the specific devices that characterize his medium, appropriating some that have been used before, adapting others, creating new ones. In so doing, he fashions a unique entity expressing its own particular reality. He discovers and records a meaning that did not previously exist and that exists now only in the delicate balances of his completed artifact. This meaning may consist of the special circumstances of a meticulously delineated concrete situation; it may inhere in a carefully wrought formal design; it may lend itself to the formation of a conceptual abstraction. Whatever its particular constitution, however, it is this meaning that the performed play instills in the consciousness of the spectators who witness it.

This book is concerned with the potential dramatic form.

Since it seeks to examine the process by which the "poet" sees "in such a way that whatever is seen is perceived by the audience just as the poet saw it," it may well be regarded as an elaborate footnote to Ibsen's observation. By "poet" Ibsen meant, of course, the dramatic poet, whether he writes in verse or prose, and this study is an examination of the dramatic poet's peculiar "idiom," the formal devices by means of which he compels his spectators to view the staged experience in one perspective rather than another. More precisely, this study seeks to define the various devices, verbal and nonverbal, that constitute the dramatic form and to show how these devices, singly or in combination, create the kinds of meaning that the spectator experiences while he is watching a play.

The book is divided into four parts. Part I consists of two chapters of an introductory nature which define in a general way the peculiar blend of words and nonverbal signs that make up the dramatic medium; it focuses on the chief limitation of dramatic speech—the absence of a single expressive voice—and the corresponding compensation provided by the aural and visual qualities of drama. This section ends with a distinction between a play's two "levels": the immediate action, or concrete situation, and the action of depth, or the accumulated implications that endow the concrete situation with more than local significance. Part II examines the immediate action in greater detail by considering the various means through which the dramatist defines his characters. Part III then examines the action of depth; it describes and illustrates the various expository, stylistic, and structural devices that establish a play's more abstract and symbolic level of meaning. Part IV attempts a synthesis by treating what I call the "final fusion"; this section studies the organization of the separate devices and the effect it has on the spectator's response to individual details and to the dramatic experience as a whole.

Three features of the book require special comment. First, many—indeed most—of the devices that I isolate, define, and illustrate are by no means peculiar to the dramatic form but are characteristic of other literary forms as well. Nevertheless, after the two opening chapters, and with the exception of occasional remarks such as those on the visual extension of verbal imagery, I make no attempt to distinguish between drama and other genres. This omission makes it possible to avoid constant and pointless reminders that the reader can expect to meet this or that verbal or structural device in a novel or poem as well as a play. Second, my intention is to be as thorough as possible in surveying the many ways in which the dramatist creates meaning, and therefore of necessity some of the discussion is fairly elementary. But this quality of the book is, I believe, confined to its opening chapters; and I have endeavored to give the discussion of elementary principles new interest through the concrete examples that illustrate them.

The third feature requiring special comment has to do with these concrete examples. In order to demonstrate that the devices I isolate are characteristic of drama in general, I have selected my examples from more than one period and style. In order to gain greater coherence and to avoid creating the impression that any given play specializes in one kind of device, I have tried to use the same plays for my examples throughout. As a result, though I occasionally introduce brief analyses of other plays because they best illustrate the topic under discussion, most of the concrete illustrations are drawn from three primary texts: Aeschylus' *Oresteia*, Shakespeare's *Hamlet*, and Ibsen's *Rosmersholm*. This feature of the book has given it an additional dimension: the examination of dramatic form is carried on principally by means of progressing analyses of these three plays.

My primary text for the *Oresteia* is the translation by Richmond Lattimore in Volume I of *The Complete Greek Tragedies*, edited by David Grene and Richmond Lattimore (Chicago: University of Chicago Press, 1959); quotations are by permission of the Press and the translator. For the Greek text I have used the Loeb Classical Library *Aeschylus,* Volume II (London: William Heinemann, 1930). Quotations from *Hamlet* and all other plays by Shakespeare are from *William Shakespeare: The Complete Works,* edited by Peter Alexander (London: Collins, 1951). The quotations from *Rosmersholm* are my own translations of the text of the play in Volume V of *Samlede Digterverker,* edited by Didrik Arup Seip (8th edition; Oslo: Gyldendal Norsk Forlag, 1937), though I have occasionally referred to the translations by Charles Archer and Una Ellis-Fermor; all other references to Ibsen's plays or to his drafts are to *The Works of Henrik Ibsen,* edited by William Archer (New York: Charles Scribner's Sons, 1911–1912).

Portions of my book have already been published in different form. An article on the structure of *Rosmersholm* appeared in *Modern Drama* (1963). The material on Synge's *Riders to the Sea* in Chapters 2 and 7 has been condensed from an article on the play's form that appeared in *Drama Survey* (1964). The material in Chapter 5 on the repetition of ironic reversal in *Hamlet* is a slightly different version of an article in *Studies in English Literature* (1966). I am grateful to the editors of these journals for permission to reprint.

To the Research Council of Rutgers University I am indebted for grants-in-aid which supported my research and which gave me the free time to complete the book. I am grateful to Anna Benjamin of Douglass College, who kindly reviewed my assertions about the Greek text of the *Oresteia,* and to Hans Aarsleff of Princeton, who gave me similar assistance with the Dano-Norwegian text of *Rosmersholm;* both helped me avoid serious blunders and gave me valuable suggestions. I am also deeply grateful to those who gave generously of their time in offering me encouragement and valuable criticism at various stages of composition: Travis M. Bogard, Terry Comito, Victor Doyno, Robert Lyons, Donald C. Mell, Jr., and Elliot Rubinstein. They purged the book of innumerable errors of fact and judgment and infelicities of style; for those that remain I am fully responsible. My chief debt is to my wife, whose constant encouragement and stubborn refusal to accept nonsense can never be adequately measured or repaid.

THOMAS F. VAN LAAN

New Brunswick, New Jersey
May 1969

Contents

CONTENTS

Part I: The Medium

1. The Limitations of Dramatic Speech

There is still a third difference—the manner in which each of these objects may be imitated. For the medium being the same, and the objects the same, the poet may imitate by narration—in which case he can either take another personality as Homer does, or speak in his own person, unchanged—or he may present all his characters as living and moving before us.

—Aristotle, *Poetics*

In *Each in His Own Way*, Pirandello attempts to invalidate certain common assumptions by juxtaposing three disparate versions of "reality." For some time after the curtain rises everything seems straightforward enough; *Each in His Own Way* looks like a typical example of formal realism, and as such it invites the audience to regard the dramatized experience as equivalent to reality. But suddenly, at what should be the end of the first act, the "play" turns out to be a play-within-a-play and thus only the first phase of a rather complicated action. When the curtain falls on the "first act," it rises again at once. The stage now represents the lobby of the theater; Pirandello, as all dramatists must wish to do at one time or another, has provided his own audience—which here enters to talk over the events and characters it has just witnessed. In an elaborate stage direction preceding this episode, Pirandello explains his intentions. The scene in the lobby, he declares, "will show what was first presented on the stage as life itself to be a fiction of art; and the substance of the comedy will accordingly be pushed back, as it were, into a secondary plane of actuality or reality." Further complications result from the presence in the onstage audience of a small group of "real" people who are the prototypes for the characters in the play-within-a-play. "Their appearance," Pirandello adds, "suddenly and violently establishes a plane of reality still closer to real life, leaving the spectators who are discussing the fictitious reality of the staged play on a plane midway between." All this, however, is preliminary to his main intention: "In the interlude at the end of the second act these three planes of reality will come into conflict with one another, as the participants in the drama of real life attack the participants in the comedy, the SPECTATORS, meantime, trying to interfere." [1]

This information enables the reader to comprehend Pirandello's understanding of his dramatic design. But plays are experienced by audiences, not readers, and the audience in the theater necessarily lacks access to the dramatist's bracketed prose. As the existence of this stage direction attests, Pirandello evidently felt that the distinctions and conflicts it describes are imperfectly realized in the dramatic situation and require emphasizing if they are to be fully experienced. The possible obscurity of the play's design is only part of the difficulty, however, for even if the spectator should grasp this design, he must still do without the "planes of reality" terminology with which Pirandello himself understands it. There will always remain, then, an unbridged gap between Pirandello's own precise sense of his play's action and that which can be conveyed on a stage.

Pirandello's ill fortune results in part from the nature of his form: he has tried to juggle illusion and reality with one hand

[1] Trans. Arthur Livingston, in *Naked Masks*, ed. Eric Bentley (New York: Dutton, 1952), pp. 311–312.

tied down by the leading strings of a restricted medium. His stage direction represents an attempt to escape from his difficulties by adopting a device more characteristic of other, nondramatic, literary forms: the dominant voice that serves as an agency of discursive meaning. This device is indeed crucial in much literature. It permeates poetry, fiction, and the essay, where, though it sometimes fulfills its purpose clumsily, by telling the reader what he should believe about a character, event, or the experience as a whole, it ordinarily exists only as a specific tone that establishes for the reader a point of view, that compels him, in other words, to look at the recorded experience in one perspective rather than another. Yet even this sophisticated version of the dominant voice is alien to drama. In drama, as Aristotle's distinction reminds us, every word the spectator hears is spoken by one of the characters "living and moving" on the stage. As Stephen Dedalus would add, "The artist, like the God of creation, remains within or behind or beyond or above his handiwork, invisible, refined out of existence, indifferent, paring his fingernails." [2] Though Joyce's Stephen exaggerates, the passage epitomizes the characteristic of drama that is here most pertinent, its apparent objectivity. Drama lacks the interpretive, controlling voice of poetry and fiction. In its place single speech follows single speech, each stemming from one of the characters onstage. And for the most part, no character ever understands the full significance of the total situation in which he is involved.

This condition of drama is, of course, one of its virtues, for it makes possible the continual "dramatic" irony that is a hallmark of the form. But it also raises some highly significant questions. How can the dramatist, working in such an apparently objective medium, manage to control his spectators' responses so that they ultimately see his play as he sees it himself? What authority exists in any given dramatic speech? Does the dramatist have any

[2] James Joyce, *A Portrait of the Artist as a Young Man* (New York: Viking Press, 1956), p. 215.

means by which he can explicitly define for his spectators the attitudes they must assume either for the moment or toward the action as a whole? The first question is the one of greatest importance, but its answer depends in part on a prior consideration of the other two.

Pirandello's difficulty suggests that no single speech has any real authority in itself and that therefore the dramatist's direct intervention is an impossibility. But Pirandello's difficulty arises to some extent because, though he discredits the "reality" of formal realism, he nevertheless adheres to its conventions. Despite its bold attack on common assumptions, *Each in His Own Way* attempts to convey its point in a dramatic mode whose primary characteristic is its fidelity to the familiar surfaces of everyday life. This kind of drama restricts itself to speech that imitates ordinary conversation and allows its characters to say only what actual human beings would be inclined to say in similar circumstances. This restriction threatens to put much of the play outside the direct control exerted by the dramatist's language. The dramatist will obviously find little opportunity for explicit interpretation of any kind, and, more important, he will not even be able to establish with precision the signs that imply a particular view of individual characters or events or of the whole experience. Most of the speeches he writes will necessarily lack a prescriptive rhythm, and when their content or context does not clearly indicate how they ought to be delivered, they will have to be interpreted by the actor. The actor's gestures and movements, instead of being defined by the spoken text, will be merely suggested by it or described in ignorable stage directions. Visual symbols like the setting or lighting will depend on the designer's creative reading of a limited word picture or the technician's response to an unverbalized sense of mood or atmosphere. Structural effects such as tempo will take their origin not from concrete verbal effects but from the director's conception of the dramatic design.

But formal realism is, of course, a rather late development in drama, originating with Ibsen's prose plays and the naturalistic experiments of Emile Zola and his followers. It belongs to one branch of a large family, and some of its cousins offer a vastly different impression of the possibilities in dramatic speech. The plays of Ibsen's predecessors, and of those dramatists of the twentieth century who, like T. S. Eliot, have rebelled against formal realism, reflect an art in which language predominates. In these plays most of the implications will very likely be spelled out—or embodied—in the dialogue itself.

Everyman well illustrates this more explicit technique. All effects that would seem to belong to the province of performance already exist clearly articulated in the words of the text. The aural impressions produced by the tone and stress of the actor's voice are controlled not by his own interpretation but by the rhythm of the verse in which the play is written. The actor's gestures, movements, and appearance are described in the speech as well as communicated visually. When, for example, the plot calls upon Everyman to mortify his flesh with the scourge of penance, he not only does so but accompanies his action with a spoken version of it and of its significance:

> In the name of the Holy Trynyte
> My body sore punysshyd shall be.
> Take this, body, for the synne of the flesshe!   [ll. 611–613].[3]

Larger aspects of meaning are equally explicit. The import assigned to the characters and events, which here is allegorical in nature, is clearly defined in the speeches that embody them. As part of its argument the play teaches that man's friends and relations will desert him in his utmost need; consequently, the conceptual personifications Fellowship, Kindred, and Cousin all ap-

---

[3] All quotations from *Everyman* are from the text established by Joseph Quincy Adams, *Chief Pre-Shakespearean Dramas* (Cambridge, Mass.: Houghton Mifflin, 1924), pp. 288–303.

pear for the sole purpose of revealing the falsity of their professed allegiance to Everyman once they learn that he needs
someone to accompany him on his pilgrimage to the grave. One
of them, Cousin, makes his part in this pattern clear in the dialogue: "I wyll deceyue you in your moost nede" (l. 358). And
Everyman himself then sums up the episodes in which they all
appear:

> Howe sholde I be mery or gladde?
> For fayre promyses men to me make,
> But when I haue moost nede they me forsake.
> I am deceyued; that maketh me sadde   [ll. 369–372].

Even the emotional design of the play reveals this tendency toward fully explicit articulation. If the character's feelings are of
importance, they will be expressed verbally, as Everyman here
specifies his sadness. Thus the emotional dimension of Everyman's entire progress is openly stressed by the language and its
rhythms at the same time that it is conveyed by the actor's representation of his suffering and relief. *Everyman* is by no means a
simple play, for it contains rich ironies and extremely subtle effects of structural contrast; but all of them are defined by language, as in a poem. The primary function of the nonverbal effects is to reinforce the speeches rather than to supersede them or
to establish aspects of the play that they do not express. In the
tradition of which *Everyman* is an example, then, the dramatist,
while perhaps not intervening directly, is able to provide at all
times an exact verbal equivalent of the implications arising from
the visible action and the details that constitute it.[4]

---

[4] My distinction between the two techniques has been influenced by
Harley Granville-Barker, *The Use of the Drama* (Princeton, N.J.:
Princeton University Press, 1945), pp. 43–48, and by Raymond Williams'
studies of the relationship between text and performance in drama; see
his *Drama from Ibsen to Eliot* (London: Chatto and Windus, 1952),
chapter i, and *Drama in Performance* (London: F. Muller, 1954). The
English tragedies of the mid-sixteenth century represent an even more

This distinction between the two styles of drama provides one answer to the original questions. The characters of a play written in the explicit style are extremely reliable. They possess an unusual awareness of their own feelings and motives and those of others, and they are often equally knowledgeable about the significance of their specific actions. If what they say is intended to deceive—either themselves or others—this fact will somehow be noted in the text. Consequently, the dialogue of this kind of play tends to have a great deal of authority. Nevertheless, certain qualifications are in order. *Everyman* is obviously an extreme; other plays written in the explicit style, such as those of Shakespeare, grant far more autonomy to nonverbal effects and to unverbalized implications, and much of the import of these plays naturally remains beyond the scope of explicit statement. Furthermore, though a play like *Everyman* tends to define the import of each of its details, it does not always articulate the import that emerges when these separate details combine. The explicit style does not, therefore, provide a full verbalization of a play's meaning. But it does guarantee a precise indication of the majority of the signs that convey this meaning to the spectators.

A fuller answer to the questions about the authority in dramatic speech and the dramatist's possible intervention requires the development of a further and quite different distinction, one which has to do with the kinds of characters available to the dra-

---

extreme version of the language-oriented play than does *Everyman:* "Retrospective reports and soliloquies, deliberations on things to be done in the future, emotional speeches reflecting a character's state of mind in response to a situation, detailed discussions of the pros and cons of a course of action, these are the normal methods employed; it is not the immediate event, not life lived in the present moment, that are put before us, but what has gone before and what is still to come, while anything truly dramatic, anything that gives a sense of immediacy and actuality, seems almost to be outlawed from the drama" (Wolfgang Clemen, *English Tragedy before Shakespeare,* trans. T. S. Dorsch [New York: Barnes and Noble, 1961], p. 24).

9

matist. One kind is the individualized character who has some stake in the action, and who is therefore more important as a being capable of acting and suffering and speaking than as a source of information or interpretation. What this kind of character says is of interest primarily for what it reveals about the speaker but only secondarily for what it contributes to the explanation of other characters or of the situation in which all the characters are linked. When Kroll, in Ibsen's *Rosmersholm*, describes the local "radical" movement as "this pernicious, subversive, and disintegrative spirit of the times" (I, p. 131), his extreme bitterness has no objective validity until later events partially confirm him. Yet the spectators respond to the speech at once as a revelation of Kroll's own adherence to a kind of bigotry that brands all opposition with the most incriminating labels of the day. Before the speech of an individualized character like Kroll can establish a point of view, the audience must extract from his speech the inherent bias that gives him individuality. The spectators must note not only what is said but also who says it, why it is said, how it is received by other characters, and how it relates to the whole context. The speech of the individualized character consists only of dramatic statements. It can establish meaning only through its complicated relationship to the larger design of which it is but a part.

In contrast to the individualized character is the speaker of a more functional nature. Of this sort are the Greek chorus and messenger, the frequently unnamed and unidentifiable but highly informative spokesmen who hover on the periphery of the main action in Elizabethan drama, and, more recently, the *raisonneurs* of Pirandello (when he uses them) and the narrators of Brecht. The functional figure is less involved in the action than the other characters; he is usually thinly developed and nameless; he often belongs to a cohesive group. The spectators can scarcely be interested in the functional figure for himself; they respond instead to what he says about the characters and events that do interest them. Since the functional figure is usually the only source of the information he is introduced to convey, the spectators tend to accept his statements as reliable. In so doing, they also tend to accept the attitudes and interpretations that accompany his factual information. In contrast to the dramatic statement of the individualized character, the speech of the functional figure amounts to expository statement; through it the dramatist can address his spectators more or less directly. *Everyman* again provides a useful illustration because it concludes with a summation by a "Doctor," a man well learned in theology, who has not been seen before. He speaks with the authority of his profession, his anonymity, his placement at the very end of the action, and his ability to define for the less perceptive the clear intellectual argument just enacted:

> he that hath his accounte hole and sounde,
> Hye in heuen he shall be crounde   [ll. 916–917].

When Ibsen's Kroll speaks, we wonder; but when the Doctor of *Everyman* speaks, we had better listen.

Since the Doctor of *Everyman* is so useful, and since similar functional figures occur frequently in drama, this device needs to be examined in more detail. For its limitations are immediately apparent. To begin with, not every play can accommodate this device conveniently; formal realism, for example, excludes it altogether. Other drama, less restricted by a set of limiting conventions, employs functional figures freely, but every play worthy of attention emphasizes its individualized characters: Agamemnon, Clytaemestra, Cassandra, and Aegisthus are obviously more central to the meaning of the *Oresteia* than are Aeschylus' Watchman, chorus, and Herald. Thus, even in those plays that do contain expository statement, the majority of the speeches are dramatic, and thus most of the action in a play never falls within the purview of *any* functional figure. Furthermore—and this is the really crucial point—the Doctor of *Everyman* is a special case. It would not do to assume that the contribution of every functional figure is so thoroughly or so purely explicative—to assume, for example, that the Greek chorus has "the more or less passive role of interpreters of the play." [5] In a superb study of Molière, W. G. Moore re-examines the assumption that the numerous *raisonneurs* who populate Molière's plays "express the author's mind." He concludes that they do not:

These characters have a better reason for their presence, an aesthetic reason. They ensure symmetry and roundness of comic presentation. Excess is the more distinguishable if its opposite is exhibited at the same time. Sense shows up nonsense, sobriety offsets bad temper. To insist that one should be "sage avec sobriété" is a piece of rather flat moralizing unless and until it is put in contrast to a man doing the precise opposite.[6]

Through Moore's analysis, what seems to be pure expository statement is more accurately defined as a structural device that affects the audience's understanding less for its discursive value than for its relationship to other elements of the action.

Moore's conclusion about Molière's *raisonneurs* indicates the necessity of a more specific analysis of the functional figure's role. One convention that permits the introduction of expository statement is the prologue of Greek tragedy, the extreme form of which appears in the plays of Euripides. These so-called Euripidean playbills employ a single speaker—often a god, sometimes a minor character with the knowledge of a confidant, occasionally even the protagonist. The prologue to the *Hippolytus* well illustrates the dramatist's ability to use this device for expository statement. The goddess Aphrodite appears, identifies herself, and, addressing the spectators directly (l. 9), quickly provides on her author's behalf a summary of past events, an assessment of major characters, and an outline of the following action. Her authority

[5] Frank O'Hara and Margueritte Bro, *A Handbook of Drama* (Chicago: Willett, Clark, 1938), p. 226.
[6] *Molière: A New Criticism* (2d ed.; Garden City, N.Y.: Doubleday, 1962), pp. 71–73.

is vouched for by her divine nature and by her sharing with Euripides an apparent omniscience with regard to the plot material; moreover, she insists she is telling "the truth of this story" (l. 9).[7] Thus she convincingly establishes an explanation of the metaphysical dimension of the tragedy to come when she states:

> All those that live and see the light of sun
> from Atlas' Pillars to the tide of Pontus
> are mine to rule.
> Such as worship my power in all humility,
> I exalt in honor.
> But those whose pride is stiff-necked against me
> I lay by the heels   [ll. 3–8].

Hippolytus "has blasphemed" her by ignoring her sovereignty, choosing to worship only Artemis, goddess of hunting and chastity. For his neglect Aphrodite promises to "punish Hippolytus this day" (l. 22) by exposing him to the unrestrained passion of his stepmother Phaedra. She leaves no doubt as to what has provoked Phaedra's lust: "This was my work" (l. 28). She also establishes the nature of Hippolytus, who is a blasphemous sinner (ll. 12, 21), and of Phaedra, who is a helpless and apparently blameless victim of the act of revenge:

> Renowned shall Phaedra be in her death, but none the less
> die she must.
> Her suffering does not weigh in the scale so much
> that I should let my enemies go untouched
> escaping payment of that retribution
> that honor demands that I have   [ll. 46–50].

Her information given, Aphrodite exits; the spectators are now prepared to enjoy the working out of the scheme she has so fully outlined.

---

[7] All quotations from the *Hippolytus* are from the translation by David Grene, in *The Complete Greek Tragedies*, ed. David Grene and Richmond Lattimore (Chicago: University of Chicago Press, 1959), III, and are used by permission of the Press and the translator.

But even so patent a specimen of expository statement illustrates as well the limitations on its authority. Although he often speaks for the dramatist, the functional figure, as Aristotle would have insisted, is also "living and moving before us." Even Aphrodite must appear onstage, her role taken by a living performer; for all her knowledge, therefore, she too is absorbed into the spectacle that is part of, rather than superior to, the audience's own commanding view. And rightly so, for the play is not a concrete representation of her assertions but an examination of them, one that ultimately exposes her failure to comprehend fully her own role as a natural force in the universe and in human experience. Her "omniscience," that is, does not extend far enough to recognize that Artemis also embodies a valid natural force. Aphrodite, though having the power to punish violations against her sovereignty, is really only half-right, Hippolytus only half-wrong. This aspect of the tragedy comes into focus toward the end, when Artemis herself appears. She is as one-sided as Aphrodite, whom she calls "that most hated Goddess" (l. 1301), "the worker of mischief" (l. 1400). Hippolytus, in her view, "was always just, so just that for his good name / he endured to die" (ll. 1298–1299). What Aphrodite had said in the prologue was indeed the "truth"—but not all of it: she had established only part of the play's meaning. Artemis now helps establish the rest. The whole purport of the tragedy, as Artemis herself suggests in a less heated moment, encompasses both extremes:

> This is the settled custom of the Gods:
> No one may fly in the face of another's wish:
> we remain aloof and neutral   [ll. 1328–1330].

Both forces, passion and continence, have dominion in the universe; neither can oust the other. Hippolytus, in devoting himself entirely to one, has brought on his own destruction.

The single-speaker prologues of Aeschylus and Sophocles are

ordinarily even less purely expository than those of Euripides. The prologue to Aeschylus' *Oresteia*, for example, resembles that of the *Hippolytus* only in its use of a single character who speaks directly to the spectators (l. 37). The vast and limitless *Oresteia* is introduced not by a god but by the solitary figure of the insignificant Watchman "elbowed . . . dogwise" on the palace roof, waiting for the beacon flare that will announce the end of the Trojan War. From his position atop the palace the Watchman looks down on the action physically, but he is nevertheless looking up at it socially, and intellectually he is looking on from a distance. He does, it is true, fix the place as Argos and the time as just before the homecoming of Agamemnon. He also stresses what are to be the thematic centers of this first play of the trilogy: the Trojan War, Agamemnon, Clytaemestra, and the coming catastrophe in the palace. Beyond these purely informational matters, however, his expository function does not extend, for he is unable to define the coming action with any precision.[8] He speaks of the stars he has seen during the years of his watch (ll. 4–7)—thereby creating a powerful image of the rise and fall of dynasties—but he has no idea what relevance this image might have for the play. He suggests an attitude toward Clytaemestra when he mentions "a lady's / male strength of heart in its high confidence" (ll. 10–11), but his remark is ambiguous. He is clearer in his assessment of Agamemnon, whom he loves (ll. 31–34), but since his love is so obviously a function of his role as Agamemnon's subject, it can have little influence on the audience's attitude. His fear and suspicion of the palace where Clytaemestra waits for her husband anticipate a catastrophe of some

[8] The Watchman's monologue suggests that a distinction ought to be made between those aspects of expository statement that are purely informational and those that are truly interpretive. This distinction would be less valid than it may at first appear, however. As I show in the section on exposition in Chapter 4, even the "purely informational" details almost always exert some influence on the spectators' understanding and attitudes.

sort, but what it will be he either cannot or will not say: "I speak to those who understand, / but if they fail, I have forgotten everything" (ll. 37–38).

The Watchman's limitations identify him as a part of the action rather than an external commentator on it, and therefore his monologue is primarily influential through its unverbalized implications. Since he does have some of the attributes of a functional figure, much of his significance lies in his hesitancy, his very refusal to be omniscient. "The rest / I leave to silence; for an ox stands huge upon / my tongue" (ll. 34–36) establishes the appropriate mood of fear and foreboding far more effectively than would a detailed account of the information he presumably conceals. His cautious "I speak to those who understand" (l. 37) transforms the spectators into fellow conspirators, and by this means Aeschylus informs them that what they already know about the legend of the House of Atreus is highly relevant to their understanding of the present version. Further implications result from the lowness of the Watchman's status. The end of the trilogy, which focuses on the union of Zeus and Destiny, will show that Aeschylus' decision to begin the first play with the lowliest of mortals has allowed him to dramatize a vast chain of being through which he can demonstrate both the scope and the universality of his tragedy. But the Watchman's social position has also a more immediate effect on the spectators' understanding. What he says smacks of rumor or hearsay; it implies the gossip of the servants' quarters. Since he is a slave, however, it is surprising that he has as much knowledge as he does and that he is so interested in the affairs of his masters. His partial awareness and his compulsion to speak despite his fear magnify the importance of the dramatic events: the spectators realize that the murder of Agamemnon will have repercussions even for the lives of the Watchman and his peers.

These two prologues emphatically support Moore's claim about the complexity of the functional figure. They reveal that the dramatist can use this kind of character as a device for directly controlling his audience's understanding, but they also show that the functional figure commands only a small area of the play's full import and that he does not always explicitly articulate the whole significance of the area falling within his scope; much of his expository statement, like the dialogue of the explicit style of drama, articulates the signs that convey meaning without articulating the meaning itself. Even more important, these two prologues also indicate that despite his comparative lack of involvement the functional figure, like all characters, exists only within the total dramatic situation; his status, the self-characterizing functions of his statements, and the stylistic effects of his speech necessarily evoke implications that affect understanding only through their relation to the context in which they occur. That these conclusions apply not only to the two prologues but to the functional figure in general is readily demonstrated by the great complexity that characterizes the most familiar versions of this device, the Greek chorus and the spokesman of Elizabethan drama.

The Chorus of Greek Tragedy

It is really improper, of course, to speak of *the* chorus of Greek tragedy, since, as H. D. F. Kitto points out, Greek tragedy was "a continually changing system," [9] and since, additionally, every specific chorus is unique. There are, however, certain generalizations about these many choruses which can be profitably made. The chorus' chief contribution consists of its odes, and these tend to divide the tragedy into a series of brief and separate episodes. The chorus occupies the stage by itself during its odes, and it introduces each successive episode; therefore it seems to control the action of the play. During the odes it concentrates

[9] *Greek Tragedy: A Literary Study* (2d, rev. ed.; Garden City, N.Y.: Doubleday, 1955), p. 57.

the spectators' emotions on particular themes; in the episodes it focuses their attention on particular events, almost as if illustrating through selected examples its own intellectual and emotional generalizations. While the chief characters are performing their action, moreover, the chorus becomes "an emotional sounding-board," [10] re-expressing in its verbal and physical responses the protagonists' hopes and fears.

These qualities of the chorus endow it with an aura of omniscience, so that the dramatist could, if he wished, use choral speech to introduce expository statement. In most plays the members of the chorus possess a general identity, whether that of slaves, captives, suppliants, citizens, or elders, and therefore the chorus customarily voices the specialized point of view of a circumscribed group. Often, however, this specialized point of view closely resembles that which the dramatist wanted his spectators to assume. Consequently, while using the chorus to establish necessary exposition, he could also instill in his spectators his own way of seeing past events and suggest how they ought to respond to the future action. Or he could at any time have his chorus express an assertion about the major characters, their experience, or their world. The most obvious use of the chorus for expository statement of this kind appears in its final summation of the play in a gnomic comment, like that which concludes Sophocles' *Oedipus the King:*

You that live in my ancestral Thebes, behold this Oedipus,—
him who knew the famous riddles and was a man most masterful;
not a citizen who did not look with envy on his lot—
see him now and see the breakers of misfortune swallow him!
Look upon that last day always. Count no mortal happy till
he has passed the final limit of his life secure from pain.[11]

[10] D. W. Lucas, *The Greek Tragic Poets* (London: Cohen and West, 1950), p. 43.

[11] Trans. David Grene, *The Complete Greek Tragedies*, II, 76; quoted by permission of the University of Chicago Press and the translator.

These choral epilogues frequently resemble the moral-pointing that concludes so many eighteenth-century tragedies, and like that device they tend to limit rather than express the full range of meaning. Furthermore, since Euripides used virtually the same speech to end five of his extant tragedies, there is some evidence that the Greek dramatist failed to take this function of his chorus very seriously. Nevertheless, as C. M. Bowra points out, these choral epilogues do manage "to strike a note, to give a tone, of relief or acceptance or understanding or joy, and so to put the dramatic events in their right perspective. They leave no doubt what we should feel when the play is over, what our general impression ought to be." [12]

To focus only on the chorus' capacity for expository statement, however, is to ignore some crucial facts. For one thing, the chorus is more than a disembodied omniscient voice; it affects understanding not only through its evaluative and interpretive assertions but also in other ways as well. The same qualities, for example, that tend to give it an aura of omniscience also enable the dramatist merely to underscore specific aspects of character and event without explicitly defining them. Similarly, the chorus' total contribution to understanding derives in large part from the traditional forms and images of its odes and from the music and dance that augment its verse. The odes, sung in a lyrical and archaic diction, normally echo rhythms, images, and word patterns made familiar in previous contexts, thus indicating the universality of the present theme and creating oblique perspectives like those that the Elizabethan provides through the incorporation of subplots. The music and choreography of Greek tragedy are no longer available for analysis, but they must have produced aural and visual effects of great significance. Aeschylus was his own

---

This function of the chorus is found most often in Sophocles, who usually dispensed with its other interpretive functions; see C. M. Bowra, *Sophoclean Tragedy* (Oxford: Clarendon Press, 1944), p. 7.

[12] Bowra, *Sophoclean Tragedy*, p. 9.

choreographer,[13] and his control of the choral movement undoubtedly gave him added opportunities for shaping his spectators' responses.

Furthermore, the chorus' capacity for expository statement is
not always put to use. In some plays the specialized point of view
that the chorus acquires from its members' general identity, far
from paralleling that of the dramatist, is introduced only for the
contrast it offers to the meanings established implicitly, with the
resulting interplay enriching the dramatic experience by presenting it to the spectators from opposing angles simultaneously. And
many of the choruses that do employ expository statement also
display an unusual flexibility, for though they tend to approach
omniscience in their odes, they adopt narrow and restricted personal voices in the episodes, where they become mere observers
whose speeches have little authority. It is especially this flexibility which makes the Greek chorus so supple an instrument that
its exact nature necessarily varies from play to play. Its precise
function in establishing a point of view for the spectators must
be determined from the whole context of the tragedy in which it
takes part.

The *Agamemnon* chorus is a case in point. The Argive Elders
who comprise it stand far from the center of dramatic interest;
they tend to envelop the action rather than share in it.[14] This
chorus thus has an impersonal voice through which Aeschylus
can freely shape his audience's responses. From the moment the
chorus enters until the end of the play, it has control of the action's structure. During its odes it continually remembers, con-
templates, comments, and interprets; what it cannot clearly ex-

[13] A. E. Haigh, *The Tragic Drama of the Greeks* (Oxford: Clarendon
Press, 1896), p. 69.

[14] Cf. Kitto, *Greek Tragedy*, p. 116. For an analysis of the chorus in
Sophocles' *Oedipus the King*, see Francis Fergusson, *The Idea of a Theater* (Princeton, N.J.: Princeton University Press, 1949), pp. 29–32. Kitto
studies Euripides' characteristic use of the chorus in *Greek Tragedy*, pp.
224–225. I discuss the choruses of *The Libation Bearers* and *The
Eumenides* briefly in Chapter 8.

press, it attempts to convey through imagery, rhythm, music, and dance. Each intervening episode seems to be chosen by the chorus to show the spectators something that it does not itself fully understand or that, like the effects created by the nondiscursive dimension of the odes, it cannot phrase in all its complexity. What E. T. Owen has written of Aeschylean tragedy in general is especially pertinent to the *Agamemnon:*

> The artistic purpose that controls the design, woven of intertwining odes and episodes, remains the artistic purpose of the choral hymn. The whole play is the dramatization of the choral hymn. The events of the story originally sung by the chorus in coming out of their song and taking visible shape bear the same relation to the whole as before.[15]

Because of its relationship to the action, the impersonal voice of this chorus functions like the omniscient narrative voice of prose fiction. This chorus has supreme knowledge of the past, of the war and its causes and its meanings for the play, and of the past behavior of Agamemnon. The audience learns of these from the chorus and must form its response to them on the basis of the chorus' information and attitudes. The chorus has also a profound understanding of certain general laws governing the universe, at least those laws that pertain to the themes of the trilogy, and these are the laws by which the spectators must judge the characters and events presented directly in the episodes.

During these episodes the chorus' omniscience fails; its statement is no longer authoritative. The same figures who express for Aeschylus the meaning of the past and the timeless have also a more personal voice, that of a group of Argive Elders. Aeschylus individualizes this group through its self-characterization as "dishonored, old in our bones" (l. 72)—too old, too weak to join the Trojan expedition, and sadly aware of its frailty. Later its loyalty to Agamemnon will appear (ll. 805–810), and later still

---

[15] *The Harmony of Aeschylus* (Toronto: Clarke, Irwin, 1952), p. 63.

its hatred of tyranny (ll. 1348–1365). Of the present action and of almost all that the future will bring, these Elders are ignorant. When the episodes begin, the chorus must observe with the audience, unable to comment and interpret until it has itself learned. The chorus is especially blind to the character, motives, and plans of Clytaemestra, and only when these have been revealed can it judge her in relation to universal law and to its own personal opinions. When its sure knowledge fails, the group of Argive Elders corresponds rather to the central consciousness of prose fiction, the character through whose responses the events of the experience filter, and who must learn along with, and sometimes after, the reader. Moreover, the individualization of this chorus increases its dramatic significance. As a specific group the Argive Elders stand on the next step of the social and intellectual ladder above the Watchman. Their concern and their attempt to understand both the past and the present indicate that the central experience impinges on the welfare of the leading citizens in much the same way that it affects the slaves and servants represented by the Watchman. The individualization of this chorus thus reinforces and expands one implication of the Watchman's opening monologue. Agamemnon's tragedy is social and political as well as personal. It involves not only himself but also his entire kingdom.

The Spokesman in Shakespeare

It is a commonplace that the Elizabethan dramatist, like the Greek, strove to make the course of his dramatic action and its implications fully explicit.[16] But the drama of the English Renaissance differs from Greek tragedy in one major structural re-

---

[16] See M. C. Bradbrook, *Themes and Conventions of Elizabethan Tragedy* (Cambridge: University Press, 1935), p. 127. On the general subject of interpretive and explanatory comments in Elizabethan drama, see Clemen, *English Tragedy before Shakespeare*, pp. 69–73 and *passim*.

spect that changes the nature of the conventions permitting expository statement. The Greek dramatist opens his tragedy late in the narrative, just before the catastrophe; the Elizabethan begins "at the beginning": he stages as many of the story's events as possible, presenting what the Greek dramatist would narrate through prologue, chorus, or messenger. As a result, Elizabethan drama normally contains a multiplicity of scenes, often spaced throughout a long period of time and occurring in several distinct locales. At the same time, the dramatist seldom has much to report about preceding events; *King Lear*, for example, provides the relevant exposition for both plots in the first few lines of the opening scene. This episodic technique precludes both the possibility and the necessity of a group like the Greek chorus, and therefore the various functions of the choral voice, which are assumed by a single group in Greek tragedy, are in Elizabethan drama divided among several conventions.

Some of these—such as the prologue and epilogue—stand outside the individual scenes,[17] but the most important and most often used of these expository conventions in Elizabethan drama employs a figure who participates directly in the action of the play. This figure, whose interpretive contributions were evidently considered indispensable, is the spokesman. The typical Elizabethan play abounds in minor characters, frequently unnamed, normally with few individualizing traits, who appear briefly and serve only to comment on the action and its meanings or supply evaluations of its characters. One of the most helpful of these spokesmen appears in *King Lear*, where a Gentleman, seeing the king gone mad, enables Shakespeare to control both the audience's emotion and its understanding:

[17] See Martha Gause McCaulley, "Function and Content of the Prologue, Chorus, and Other Non-organic Elements in English Drama, from the Beginnings to 1642," *Studies in English Drama*, 1st series, ed. Allison Gaw (Philadelphia: University of Pennsylvania Press, 1917), pp. 161–258.

A sight most pitiful in the meanest wretch,
Past speaking of in a king! Thou hast one daughter
Who redeems nature from the general curse
Which twain have brought her to   [IV.vi.206–209].

Less far-reaching but still informative is the Gentleman in *Hamlet* who warns Claudius of Laertes' rebellion (IV.v.95–105) and who, by the attitude implicit in his contempt for the "riotous head," for the "rabble" who have forgotten antiquity and custom, invites the spectators to respond unfavorably to Laertes and his action. Nor need the spokesman always be anonymous. At the end of *Hamlet*, Fortinbras delivers a final eulogy on the dead prince:

> For he was likely, had he been put on,
> To have prov'd most royal   [V.ii.389–390].

There is much to be said for the claim that "if we wish to know what Shakespeare intended us to think of Hamlet, we have only to read the final speech of the play." [18] Fortinbras, who has no personal motive for his words, phrases in expository statement the attitude toward Hamlet that Shakespeare has built in his audience's consciousness throughout the tragedy.

Shakespeare's tendency to make use of this common Elizabethan device is well known; [19] Walter Raleigh, for example, asserts that in almost every play Shakespeare establishes "a clear enough point of view" by including "some character, or group of characters, through whose eyes the events of the play must be seen, if they are to be seen in right perspective." [20] Nevertheless, these Shakespearean spokesmen must be studied in their full con-

[18] John Erskine Hankins, *The Character of Hamlet* (Chapel Hill: University of North Carolina Press, 1941), p. 82.
[19] See especially Levin L. Schücking, *Character Problems in Shakespeare's Plays* (New York: Holt, 1922); Arthur Colby Sprague, *Shakespeare and the Audience* (Cambridge, Mass.: Harvard University Press, 1935); and Alfred Harbage, *As They Liked It* (New York: Macmillan, 1947).
[20] *Shakespeare* (London: Macmillan, 1961), p. 152.

texts. The various knights, messengers, and gentlemen who suddenly enter for a speech or two cause no trouble—their words convince because nothing can detract from them. But as soon as individuality or a clear relationship to the situation gives the character some focus of his own, his speech becomes just one of a number of effects in a composite image. It is of such apparent spokesmen as Thersites in *Troilus and Cressida* and Apemantus in *Timon of Athens* that Alfred Harbage correctly writes: "Whenever in a play by Shakespeare there is a commentator on the worth of the other characters or the significance of the action, there is always something about him to prevent our relying too implicitly upon his words." [21] These figures possess specialized and excessive points of view which Shakespeare has included not to control the audience's understanding but to temper it.

This point is well illustrated by the contribution to *Antony and Cleopatra* of Philo, whose speech, according to Raleigh, "interprets to the audience the meaning of what is going forward on the stage." [22] Philo begins the play unintroduced; his name is never spoken. His sole function, quite obviously, is to give the spectators an account on Antony's present situation, and his words clearly express his opinion of his general's "dotage." According to Philo, Antony has abandoned his duty in submitting to Cleopatra's charms. The great soldier has "become the bellows and the fan / To cool a gipsy's lust"; "the triple pillar of the world" has been "transform'd / Into a stumpet's fool"; Antony is no longer Antony (I.i.57–59). Philo's language is especially significant, for it connotes excess and the dissolution of a necessary firmness. Antony "o'erflows the measure"; his eyes "now bend, now turn"; his captain's heart "reneges all temper." Every word Philo speaks evokes the disgust and regret aroused in him by his general's pathetic fall from the ideal. And, like a chorus, he even offers Antony and Cleopatra's entrance as visual proof: "Behold and see."

[21] *As They Liked It*, p. 110.   [22] *Shakespeare*, p. 125.

A clear picture. But if the spectators rely on it alone, a false one. Philo is in conversation with Demetrius. The play's first words—"Nay, but"—show that they have been talking for some time, and that Philo's remarks constitute an argumentative reply. Thus a dramatic situation presents itself, and Philo's assessment belongs to the whole situation. When he characterizes Antony's change as a falling away from a standard, he acknowledges his own devotion to a specific conception of human behavior. His use of "measure" reveals his belief that man's proper concerns should not extend beyond fixed boundaries. He prefers the military way of life to any other. He equates nobility only with political leadership. The total situation of which Philo is but one part also includes Antony and Cleopatra, however. Their speeches, which immediately follow his, confirm the facts of his interpretation, but they offer a completely different assessment of these facts. Against Philo's concept of measure, Antony places infinity: "There's beggary in the love that can be reckon'd"; if Cleopatra would "set a bourn how far to be belov'd," she must "needs find out new heaven, new earth." Antony scorns military conquest and political leadership: "Kingdoms are clay"; for him the "nobleness of life" is just that liaison with Cleopatra which Philo deplores. Antony and Cleopatra, the most important figures on the stage, have just made a splendid entrance, and these emotional factors give Antony's words a great deal of authority. If Philo is a spokesman, then, he is of a special kind. Shakespeare develops the action of this play at least in part on the basis of a contrast between the Roman view of life and that of Antony in Egypt. Philo speaks not for Shakespeare but for Rome. He is Shakespeare's means of introducing at once the Roman point of view by presenting *its* attitude toward Antony and Egypt. *Antony and Cleopatra* opens, in other words, not with an absolute placement of Antony, but with a placement of him in relation to another point that is itself within the dramatic experience.

Philo's contribution is much like that of Molière's *raison-neurs:* what seems to be expository statement is really something else and something more. But through his skillful employment of functional figures Shakespeare could also achieve the equivalent of expository statement in speeches that seem purely dramatic. *Hamlet* offers an example of the spokesman which closely approximates the classical chorus in its more subtle functions. Coleridge long ago observed to H. C. Robinson that in Shakespearean tragedy the Fool replaces the ancient Greek chorus: he is disinterested, while all the other characters are involved. In *Hamlet*, Coleridge went on, "the Fool is, as it were, divided into several parts, dispersed thro' the piece." [23] In *Hamlet* the Fool appears at least once in the form of two characters, the gravediggers, whose contribution to the play is indeed much like that of a Greek chorus.[24] The Greek chorus was certainly not indifferent, as Coleridge suggests, but its capacity for detachment often allowed it to control the spectators' attitudes by intervening between them and the activity of the principal characters. Both gravediggers have individuality, especially the one who remains to chat with Hamlet, and Shakespeare permits them no direct explanation that might define and thus limit the meaning of the action. But the gravediggers do possess a detachment lacking in the other characters of the play. Shakespeare uses their brief scene to adjust the audience's point of view without its being quite aware of what has happened, much as the Greek dramatist did through the allusions, rhythms, images and traditional forms of the choral odes.

Throughout the play, before the entrance of the gravediggers, Denmark's basic rottenness has been continually stressed, espe-

[23] Diary of H. C. Robinson, Jan. 29, 1811, *Coleridge's Shakespearean Criticism*, ed. Thomas M. Raysor (Cambridge, Mass.: Harvard University Press, 1930), II, 211–212.

[24] Cf. H. D. F. Kitto, *Form and Meaning in Drama* (London: Methuen, 1956), p. 283.

cially through the metaphor of the cancerous ulcer. In the fifth act the ulcer will burst, discharging its poison until all but a few are destroyed, and Shakespeare has so shaped his spectators' point of view that they cannot help anticipating wholesale destruction. Nevertheless, this final exhibition of rottenness will be accompanied by the assertion of its opposite: the ulcer even as it bursts will evidently heal over; soundness will be restored to Denmark. Shakespeare must therefore adjust his spectators' attitudes so that they can accept the restoration as well as the destruction. He accomplishes this by presenting in a totally new perspective not the characters and their activity but the motifs that have obsessed Hamlet and disturbed most of the others: rottenness, sin and judgment, disorder, madness, mutability, and death.

The clowns discuss these matters, but they remain detached. Their attitude is comic and therefore healthy. They have cut the disorder in the state down to size by translating it into the age-old complaint of the underprivileged that their social betters are exempt from some of the rules: "the more pity that great folk should have count'nance in this world to drown or hang themselves more than their even Cristen" (V.i.26–28). Sin—and with it Hamlet's compulsion to reason out his situation—is reduced to a debate in garbled Latin about whether a man goes to water or the water comes to him. The First Clown further parodies Hamlet's attempts to make careful distinctions when he equivocates about the ownership of the grave he digs. His attitude toward Hamlet's madness is reassuringly matter-of-fact: madness must be relative, he suggests; otherwise Hamlet would not have been sent to England. His explanation of the cause of the madness is eminently sane: Hamlet became mad because he lost his wits. Rottenness abounds in the First Clown's talk of "pocky corses" (l. 161), but it is transformed by his joke that a tanner's body will last longer than another because "his hide is so tann'd with his trade" (l. 165). The major emphasis in the graveyard scene is, of course, on death, and the clowns are equally matter-of-fact and unemotional about this: they imply that, in Gertrude's words in Act I, " 'tis common." Death is the ordinary end of everything that lives. Thus "a grave-maker" solves the riddle of who builds the strongest. Thus the corpse of Ophelia is neither man nor woman but a dead body. Thus a skull is much like a stone: it can slow up the digging.

The gravediggers' scene effects its shifts in the spectators' point of view by the natural implications of its central attitudes. The clowns, by their anonymity and detachment, speak more for the dramatist than for themselves. It is as if Shakespeare were to appear in his own person to announce that sin and death and madness need not be dwelt on obsessively; such things happen; one corrects them if one can or else adapts oneself to them. Through his clowns' attitudes Shakespeare reminds his audience that an awareness of the imperfections of life need not be morbid, that it can, indeed, be a sign of the healthy recognition of the basic facts of existence. This new attitude, suggested by the conversation of the clowns, is confirmed for the spectators when Hamlet expresses a similar detachment. It is this new attitude, which Hamlet retains throughout Act V and which he persuades the spectators to retain with him, that opposes and modifies —though without nullifying—the excess of death and destruction during the final scene of the play.

Individualized Character and Expository Statement

The problematic nature of the functional figure demonstrates that my distinction between the two kinds of characters in drama, despite its basic validity, is not without complications. Similar though less extensive qualifications are in order for the individualized character, whose speech, which normally possesses no objective authority, can under certain conditions be made to approximate expository statement. One source of this effect is the flexibility of the individualized character in Elizabethan drama:

Sometimes the dramatis personae exchange speeches in the modern manner, where each character has his limited role and remains inside it; sometimes the character, still inside his role, will approach the spectators; sometimes again a character may transcend the limits of his special role and assume a kind of choric speech, in which he states the total situation and expresses the "moral" or central significance of the play.[25]

An example of this transcendence, though on a minor scale, is the speech in *Hamlet* in which Gertrude describes Ophelia's drowning (IV.vii.167–184). In this speech Gertrude transcends her special role as wife of Claudius, mother of Hamlet, and widow of the Ghost; as Sir John Squire puts it, "No attempt is made to give the Queen's individual reactions; she does not speak in character but, for the moment, becomes the mere mouthpiece of the most mellifluous of poets." [26] The pity Gertrude had previously shown the mad Ophelia (IV.v.17–20) reflected more upon herself; her remorse usurped the central focus. Here, however, her pity, purified of self-revelation, has become impersonal. The speech therefore serves only to characterize the event it describes, and this allows Shakespeare to use the details of the speech to alter the response to Ophelia in death. Her fate is idealized by the emphasis on the setting with its contrasts between nettles and daisies, "cold maids" and "liberal shepherds," "muddy death" and "melodious lay." Life's complexities drove Ophelia to madness, but in death she is raised to the mythic dimension suggested by the personification of inanimate objects, and in this

[25] Bradbrook, *Themes and Conventions of Elizabethan Tragedy*, pp. 111–112.

[26] *Shakespeare as a Dramatist* (London: Cassell, 1935), p. 215; cf. S. L. Bethell, in *Shakespeare and the Popular Dramatic Tradition* (Durham, N.C.: Duke University Press, 1944), who cites this passage as an example of "depersonalization": "The writer has so concentrated on the content of a speech, as apparently to have ignored the speaker's identity" (p. 109).

dimension all opposites fuse into the tranquil harmony evoked throughout the speech by its tone of detachment.

Expository statement by individualized characters occurs most frequently in Elizabethan drama, however, through those conventions that permit the character to speak directly to the audience, especially the soliloquy. Schücking conveniently distinguishes two types: "a means which the author uses in order to instruct his audience about the events, or about the plans and character of the personage speaking," and "the expression of an individual who, thinking aloud, renders account of his most intimate thoughts and feelings." [27] The first type is the ordinary Elizabethan soliloquy; its expression is largely expository. Since the character's remarks are addressed to the spectators, he has nothing to conceal. He can speak for the dramatist by telling the audience what it must know to comprehend the surface level of the action. He temporarily lays aside the limitations of his personal involvement to explain frankly his reasons for previous activity and to share with the audience his future plans. When he talks about other characters, he tells the spectators what the dramatist wants them to know. Even the villain candidly admires his opponent's good qualities and despairs at the failings of his own associates.

The second type of soliloquy, more subjective in nature, provides the dramatist an opportunity to explore the speaker's "inner life," for his deepest feelings emerge even as they take shape in his own consciousness. The effect on the audience is that of greater knowledge of the speaker and, at the same time, of a more intense emotional relationship with him. As a result, this kind of soliloquy has also a special significance for the spectators' attitude toward the entire play. Wylie Sypher compares it to "one of the most dramatic devices of mannerist painting," the *Sprecher*, or "speaker"—"like the man in the left-hand corner of

[27] *Character Problems in Shakespeare's Plays*, p. 29.

Tintoretto's Presentation of the Virgin—a sharply accented fore-ground figure who faces outward toward the spectator, yet twirls inward, gesturing or glancing toward the action behind him." [28] The soliloquy of this type creates an intimacy with its speaker that forces the audience to observe the drama almost entirely through the eyes of a single speaker, much as the *Sprecher* invites study of the painting from his oblique angle. When the focus widens from the soliloquy back to the group, the spectators take with them not only a keener understanding of the speaker but also a sharper awareness of the principal issues in the play. By temporarily closing the gap that separates them from the action, this kind of soliloquy, like the chorus of Greek tragedy, heightens the spectators' participation. For a moment they become a part of the experience enacted on the stage.

Hamlet's soliloquies belong to this category. His first, for example, informs the audience how the world simultaneously bores and disgusts him and how he longs for death. His love for his dead father is so intense that it momentarily obscures the hatred for Claudius which he had previously given primary emphasis; indeed, the hatred appears only in the brief comparison of the two kings: "Hyperion to a satyr" (I.ii.140; cf. l. 152). Even more intense, however, is his obsession with his mother. The spectators see her through her son's assessment of her inconstancy, which enlarges into the generalization, "frailty, thy name is woman!" (l. 146), and then centers on her hasty and improper marriage: "O, most wicked speed, to post / With such dexterity to incestuous sheets!" (ll. 156–157). Hamlet's statements have to be taken as sincere; they express without concealment his feelings as he comprehends them himself. But the attitudes are his own, not Shakespeare's. In soliloquy of this kind the character can communicate directly with the audience while the dramatist cannot. This kind of soliloquy is not expository but dramatic.

[28] *Four Stages of Renaissance Style* (Garden City, N.Y.: Doubleday, 1955), p. 143.

As such, it reveals that the dramatist can communicate *indirectly* even through the speech of an individualized character who has not temporarily abandoned his role. For Shakespeare is not entirely absent. To the extent that this first soliloquy presents Hamlet's attitudes more fully than might otherwise be possible, it resembles the narration of the central consciousness in fiction. And such narration, as Henry James's *The Ambassadors* shows, can be qualified by the author so that it establishes contributions to meaning that do not suffer from the limitations of the necessarily restricted observer. Shakespeare enriches Hamlet's soliloquy in the same way that James adds overtones to the thoughts of Lambert Strether, for Hamlet's words convey much more than the mere expression of his present mood. In order to make himself understood, he necessarily informs the audience how recently the old king died and how quickly his widow remarried. By insisting on his father's excellence as king, husband, and man, he unknowingly reinforces Horatio's evaluation of old Hamlet in the first scene of the play. In giving his opinions of others, he indicates his own capacity for love and hate, and throughout the speech he manifests the intensity of his feelings. Finally, through his choice of images, which initiates one strand of the leitmotif expressing the rottenness in Denmark, he enables Shakespeare to suggest at least one aspect of the play's larger design. But it is not just a matter of what Hamlet says, for the structural placing of the soliloquy is also important. It is Hamlet's first opportunity to share his feelings intimately with the spectators, and "we naturally take it to be our key." [29] In addition, the soliloquy provides a point of rest after an important scene involving several characters in an exchange of dialogue. It narrows the focus from a group of speakers to a single figure. It substitutes a continuous speech of substantial length for a succession of briefer speeches divided among a number of separate voices. It changes the tempo

[29] A. J. A. Waldock, *Hamlet: A Study in Critical Method* (Cambridge: University Press, 1931), p. 13.

by converting action to reflection. All these effects vastly increase the impact of the soliloquy and thus prompt the audience to respect not only Hamlet's information but even his attitudes.[30]

Except that it is a soliloquy and that it is expressive rather than symptomatic, Hamlet's speech exemplifies the condition of most dialogue in drama: though spoken by individualized characters who remain within their roles, it can still be fully as informative as the most patent example of expository statement. For the dramatist's relation to his characters resembles that of James to his central consciousness: while the character observes, the dramatist observes with him from a point just over his shoulder.[31] The dramatist sees more accurately and he sees more extensively, and to convey the fullness of his own vision he must employ what Moore, in his study of Molière, calls the "dramatic trick of forcing a man to say two things when he thinks he is only saying one." [32]

The various means through which the dramatist accomplishes this "trick" demand fuller analysis, and they are explored in the following chapters. To complete this survey of expository statement, however, a final point must be made. For there is one set of circumstances in which the speech of an individualized character can approximate expository statement even when he remains firmly anchored within his role, as Hamlet does in his soliloquy. These circumstances arise when the two things the dramatist wants his character to say coincide. An example occurs in the

[30] This conclusion about the emphasis given Hamlet's soliloquy by structural effects is generally applicable to any occasion in drama where the focus narrows from a scene of varied action to the long reflective speech of a single, isolated character; see the analysis of *The Spanish Tragedy* by Clemen, in *English Tragedy before Shakespeare*, p. 102.

[31] Cf. Henry James, *The Art of the Novel: Critical Prefaces* (New York: Scribner's, 1934), p. 304.

[32] *Molière*, p. 58.

final act of *Rosmersholm*, when Rebecca explains to Rosmer why she has surrendered the happiness she fought for just at the moment it seemed to be hers. She has, she realizes, succumbed after all to Rosmersholm and its ways, and they have changed her: "The Rosmer view of life ennobles . . . but it kills happiness" (IV, p. 203). Rebecca has not suddenly transcended her role, as Gertrude does in *Hamlet*. The statement is in keeping with her character, and it has nondiscursive value because it indicates to the spectators the growth she has achieved in adjusting her own point of view so that it can equate with the more inclusive dramatic point of view. But by summing up what Ibsen has implicitly expressed through the action as a whole, Rebecca's speech also fulfills the function of expository statement. For the meaning of *Rosmersholm*, her remark is as vital as the speech of a Greek chorus in its role as "ideal spectator" or that of an Elizabethan spokesman like the Gentleman who summarizes the action of *King Lear*.

Mature realization amounting to expository statement is common at climactic moments of plays that exclude functional figures. And though my example of this device comes from formal realism, it should be obvious that its use is characteristic in drama of every kind. In plays like the Greek and Elizabethan, which employ functional figures and other conventions for expository statement, the mature realization of individualized characters allows the dramatist one more means of speaking "in his own voice." It is, after all, Lear himself late in the play who best sums up what he has always been:

> I am a very foolish fond old man,
> Fourscore and upward, not an hour more nor less;
> And, to deal plainly,
> I fear I am not in my perfect mind   [IV.vii.60–63].[33]

[33] I discuss in Chapter 4 a special case in which the speech of an individualized character takes on the authority of expository statement.

Speech through which the dramatist can directly control his spectators' attitudes and understanding is available to some extent in almost every style of drama. But its use is severely limited. In formal realism the instances of expository statement are few and brief; they depend on the presence of characters capable of insight, and they serve only to express a meaning already implicit. In Greek tragedy and Elizabethan drama the functional figure is freely employed, but he must finally yield the stage to the more interesting individualized characters. Like the *Agamemnon* chorus, the functional figure never knows all. Even the Doctor of *Everyman* merely condenses into a few words an import that has been elaborated in many speeches accompanied by visual action; and despite his conceptual knowledge, he makes no attempt to articulate the more sensuous and emotional meanings of the play. Furthermore, the functional figure, like all characters in drama, is living and moving before the spectators, and the opportunity for nondiscursive contributions which this aspect of his role provides is one more proof of the greater importance of the implicit rendering of meaning. Expository statement is important in the final analysis only as it supplements the implicit effects, explicates portions of them, or suggests general limits for the area of meaning explored by the whole play. For the most part, then, the discursive content of the given speech has no authority whatever in itself; the speech can influence the spectators only through suggestion, through the effects of the style in which it is written, and through its complicated relationship to everything else that takes place on the stage. That this restriction is really a "limitation," however, is extremely doubtful. It keeps the dramatic situation more immediate and therefore more capable of rendering the nuances of experience. And it enables the dramatist to make each speech accomplish several different objectives at one and the same time.

2. Drama on the Stage

The text of a play is a score waiting performance.
—Harley Granville-Barker, *Prefaces to Shakespeare*

In *Riders to the Sea,* to characterize the impersonal antagonist that relentlessly pursues and destroys its human victims, John Millington Synge establishes a highly expressive contrast. The nets, oilskins, and new boards that can be seen in the cottage kitchen at the beginning of the play are supplemented, as the action develops, by additional concrete objects: the bundle of clothes, the turf, the rope, the shirt of the dead man, and the stitches of his stocking. Cathleen's initial activity (kneading and spinning) introduces a pattern of basic human actions which also includes Maurya's stirring the fire and the various arrivals and departures to which the characters give so much attention. These concrete objects and basic actions combine to evoke the austerity and simplicity of human life as it is here pictured. They form one side of the contrast; the other is formed by the almost monotonous references to wind, sea, and tide.

The remarkable feature of this contrast is that Synge has managed to express each of the opposites differently: the realm of human life is directly represented by concrete visual symbols, but the realm of nature is only evoked through suggestion or alluded to in words. This feature of the contrast effectively emphasizes the invisible quality of nature, and since nature remains invi-

37

sible, it remains mysterious and awesome, scarcely comprehensible from the point of view of the visible and uncomplicated human realm. When Synge combines the two realms in composite images, he expresses the relationship that links them. The nets and oilskins are concrete objects of human manufacture designed for use on the sea; the new boards represent a natural object adapted to human needs; both images suggest man's attempts to conquer nature. The other composite images, however, reveal the futility of such efforts by demonstrating nature's power and destructiveness. At one point in the action the invisible wind blows open the door. Shortly afterward, Cathleen notices that the pig with the black feet, which is never seen, has been eating the bit of new rope, an object visible on the stage. The twice-mentioned floating man is the most striking of these composite images, and in this purely verbal linking of the two realms, the human has been destroyed by the natural, the visible has been made invisible.[1]

Synge's contrast between that which is seen and that which is heard illustrates a basic characteristic of communication in drama. For if the nature of his form imposes a restriction on the dramatist by limiting his direct verbal intervention, it also provides ample compensation. A play is written to be performed, and performance equips the dramatist with a wide variety of tools.

Method of Production

Every play presupposes one kind of production rather than another, and while individual differences in modes of production are not always meaningful, an important if broad distinction is in order, a distinction similar to that which separates formal realism from plays more explicit in style. The import of all drama is simultaneously intellectual *and* emotional, abstract *and* concrete,

[1] *The Complete Plays of John M. Synge* (New York: Random House, 1960), pp. 84, 85, 90, 91.

but most plays stress one kind of meaning more than another, and this emphasis will be implicit in the nature of the production that the play receives. Formal realism, as in *Rosmersholm*, demands a darkened auditorium, a framing proscenium with its suggestion of a missing "fourth wall," and what Richard Wagner called the "mystic gulf" between the spectators and the stage.[2] This kind of drama carefully excludes all effects that might violate a naturalistic perspective. Its intention is to present a slice of reality, in which the action on the stage seemingly duplicates life itself, and therefore it pretends that its audience does not exist. It invites the individual spectator to regard himself as a solitary, privileged eavesdropper. Vastly different in production technique but similar in ultimate effect is the kind of drama—like Artaud's "Theater of Cruelty"—which combines an unusual emphasis on spectacle with an attempt to assign the spectators a role in the action. Both methods of production tend to appeal more to the spectator's emotions than to his intellect. They urge him to participate directly or vicariously in the staged action and thus experience an emotional response that either induces understanding or forms by itself the essential meaning of the play.

In obvious contrast to these methods is the kind of production insisted on by Bertolt Brecht. Brecht scorned the early-twentieth-century "entertainment emporiums" that specialized in formal realism and accused them of having "degenerated into branches of the bourgeois narcotics business." His own plays, without sacrificing drama's inherent entertainment value, were designed "to transform the means of enjoyment into an instrument of instruction, and to convert certain amusement establishments into organs of mass communication." To these ends he evolved his theory of "estrangement," or "alienation." This theory dictates that the actor remain detached from the character he portrays so that his performance will serve not as a representation but as a commentary. Similarly, individual episodes of the

[2] Quoted by Mordecai Gorelik, in *New Theatres for Old* (New York: Dutton, 1962), p. 288.

play "have to be knotted together in such a way that the knots are easily noticed." Titles, indicating the point of each episode, should be introduced on stage, and the spoken dialogue should frequently be interrupted by songs. Above all, the whole performance must unmistakably convey the impression that it has been thoroughly and carefully rehearsed. This kind of production, Brecht felt, would prevent the spectator from surrendering himself to the staged experience. It would allow him to retain intellectual detachment and a critical attitude. It would prompt him to exercise his judgment. As Brecht sums it up, "The finished representations have to be delivered with the eyes fully open, so that they may be received with the eyes open too." [3]

Brecht's conscious awareness and some of his specific devices may have been new, but his method of production in its general form is as old as drama itself. Most plays written before the middle of the seventeenth century were performed out of doors in broad daylight, and under such circumstances the audience's presence cannot very well be denied. Indeed, such plays as the *Oresteia, Hamlet,* and other examples of the explicit style often acknowledge the audience as an audience: devices like the Watchman's direct address or Hamlet's asides draw the spectator more intimately into the staged experience, but they do not do so without also reminding him of his actual relationship to the play. Moreover, other aspects of this kind of drama—the use of verse, the clear verbal articulation of almost every detail, the ritualistic quality of much of the action, and the employment of functional figures—call for a stylized technique that makes naturalistic perspectives irrelevant. This method of production continually advises the spectator that the play before him is only a play. The kind of emphasis implicit in this method and the general effect it has on the audience are well described in Arnold Hauser's account of neoclassic art:

[3] "A Short Organum for the Theatre," trans. John Willett, in *Brecht on Theatre* (New York: Hill and Wang, 1964), pp. 179, 194, 201, 204.

Classicism . . . desired to be stimulating and arouse feelings and illusions in the reader or beholder—what art has not desired to do so!—but its representations were always in the nature of an instructive example, an analogy or a symbol full of implications. The audience reacted not with tears, raptures and fainting fits but with reflections, fresh insights and a deeper understanding of man and his destiny.[4]

The Physical Theater

Whatever its method of production, a play, in being performed, must be performed somewhere, and the dramatist, familiar with his theater and its physical characteristics, will obviously use them to support his presentation of meaning. The Greek theater, for example, placed its audience in a semicircle on a hillside, looking down on a flat, hard-packed orchestra, which had a permanent altar at its center and behind that a narrow, rectangular structure with simple architectural lines. The altar, the temple-like structure, and the theater's association with the festival of Dionysus endowed each performance with some of the quality of a religious experience, and this effect helped reinforce the theological dimension of the play. The Greek theater also provided a chorus that simultaneously united the spectators with, and separated them from, the acted events and through its flexibility allowed the dramatist to widen or narrow the gap at will. This chorus was able to surround and envelop the major characters, as in the *Agamemnon,* or present them from a single oblique angle, as in *The Eumenides,* or merge with them and contribute to their activity, as in *The Libation Bearers.* The chorus thus served as a means to direct the audience's attention wherever the dramatist wished. It could focus in ever narrowing perspective

[4] *The Social History of Art,* trans. Stanley Godman, III (New York: Vintage Books, 1958), 177. For a fuller analysis of the psychological effects involved in this distinction between methods of production, see Paul Goodman, "The Shape of the Screen and the Darkness of the Theater," *Art and Social Nature* (New York: Vinco, 1946), pp. 72–85.

upon the protagonist, whose dignity and isolated majesty were augmented by his placement against the bulk and strong, clear outlines of the façade. Or it could direct the audience's attention to the unchanging features of the universe, and the audience, while it watched the action in the orchestra, could also see the area surrounding the theater: the sky, the hills and valleys, and the harbor in the distance. The awareness of these components of nature suggested the gods associated with them and thus affirmed the presence of the gods even when they were not included in the dramatis personae. The final ordeal of Orestes—his isolation from the rest of mankind, his naked exposure to the universe, and his suspension between a friendly god and a hostile chorus—was, then, to some extent already implicit in the basic composition of the theater in which the spectators experienced it.

The Elizabethan stage, with its delocalization in time and its freedom of movement from place to place, encouraged the creation of brief and separate scenes. These characteristics allowed the dramatist to present every facet of his theme directly and to achieve such special effects as the implicit insistence in *Antony and Cleopatra* on the thematic importance of the entire known world. The freedom of movement also allowed the dramatist to place contrasting and complementary scenes in immediate juxtaposition and to provide subsidiary episodes that might help control understanding of the main action by mirroring it in various ways. Another important feature of this theater was the long, wide platform that projected into the spectators' midst, for this made possible a close contact between audience and actor which increased the intimacy of performance. The proximity of the spectators ensured recognition of them in the use of direct address, aside, and soliloquy, and thus the audience could act as a character's confidant and be rewarded by a heightened awareness of his precise attitudes. As in the Greek theater, the purely visual element was also supremely important. The action on the Elizabethan stage could do without specific localization because the physical structure of the theater constantly asserted that the true setting was nothing less than the universe itself. The platform was the earth, its four corners suggesting the four corners of the world. At its rear rose the walls—of city or castle. Beneath was the hell from which ghosts could rise and into which villains could fall. Above, the power of the stars and of other elements controlling the affairs of men was continually symbolized by the designs that decorated the projecting "heavens." [5] It is especially these qualities of the Elizabethan theater that make Hamlet's Denmark a microcosm, an epitome of the larger world.

As the theater changed throughout the seventeenth and eighteenth centuries, the forestage was shortened and the platform raised. This development thrust the audience away from the action and increased the prominence of the proscenium frame. The importance of this second effect is obvious, for the lines of the proscenium, like the edges of a painting, create boundaries to enclose the mass and focus on the subject, thus setting definite limits to the audience's view and fixing its point of concentration. The proscenium's increased prominence also brought it into the spectators' field of vision, so that it became an additional influence on their emotional response to the play. The audience of Racine, for example, could not watch the action on the stage without also being aware of the gilt and baroque ornamentation that surrounded it. But between the architecture and the action there existed a harmony that would be shattered if plays of a different tone—*Desire under the Elms* or *The Lower Depths*—were to appear on a seventeenth-century stage, even though they too were written for a theater with a proscenium frame.[6]

[5] For a discussion of the relevance of the physical characteristics of the Elizabethan theater to an understanding of *Antony and Cleopatra*, see Maurice Charney, *Shakespeare's Roman Plays* (Cambridge, Mass.: Harvard University Press, 1961), pp. 81 ff.

[6] Cf. Gorelik's reconstruction of the original performance of Elkanah Settle's *The Empress of Morocco* (1673), in *New Theatres for Old*, pp. 80–93.

Another important development was the increasing prevalence of the naturalistic setting; this greatly affected the action of drama by giving it an exact location, usually indoors. The solid walls of the interior setting, abetted by the proscenium frame, tend to create a boxlike effect that dissociates the action on the stage from the world that lies beyond it. Since this effect limits the spectators' attention to the area brought to life by the actors and technicians, it makes possible the popular success of plays whose significance is entirely limited to the immediate surface of their action. But the box can also serve as an effective means of magnifying significance. In *A Doll's House*, Helmer's flat represents the typical middle-class home which is his appropriate milieu, but Ibsen transforms the import of this setting by emphasizing the boxlike characteristics. All the action occurs within the high thick walls of the living room, and the only exits lead not directly to the outside world but to the hall and to the study. As a result, the setting comes to represent not only a milieu but also a prison, the cage in which Helmer confines his twittering lark. In the last act, when "from below is heard the reverberation of a heavy door closing," [7] the significance of Nora's release from her husband and his world gains the added implication of the shattered box, the burst cage, the sudden coming into existence of the freedom of the outside world where the lark can try her wings.

The Fusion of Effects in Performance—
Ibsen's *Rosmersholm*

It is, of course, the experience that takes place on the stage which ultimately fulfills the task of creating and communicating meaning in drama. Performance supplies the dramatist with numerous "collaborators": the designer, the technician, the direc-

[7] *The Works of Henrik Ibsen*, ed. William Archer (New York: Scribner's, 1911–1912), VII, 191.

44

tor, the actors. These collaborators ensure that his words receive their proper tone and stress, but more important, they also produce in concrete form the nonverbal effects—the sights, the sounds, the particular tempo, the living vehicles of emotion—which emphasize, clarify, support, supplement, or qualify these words. The written text is primary, not only because drama is a literary art, but also because it is the text that determines, whether implicitly or not, both the scope and the nature of the nonverbal dimension of performance. Yet without these nonverbal effects, the dramatist's communication would be less complete.

To illustrate the various additional effects in individual analyses is unnecessary; such a procedure would, moreover, create a distorted impression of what they contribute, because it would isolate them from each other and from the verbal effects they supplement. Meaning in drama results not from a single device but from the interplay of many devices, and any examination of the way a play works in performance must concentrate on the composite image produced by the intermingling of all kinds of effects, both verbal and nonverbal. For this purpose, I have selected Ibsen's *Rosmersholm*. It has no functional figures, and its use of expository statement is both minimal and restricted to those occasions late in the play when the characters and the spectators have had an opportunity to make discoveries about the world that the play embodies; necessarily, therefore, the meaning that *Rosmersholm* instills in its spectators' consciousness is the product of a countless number of juxtaposed effects, each of which implants a few tentative suggestions. The following analysis of the play treats its first act up to the entrance of Ulrik Brendel.

When *Rosmersholm* begins, the audience is presented with a tableau of suggestive visual details which includes the setting with its furnishings and decorations, and Rebecca West crocheting her shawl near the window. The spectators see and respond to these separate effects simultaneously, and during the pause that Ibsen calls for in his first stage direction, the suggestive value of the picture has time to form a complex pattern of understanding in their consciousness. The room in which Rebecca sits is "spacious, old-fashioned, and comfortable." Its high, solid walls add to the boxlike effect that tends to separate the life on the stage from the life outside. The old-fashioned sofa and easy chairs and the series of "old and more recent portraits of clergymen, military officers, and public officials in uniform" attribute to the house and its inhabitants an air of respectable, conservative tradition. At the same time, however, the room is decked with fresh flowers and cut branches, the window on the left is open, admitting the tranquil blow of summer twilight, and the doors at the rear of the room stand wide, showing the hall, and through the open house door, a row of "huge old trees." The effect of the box and the suggestion of quiet conservatism clash with the sense of freshness, beauty, and vitality contributed by the flowers and by the gaps in the box's structure. The row of stately trees makes this conflict even more complex: in their natural growth they are part of the vitality, yet they are also old and long-established, and this suggests the settled tradition.

The woman who sits in this room is still young. Her youth, her proximity to the flowers, and the searching glances she darts through the open window to the life beyond the box prompt the spectators to associate her with the element of vitality in the setting. But the conflict evident in the room also extends to her, for as she sits, she "crochets a large white woolen shawl, which is almost finished." In an earlier version of the play, the character who became Rebecca operated a sewing machine;[8] the change substitutes an old-fashioned task for one more intrinsically modern, and, as Alan Downer remarks, "the crocheting of a large shawl is work for an old woman, or for a young woman who has

[8] *Works*, XII, 266.

little to do but watch and wait and ponder." [9] The shawl therefore conflicts with the youth and the flowers; it links Rebecca to
that element of the setting which suggests quiet routine. The
spectators absorb these conflicting impressions simultaneously as
a single complex statement about Rebecca. Her presence within
the tableau strengthens for them the implication that the play
will be concerned with some kind of conflict between stagnancy
and vitality, between old and new.

The entrance of Madam Helseth breaks the tableau, and while
the two women talk together on the stage, they introduce and
emphasize two important verbal motifs: the footbridge over the
millrace and the enigmatic "white horse." Ibsen stresses the importance of the footbridge through the concern the women show
for it and for the two men who approach it separately. Rebecca
and Madam Helseth watch Pastor Rosmer walk toward the
house, and both of them, especially Rebecca, reveal their eagerness to see whether he will use the bridge. But he does not, and
the audience at once senses Rebecca's extreme disappointment,
for she wearily turns from the window. Madam Helseth is more
resigned: "It's not surprising it bothers the pastor to walk over
that bridge. *There*, where a thing like that's happened." Rebecca's reply instantly magnifies the audience's interest: "They cling
to their dead for a long time here at Rosmersholm." The speech
creates an air of mystery; by heightening suspense it elicits a desire for further knowledge and thus commits the spectators to
the action of the play. But the speech has also a more significant
effect on their understanding, for it puts into words the feeling
evoked by the traditional elements of the setting.

Although Rosmer seemed afraid of the bridge, the second
man, whom Rebecca identifies as Rector Kroll, shows only in-

[9] Introduction to *Twenty-Five Modern Plays*, ed. S. Marion Tucker
and Alan S. Downer (rev. ed.; New York: Harper, 1948), p. xv; cf.
Harley Granville-Barker, *On Dramatic Method* (New York: Hill and
Wang, 1956), p. 174.

difference. Now it is Madam Helseth who expresses concern: "He goes straight over the bridge, he does. And yet she was his own sister." The spectators already know from the program that Kroll is Rosmer's brother-in-law. They realize that the woman to whom Madam Helseth refers must have been Rosmer's wife and that her death and the footbridge are somehow related. Rosmer's fear and the concern of the two women indicate that the death was an event of such consequence that it still affects, perhaps even threatens, the lives of those who belong to Rosmersholm. The vague sense of a brooding, threatening past, already suggested by the setting and by Rebecca's remark about the dead, now takes on concreteness in the shape of a specific incident that Rosmer, Rebecca, and Madam Helseth cannot forget but from whose influence Kroll is somehow exempt.

The second important verbal motif, which also helps Ibsen arouse in his spectators desired attitudes toward the established conflict, calls attention to itself by its very oddity. Madam Helseth objects to Rebecca's remark; she believes rather that the dead cling to Rosmersholm, that they cannot leave "those who remain." It is this, she adds, that explains the visits of the "white horse." Nothing more specific is said at this point to satisfy the spectators' curiosity about the nature of this cryptic symbol, but Madam Helseth has associated it with death, and it suggests some kind of local superstition. Significantly, it is introduced not by Rebecca but by Rosmersholm's housekeeper, whose place in the conflict was fully established at her entrance, when she immediately began closing the doors and windows, shutting up the gaps in the box and thereby emphasizing the more permanent features of the house. The white horse is thus related not only to the dead wife but also to the traditional aspect of the setting; it serves as one more symbol of the past that continues to haunt the present. Rebecca's attitude toward this symbol differs from that of Madam Helseth, who speaks of it with awe. Rebecca wants to know exactly what this white horse is; she shows amusement that

Madam Helseth evidently believes in such things. Rebecca's skeptical response reinforces the earlier impressions that suggested her opposition to the imagery of the past, and it prompts the spectators to admire her, for the note of superstition is one more effect compelling their disapproval of the spirit that seems to dominate Rosmersholm. Yet even while Rebecca scoffs, she is busily folding up her work, the white shawl, and the identity in color of the shawl and the horse indicates that whatever her conscious attitude may be, she is by no means entirely free from the implications that the horse conveys.[10]

Kroll's arrival engages Rebecca in a new conversation; this one defines the central conflict more precisely, places Kroll in relation to it, and clarifies Rebecca's role in the action. She was delighted when she saw Kroll approach, but now that he confronts her, she reveals uneasiness. He has not dropped in to visit lately, and their present interview is strained: they are not casual enough; there is too much formal politeness; he remains stiff while she makes excessive attempts to please. Kroll relaxes this tension near the end of their conversation by professing his admiration for her, but while the tension lasts, it provides a dramatic metaphor to suggest that these two are fundamentally opposed.

Kroll, in visiting Rosmersholm, reinforces the impression conveyed by its more permanent features; his nature and attitudes make the influence of the past more firmly felt. He is headmaster of a school for young people and therefore an easily acceptable symbol of tradition and conservatism. His indifference to the footbridge has shown that he is at peace with the specific elements of the past that disturb Rosmer and Rebecca. As he now announces, he has recently earned a name for himself in the community as a political agitator, and his desire to support the forces of tradition has transformed him into a keen fighter. Even here,

[10] For the significance of the shawl's color I am indebted to John Northam, *Ibsen's Dramatic Method* (London: Faber and Faber, 1953), p. 111.

alone with Rebecca, he cannot refrain from voicing his extreme bitterness toward the radicals who oppose him in the "civil war" now raging in the town:

You have read then, I suppose, how these gentlemen of the "people" have been pleased to abuse me? What infamous obscenities they have dared to resort to . . . ? Now I've tasted blood. And they shall soon get to feel that I'm not the kind of man who willingly gives up a cause.

Kroll's quarrel with the radicals gives the central conflict a new dimension and confirms the earlier suggestion that this conflict pits the old against the new. Furthermore, since Kroll so unconditionally aligns himself with the past, the characteristics Ibsen has assigned him help dictate the attitudes that the spectators must assume toward each of the opposing sides. Kroll's sincerity and determination are obvious; he is so devoted to his single view of life that he flushes with joy when Rebecca assures him that he gave as good as he got. Far more influential in determining the attitudes of the audience, however, are his offensive self-complacency, his vicious, almost cannibalistic eagerness for revenge, and his unyielding narrow-mindedness. His denunciation of the radicals includes an expression of contempt for those whose social rank is beneath his own, and to Rebecca he expresses his conviction that it makes no difference if a woman reads the radical newspapers he abhors with such intensity: no one can expect a mere woman to involve herself in anything so momentous as civil strife. Kroll's dominant qualities are such that they prompt the spectators to reject him, and to reject with him the traditional conservatism he so obviously represents.

While Kroll antagonizes, Rebecca elicits an entirely different response. Despite the absence of expository statement, Ibsen manages to articulate a fairly elaborate assessment of her character through Kroll's review of her past career: "You know—there's something fine in a woman's sacrificing her whole youth for oth-

ers, as you have done. . . . When you first came here you had
that perpetual labor with your crippled, demanding foster father." Rebecca substantiates the import of this assessment dramatically—by denying its significance. Her protests multiply: she
had nothing else to live for; Mr. West was not so difficult up in
Finmark; it was only the last two years of his life—after they
had come "down here"—which were at all hard on her. The
years that followed, the years she spent at Rosmersholm, were
certainly not unpleasant, since she was "so fond of Beata" and
knew how "dreadfully she, poor dear, needed care and sympathetic companionship." Kroll, with a ring of sincerity noticed
even by Rebecca, voices the appropriate response: "You deserve
thanks and praise for remembering her so charitably." And he recalls how, in Beata's "last unhappy years," it was Rebecca, and
Rebecca alone, who directed the household affairs.

This brief revelation of Rebecca's career and her reaction to
Kroll's praise characterize her as a woman to be respected—practical, highly competent, with the strength and courage to withstand years of hardship, yet self-effacing, warm, and thoughtful,
living only for the sake of others; she forms a sharp contrast to
the savage and revengeful Kroll. The spectators are thus compelled to view her with approval, and even Kroll is won over, as
his belated acceptance of her indicates. Pleased by what he now
sees in her, he is willing to hint that he would have no objection
if she became Rosmer's second wife; and this sign of approval increases the spectators' own favorable attitude toward her. But
Kroll's suggestion shocks Rebecca; she accuses him of joking and
refuses to hear him out. Later the spectators will be able to recall
this exchange and realize that it contained rather sinister implications, but at this point Rebecca's reaction merely confirms their
belief in her self-abnegation.

The spectators' response to Rebecca entails far more than the
approval of a human being. This conversation clarifies her role in
the action by stressing those aspects of her nature which place

her in opposition to the permanent features of the setting. She now emerges as a clear representation of the spirit of freshness and vitality which wars with the forces of tradition embodied by Rosmersholm and Kroll. The association between her and the flowers becomes explicit when Kroll notices them and marvels at the way she has brightened up "the old room." He then recalls that "poor Beata could not stand the odor," and Rebecca adds, "Nor their colors either. She became quite disturbed." These speeches bring out the full symbolic value of the flowers, which not only represent the new but also serve as a means for contrasting Rebecca to Beata, whose death provides a primary symbol of the past and its essential quality. Nor are the flowers the only device that establishes Rebecca's allegiance to the new. The account of her career reveals that she has come from Finmark, a region long associated—at least for a Norwegian audience—with the insurgent forces that challenge respectable tradition: Finmark is "the ancient stronghold of paganism, the country which, together with Finland, the Norseman's imagination to this day peoples with witches and demons." [11]

Ibsen thus prompts his spectators to reject Kroll and the past while embracing Rebecca and the spirit she symbolizes. But the conflict is more complex than a simple clash of pro and con: Ibsen is careful to ensure that his spectators will receive the action not as an allegory but as an artistic shaping of experience. Kroll, the militant conservative, has assumed the mode of the new in order to defend the traditions of his society. If his adversaries seek a battle, he is prepared to fight to the death, even to adopt their tactics, so long as they prove effective. Furthermore, despite his dominant qualities, he is not wholly objectionable. Even though the spectators see him as essentially self-centered, proud, narrow-minded, and contemptuous, they must also admire his obvious courage, sincerity, and determination. And his

[11] Hermann J. Weigand, *The Modern Ibsen* (New York: Holt, 1925), p. 206.

ultimate acceptance of Rebecca invites a corresponding acceptance of him.

Similarly, the spectators' admiration for Rebecca does not entirely eliminate all doubts. Beata's death has enabled Rebecca to
replace her as household manager at Rosmersholm—to acquire,
as she puts it, "the position I desire"—and this death remains
unexplained. Moreover, the fact that Rebecca now holds this position complicates the contrast between her and Beata; like the
shawl, it suggests that the past extends its influence even over
her. As Rebecca admits to Kroll, she had not planned to stay at
Rosmersholm, but she has grown "so familiar with the place"
that she feels almost as if she belonged to it. Rebecca is the
human embodiment of the freshness and vitality that oppose
the forces of tradition; she is the new in the house of the old.
But the spectators cannot ignore the suggestion that she and
with her the spirit she embodies have partially succumbed to the
thick walls, the rows of portraits, and the old-fashioned comfortable furniture: the spirit that opposes the past is perhaps as
fragile and temporary as the fresh flowers and the glow of twilight which symbolize it. And even as Kroll and Rebecca talk,
the spectators can see the twilight fade and the room grow
steadily darker.

Because of the complexity of the responses Ibsen has elicited,
the spectators become thoroughly committed to the moral conflicts of the play. They have been invited to desire defeat for the
past, yet they also realize its strength, and their awareness that it
is not wholly evil disturbs them. They are anxious for the entrance of Rosmer, to place him in relation to the central conflict
in order to complete their understanding. Their attitude toward
him is already partially formed, for Rebecca, when she watched
him approach, displayed an excitement indicative of strong personal attachment, and Kroll has directly expressed his affection
for "our good Johannes Rosmer." Both of these favorable attitudes naturally influence the spectators, yet they also remember

Rosmer's timidity by the footbridge. Once he has entered, more-over, they soon realize that it is Rosmer who really stands at the center of the basic conflict.

Rosmer is already firmly associated in the spectators' con-sciousness with the spirit of the past: Rosmersholm is his house; the old furniture and portraits belong to him; he has been identi-fied as a pastor, an obvious supporter of tradition and conserva-tism; and he has his own personal past that haunts him in the form of the bridge where Beata died. All these implications are amply confirmed by the warm affection for Kroll that Rosmer exhibits both verbally and visually. He is especially pleased by this visit because, as he soon remarks, Kroll has always been his personal adviser.

Nevertheless, Rosmer is just as firmly associated with the spirit that opposes the past. From the conversation between Kroll and Rebecca the spectators have learned that Rosmer enjoys having fresh, growing flowers around him. This characteristic separates him from Beata; it also tends to link him with Rebecca, and their actual relationship, as Ibsen now indicates, is a close one:

ROSMER. No, really, the thought of Beata is not painful for me. We speak of her every day. We feel almost as if she was still a part of the house.
KROLL. Do you really?
REBECCA (*lights the lamp*). Yes, we do indeed.
ROSMER. It's quite natural. We were both so deeply attached to her. And both Rebec—both Miss West and I, we know in our hearts that we did everything we could for the poor afflicted woman. We've nothing to reproach ourselves with. So I feel there's some-thing tender and peaceful in thinking of Beata now.

Rosmer here asserts his freedom from the past as represented by Beata, though his behavior at the bridge makes the assertion doubtful. Much more positive and significant is the implication evoked by the way he speaks. He begins with the single self-reference *me*, immediately alters it to include both himself and

Rebecca with the repeated *wes*—echoed by Rebecca as she looks up from the lamp—the *boths,* and the *Miss West and I,* and then completes the pattern by returning to the original self-reference, but with *I.* The inadvertent use of Rebecca's first name, which he quickly corrects to *Miss West,* reinforces the impression conveyed by the passage as a whole—that Rebecca and Rosmer are so close that what concerns him must also concern her in the same way. But the correction reveals that he is unwilling to let their intimacy be known.

The spectators become still more thoroughly convinced that the dramatic conflict pits the old against the new and that Rosmer stands at its center when, throughout the rest of the scene, they watch both Kroll and Rebecca seek to strengthen their hold on him. Kroll, for his part, fights fiercely to persuade Rosmer that a "pernicious, subversive, and disintegrative spirit" has arisen, and to assure him of the deadly seriousness of the war between conservatism and liberalism. As he argues, he continually reveals through his tone and his language his unqualified, unyielding commitment to his own narrow point of view. He has been forced, he declares, to become an "active politician" because the radicals have "shockingly" come into power. His eyes were "opened for sure" when the worst of evils occurred in his own little world: "Now the spirit of revolt has invaded the school itself." The old way of life, the Rosmersholm way, is fighting for survival and needs all the help it can get. It is clearly "high time" that every right-thinking man fulfill his "compulsory duty" and join him in the battle to save society.

With each word he speaks, Kroll increases the spectators' opposition, until he virtually loses what little sympathy he has been able to elicit. His speeches continually backfire. The spirit of revolt, he announces, has even penetrated into the sanctity of his family circle, for his own son and daughter are the ringleaders among the youth. His wife, who has always obeyed him—"in great things and small alike"—is now inclined to side with the children. Unaccountably, Kroll feels, she blames him for their recent trouble: "She says I tyrannize over the children. As if it weren't necessary to. . . ." A few minutes later, he is denouncing the publisher of the town's leading radical newspaper for his "soiled past" and his "immoral behavior." But Kroll is not only a petty tyrant and a contemptible opponent; he is also a poor advocate: his support of his own views tends to enhance the stature of his enemies. He charges that the radical newspaper poisons the minds of his students in the sixth form, but he must add that it is only the cleverest among them who have responded, and this is an unintentional admission of merit in the new spirit of revolt.

Rebecca's exertion of influence upon Rosmer is quieter and more restrained than Kroll's, but equally firm. While Kroll exhausts himself in an abundance of words, she has little to say, and this contrast presents a vital distinction between them: Kroll must talk, but Rebecca's strength does not depend on rhetoric. To maintain this contrast, Ibsen establishes Rebecca's influence by means of a visual device. Since Rosmer's entrance the room has grown darker, and Rebecca now circles about the men, going from lamp to lamp, busying herself by igniting them and bringing light into the darkness.[12] Her battle with the gloom of evening, like the flowers with which she has brightened the house, is an indication of her attempt to supplant the old spirit of quiescence and stagnation with the new spirit of freedom and life, and in this instance her effort pertains directly to the contest for Rosmer's soul. When the conversation momentarily lags and Kroll walks away, perhaps to gather strength for a renewed assault, Rebecca has her opportunity to speak privately to Rosmer: "Do it!" Despite his hesitant "Not this evening," she remains firm:

[12] Ibsen's stage directions make two references to Rebecca's activity with the lamps. But she seldom intervenes in the conversation between Kroll and Rosmer, and, when given the opportunity to speak to Rosmer, she must move closer to him. The implication is that Rebecca performs the regular evening task of lighting the several lamps that serve the sitting room.

"Yes, right now." And she then moves to the table, once more busying herself with a lamp. Her urgent words are a plea for Rosmer to break off Kroll's tirade by making his own position known, to begin the task of having the heart-to-heart talk with Kroll he had requested earlier. She is, as her action with the lamps suggests, urging Rosmer to give light also, both to Kroll, who misunderstands his position, and to himself by coming to grips with his new beliefs through confessing them publicly.

An early draft of *Rosmersholm* (the second) points up by contrast the full symbolic value of Rebecca's activity with the lamps. Act I of the draft ends without Rosmer's declaration to Kroll that the two no longer agree in their social and political beliefs. Rebecca (Mrs. Rosmer in the draft) is upset by his failure; she believes that complete emancipation cannot occur until open avowal has dissolved the former shackles once and for all: "We must have light, Rosmer." Just then the housekeeper enters, bringing with her the symbol of that light: "Here is the lamp, ma'am." [13] The final version is a brilliant improvement over the crude draft: here the symbol is not only introduced naturally but its import is conveyed by visual effect alone. It represents an order of expression entirely different from Kroll's orations. At the same time, the change also transfers the act of producing light from the servant to Rebecca so that it may affect the spectators' emotional relationship to her. As I have already noted, Rebecca's action is the first concrete display of her continual effort to battle the gloom of Rosmersholm, but more is involved than this. Since the lighting of the lamps is a regular household task, one which would have been performed in the past by Beata, it also provides a new example of the paralleling that complicates the contrast between Rebecca and Beata. Furthermore, during the earlier discussion of Beata, Rebecca had busied herself with a lamp, almost as if she were trying to rid the room of Beata's shadow. But the image of her death at the footbridge produces a

[13] Trans. A. G. Chater, *Works*, XII, 289.

cloud of unresolved mystery which is quite different from the gloom of evening, and against this darkness Rebecca's lamps are rather ineffectual. The lighting of the lamps is therefore not only a sign of her embodiment of the new; it also tends to strengthen the note of suspicion that prevents the spectators from granting her their full approval.

As Kroll nears the heart of his tirade, the spectators learn why Rosmer readily fulfills the role of pawn in the struggle between the opposing forces. His timid rebuttal of Rebecca's demand initiates a series of impressions that reveal his major trait, a basic passivity. When Kroll insists that Rosmer "take a hand" in the current strife, this trait is exposed implicitly—through the fact that it is Rebecca who answers—and then articulated:

REBECCA. But, Rector Kroll, you know very well Mr. Rosmer's distaste for such things.

KROLL. He must see to it that he overcomes his distaste, then.— You don't keep abreast of things, Rosmer. You sit here and wall yourself in with your historical collections. God knows—all due respect for genealogical tables and everything that goes with them. But this is no time for that sort of thing—unfortunately. You have no idea how things stand all over the country. In a word, every single notion's been turned topsy-turvy. It will be a herculean task to get all the errors rooted out again.

ROSMER. I quite agree. But I'm no good at that kind of work.

However their purposes may differ, all three speakers agree on the main point, Rosmer's "distaste" for decisive, public action. His own remark, perhaps, merely constitutes an attempt to avoid allying himself with Kroll, but if so, his evasiveness confirms the general impression. By emphasizing his timidity and passivity, these speeches characterize Rosmer as a man who will succumb to that side of the central conflict which is the more powerful. Kroll's image of Rosmer walling himself up within the house, surrounded by emblems of the past, suggests that the battle is already won, that Rosmer, despite his resistance to Kroll's demands and despite his apparent agreement with Rebecca, has never really freed himself from the forces of tradition.

Further evidence of Rosmer's indecisiveness emerges when Rebecca counters Kroll's attack by expressing for the first time what it was she had urged Rosmer to confess: "I think Mr. Rosmer has come to take a more open view of life . . . or freer, if you like. More unprejudiced." Her prefacing the comment with "I think" and her careful phrasing indicate anew the subtlety that supplies her with strength, for she has left the major admission to Rosmer. But once more he disappoints her. His hesitant confirmation of her statement is decidedly feeble: he claims he really understands very little about politics, but it seems to him "that in recent years people have acquired, as it were, more independence of thought." His failure to acknowledge fully the direction of his beliefs now that the proper occasion has arisen convincingly demonstrates his lack of moral courage. It forces the spectators to modify their positive attitude toward him with an element of contempt.

Despite his unwillingness to follow Rebecca's lead, however, Rosmer at least shares her ideas, and therefore the battle is in reality far from over. In the concluding movement of the scene each of the opposing forces continues to assert its strength as now Rebecca, now Kroll, seems to secure a hold on Rosmer. Rebecca lets it be known that Mortensgaard's radical newspaper is read with interest at Rosmersholm and that at least to this extent Rosmer has joined Kroll's enemies. When Kroll asks Rosmer to become editor of the *County News*, a paper that he and his fellow conservatives have set up in opposition to Mortensgaard, Rosmer expresses his complete antipathy to the idea through the look of near terror on his face and through the shocked tone of the only word he can manage in reply: "I!" But Kroll applies persuasion, and the balance is restored. An editor's work, he argues, would surely not be too conspicuous. If nothing else, might they at least have the use of Rosmer's name? That in itself would make their cause more palatable: "Your gentle, honest disposition—your fine habits of thought—your unassailable honor—these are known and valued by everyone around here." This evaluation helps restore for the spectators the more favorable attitude they have been invited to assume toward Rosmer, but far more important at this point is the accumulating stress Kroll places on Rosmer's association with the forces of the past.

In Kroll's mind Rosmer's nobility derives less from his personal nature than from his station in life: "And then there's the esteem and respect your former position as a clergyman has brought you. And of course, ultimately, your venerable family name!" Then, pointing decisively at the portraits, Kroll verbalizes a constant visual effect when he summarizes the impression made by the house and its evocation of traditional conservatism: "Rosmers of Rosmersholm—clergymen and military officers. Highly trusted public officials. True men of honor, every one of them—a family that for nearly two hundred years now has stood first in the district." Kroll's gesture and words reaffirm his own attachment to the entrenched past symbolized by Rosmersholm and its portraits. His determination to hold Rosmer to this past, as he fights to preserve it inviolate, is conveyed by a visual effect: still pointing at the portraits, he lays his free hand on Rosmer's shoulder and demonstrates more conclusively than ever before his role as the primary link between Rosmer and the past. But Kroll, as always, must also express himself verbally: "Rosmer—you owe it to yourself and to the traditions of your family to join us and defend all those things that have until now been held sacred in our society."

The next moment epitomizes the whole preceding scene. Kroll, luxuriating in the force of his persuasion, turns to ask Rebecca for her opinion. Her reply is soft laughter, and it clashes with his declamation on the sacredness of tradition like a pagan chant in a cathedral. The startling aural effect of the woman's soft laughter breaking into and silencing the harsh, persistent tones of the man promises the ultimate victory of vitality over stagnation. This effect and Rebecca's own unequivocal commitment to the new, free way of life are confirmed by her utter inability to accept Kroll's point of view: "My dear Rector, all that strikes me as unspeakably ludicrous." Kroll looks from Rebecca to Rosmer, his amazement signifying his defeat. The conflict has almost reached an open break, but Rosmer—who stands to one side voicing his protests ("No, no—be quiet! Not now!")—is temporarily spared by the entrance of Ulrik Brendel.

Some Preliminary Conclusions

Apart from its primary purpose of illustrating the interplay of verbal and nonverbal devices, the preceding analysis demonstrates three other basic characteristics of drama. The first of these is an element of performance which, like each of the concrete verbal and nonverbal effects, helps shape understanding and attitudes but which is too complex for brief illustration. This element of performance is the emerging gestalt, the *configuration* of effects—what Ronald Peacock has called "the *whole* conception in its unity of idea or impression." [14] Ibsen begins with a few suggestions, adds more, qualifies some, rejects others, and ultimately completes—not before the end of the play, however—a totality of meaning that derives from the individual effects but transcends what might be called their "sum." Thus the various details of the opening tableau *seem* to project a conflict between two opposing forces. When Kroll and Rebecca are distinguished, at least in part, by means of this conflict, the opening implication becomes more firmly established. It then solidifies in the spectators' consciousness as the thematic center of the play when they see Kroll and Rebecca, who embody the opposing forces, engage in a battle for Rosmer's allegiance. The same episodes that focus ever more clearly on the existence of this conflict also contin-

[14] *The Art of Drama* (New York: Macmillan, 1957), p. 208.

ually provide new indications of its precise nature. The significance of this emerging totality lies in its capacity to crystallize preceding implications and, especially, to illuminate subsequent details that in themselves would have little to convey. This element of drama undoubtedly constitutes the chief instrument for creating meaning throughout the major portion of a play.

The second characteristic has to do with the general nature of the moment-to-moment action occurring on the stage. Ronald Peacock has said that the primary quality of drama is "tension," [15] and though his term is applicable to all forms of serious literature, it is particularly suited to drama because it connotes not only the traditional idea of grand-scale conflict—the hero's struggle with other characters, with his environment, with his universe, or with himself—but also the momentary "conflicts" that enrich the larger design: the constant ironic qualification of one impression by another. This second kind of tension is certainly evident in the opening moments of *Rosmersholm*, and though it appears in everything that is said and done, it probably manifests itself most clearly in the personalities of the three main characters, those "bundles of opposite qualities," as John Northam called Ibsen's characters in general.[16] Rebecca, Kroll, and Rosmer unquestionably possess that "richness of the soul-complex" which, as Strindberg argued, the naturalistic dramatist could create,[17] and which, as he might have added, is the basic attribute of almost every successful dramatic character. But this kind of tension, this fusing of conflicting effects in a single complex impression, does not pertain to character alone; it pervades the entire staged experience: "the dramatic act can accommodate opposites as logic cannot." [18]

[15] *The Art of Drama*, p. 160.   [16] *Ibsen's Dramatic Method*, p. 12.
[17] Preface to *Miss Julie*, trans. Elizabeth Sprigge, *Six Plays of Strindberg* (Garden City, N.Y.: Doubleday, 1955), pp. 64–65.
[18] Wylie Sypher, *Four Stages of Renaissance Style* (Garden City, N.Y.: Doubleday, 1955), p. 162.

The source of this tension lies in the peculiarity of drama that I have been exploring throughout the first two chapters. Sophocles' *Oedipus the King*, Francis Fergusson writes in *The Idea of a Theater*, "is so arranged that we see the action, as it were, illumined from many sides at once." [19] Sophocles' tragedy is surely something out of the ordinary, but as the remainder of Mr. Fergusson's book demonstrates so brilliantly, all good drama partakes of this quality. Because drama directly presents a number of speakers, each voicing his own limited point of view, and because it is made up not only of words and their implications but also of visual, aural, and other nonverbal effects, the spectators receive innumerable disparate glimpses of the people, events, and themes from many diverse angles at one and the same time. By presenting his material "in the round," [20] the dramatist establishes in his spectators' consciousness a fusion of multiple and perhaps conflicting realizations into a single meaning. The resulting richness is an essential element and the final cause of the dramatic experience in general.

A specific element of this ultimate richness is the third characteristic of drama to be extracted from my analysis of *Rosmersholm*. The opening scenes initiate not one but three levels of action, all three of which develop together throughout the play to its conclusion, comprising in their integrated movement the dramatic action as a whole. The first level is the immediate action; it consists of the characters and the human situation in which they are presently involved. This level is directly experienced by the spectators, though some of its events, such as the behavior of Rosmer and Kroll at the footbridge, are described rather than shown. Even in the opening moments of the play, the immediate action already bristles with tension, promising the complete break between Rosmer and Kroll that is to take place in the second act. Kroll, standing solidly in support of his reactionary

[19] Princeton, N.J.: Princeton University Press, 1949, p. 17.
[20] Fergusson, *The Idea of a Theater*, p. 39.

views, cannot be budged from his purchase; Rosmer, hesitant and wary, unsure of himself and his revised opinions, is held firm by Rebecca. If the play consisted only of this tense situation and its aftermath, it would still rightly command the spectators' attention.

But *Rosmersholm* also includes a fourth character almost as important as these three: Beata. She is never seen; she exists only on the second level of the play, the retrospective action that consists of the exposition established in the opening scenes by the characters' unelaborated hints about the footbridge and about Rosmer's former wife.[21] The spectators' knowledge of the events that have preceded the immediate action will increase in subsequent scenes to such an extent that it will eventually alter the point of view from which they see Rebecca and her involvement with Rosmer. But in the opening moments the function of the oblique references to the retrospective action is to qualify only slightly the audience's understanding of the present situation. Madam Helseth's allusions to Beata help reveal her own somewhat superstitious nature, and this reflects on the house with which she is associated. Hints about Beata's fate and Rosmer's reaction to it establish the existence in his past experience of an episode that still influences his present behavior, though it has no effect on Kroll. Repeated contrasts between Beata and Rebecca help indicate Rebecca's adherence to the new way of life, but they also produce subtle implications that darken her image.

Like the retrospective action, the third level of *Rosmersholm* also remains unseen. It is neither directly presented nor specifically referred to but emerges only through the various implications established by the words and visual objects of the immediate situation. This level is the action of depth, the background or context within which the other two levels are set, which derives its existence and meaning only from them but gives them in re-

[21] I owe my distinction between immediate and retrospective action in *Rosmersholm* to Granville-Barker, in *On Dramatic Method*, pp. 176–177.

turn a larger significance. The action of depth in *Rosmersholm* is
the level of the abstract conflict between the old and the new, between tradition and progress, between death and life. The audience perceives this deepest level through the visual details of the
setting with its juxtaposition of stagnancy and growth, through
the repeated discussions of the local battle between conservatives
and liberals, through symbols like the white horse, and through
the effects that tend to identify the characters with opposing
sides in the abstract conflict. At the same time, Ibsen induces his
spectators to assume attitudes toward both sides. The past connotes death and superstition and darkness; Kroll, whom the spectators are prompted to dislike, is its staunchest defender. The
new, in contrast, connotes progress and freedom, physical and
spiritual enlightenment, and the freshness and vitality of youth.
Rebecca, generally admirable from the spectators' point of view,
supports the new calmly yet steadfastly.

In applying this distinction between the levels of action in
Rosmersholm to drama in general, it is necessary to ignore the
retrospective action, which might better be regarded as another
dimension of the immediate action: it is, after all, Ibsen (and
Sophocles in *Oedipus*) who more than anyone else employs the
retrospective action as a distinct level. In most drama, especially
before Ibsen, the revelation of past events is completed rather
early, as in *Hamlet*, even though the dramatist continually plays
on the spectators' knowledge of these events right up to the end.[22]
But the rest of the distinction is quite useful. The immediate action, then, is the concrete anecdote, the story. The action of depth,
on the other hand, is whatever broader significance this anecdote
acquires. On the level of immediate action the dramatist's concern
is to let his spectators know what is occurring and to involve
them in it. Hence, on this level, his effects are devoted to clarifying the story line, establishing the nature of his characters,

---

[22] Exposition that reports present offstage events belongs to the immediate action.

arousing and fulfilling expectations, creating irony of circumstance, and performing the myriad other tasks that make a play both entertaining and humanly relevant. On this level the characters and their activity are predominant. What matters most in the immediate action of *Hamlet*, for example, is the hero, his pursuit of Claudius, his frustrations, his agonies, his brief moments of satisfaction, his continual and varied encounters with the minor figures who surround him, and the matchless complexity of the language with which he expresses his thoughts. In the action of depth, on the other hand, particularized character and localized incident lose their autonomy to become symbolic representations that form a design having universal import. This design may be didactic, as in a thesis play—or as in a morality, where the allegory of the action of depth almost eliminates the human involvements of the immediate action. Most plays, however, are exploratory rather than didactic, and in these the design presents the spectators not with a message but with an ordered vision of life. This deeper level is not static; as the immediate situation alters, so also does the organization of images, symbols, and ideas which forms the larger design. The two levels, immediate action and action of depth, have been well distinguished for the *Oresteia* in a brief but penetrating statement by William Chase Greene: "The *Oresteia* contains two dramas: first, the external fortunes of Agamemnon and his family; and, behind this drama, the vindication of the moral law of fate." [23]

The relationship between the two levels admits of several possible combinations. The action of depth may constitute no more than a mere rendering of the concrete events in abstract terms. An earlier *Hamlet*, an "Ur-Hamlet," if it ever existed, might well have been an ordinary revenge play, signifying only that revenge can be a pretty difficult job. Another *Hamlet*, unquestionably an imaginary one, might even allow its audience to accept the notorious "This is the tragedy of a man who could not make up his

[23] *Moira: Fate, Good, and Evil in Greek Thought* (New York: Harper and Row, 1963), p. 125.

mind" which is spoken by a narrator at the beginning of the Olivier film version of Shakespeare's play. Far more often, however, as in *Rosmersholm*, the action of depth thickens the significance of the concrete anecdote by demonstrating a pattern of abstractions that are meaningful in themselves and that illuminate the characters' relationships to one another and to their environment. In what is perhaps its most complex form the action of depth evolves a dramatic pattern that is not ostensibly the subject of the immediate action: thus in the real *Hamlet* the immediate action's concern with revenge yields in the action of depth to an exploration of the nature of the universe. Whatever their relationship, the two levels exist, in *Hamlet* and in drama generally. In the well-ordered play the two levels are fused throughout. From their interrelated and simultaneous development emerges the basic meaning of the whole.

One reason for the fusion is that the action of depth exists only by means of the immediate action, through its words and their implications, through its visual and aural symbols, and through the unchanging features of the theater in which the play is staged. The action of depth emerges through the immediate action like light through a prism, and just as the prism receives its color and design from the light filtering through it, so also the action of depth gives the immediate action the richness of texture that makes it something more than a mere reproduction of life's surface. But at the same time, the prism refracts the light, alters its structure, and distinguishes its components; in the same way the immediate action gives the action of depth its flesh and blood and therefore its relevance to a human spectator. Without the light the prism would be less interesting; without the prism the properties of the light cannot be examined. The abstractions of the action of depth deserve our attention if we are to understand the play. But since they owe their existence to the immediate action, we cannot strip it away and focus directly on the larger design. Nor would it be right to do so.

Part II: The Immediate Action

3. Presentation of Character

The action of drama tends to be chiefly interpersonal. It is action, that is, which is not confined to the purely private sphere, as is so often the case in lyric poetry; it is in the main something done by someone to someone else, of such a nature as to affect his condition or future. In a word, it is action in which people act upon each other.
—Elder Olson, *Tragedy and the Theory of Drama*

On the level of immediate action, as I have said, character is predominant. But the dramatic character is a "fiction" in more than one sense. In the first place, he has no existence beyond the experience of which he is a part. It is not possible, for example, to determine what Hamlet did before and between the scenes—unless that activity is described within the play, as in Ophelia's account of his visit to her chamber (II.i)—or to know how he would have ruled Denmark had he lived. Hamlet could not have lived: his nature is inseparable from the fact, time, place, and circumstance of his death. Nor is it possible to describe the girlhood of Shakespeare's heroines. They, like Hamlet (or Rebecca, or Clytaemestra), are not people; they are representational images established only by the actual impressions of the play. Furthermore, the character does not even exist autonomously *within* the dramatic experience. His nature consists partly of words that also belong to a larger design which continues whether or not he is on the stage, partly of various acts that at the same time form but a single strand of the action as a whole, partly of the words and acts that simultaneously constitute the nature of other characters.

What is normally called a character is therefore two separate things. He is, on the one hand, a series of impressions woven into the composite pattern formed by the entire play. This series of impressions clusters around a single label—for example, Hamlet—and acquires substance from the personality of the actor, whose continued identification with the label focuses and sustains the implications of the related impressions. On the other hand, the character is a perception that takes shape in the consciousness of the spectators and consists of the realizations and attitudes that the received impressions awaken. As they watch the actor performing his part, the perception and the visible figure coalesce. For them the actor thus perceived becomes an individual possessing a nature that can be described in terms of the human personality; for them the actor thus perceived *is* Hamlet.

The dramatic character is not, in other words, a separate entity with autonomous existence. But it is possible to isolate him arbitrarily in order to study the methods by which his creator establishes the effects that instill the spectators' perception. These methods, for the sake of convenience, can be arranged under four general categories: audience foreknowledge, extratextual signs, the character's relationships with others, and his own activity and speech.[1]

The Methods

Audience Foreknowledge. This category pertains generally to each of the others, because the dramatist, working in a medium

[1] For somewhat similar lists that have influenced mine, see Gilbert Norwood, "The Nature and Methods of Drama," in *Euripides and Shaw* (London: Methuen, 1921), p. 133; Frank O'Hara and Margueritte Bro, *A Handbook of Drama* (Chicago: Willett, Clark, 1938), pp. 89–94; and Sir John Squire, *Shakespeare as a Dramatist* (London: Cassell, 1935), pp. 138–144.

especially dependent on inference, anticipates a group of spectators capable of apprehending his effects and interpreting them in relation to its own experience. He relies, in other words, on a sure knowledge of his audience's expectations, values, beliefs, ideas, prejudices, and emotions. Sometimes the precise significance of the dramatist's effects depends on local and temporary notions, and can be recovered only by historical investigation. But this is not always as great a problem as it might seem. To properly understand Apollo in Aeschylus' *The Eumenides*, it is helpful but not entirely necessary to know how a Greek audience would react to his argument that the Furies, who punish crimes against blood relations, have no right to pursue Orestes for killing his mother:

> The mother is no parent of that which is called
> her child, but only nurse of the new-planted seed
> that grows. The parent is he who mounts. A stranger she
> preserves a stranger's seed [ll. 658–661].

The modern spectator would undoubtedly condemn this speciousness out of hand. But not the Greek, who would probably view the argument with considerable ambivalence.[2] Fortunately, however, the change in assumptions about blood relationship does not greatly handicap the modern audience in its understanding of Apollo. Although it would intellectually reject the substance of his argument, it also has an emotional involvement in the play: it desires Orestes' release, and consequently it would emotionally approve *any* argument put forth on his behalf. The resulting tension between the intellectual and the emotional responses therefore produces an ambivalence toward Apollo much like that which would be aroused in the Greek audience by his argument alone. Thus, even when a particular effect has been shorn of the frame of reference to which it appeals, its function will very likely be fulfilled by the context in which it occurs.

[2] See Chapter 8, p. 337.

Exact knowledge of the world view for which a play was written obviously increases appreciation and understanding, but most
plays that endure do so because the dramatist, in creating his implications, has addressed himself principally to the more permanent intellectual and emotional qualities of the human consciousness.

The category of audience foreknowledge becomes significant
in itself, however, only when the dramatist has assumed that his
audience possesses knowledge and expectations of particular relevance to his play, and therefore this category is most meaningful
for those plays, like the Greek and the Elizabethan, which take
their plots from legend, history, or popular tales. In the *Agamemnon*, for example, Aeschylus presupposes in his spectators a
knowledge of Clytaemestra's nature. Until she has murdered
Agamemnon she plays flawlessly the role of the faithful wife eagerly awaiting her lord's return, and since she is sufficiently convincing to deceive the chorus of Argive Elders, the spectators
must already have some awareness of her character or they cannot understand her activity at the altar during the long first choral ode. The legend of the House of Atreus was easily familiar to
every Greek spectator. Homer's *Odyssey*, which itself assumes
so thorough a knowledge of the legend that it refers to its events
only obliquely in analogy to Odysseus' adventures, was given
public readings in Athens at least every four years during the
Panathenaic festival.[3] During these readings the Greeks could
hear from Agamemnon's own lips—when he speaks to Odysseus
in the underworld (Book XI)—that Clytaemestra was a traitress,
an accursed deceiver, the epitome of the treachery of all women.
The universal knowledge of her character is also indicated by the
account of her crime in Pindar's "Eleventh Pythian," in which
the poet tells how Agamemnon fell, "cut down by Klytaimnes-
tra's / strong hands," and wonders which of several possible mo-

[3] Moses Hadas, *A History of Greek Literature* (New York: Columbia
University Press, 1950), p. 27.

tives "vexed her to drive in anger the hand of violence," what "set her awry." [4]

It is foreknowledge of this sort that Aeschylus calls up in his spectators' consciousness through the Watchman's reference to "a lady's / male strength of heart in its high confidence" (ll. 10–11). When Clytaemestra professes to the chorus that her supreme joy upon hearing of Agamemnon's safe homecoming stems from a desire to have her husband with her again, the spectators know she is lying. They know that she is bursting with hatred, impatient for her husband's return only because she wishes to kill him. The unsuspecting chorus is fooled, but the spectators realize that behind her pose of innocence she hides a will primed to the act of vengeance. As a result, her silent activity at the altar during the first choral ode evokes sinister implications. What seems to be the appropriate act of the faithful wife is in reality both a thank offering for the deliverance of Agamemnon into her hands and a prayer requesting divine aid in carrying out her intentions. Clytaemestra is the most prominent character in the play, but until she has killed her husband she refuses to speak openly. Therefore the audience's understanding of her is controlled almost entirely by two devices: prior knowledge of her character, and her attempt to conceal her treachery, with the second device serving to increase the hostility already instilled by the first.

Reliance upon the spectators' prior knowledge of a character is widespread in Greek tragedy. Sometimes, as in the example of Clytaemestra, this foreknowledge completes an image; sometimes it becomes a source of profound ironies, as in Sophocles' Oedipus; sometimes—quite often in Euripides—it provides an unverbalized contrast to emphasize the significance of the dramatist's new interpretations of familiar characters and events. Similar possibilities were available to the Elizabethan dramatists: such char-

[4] The Odes of Pindar, trans. Richmond Lattimore (Chicago: University of Chicago Press, 1947), pp. 90–91.

acters as Faustus, Prince Hal, and (perhaps) Hamlet possessed established reputations, and the audience who witnessed the first performance of *King Lear* probably knew both the legend and the old play and would realize in advance the true depths of Cordelia's love, a knowledge that helps clarify her behavior in the first scene and heighten her father's folly. More recent dramatists have less occasion to anticipate specific foreknowledge in their audiences, but it is still pertinent for plays like *Look Homeward, Angel,* which dramatize novels, or plays like *Saint Joan,* which portray historical figures. The most important use of it in modern drama, however, is by those dramatists, like Eliot, Sartre, Anouilh, and Giraudoux, who specialize in the reinterpretation of myth.

Extratextual Signs. The devices of this category, which consist of direct authorial assertions, are also logically prior to anything the characters themselves say or do. Some of these devices are purely visual; those which need to be introduced by an onstage speaker in no way depend for their validity on the speaker's reliability. Independent of the complexity that characterizes speech in drama and of the subtleties attendant upon self-revelation, these devices provide the spectator with a set of "given" facts about the character.

One of these devices is the "charactonym," or label name, which provides a shorthand method of epitomizing the character's nature, function, or both. A staple of the morality tradition, this device also appears in comedy from Aristophanes to Shaw. It is rarer in melodrama and tragedy, but Lillo's *The London Merchant* has such character labels as Thorowgood, Trueman, and Blunt, and in *The Revenger's Tragedy,* Vendice declares, for those whose Italian is weak, that his own name means "a revenger" (IV.ii.193).

Formal realism, normally unfriendly to all unrealistic conventions, often retains a subtle version of the interpretive name. Ibsen had occasionally used the charactonym in his early verse plays—Brand, for example, means both "fire" and "sword"—and he always remained conscious of the possible connotative value in a name. A study of his drafts reveals the extraordinary care he took with this feature of his drama. A new revision of a play ordinarily introduces a new name for each character, and often the names change abruptly in the course of a single draft. In the drafts of *Rosmersholm*, Kroll is first called Hekmann and then Gylling before he ultimately receives his final name in the finished version.[5] The name Kroll, with its single tense syllable, corresponds aurally and kinesthetically to the character's stiff and unyielding manner. More important, the name also sounds suspiciously like *trold*, or troll, a creature recurring frequently in the Norse imagination and in Ibsen's plays as something to be detested and feared, a diabolic creature which, as M. C. Bradbrook describes it, represents "humanity minus the specifically human qualities; at once a hideous parody of man and yet only the isolation of his worst potentialities."[6] Rosmer's name, which Ibsen quickly changed from S. to Boldt-Römer to Rosenhjelm to Rosmer, was one of the earliest to be selected in its final form. Both the second and third versions are long-established and respected family names in Norway,[7] and the final choice remains enough like them to preserve the connotations of tradition and respectability. In addition, it brings into greater prominence a syllable that must have been important to Ibsen's conception of the character. The similarity of sound (-Römer, Rosen-, Rosmer) suggests he was trying to associate the name in his Norwegian audience's consciousness with the denotations of the Norse *ros* (praise, encomium), just as the man himself attracts the praise and admiration of his acquaintances, both through his position in life and through his quiet, generally noble nature.

But the charactonym, whether explicitly allegorical or subtly

[5] *The Works of Henrik Ibsen*, ed. William Archer (New York: Scribner's, 1911–1912), XII, 268, 273.

[6] *Ibsen the Norwegian* (London: Chatto and Windus, 1946), p. 56.

[7] Halvdan Koht, *The Life of Ibsen*, trans. Ruth McMahon and Hanna Larsen (New York: Norton, 1931), II, 230.

suggestive, is not the only means by which the dramatist can directly define his character. The "List of Characters" that heads the printed version of *Rosmersholm* exemplifies another, for both Kroll and Rosmer are there assigned professions that pertain, however remotely, to their natures and their functions, and these professions are specifically mentioned in the opening minutes of the play. Kroll's job as headmaster may not tell an audience very much about him, but it certainly fits the conservatism to be established by the details of his speech and activity. Rosmer, according to the "List," is a "former clergyman," and again, while nothing very elaborate is expressed, the epithet prepares for the tension between one belief and another which his behavior manifests. But details of this kind—profession, status, sex, and so forth—are ordinarily more pertinent in plays of the past, when they belonged to well-ordered, hierarchical systems of value. To the Greeks, Agamemnon was ruler of his land, while Clytaemestra was only his wife. Shakespeare's Lear is king, father, and old man, and his tragedy cannot be fully appreciated without a realization that each of these roles would exact from an Elizabethan audience an immense amount of respect.[8] Undoubtedly, however, this method of characterization has its greatest importance for those dramatists who subscribe to such rigid formulations as the Renaissance doctrine of decorum, which dictates that a character behave in accordance with his nationality, age, sex, social position, and the situation in which he is placed.[9]

The remaining extratextual signs—which are visual rather than verbal—stem from the material details associated with the character: his appearance, his costume, his possessions, his milieu. As with his name and status, the specific techniques employed depend a great deal on the audience's particular frame of reference.

[8] See William Rosen, *Shakespeare and the Craft of Tragedy* (Cambridge, Mass.: Harvard University Press, 1960), pp. 1–2.

[9] See Madeleine Doran, *Endeavors of Art* (Madison: University of Wisconsin Press, 1954), pp. 77–79, 217–232.

Shakespeare can accomplish much in the way of character definition by endowing Richard III with a hump or Caliban with fins, or by having his stage manager paint Aaron the Moor black.[10] But if Ibsen wants to define one of his characters through his appearance, he must rely on his spectators' ability to respond to vague suggestions. When Peter Mortensgaard first arrives, in *Rosmersholm*, he "enters softly and quietly"; he is a "small, slender man with thin reddish hair and beard" (stage direction, II, p. 159). His appearance awakens no automatic response, but it is indeed significant; as John Northam points out, Mortensgaard's appearance matches his nature: "The play tells us that he is foxy— colour, size, and gait suggest a wary, cunning animal. Even the thin hair suggests a meagre personality." [11]

The same dichotomy pertains to costume. Nothing could be more confident than the tone of Donatus describing Roman comedy in the fourth century A.D.:

The old men in comedies wear white costumes, because they are held to be the oldest sort. Young men wear a variety of colors. The slaves in comedy wear thick shawls, either as a mark of their former poverty, or in order that they may run the faster. Parasites wear twisted *pallas*. Those who are happy wear white robes; the unhappy wear soiled robes; the rich wear royal purple, paupers wear reddish-purple; the soldier carries a purple *chlamys;* a girl wears a foreign robe; a procurer, a robe of many colors; yellow, to designate greed, is given to the courtesan.[12]

---

[10] See J. Dover Wilson, *"Titus Andronicus* on the Stage in 1595," *Shakespeare Survey,* I (1948), 17–22, 32.

[11] *Ibsen's Dramatic Method* (London: Faber and Faber, 1953), pp. 118–119.

[12] *De Comoedia et Tragoedia,* trans. Mildred Rogers, in *European Theories of the Drama,* ed. Barrett H. Clark (New York: Crown, 1947), p. 45. For a similar account of the function of masks in classical tragedy, comedy, and satyr play, see Julius Pollux, *Onomastikon,* reprinted in *A Source Book in Theatrical History,* ed. A. M. Nagler (New York: Dover, 1952), pp. 10–15.

But when Strindberg wishes to establish a point by means of costume in *Miss Julie*, he must do so with great care. Jean first appears in his livery, but he soon changes—at Julie's insistence—to his fancy-dress black coat, which serves to symbolize his ascendency above the woman who has been his superior. Later, when her father's bell rings, he quickly changes back to his livery even before he replies through the speaking tube. Jean himself indicates the symbolic value of his uniform:

I don't know why—I can't now—I don't understand. . . . It's just as if this coat made me—I can't give you orders—and now that the Count has spoken to me—I can't quite explain, but . . . well, that devil of a lackey is bending my back again. I believe if the Count came down now and ordered me to cut my throat, I'd do it on the spot.[13]

By means of costume the spectators are shown that Jean is still inherently the servant, that he cannot rise above himself even in his own mind. Julie needs his dominance despite his failure, however, needs him to give her the final command before she can go through with her suicide. The costuming, by indicating that Jean has not really risen, implies the great depth to which Julie has fallen. But no spectator could safely do without Jean's own spoken realization.

Stage properties are equally problematic. Those of the Shakespearean theater—the thrones, the crowns, the books, and the mirrors—are few and usually related to fixed codes of iconography. But to define Rosmer through his possessions, Ibsen requires a well-filled stage, like that described in the first stage direction in Act II of *Rosmersholm*. This act takes place in Rosmer's study, which contains "a writing table covered with books and papers"; shelves and cases of books surround the desk; the furniture, which is "plain," includes "an old-fashioned couch." This

---

[13] Trans. Elizabeth Sprigge, *Six Plays of Strindberg* (Garden City, N.Y.: Doubleday, 1955), p. 113.

setting stresses those qualities of the first-act sitting room which embody the deep-rooted conservatism of Rosmersholm: Rebecca's touch is nowhere in evidence. Since this is Rosmer's room, its furnishings strengthen the suggestion of his personal attachment to the old-fashioned life. His bookish nature, asserted verbally in Act I, is here made visible by the generous supply of books, particularly those scattered on the table and apparently in frequent use. But Rosmer now ignores the books; as he sits at the desk, "he cuts and flips through the pages of a pamphlet and reads a little here and there." The uncut pages of the pamphlet signify its newness, and a pamphlet, like a newspaper, is the verbal weapon of the latest cause. Rosmer, surrounded by his old-fashioned furniture and his volumes of genealogies, is nevertheless more interested in current ideas: the conflict within him between his conservative past and his radical idealism manifests itself even in the nature of his room.

The Relationship between Characters. Character is rarely defined in isolation from its context, and this context includes the numerous effects arising from the simultaneous presence of other characters. One of the most important devices guaranteed by the interpersonal nature of drama is the evaluation of one character by another, whether explicitly formulated or left to the actor to communicate through his gestures, facial expressions, and intonations of voice—though, as my first chapter argues, these evaluations are of more than one kind and have varying degrees of authority. Furthermore, since drama is a dynamic, constantly changing experience, one character's impression of another seldom carries a great deal of weight with the audience. On the whole, each evaluation that is sufficiently authoritative, consistently reiterated, or agreed on by a number of observers without adequate persuasion to the contrary will earn its place as a major definition of its subject. But some evaluations pertain only to the character's immediate involvement in a peculiar set of circumstances or to the immediate response to him by others. Some evaluations have little effect because of the obvious prejudices of the characters who initiate them. Others may lose relevance when obscured by more important issues. Still others will lack force because the audience has already formed its own impression.

The impossibility of establishing a general rule is well exemplified by Hamlet's evaluation of Claudius as a "Remorseless, treacherous, lecherous, kindless villain!" (II.ii.576). As I will show in the next section, these words are excessive even in their immediate context. In addition, Claudius' future behavior, in aside (III.i.49–54) and soliloquy (III.iii.36–72), will provide a quite different view of his nature, one that stresses the agony of his remorse. But the original assessment is Hamlet's—which gives it immense value for the spectators—and Hamlet consistently advances it. Moreover, despite the complexity with which Shakespeare endows Claudius, the extreme view of him is the most useful dramatic attitude for the final scene, when Hamlet at last punishes the villain for his unnatural treachery. Further complications are added to Hamlet's words by an additional and extremely important aspect of the relationship between characters. Every evaluation serves two functions: it not only helps define the character evaluated, but it also acts as a key effect for defining the speaker, since he will call attention only to that which his own nature and involvement permit him to see. As Shaw knew, "a man always describes himself unconsciously whenever he describes anyone else." [14]

Apart from his spoken and implicit attitudes, the mere presence of a second character provides valuable insights for the audience's understanding of the first. The spectators perceive Rebecca's nature more clearly because Ibsen places her in contrast to Kroll—and vice versa. With most dramatists this revelation by contrast acts as a major device; Shakespeare, for example, is fond of creating triads. In *1 Henry IV*, Prince Hal stands somewhere between Hotspur's extreme, with its fanatical devotion to cause

[14] Preface to *Saint Joan* (Baltimore: Penguin Books, 1951), p. 42.

and its conception of honor as an absolute that dictates the behavior of men, and Falstaff's opposite extreme, which jocularly disregards any abstractions that might interfere with bodily ease and pleasure. The triad in *Hamlet* consists of three sons, each seeking to avenge the death of his father. Its value lies in the various individual contrasts it creates and especially in the way these contrasts help illuminate Hamlet and his situation. On one side is Laertes, whose impetuosity makes him forget custom, religious precept, and the social order. He would sacrifice all to his intention:

> To hell, allegiance! Vows, to the blackest devil!
> Conscience and grace, to the profoundest pit!
> I dare damnation. To this point I stand,
> That both the worlds I give to negligence,
> Let come what comes; only I'll be reveng'd
> Most throughly for my father   [IV.v.128–133].

At the other extreme, Fortinbras, less deeply moved, bides his time, aloofly awaiting his opportunity. He expresses his sense of conviction in a far different idiom:

> I have some rights of memory in this kingdom,
> Which now to claim my vantage doth invite me
> > [V.ii.381–382].

In between these extremes, Hamlet suffers, too deeply involved to be a Fortinbras, too sensitive to the full implications of human action to be a Laertes. He faces a dilemma, a choice in which neither alternative is acceptable. To wait would be to incur the remorse that stings him when he neglects his vow; to act would be to commit himself to a code of behavior that grossly simplifies his understanding of life's complexities. So he operates according to the circumstances of the moment, sometimes in undue haste, as when he stabs Polonius, sometimes not at all, as when he spares Claudius, but never, until the end perhaps, approaching the calm indifference of Fortinbras.

Contrast is not the only means by which the presence of one character illuminates the nature of another. The opening scenes of *Rosmersholm* present a triad of a different sort, one which utilizes parallelism rather than contrast. Rosmer's inner conflict between the traditional conservatism of his family heritage and the new liberal idealism he seeks to activate emerges clearly in the spectators' view only because Kroll and Rebecca occupy the stage with him. Rosmer's conflict is internal and temporarily remains so; the spectators can perceive it not through anything he says or does but because Ibsen dramatizes it much in the manner of a morality play. In the long battle for his allegiance, Kroll and Rebecca, without losing their own autonomy, serve as external representations of the two forces at war in Rosmer's mind. They thus resemble the Good Angel and Bad Angel who stand on either side of the hero in the moralities (and in *Doctor Faustus*), articulating the alternatives that foment his inner turmoil. Kroll's proximity throws attention on those aspects of Rosmer that still link him to staunch conservatism. Rebecca's proximity provides a parallel to highlight Rosmer's tendency toward a "freer, more unprejudiced" view of life. Without the parallels their presence establishes, Rosmer's inner conflict would be far less obvious. Its presentation would depend on such material details as the house he owns and the flowers he so warmly responds to, and on the hints supplied by his behavior and the few things he is willing to say.

The Character's Activity and Speech. This category, the most important of the four, consists of the character's self-revelations: the things he does, the things he says, and the way in which he says them. Its typical effects are well illustrated by the soliloquy with which Hamlet concludes Act II (II.ii.542–601).

What Hamlet *does* here is seize an opportunity to speak, to unburden himself. And this is characteristic of him: it is his fourth soliloquy of the play, and it joins as well a whole series of speeches—such as his insistence that he knows "not seems" (I.ii.76–86), his account of the "vicious mole of nature" (I.iv.23–38), and his description of man (II.ii.292–309)—which are addressed to others but serve principally to summarize those few deep concerns that he may safely make public. Insofar as this soliloquy is a speech that allows him to express his feelings, then, it belongs to that rich strand of impressions which characterize him as a man who needs to "unpack [his] heart with words," as he puts it here (II.ii.581). But this speech has no onstage listeners; it repeats the situation of the first soliloquy, in which Hamlet also saw the exit of the others as a cue for formulating verbally the feelings he thought he must suppress when speaking to them, and it emphasizes this situation in its opening statement: "Now I am alone" (l. 542). It thus helps establish Hamlet's sense of isolation. The very act of soliloquy suggests a man on the defensive, a man who must watch and wait and proceed with caution, a man well aware that he is being spied on.

What Hamlet *says* in this speech is that he has basely neglected fulfilling his vow of revenge (ll. 542–583) but that he will now at least make a beginning by using the play to confirm the Ghost's accusations (ll. 584–601). The entire sixty lines therefore focus on the subject of revenge. What is significant, however, is not the subject—that comes as no surprise—but the emphasis given it at this particular point. Hamlet's purpose has not been mentioned overtly anywhere in the act—some seven hundred lines. He has himself been present more than half of this time, talking with Polonius, with Rosencrantz and Guildenstern, and with the players about a variety of things, but mostly about the theater. He has played the madman, shown contempt for Polonius, expressed dissatisfaction with the world, and been delighted by the arrival of the players. Now, suddenly, the theme of revenge re-emerges. The effect is twofold. On the one hand, his sudden return to this theme the moment he has the opportunity to speak unheard indicates how fully he has committed himself to his vow. It suggests that the commitment has dominated his thoughts throughout the preceding scene, in which he was presumably concerned with other matters. And it suggests, therefore, that his commitment is always there, just below the varied surface of his many public dialogues. On the other hand, the sudden mention of revenge contrasts sharply with the almost casual, almost irrelevant chats with Polonius and the others, and the contrast dramatically underscores Hamlet's own insistence that he ignores his duty.

Equally important is his *manner of speaking*, for it illustrates a number of common dramatic devices that belong under the general heading of definition by speech. One of these is self-assessment. Hamlet calls himself "a rogue and peasant slave" (l. 543), "a dull and muddy-mettl'd rascal" (l. 561), "an ass" (l. 578); he compares himself to a whore, a drab, and a scullion (ll. 581–583); he implies that he is "pigeon-liver'd and lack[s] gall" (l. 572). Self-assessment—whether explicit like Richard III's "I am determined to prove a villain" (I.i.30) or implicit like Rebecca West's denial that life in the service of others has caused her hardship—occurs frequently in drama. The spectators would probably believe Richard, because he speaks to them as prologue of his play and because his statement fits his reputation; and Richard, of course, never disappoints them. They would probably believe Rebecca because in making her denial she deliberately silences Kroll's praise of her, and the purpose of the speech thereby affirms the self-effacement implied by its content. But Hamlet's words work otherwise. No impression Shakespeare has thus far given of him justifies so severe an evaluation. Because they are exaggerated, Hamlet's self-denunciations create a false picture that is easily rejected. Nevertheless, the exaggeration itself helps convey the intensity of his feeling: the tone is that of a man who unjustly castigates himself through overwhelming remorse.

Devices of style provide further evidence of his deep remorse and also suggest a far more significant aspect of his nature. The soliloquy has a ring of violence. For two-thirds of it, at least, the sense pattern of the words varies so widely from the underlying metrical pattern of the blank verse that only two or three syllables per line receive any stress, and these an abnormal amount. This portion of the soliloquy is a series of rapid-fire questions and exclamations. The normal unit between emphatic pauses is not the single line or the verse paragraph but the phrase or word. The whole effect is epitomized by the short ejaculatory lines that punctuate the speech and further heighten its irregularity: "For Hecuba! (l. 551); "Yet I" (l. 560); "Ha!" (l. 570); "O, vengeance!" (l. 577); "Fie upon't! foh!" (l. 583). All these qualities of the verse dramatize Hamlet's deep-seated agitation; he is quite obviously trying to goad himself into action. This suggests not only his remorse—like the self-denunciations, the tension in the verse seems almost a physical scourging, a penitential bodily mortification—but it also suggests a reason for his failure to carry out the vow: he must goad himself because something in his nature prevents him from acting otherwise. His diction adds to this impression; here, for example, is his evaluation of Claudius:

Bloody, bawdy villain!
Remorseless, treacherous, lecherous, kindless villain! [ll. 575–576].

The words may accurately convey Hamlet's opinion of his uncle, but they are excessive, and the excess is emphasized by the repetition, the alliteration, and the rhyme. Hamlet is caught up in these words; he expends his rage in *them* rather than in physical action; he is destroying Claudius verbally because, evidently, he cannot bring himself to destroy him in fact.

Even the emotional structure of the soliloquy is revealing in this respect. It begins with restrained excitement while Hamlet works out, in a somewhat orderly fashion, the comparison between himself and the player who weeps for Hecuba. Once that comparison accuses him, however, he gives way to the uncontrolled emotional debauch that forms the center of the speech.

Then, suddenly, he restores control—"About, my brains" (l. 584)—and the rest of the soliloquy, which expounds his plan to trap Claudius, is both calm and orderly. The pattern reveals that Hamlet, despite the deep intensity of his feelings, can nevertheless still keep himself in hand. Yet in emphasizing this capacity, it throws added focus on the means by which he does so, and this detail creates its own significant effect. Hamlet has driven himself almost to a frenzy because he has failed to act; the expectation is that only a decision to now act in earnest can relieve his excitement. As a matter of fact, however, he finds a reason to continue waiting, a reason he can cling to without any worry— for the time being—that he is guilty of procrastination.

Hamlet's soliloquy thus exemplifies a number of the possibilities available to the dramatist for defining character through activity and speech. In this soliloquy Shakespeare combines act, statement, and style to present the impression of a man in painful conflict because of his commitment to a vow and his inability or unwillingness to carry it out. To say that this soliloquy tells the whole story, however, would be an exaggeration as gross as Hamlet's self-assessments. For this speech is one moment of action that follows many others devoted to Hamlet and precedes a great many yet to come. It does not therefore *define* Hamlet; it instead highlights some rather important aspects of his nature while neglecting others. Insofar as it emphasizes his need to expend his feelings in words rather than action, it simply ignores the unhesitating eagerness with which, in the preceding act, he went in pursuit of the Ghost. And insofar as it stresses revenge as a concern so dominating that it usurps control of his private thoughts, it will be refuted by the next soliloquy—about fifty-five lines later (III.i.56–88)—which never mentions it. Like all moments of action that help reveal character, this soliloquy elaborates rather than replaces the developing pattern of which it forms a part.

As a part of that whole pattern, Hamlet's soliloquy also illustrates a further means of defining a character through his speech. The self-assessments, rhythms, and structure of the speech pertain most directly to the particular moment. But when Hamlet refers to "John-a-dreams" (l. 562) or talks of tweaking noses (l. 568) or expounds a bit of popular theater lore, his words belong less to the moment than to his whole nature, for he here draws on the kind of imagery that pervades all his speeches. As Mikhail M. Morozov has shown, Hamlet's typical imagery is characterized by its unlimited range, its simplicity and prosaism, and its frequent recourse to riddles, popular sayings, proverbs, games, and hunting. In general, Morozov concludes, Hamlet's imagery stresses his determination "to understand life to the end, to approach it directly and face to face." [15] The range and variety of Hamlet's images tend to define him in a general way. More important, perhaps, is the effect upon the spectators' attitude toward him, for the nature of his images should and does make him especially attractive, and the revelation of his passionate involvement in all phases of life vastly increases the significance of his intense suffering.

As the consistency of Hamlet's imagery suggests, a character's typical style may well be itself an important means of establishing his nature, as it unquestionably is in the later Shakespeare. [16] Nor is this device confined to verse drama: Una Ellis-Fermor, a translator of *Rosmersholm*, shows that in the original Norwegian each character speaks in a prose style peculiar to himself. Her account is worth quoting in full:

Each of these characters has his own distinctive language; syntax, vocabulary, and rhythms all image the mind. Rosmer speaks the grave, natural prose of an old-fashioned gentleman; Kroll passes,

[15] "The Individualization of Shakespeare's Characters through Imagery," *Shakespeare Survey*, II (1949), 93–101, 95.

[16] For an elaborate analysis of one character's speech style, see Una Ellis-Fermor's examination of Coriolanus, in *Shakespeare the Dramatist*, ed. Kenneth Muir (London: Methuen, 1961), pp. 132–138.

when roused, from his slightly pompous manner, with its occasional German constructions, into the language of the platform and sometimes to that of hustings; Mrs. Helseth's idiom is homely and wholesome; Brendel's a bewildering confusion of the colloquial and the inflated, full of clichés and imperfectly remembered foreign phrases; Mortensgaard's a flashy mixture of the colloquial and racy, but, when he is strongly moved, plain and manly; Rebekka's is at once the easiest and the most direct, changing from fluency to terseness as the tension grows.[17]

Rebecca's style, which seems to be the least expressive, substantiates by its simplicity her no-nonsense practicality and clear-headed competence. As an independent effect Rebecca's style might signify very little; in the play, of course, it is heard and felt as it contrasts with the styles of the other speakers.

The Methods in Context

In cataloguing the various devices that present character, I have isolated each from its dramatic context; during the synthesis of performance, however, each effect these devices produce is modified by its juxtaposition to others, and a single moment of action incorporates several devices that may simultaneously establish impressions of many different characters. For when two characters face each other, each is engaged in activity; each exhibits his attitude toward the other; each exposes his own nature through his speech; each is a visible object. Nor do the devices all have equal value: activity is more reliable than words; evaluations admit of innumerable qualifications; audience foreknowledge and extratextual signs have less influence than the more immediate effects of drama. Because of his temperament, or because of the conventions he works with, a dramatist will employ

[17] Introduction to *The Master Builder and Other Plays by Henrik Ibsen* (Harmondsworth, Middlesex, Eng.: Penguin Books, 1958), p. 15.

some devices more readily than others. As his purposes change, he will introduce the devices in different arrangements. While the Greeks, with their prologue, chorus, and messenger, frequently define a character through expository statement, and the Elizabethans emphasize the evaluation of a character through detailed assessments by others, the practitioner of formal realism gives equal weight to devices of every kind. These and other complexities of character definition warrant the examination of a few dramatic characters in their specific contexts.

Agamemnon. Aeschylus' method of controlling his audience's relationship to Agamemnon illustrates the Greek tendency to define character through expository statement, but it also illustrates a technique common to all drama, the technique of defining and evaluating a character before he actually appears. The spectators come to the play with a preconceived notion of Agamemnon. The title, which designates him as the central character, prompts them to pay special attention to the indications of his nature conveyed by the expository statements of the Watchman, chorus, and Herald, and by the implications of Clytaemestra's speech and activity. When Agamemnon himself finally enters at the beginning of the carpet scene, his own speech and activity and the material details associated with him confirm the validity of the point of view already established.

The Watchman's brief mention of his king is not an assessment; instead, it phrases for the spectators one of the potential attitudes toward him, that of his loyal slave. The Watchman's point of view is thus limited, but the limitation is an advantage, for it allows Aeschylus to indicate Agamemnon's public character as governor of his household. The weary Watchman is glad that the war has finally ended. His joy at first reflects little more than relief at the completion of his sleepless vigil, but it then becomes a symbol of the eagerness with which he looks forward to the imminent return of his king:

my lord's dice cast aright are counted as my own,
and mine the tripled sixes of this torchlit throw.
May it only happen. May my king come home, and I
take up within this hand the hand I love   [ll. 31–34].

The Watchman's approval may be uncritical, but it nevertheless has some effect on the spectators' own attitude, for it is the first impression that Aeschylus gives them of Agamemnon, and it substantially agrees with the evaluation of him they have already derived from other versions of the legend.

When, however, the chorus, with its infallible knowledge of the past, narrates in expository statement the sacrifice of Iphigeneia, it presents a quite different view of Agamemnon. The chorus acknowledges the impossibility of avoiding the sacrifice; it also notes Agamemnon's weeping and hesitation—and these details tend to validate the attitude evoked by the Watchman. But Agamemnon went too far:

when necessity's yoke was put upon him
he changed, and from the heart the breath came bitter
and sacrilegious, utterly infidel,
to warp a will now to be stopped at nothing   [ll. 218–221].

This insistence on the enthusiasm with which Agamemnon carried out the actual slaughter urges condemnation of him, especially since it is coupled with a highly sympathetic portrait of the "stainless" Iphigeneia. The extreme contrast that the chorus develops between her former glory and her brutal fate endows her slayer with the qualities of a cruel and vicious monster.

The spectators' acceptance of these two opposing attitudes gives them a complex view of Agamemnon. With the Watchman, they feel adoration for him; with the chorus, they regard him as a heartless murderer who enjoyed the crime he was forced to commit. The second attitude does not supersede the first. Even as the chorus sings about the sacrifice, the activity of Clytaemestra visually and indirectly reinforces the Watchman's positive view. Clytaemestra, already defined by legend as an evil murderess, stands busy at the central altar, absorbed in her silent oblations. The spectators know her intentions and realize that through her prayer she requests divine help to strengthen her in murdering her husband. While she sacrifices, the chorus recites the prophecy of Calchas that the killing of Iphigeneia inspired:

> the terror returns like sickness to lurk in the house;
> the secret anger remembers the child that shall be avenged
> [ll. 154–155].

Clytaemestra's presence and activity convert these words into an unequivocal announcement that Agamemnon must die. Her purpose, kept hidden by her secrecy, is more terrible than if it were overt; it thus elicits sympathy for her victim. The analogy between the two altars is also significant, for Agamemnon was at least initially hesitant, but Clytaemestra never pauses. The spectators, even while hearing the chorus' condemnatory account of Agamemnon's behavior at Iphigeneia's altar, are nevertheless, because of Clytaemestra's activity at her altar, moved to feel pity for the majestic giant who will come home in glory only to be cut down by his wife. Since different devices assert the two attitudes simultaneously, the spectators must accept both.

This double view is consistently advanced. The direct communication of expository statement once more appeals to the spectators' tendency to admire Agamemnon when the Herald, arriving sooner than his lord, addresses the "great hall of the kings and house beloved; seats / of sanctity; divinities that face the sun" (ll. 518–519), and his apostrophe, while conventional, emphasizes the glory, majesty, and awe bestowed on Agamemnon by his position as lord of Argos. The Herald also expresses the admiration more directly, in words that seem addressed as much to the spectators as to the citizens gathered on the stage:

> look now with kind and glowing eyes
> to greet our king in state after so long a time.

He comes, lord Agamemnon, bearing light in gloom
to you, and to all that are assembled here.
Salute him with good favor, as he well deserves.

. . . . .

he comes, the king, Atreus' elder son, a man
fortunate to be honored far above all men
alive   [ll. 520–532].

Yet even while he recites this assessment in expository statement, other aspects of the immediate context reinforce the opposing view. Clytaemestra's presence and purpose underscore the irony in the Herald's formula about Agamemnon's good fortune, and this effect ridicules both the speaker and his subject. Moreover, before the Herald's arrival, Clytaemestra had pointed out the supreme danger that would befall the conquerors of Troy if they failed to honor the Trojan gods. The Herald, attempting to enhance the magnitude of Agamemnon's accomplishment, unwittingly reveals that once again he has overstepped accepted limits: "Gone are their altars, the sacred places of the gods / are gone" (ll. 527–528). To the guilt incurred when sacrificing Iphigeneia, Agamemnon has added the more horrendous sin of blasphemy.

When Agamemnon finally enters after some 780 lines, he arrives in his chariot; seated beside him amid the captured booty of Troy is his prize of victory, the Trojan prophetess Cassandra. This spectacular arrival makes him a vivid symbol in which the conflicting emotional attitudes merge. The entrance of a long-awaited character has a powerful dramatic effect. The spectators' attention is magnetized by him; all that has been said of him and all that has been felt about him cohere in their consciousness to the image of the actor playing his role. Aeschylus' spectators finally see, concentrated in the single human figure before them, the great king, the lord and master respected and revered by his subjects, the hero "who tore up Ilium by the roots" (l. 1227), the father who came to enjoy the sacrifice of his own daughter, the proud blasphemer who smashed the gods of Troy, and the victim who must pay for his crimes with his life. The visual presence of Agamemnon tends to fuse these contradictory impressions. Seeing him, the spectators do not feel that he is either one or another, or this or that by turns, but that every one of these impressions is true of him simultaneously. And the complexity of their view is increased by the new effects emerging from the tableau created by his entrance and from the action of the carpet scene.

Surrounded by the chorus, with Clytaemestra behind at the palace gates, Agamemnon forms the center of a richly evocative stage picture. The material details that accompany him enhance his majesty even while they add to his guilt. In his chariot the spoils of Troy create a sumptuous display of wealth and glory. The most impressive item of this booty is Cassandra, whom Agamemnon calls the "flower exquisite / from all my many treasures" (ll. 954–955). She sits silent and motionless, yet by her presence alone she arouses ambivalent responses. The spectators, through their familiarity with legend, know that she too has come to Argos to be murdered. The doomed innocence reflected in her static helplessness demands for her a compassion that would include as well her fated partner, if her situation did not so strongly recall the corresponding helplessness of Iphigeneia. And Cassandra, as Agamemnon's concubine, visually indicates his luxury and sensuality, tainting by extension the other wealth beside her in the chariot, the material details that reflect his character. As his concubine her presence is also an injustice to the waiting wife, furnishing her with a valid motive for her proposed vengeance. Cassandra is, therefore, not only a sign of Agamemnon's greatness but also one more justification of his coming punishment.

The chorus surrounds Agamemnon; its placement, speech, and activity display to the spectators homage, reverence, and exultation at the king's safe return. The chorus has shifted from its function as the omniscient narrator capable of describing the evil sacrifice to its secondary role as minor participant in, and viewer

of, the action. In this role it confirms on a higher social level the
adoration of the Watchman. To emphasize its implicitly revealed
homage, Aeschylus has his chorus contrast its present love with
past hatred:

> when you marshalled this armament
> for Helen's sake, I will not hide it,
> in ugly style you were written in my heart
> for steering aslant the mind's course
> to bring home by blood
> sacrifice and dead men that wild spirit.
> But now, in love drawn up from the deep heart,
> not skimmed at the edge, we hail you.
> You have won, your labor is made gladness   [ll. 799–807].

The chorus assigns the conflicting attitudes to separate occasions,
but through its words Aeschylus manages for the first time to
combine both the relevant attitudes toward Agamemnon in a single speech.

Clytaemestra completes the splendid tableau. The audience can
see her standing at the rear of the orchestra, before the door of
the palace where the slaughter will take place, watching the
killer of her daughter, watching her husband's concubine. Her
presence keeps vivid in the audience's consciousness the tension
of her resolve and the insistent awareness that Agamemnon must
shortly fall. She is an urgent visual effect translating the arrangement of the tableau into an intellectual design that epitomizes the
entire immediate action of this first play of the trilogy: Agamemnon, a man both good and evil, has come home in triumph and to
die.

The scene that follows his entrance restates through speech
and activity the implications of the tableau. The content of Agamemnon's first speeches augments the pattern urging approval of
him. Although he credits the gods with only a helping hand in
the defeat of Troy, he does realize that his first act upon homecoming must be a demonstration of his reverence for them. This

done, he will assert his authority by reorganizing the state, preserving the pure elements and purging the evil. Both acts are to be expected of a king just returned in victory from a long war, and Agamemnon convinces the spectators of the excellence of his leadership by promising to fulfill their expectations. His declarations have even more influence through contrast with the false statements of Clytaemestra, who now steps forward to present herself to her husband in the pose she has simulated throughout, to paint her pathetic self-portrait as the waiting wife who trembled at the arrival of every piece of news, every rumor, to tell how report of his wounds almost drove her to suicide. Agamemnon's blindness to her true nature wins for him some of the pity due the helpless victim, for this is what her confident manipulation transforms him into.

The spectators know, of course, that Clytaemestra's protestations are designed to put Agamemnon off guard so that she can more easily compel him to condemn himself through his activity. She wants from him, as she urges him to walk upon the carpet spread by her handmaidens, a display of *hybris*, for *hybris* is a sin against the gods. Because of the complexity of the attitudes Aeschylus has instilled in his spectators, they hope he will resist her, but they fear he cannot. Clytaemestra works upon a pride already existent when she calls him "my lord, / sacker of Ilium" (ll. 906–907). Agamemnon is wary and at first refuses to step upon the carpet. He knows the act would signify arrogance. He is not an Asiatic. Priam might have done this; he will not. But his chariot filled with Asiatic plunder, with Priam's wealth, is there to see: material details contradict his statement. And his next words, in response to Clytaemestra's continued urging, form the most influential of his self-revelations: "My will is mine. I shall not make it soft for you" (l. 932). The statement expresses unequivocally the implications of Agamemnon's excess with Iphigeneia and at Troy. The spectators realize that he must walk upon the carpet, that this activity, the most convincing evidence of his *hybris*, will be only a symbolic presentation of a quality already inherent.

All the impressions that emerge during the conclusion of this scene focus on Agamemnon's *hybris* and thus produce a final summation of the complexity that is his nature. This complexity, asserted by the conflicting evaluations of expository statement and implicit suggestion and confirmed by the speech, activity, and material details occasioned by Agamemnon's entrance, is now visually symbolized by the carpet on which he is to walk. The carpet resembles blood spilled upon the ground,[18] suggesting both the blood he has shed and his own blood that must yet be shed in payment. Ultimately, it is his actual walking on this carpet that most conclusively ensures the audience's condemnation, but even here the opposite view remains in force, because while Agamemnon manifests his *hybris*, he recognizes it as such. In the very midst of his activity he feels the extravagance and shame the audience expects from a heroic king who has won their sympathy and admiration. And *hybris* is itself a concept that arouses ambivalent responses, for the man who suffers from it has been raised up by the gods to such a height that they must now cast him down.

Hamlet. The portrait of Agamemnon, despite Aeschylus' insistence on a double view, exhibits a clarity and simplicity of outline that is alien to the characterization of Elizabethan drama. Minor characters are often defined in a word or two or in a single decisive speech or act, and the frequency of explicit evaluation allows the dramatist to rely, if he chooses, on labeling rather than defining. But most of the characters with any prominence in the action inevitably evade easy categorization, for Elizabethan drama is simply so abundant in characters, all of whom delight in evaluating their fellows, and so varied in incidents, all of which

[18] On this aspect of the carpet's appearance, see Robert F. Goheen, "Aspects of Dramatic Symbolism: Three Studies in the *Oresteia*," *American Journal of Philology*, LXXVI (1955), 116.

provide a character with new opportunities to reveal his own nature, that the spectators can see the typical character of Elizabethan drama only through a multiplicity of distinct and limited points of view. Sometimes the various glimpses coincide to fix for the audience a clear, precise, and uncomplicated image. At other times each view adds a specific detail to a richly developed but consistent portrait. In many cases, however, especially in Shakespeare, the various points of view remain in conflict; indeed, the Shakespearean character is likely to be a harmonized balance of separate and apparently incompatible details.

The attempt to define Hamlet's precise nature has provoked one of the numerous unending arguments that fill the pages of *Hamlet* criticism, but the commentators tend to agree on at least one point: it has become customary to assert the multiplicity of his nature, even to the extent of describing it as a union of opposites. Several attempts have been made, moreover, to explain how Shakespeare conveys this multiplicity to his audience. Millett and Bentley conclude that "with the possible exception of Lear, no other character in Shakespeare is illuminated from so many and so diverse points of view." [19] Wylie Sypher sees Hamlet as the most fully developed literary counterpart of the mannerist statue, a "flamelike statue" that "cannot be satisfactorily seen from any one point of view" but requires for its examination what he calls a "revolving view": "We must circulate about its changing contours and supplement our immediate view of it by imagining other available views." [20] The specific source of these many views of Hamlet has been suggested by Mark Van Doren: "We see Hamlet in other persons even more clearly than in himself. His relation to each of them is immediate and delicate; his least gesture records itself in them—in their concern, their pity, their

[19] Fred B. Millett and Gerald Eades Bentley, *The Art of the Drama* (New York: Appleton-Century, 1935), p. 209.

[20] *Four Stages of Renaissance Style* (Garden City, N.Y.: Doubleday, 1955), pp. 156–157.

love, their anger, or their fear." [21] As these comments indicate, Shakespeare defines Hamlet at least in part through a technique similar to that with which Aeschylus presents Agamemnon: the other characters surround him, observe him, and report what they see. Nevertheless, the process that defines Hamlet is infinitely more complex and, despite this partial similarity, ultimately quite different.

The evaluations of Hamlet begin in Act I, scene iii; during the long, extremely static second scene of Act II, "we learn to know our man, as it were, at leisure"; [22] the whole process is then essentially completed in Act III, scene i. During these scenes the spectators view Hamlet through the reflecting mirrors provided by the varied attitudes of Laertes, Polonius, Ophelia, Rosencrantz and Guildenstern, Claudius, and Gertrude. To Laertes, Hamlet is a trifler whose advances Ophelia must parry with extreme caution if she is to preserve her honor (I.iii.5–44). Polonius at first echoes this sentiment (ll. 91–131), but he soon comes to see Hamlet as a deeply sensitive soul suffering the agonies of unrequited love (II.i.102–110, II.ii.106–150, III.i.176–178). To Ophelia, who describes him as the ideal courtier, scholar, and soldier (III.i.150–160), Hamlet is the true pattern of nobility, while Rosencrantz and Guildenstern notice only that he is excessively ambitious (II.ii.251–258). Claudius regards him as an immediate danger to the kingdom and particularly to his own personal safety (III.i.164–167). Gertrude, who never attempts a full assessment of her son, suggests only that he is probably too obsessed with the death of his father and her own "o'erhasty" remarriage (II.ii.56–57), and she hopes that Polonius is right (l. 151). Her real view, however, is demonstrated throughout by her general treatment of him and epitomized when she says, "But look where sadly the poor wretch comes reading" (l. 167); she

[21] *Shakespeare* (Garden City, N.Y.: Doubleday, 1954), p. 171.

[22] Harley Granville-Barker, *Prefaces to Shakespeare*, I (Princeton, N.J.: Princeton University Press, 1946), 41.

thus sees him as pathetic and helpless, a far cry from the threatening monster conjured up by Claudius. The simultaneous assertion of all these often mutually exclusive views can only suggest to the spectators that Hamlet's nature, if these reflect it, is a compound of irreconcilable opposites.

Although these views are given prominence rather early, one aspect of the nature of drama prevents their being decisive. The spectators cannot accept the assessments at face value because they must absorb them from the more inclusive point of view created by their accumulated experience of what has gone before. The spectators cannot accept the opinion of any one character because their knowledge surpasses that of all the characters. Before they hear or infer the individual attitudes, they have already learned of the condition of Denmark, already seen the first gathering of the court and felt the gulf separating Hamlet from the others, already enjoyed the privilege of participating in some of Hamlet's inmost thoughts. They realize, therefore, that his observers do not know Hamlet as well as they themselves have come to know him. Their more advantageous point of view prevents them from giving much credence to Laertes' notions about the philandering Hamlet, for they have previously heard nothing that might confirm this view, they know from Hamlet's first soliloquy that he is unlikely to engage in frivolous emotional involvements, and even while Laertes speaks they can perceive the denial implicit in Ophelia's refusal to take him seriously. Before they learn the attitudes of the remaining characters, they first hear Hamlet telling Horatio he might assume an antic disposition, and having seen and heard the Ghost, they know the reason for his behavior. They realize that all Hamlet's observers have two severe limitations on their authority: all speak from the rather questionable assumption that Hamlet is mad; none speaks from a knowledge of Hamlet's meeting with the Ghost.

Since Shakespeare thus conditions the spectators' reception of the various views of Hamlet, the focus shifts from subject to speaker. The way in which each speaker presses one view, and only one, of Hamlet's nature leads the spectators to a discovery about the speaker himself. The best explanation for the content of any given evaluation is that each observer can recognize and isolate only that quality of the prince that matches a strong element in his own nature. The spectators realize, for example, that Polonius' view of Hamlet betrays a mind unable to cope with new evidence and changing situations: once he performs the simple act of reversing his original opinion, he never deviates from his new one. More striking, however, is the fact that both his opinions of Hamlet, as Polonius himself unintentionally reveals, are determined by specific aspects—real or imagined—of his own limited experience. While he still doubts Hamlet's intentions, he does so because "I do know, / When the blood burns, how prodigal the soul / Lends the tongue vows" (I.iii.115–117). But after he formulates his primary view of Hamlet, he then recalls, "truly in my youth I suff'red much extremity for love. Very near this" (II.ii.188–189).

The others also tend to assess Hamlet's character in terms of their own. Laertes' shallow opinion has a touch of the haste with which he makes all his superficial decisions; since Ophelia hints at a discrepancy between his advice and his behavior (I.iii.46–51), and Polonius is suspicious enough of the way he conducts himself to send a spy after him, his opinion may also reflect the moral quality of his own approach to love. Ophelia's love for Hamlet, and her own youth and innocence, motivate her idealistic view of him as a model of perfection. Gertrude's assumption that Hamlet is disturbed by his father's death and the quick marriage that followed should suggest to the spectators her own troubled attitude toward these events, and indeed she later reveals a hint of this in an aside (IV.v.17–20). But her primary view of Hamlet suggests something else, for it matches exactly the pathetic helplessness and incapacity for understanding she often demonstrates in her own behavior. The spectators readily understand why Rosencrantz and Guildenstern charge Hamlet with ambition when they see the manner in which the two courtiers fawn upon Claudius and the ease with which they are willing to betray friendship for the sake of their own advancement. Claudius quite rightly looks on Hamlet as an ambitious threat, for Claudius himself played that role when his brother was king; and, significantly, Shakespeare has Claudius introduce the first admission of his guilt in the same scene that reveals his attitude toward Hamlet (III.i.49–54). Each of the attitudes these characters exhibit toward Hamlet exemplifies a point I have already made. Laertes, Polonius, and the others exist apart from and in addition to the evaluations they make. They have action of their own to perform; they are individualized characters rather than dramatic spokesmen, and thus their speech is self-focusing. While the views they put forth may suggest valid facts about Hamlet, each view is more important for the information it conveys about its originator. Each of these evaluations of Hamlet serves as an explicit characterization of the observer who has voiced it.

The full extent of Shakespeare's economy appears in the method by which he confirms the unintentional self-characterizations. For even while the others evaluate Hamlet, Hamlet perceives in their natures the very traits they inadvertently unveil. It is Hamlet who compels the spectators to regard Polonius as merely a tedious fool, to emphasize, that is, the limitations Polonius reveals when drawing his conclusions about Hamlet. It is Hamlet who continuously urges the guilt of the "remorseless, treacherous, lecherous, kindless villain," Claudius. And it is Hamlet who calls Rosencrantz a sponge "that soaks up the King's countenance, his rewards, his authorities" (IV.ii.15–16). Nor are Hamlet's perceptions without relevance for an understanding of his own character: they provide one more demonstration of his extreme sensitivity to his surroundings, of his amazing capacity to discern the fundamental quality of that which confronts him.

One question remains, however: since the evaluations of Hamlet are primarily of significance for the light they throw on their speakers, have they any contribution to make to an understanding of Hamlet himself? They are not, as I have shown, extremely influential. The presentation of Hamlet is in direct contrast to that of Agamemnon, for Agamemnon enters into and validates a context already established by others' evaluations of him, but the spectators' response to Hamlet tends to take shape before any evaluations are attempted. The spectators learn to know Hamlet through the gropings of his soliloquies, through his comfortable meetings with Horatio, where he feels no need to pose, and through his responses to the events and people that comprise his basic environment. Even in those scenes that include the comments of others, the most important impressions of his nature emerge from his complaints about Denmark, man, and the world, from his delighted reception of the players, from the sudden thoughts that surge up during the soliloquies in Act II, scene ii, and Act III, scene i, and from the ambivalent treatment of Ophelia and the vicious self-assessments of the nunnery scene (III.i). One of the most influential of the impressions during this part of the play is produced by the way he toys with most of his interpreters, now admitting that they are essentially correct, now wholly rejecting their misconceptions. Both his acuteness and his wit show strongly when, in welcoming the others to the performance of his play (III.ii), he becomes the quick-change artist, the man of many faces, mockingly performing for each the only Hamlet that character knows.

At the same time, the evaluations of Hamlet are not entirely without effect; they fill in or articulate certain details of the image already taking shape in the audience's consciousness. Several of the evaluations formulate impressions the audience has previously felt. Polonius' supposition is not a complete fabrication; it but distorts the actual love of which Ophelia is convinced in Act I, scene iii, and which compels Hamlet's later visit to her. Ophelia's long portrait of his nobility gives verbal extension to numerous suggestions, especially those arising from his treatment of Marcellus and Horatio. Gertrude's belief in his pathetic helplessness provides a perspective to account for his futile petulance in the first exchange with Claudius, his strong desire for suicide, his tendency to give way to excitement, and his failure to fulfill his vow—a failure which, as he himself emphasizes at the end of Act II, is not fully explicable. And that Hamlet is actually ambitious is a distinct possibility even he will later admit when he observes to Horatio that Claudius "popp'd in between th' election and my hopes" (V.ii.65). Thus the various evaluations of Hamlet serve to magnify individual traits otherwise demonstrated. Their usefulness derives not from their announcement of these traits but from their highlighting of them. In this way the evaluations help ensure the audience's full understanding of a character so composed of opposites that J. Dover Wilson could describe him as "at once mad and the sanest of geniuses, at once a procrastinator and a vigorous man of action, at once a miserable failure and the most adorable of heroes." [23] Hamlet's character is presented to the audience, as Wylie Sypher suggests, in a revolving view. But the separate views having most force are created by his own speech, activity, and emotional effect, with certain aspects of the resulting complexity emphasized by the evaluations of the observers who try to pluck out the heart of his mystery.

Ulrik Brendel. The presentation of Ulrick Brendel in *Rosmersholm* illustrates the standard method of defining character in the drama of formal realism, which, in keeping with its tendency to rely heavily on implication rather than articulation, reduces the number and scope of spoken evaluations and vastly increases the

[23] *What Happens in Hamlet* (3d ed.; Cambridge: University Press, 1951), p. 229.

role played by visual impression. Moreover, since the presentation of Brendel differs markedly from those of Agamemnon and Hamlet, it also illustrates a third general technique of characterization, one in which all the devices are used freely and simultaneously rather than separately and in carefully determined sequences.

Since Brendel arrives at the back door of Rosmersholm, it is immediately apparent that, from his own point of view at least, he does not belong to Rosmer's social level. Madam Helseth emphatically agrees. She is so unfavorably impressed by Brendel that she will not show him in without Rosmer's approval, and even when he grants it, she remains hesitant: "But he doesn't look like the sort of person you can let into the sitting room. . . . He isn't much to look at, that's certain" (I, p. 134). Kroll, who recognizes Brendel's name, echoes and intensifies Madam Helseth's contempt in a derogatory assessment. Kroll calls Brendel a "black sheep" (p. 135), happily remembers a rumor that he was in the workhouse, and can hardly believe that Rosmer would let him come in. What obviously disturbs Kroll most is that Brendel, who had once been Rosmer's tutor, "went and crammed your head full of revolutionary ideas." It was only fitting, Kroll feels, that Rosmer's father had finally driven Brendel away "with his horsewhip." Kroll's bitter dislike of Brendel is heavily stressed and necessarily has some effect on the spectators' own response. But by now they have learned that neither Kroll nor his opinions entirely deserve their respect, and Kroll has especially shown that no one who disseminates "revolutionary ideas" could get a fair hearing from him. Furthermore, there is some indication that other, quite different views of Brendel are also possible. Rebecca, who describes him only as "that strange—" is noncommittal, but Rosmer seems determined to refute Kroll, if only indirectly. Despite the objections of Madam Helseth and Kroll, Rosmer repeatedly insists that Brendel be admitted. Kroll associates Brendel with the workhouse, but Rosmer remembers that he was traveling with a theater company. And to Kroll's remark about his father, Rosmer bitterly replies, "Father was a major here in his house, too."

The next impression of Brendel, which is established by material details, strengthens the ambivalence. When Brendel enters, it becomes clear at once that the primary function of Madam Helseth's earlier evaluation is to call particular attention to his physical appearance:

He is a handsome man, somewhat gaunt but brisk and alert, with gray hair and beard. As for the rest, he is dressed like a common tramp: threadbare coat, worthless shoes, no shirt to be seen. He wears a pair of old black gloves, has a soft filthy hat stuck under his arm, and carries a walking stick in his hand   [stage direction, p. 135].

Madam Helseth has drawn her conclusions from but one aspect of the material details associated with Brendel, but the spectators, because of the stress on his appearance, will perceive "the handsomeness in rags" with its implication of " 'good material gone to seed.' " [24] This contrast, which opposes his gentlemanly features and bearing to his disreputable clothing, strongly suggests that Brendel is either unable or unwilling to "compromise with conventional life." [25]

Everything about Brendel adds to the initial ambivalence. Since he was once Rosmer's tutor, it is evident that at one time, at least, he was able to secure, if not hold, a position of some respectability. He has evidently not forsaken the "revolutionary ideas" he then held, for he is on his way into town to lay his "mite on the altar of emancipation" (p. 138), and this link with Rebecca, which is reinforced by the implication that in the past he played the same role for Rosmer that she now plays, endears him to the spectators. Other effects call for a quite different re-

[24] Northam, *Ibsen's Dramatic Method*, p. 114.
[25] Cleanth Brooks and Robert Heilman, *Understanding Drama* (New York: Holt, 1945), p. 270.

sponse, however. When he first enters, he hesitates momentarily, and then mistakes Kroll for his old pupil—a mistake which betrays a weakness of memory and, perhaps, a corresponding deficiency of intelligence. He also assumes that Rebecca is Mrs. Rosmer, and even though Rosmer corrects him at once, he continues to address her throughout the scene by formal titles that identify her as Rosmer's wife.

But it is his speech that is most incriminating, for it is whimsical and caricaturish, larded with unnecessary and inaccurate foreign phrases, biblical allusions, and such fantastic coinages as "storm-tossed solstice time"; he also stacks up modifiers unmercifully, as when he asks Kroll if there can be found "a somewhat decent, respectable, and commodious meeting room in your esteemed town" (p. 137). Especially significant is the imagery of satiation and intoxication which runs through everything he says. He refers to his past liberal writings, which Rebecca admires, as "trash" (p. 138), and his word (*pøjt*) also means "weak drink." What really matters to him are the works he still intends to produce, which have not yet been written because, he confesses, he has always been "a sybarite. A *Feinschmecker*." He prefers to enjoy—in the sense of enjoying food—his thoughts in solitude, where "golden dreams" have shrouded him in mist—or made him drunk—and new, "giddy," wide-ranging thoughts have been "fed" to him: "Oh, how I've tasted and swallowed in my days!" In sum, his solitary conceptions have "satiated" him "with a joy —oh, such an intoxicatingly vast . . . !" (p. 139). But he has written down none of these thoughts and dreams because, as he adds in a superb climax, "the flat labor of writing has always awakened a nauseous distaste in me." Brendel's speech can only affect the spectators adversely. Kroll is pompous, but he at least tries to be straightforward; here, in Brendel, is someone evidently more captivated by words than Kroll himself, and every one of them helps expose his utter impracticality. Brendel may be amusing, but he is obviously of little consequence. The spectators realize that a man who expresses himself in this way will be able to do little to aid any cause; and the pure thoughts, the grandiose ideas that he plans to sacrifice "on the altar of emancipation" exist only "in the rough outlines, you understand" (p. 138).

But even while Brendel's speech exposes his folly, other aspects of the scene salvage some measure of sympathy and admiration for him. Kroll's behavior indicates that his attitude remains what it had been before Brendel entered, but during Brendel's visit he manages to contain himself rather successfully; as a result, the attitudes of Rosmer and Rebecca become more prominent and more influential. Rosmer is still careful not to commit himself in Kroll's presence, but he listens attentively and with apparent interest to Brendel's extravagant outpourings, consistently treats him in a friendly manner, and willingly lends him clothes and money. Rebecca's attitude, which now emerges, is even more favorable than Rosmer's. She listens not only with interest but also, apparently, with complete belief, and she seems impressed: "This is wonderful of you, Mr. Brendel! You are giving the most valuable thing you possess" (p. 139). She then underscores the contrast between Brendel and the hesitant Rosmer when she looks "significantly" at Rosmer and asks, "How many are there who do so? Who *dare* do so?" It is, however, the result of Brendel's visit more than anything else which most endears him to the spectators, for Rosmer finally satisfies their desire that he take his stand against Kroll only because Brendel, in declaring his intention to combat the warriors of conservatism, has set an example.

Before this particular impression has time to solidify, however, Ibsen reinforces the more negative side of Brendel's character through the report of his subsequent activity which Kroll narrates in Act II. Kroll is eager to provide Rosmer with evidence of Brendel's improper and irresponsible behavior. He has, says Kroll, taken up quarters "in a shabby hotel—in the meanest company, naturally" (p. 151), drunk up Rosmer's money, pawned Rosmer's clothes, and—worst of all—fallen into the hands of "the noble Mr. Mortensgaard," the radical with the evil past. The vocabulary in which this report is cast reflects Kroll's own attitudes, of course, and his satisfaction in being able to tell all this to Rosmer is a further manifestation of his character. But the facts are never denied, and the behavior sounds typical of someone with Brendel's inability to discipline himself. Much of the report therefore has the effect of activity actually witnessed, and the spectators' interpretation of it necessarily resembles that which Kroll has given.

Brendel's complexity remains throughout. In Act IV, Ibsen completes his characterization of him through a structural device: he offers Brendel's second visit for comparison with the spectators' memory of the first. When Brendel returns to Rosmersholm, completely disillusioned about himself and the cause he has hoped to foster, his material details, speech, and activity all contrast sharply with their earlier counterparts. The conflict between his person and his clothing no longer exists; he now wears a "white shirt, a black coat, and good shoes" (p. 205). He has, as his speech confirms, succumbed to conventional life and his own insignificant position in it. Much of the whimsey is still evident in his speech, but now he reports facts rather than dreams, and these facts allow the spectators to hear from his own lips contempt similar to that voiced by Kroll. Brendel realizes that he has no great ideas to disseminate, that, in fact, he never had any:

For five and twenty years I've sat like a miser on his locked-up money box. And then yesterday—when I open it and wish to fetch the treasure out—there is nothing! The teeth of time had mashed it to dust. There was *nichts* and nothing in the whole show   [p. 206].

Brendel's ability to finally see himself clearly is disheartening, but it does generate some admiration for him. A different effect results from his new-found capacity to judge the world of action, for on this topic Brendel has become a cynic. He now asserts that values are entirely meaningless, that only the practical men—the

Peter Mortensgaards—can ever accomplish anything, because they are capable of doing their work without ideals: "And *that* —you see—*that* is exactly the great secret of action and victory. It is the sum of the whole world's wisdom" (p. 207). Brendel's change from his former foggy idealism to his new bitter cynicism rids him of much of his foolishness, but it also destroys the amusing oaf who could inspire Rosmer to perform his noblest act.

It is in this last respect, however, that the second visit provides a parallel rather than a contrast to the first, because once again Brendel inspires a noble act. This time, in keeping with his transformation, he presumably realizes it. He may speak with a bitter self-mockery and with a new ironic twist to his old whimsey, but he nevertheless deliberately tells Rebecca that Rosmer can reach his great goal in life only through her self-sacrifice. Since his words help motivate their double suicide, Brendel himself shares some of the rich ambiguity of the play's ending. In his exit as in his entrance, then, Brendel demands an ambivalent response. He remains to the end what his own speech and activity, his physical appearance, and his fellow characters have all declared him to be, at once both worthwhile and worthless.

In addition to illustrating the way in which different dramatic conventions affect the presentation of character, the preceding analyses exemplify three common methods of combining the various devices. Agamemnon is characterized in words before his own entrance confirms the validity of the pre-established attitudes, and this technique tends to distance him so that the spectators can view him objectively. Hamlet is a character whose relationship to the spectators is essentially fixed by means of his speech and activity before the evaluations made by others highlight certain qualities of his nature, and this technique has a double result: it increases the spectators' sense of Hamlet's central and autonomous importance even while it also convinces them that his observers are too limited in vision to provide satisfactory interpretations of him or of *any* element of the action in which they participate. The presentation of Ulrik Brendel employs a seemingly artless method in which every kind of device contributes equally and imperceptibly to the creation of a continuously developing image, and this technique is also appropriate to its context, for Brendel, like all the characters of *Rosmersholm*, must pass for a real human being in a lifelike situation. Despite these significant differences, the analyses also demonstrate that plays of every period employ the same devices for presenting character, however the combination of these devices may be affected by differences in purpose and by the prevalence of one set of conventions rather than another. Finally, as is equally clear, the fully developed dramatic character, whether he be Agamemnon, Hamlet, or Ulrik Brendel, is ordinarily exhibited from many angles of vision simultaneously.

From their understanding of the characters, the spectators acquire their point of view for the immediate action. And since this understanding enables them to determine the reliability of each character's attempt to explain the experience in which he is involved, it also provides them with one means of perceiving the exact contours of the action of depth.

Part III: The Action of Depth

4. Expository Devices

This in fact I have ever found rather terribly the point—that the figures in any picture, the agents in any drama, are interesting only in proportion as they feel their respective situations; since the consciousness, on their part, of the complication exhibited forms for us their link of connexion with it. But there are degrees of feeling—the muffled, the faint, the just sufficient, the barely intelligent, as we may say; and the acute, the intense, the complete, in a word—the power to be finely aware and richly responsible. It is those moved in this latter fashion who "get most" out of all that happens to them and who in so doing enable us, as readers of their record, as participators by a fond attention, also to get most.

— Henry James, "Preface to *The Princess Casamassima*"

One of the great virtues of drama is its capacity to portray character in action accurately, immediately, and interestingly. Achievement of this sort is rare enough, and as spectators we would be satisfied to witness no more than the sensitive delineation of the ironies that arise from Agamemnon's *hybris*, or the frustrations, agonies, and ramifications of Hamlet's dilemma, or the lifelike embodiment of conflicting opposites that constitutes Ulrik Brendel. But the dramatist seldom contents himself with a re-creation of the surface of life, however sensitive or accurate. He is concerned not only with action but with the meaning of action; he seeks to place the event in relation to all events, the character in relation to human nature in general; he is, as Aristotle noted, more philosopher than historian. Therefore he unavoidably creates an action of depth consisting of the abstractions, emotional impressions, general ideas, analogous experiences, mythic parallels, and cosmologies in relation to which the characters and their affairs must be seen if they are to be seen in all their significance. The existence of the action of depth enriches the dramatic experience, but it also raises the further question of how its materials become known to the spectators.

Understanding in drama normally results from the impact of the particular experience the dramatist presents in his play and the general experience of his audience. With most plays, however, this understanding also depends on a third coordinate, a *specific* prior experience. The *Oresteia* dramatizes a well-known legend. Racine's *Phèdre* is based on plays by Euripides and Seneca. Both the *Oresteia* and *Phèdre* belong to a familiar dramatic genre, tragedy. On the level of the action of depth as on the level of immediate action, then, specific audience foreknowledge constitutes a primary source of understanding. The relationship between the individual play and the particular awarenesses and assumptions to which it directly appeals often serves to indicate both the existence of the action of depth and some of its fundamental content.

Of all the possible versions of this relationship, that which links the play to the legend on which it is based is the most difficult to define with full accuracy. It is impossible, for example, to compare the *Oresteia* with the legend of the House of Atreus as the Greeks knew it, for most of the sources, both oral and written, have long since disappeared, while those that still exist, such as Homer's *Odyssey*, present only fragmentary accounts. Nevertheless, it is reasonably certain that the Greek spectators came to Aeschylus' trilogy not only with preconceptions about Clytaemestra, Agamemnon, Cassandra, and Aegisthus but also with a knowledge of the general outlines of the legend. They already tended, that is, to regard its material as embodying an endless cycle, a sequence of repetition in which each act is both effect and cause, and this foreknowledge would certainly alert them to the meaningful arrangement that Aeschylus has given the *Oresteia*.

Other effects, more general in nature and thus applicable to any play deriving from a familiar legend, can also be singled out. Since a legend is a part of a cultural heritage, its importance is guaranteed; those who cherish it assume that it is somehow meaningful, somehow relevant to human experience, or it would not have endured. This fact elicits a particular anticipation from the spectators: assuming that what they have come to see is more than a story, more than a few hours' entertainment, they look for the concrete specificity that the dramatist's shaping of the legend has given its inherent meaningfulness, and it is this expectation more than anything else which makes such speeches as the interpretive odes of the *Agamemnon* chorus unusually influential. In addition, an audience is never more aware of the contributions of selection, focus, and emphasis than when it is watching a play whose story is already familiar. Aeschylus, as O'Neill complained, ignores the "imaginative tragic possibilities" in "Electra's life after the murder of Clytemnestra." [1] For that matter, he also ignores the years of suffering she had to face before the return of Orestes: the *Oresteia* dismisses these possibilities and others as well; Aeschylus chooses only the murders—and the motives and intentions they embody—and therefore quite clearly defines his theme.

Selection also involves exclusion, and here again the familiarity of legend offers a valuable advantage. In dramatizing *King Lear*, for example, Shakespeare omits the reasons why the characters in his main plot behave as they do. Unlike the author of the older

[1] Eugene O'Neill, "Working Notes and Extracts from a Fragmentary Work Diary," in *European Theories of the Drama*, ed. Barrett H. Clark (New York: Crown, 1947), p. 530.

True Chronicle History of King Leir, who devotes almost a third of his play to preparing for Leir's division of the kingdom, Shakespeare takes this episode for his starting point. He does not bother to explain the obstinacy of Lear, the loyalty of Kent, the evil of Goneril and Regan, and the goodness of Cordelia. Nor, since he has appropriated a familiar action and a given set of characters, does he need to. A story with legendary status has the quality of a *fait accompli;* most of it has solidified into narrative fact and no longer remains open to question. The spectators accept Shakespeare's characters as they are, in other words, because this is what they—or rather, their counterparts—have *always* been. As a result, if Shakespeare had wanted to make their motives a relevant concern, he would have been obliged to focus on them explicitly. The omission shows that his primary emphasis is less psychological than metaphysical; it directs the audience's attention away from an interest in "inner life" and experiential antecedents and places it squarely on what really matters: the significance for experience in general that the familiar action can be made to yield.

King Lear does not, of course, always observe the sanctity of the legend. The deaths of Cordelia and Lear have a tremendous impact that for the original spectators must have been compounded by their familiarity with the entirely different outcome in every other known rendering of the story. This deliberate reversal of an expectation, occasional in a play based on legend, is more characteristic of the many plays that, like *Phèdre,* are based not on legends but on other plays. From Euripides on, for example, the *Oresteia* has been especially fertile in producing offspring, both legitimate and bastard. Plays like O'Neill's *Mourning Becomes Electra,* Eliot's *The Family Reunion,* and— less obviously—Strindberg's *The Father* contain new stories that in specific detail or in over-all form imitate Aeschylus' trilogy. The analogy thus established is supposed to convince the spectators of the universality and magnitude of the new experience, though all too often the new experience and its characters are merely, as Eric Bentley puts it in a comment on O'Neill's play, "inflated with cultural gas." [2] The more legitimate offspring, which are the ones of moment here, originated with Euripides' *Electra* and its parody of the recognition scene in *The Libation Bearers*. This mockery may have been mere impertinence, as Kitto suggests,[3] but the same cannot be said of Euripides' other parody of Aeschylus—the *Orestes*—for in this play Euripides ridicules the whole Aeschylean solution by juxtaposing Apollo's bald narration of it to the display of sheer insanity that has fallen upon the descendants of Atreus; he evokes, that is, a profound sense of cosmic and earthly disorder by stressing the incongruity of the Aeschylean harmony. Similarly, in Sartre's *The Flies*, a modern play based on the *Oresteia*, the traditional Aeschylean values accompanying the legend emphasize by contrast the new values Sartre wishes to assert, especially the rejection of externally imposed order and the glorification of existential choice as the only true source of authority. Both *Orestes* and *The Flies* offer not a new story but a new examination of the old. The import of each play lies not only in what it is in itself but also, and deliberately, in the sharp distinction between *its* dramatization of the story and the quite contrary rendering already established by Aeschylus.

There is, finally, one version of the relationship between the individual play and its antecedents in which almost all drama participates. No play is entirely new. Even those that make no use of legends or earlier plays must necessarily remind their audiences of prior theatrical experiences and consequently call up a set of more or less definite expectations inspired by a particular dramatic genre or style. Certain kinds of drama—farce, melodrama, much traditional comedy, and perhaps neoclassic tragedy

[2] *In Search of Theater* (New York: Vintage Books, 1955), p. 232.
[3] H. D. F. Kitto, *Greek Tragedy: A Literary Study* (2d, rev. ed.; Garden City, N.Y.: Doubleday, 1955), p. 359.

—realize a great deal of their significance from the way they satisfy anticipations of tone, characterization, and form. With other
plays, it is the difference between expectation and result which is
meaningful. A spectator who has seen *Titus Andronicus* and *The
Spanish Tragedy* will soon discover that *Hamlet* has some of the
basic characteristics of the revenge tragedy. What is important,
however, is the emphasis this discovery gives to those aspects of
Hamlet through which it transcends the limits already established
by these earlier examples of the genre. This kind of effect may
not be the result of conscious design—the relationship between
Doctor Faustus and the medieval morality suggests as much—but
for the highly sophisticated dramatist, deliberate toying with the
expectations aroused by particular genres is a customary and
fruitful device.[4]

In any of its forms, then, the relationship between a play and
its specific antecedents is an important source of understanding.
Nevertheless, its contribution is ultimately far less influential
than that of those revelations of the action of depth which occur
within the play itself, and it is these that require and deserve extended consideration. The most obvious class of these internal
revelations—and the one with which the rest of this chapter will
be concerned—comprises the various informational, evaluative,
and interpretive statements explicitly supplied by the characters.

Direct Statement

In its prayer to Zeus, the chorus of the *Agamemnon* helps clarify the ultimate meaning of the whole trilogy by describing the
universe within which the immediate action is set. The prayer
occurs during the first ode, after the chorus has discussed in general terms the significance of the expedition against Troy and has

---

[4] See Martin Meisel's excellent study of Shaw's mastery of this device:
Shaw and the Nineteenth-Century Theater (Princeton, N.J.: Princeton
University Press, 1963).

begun to tell how Agamemnon cruelly sacrificed his daughter
Iphigeneia. The chorus realizes that her agony was a necessary
prelude to the just destruction of Troy—"Sing sorrow, sorrow:
but good win out in the end" (ll. 121, 138, 159)—yet the realization only increases its perplexity. Therefore it pauses in its recol-
lections to appeal to the highest power in the universe: "Zeus:
whatever he may be, if this name / pleases him in invocation, /
thus I call upon him" (ll. 160–162). During this prayer, it transforms its discovery about Iphigeneia's fate into universal law, for
it assures the spectators that "Zeus, who guided men to
think . . . has laid it down that wisdom / comes alone through
suffering" (ll. 176–178).

The chorus admits its inability to understand why such a law
must exist (ll. 164–166), and it also protests the law's harshness:

> Still there drips in sleep against the heart
> grief of memory; against
> our pleasure we are temperate.
> From the gods who sit in grandeur
> grace comes somehow violent   [ll. 179–183].

Nevertheless, the chorus cannot deny the existence of the law.
By this means Aeschylus outlines for his spectators the metaphysical core of his tragedy. Introduced along with the focus on
Troy and Iphigeneia and sung in the presence of Clytaemestra,
the principle of wisdom through suffering attaches in the audience's consciousness to all the major events. The suffering forced
on Troy and Iphigeneia has been fierce and cruel. More suffering
will come for Agamemnon and Clytaemestra. Since these victims
lack both the complete guilt of the city and the complete innocence of the girl, the suffering to follow will be even more terrible, but from it in the end will emerge a wisdom otherwise impossible.

It is not, however, merely the principle of wisdom through
suffering which gives this prayer its great importance. When the

chorus recalls Zeus's victory over the older gods, it broadens the significance of the human tragedy in another way by relating it to the dynastic struggles of the gods:

> He who in time long ago was great,
> throbbing with gigantic strength,
> shall be as if he never were, unspoken.
> He who followed him has found
> his master, and is gone.
> Cry aloud without fear the victory of Zeus,
> you will not have failed the truth   [ll. 168–175].

These lines, set in a context dramatizing the endless cycle brought about by the family curse, imply that Zeus's victory has no more finality than those preceding it, that it is just one more step in a continual series of victories and defeats as new dynasties of gods keep replacing the old. This theme will be reawakened in the spectators' consciousness when, during the third play of the trilogy, they see the conflict on the human level fuse with a conflict between old gods and new. But already the introduction of this theme establishes the inseparability of things human and divine. The struggles of the gods reflect the vicissitudes of the human action. The situation of Agamemnon, his family, and his kingdom remains unsettled because the gods' own struggles have not yet come to an end. Significantly, this very prayer seems to assert two Zeuses. The first is the Zeus who has won the current victory and now reigns as the present king of heaven. The second, the Zeus who has laid down the principle of wisdom through suffering, is a greater, more eternal force, which the chorus addresses by this name only because it knows no other: "Zeus: whatever he may be" (l. 160). These two Zeuses, Aeschylus seems to suggest, must merge before any of the turmoil can be resolved.

The prayer's statements and implications about the nature of the *Oresteia* universe demand acceptance for several reasons. The

characters who express them belong to a chorus and thus automatically inherit an aura of omniscience. This particular chorus
has already demonstrated its authority by showing considerable
knowledge of past and remote events. The manner in which it
presents its information forestalls the possibility of skepticism, because rather than focusing directly on the universal attributes, the
chorus guarantees their authenticity by emphasizing instead the
mental and physical distress they cause in man. Finally, Aeschylus further ensures the effectuality of the original assertions by
repeating one of them with an interesting variation. After its
prayer the chorus returns to the story of Iphigeneia and describes
her agony in great detail. The notion of suffering is in this way
made more concrete, yet the conclusion of the ode evokes a sense
of hope. The chorus repeats the universal law it has just introduced—"Justice so moves that those only learn / who suffer" (ll.
250–251)—but its attitude toward this law has changed; this
time it focuses not on the operation of the principle but on its
outcome: "All will come clear in the next dawn's sunlight" (l.
254). What was first felt with pain now comforts. The repetition, then, stresses the principle by restating it; the new attitude,
which regards the principle as a source of release, makes belief in
it under present conditions mandatory.

   The care Aeschylus has taken to ensure acceptance of his chorus' claims suggests that direct statement is an uncertain means of
defining the action of depth even when functional figures are
available. When the direct statement is that of an individualized character, the likelihood of its convincing a spectator, as I
have argued in Chapter 1, almost ceases to exist. There are, however, exceptions. Rebecca West's discovery that "the Rosmer
view of life ennobles . . . but it kills happiness" is convincing
because it sums up the spectators' own growing awareness. It is
even possible, moreover, for the speech of an individualized character to win acceptance when the spectators' growing awareness
is not involved, when the speech voices an assertion unsubstanti-

ated by other effects. An example is Hamlet's fifth-act insistence that his experience has a particular meaning. His statements about providence take on the authority of expository statement because Shakespeare has so controlled the design of his action that the spectators must ultimately accept Hamlet's point of view as virtually equivalent to their own.

The spectators' tendency to see the action as Hamlet sees it originates with his first soliloquy, in which the activity of the other characters pauses while Hamlet comments on it and reveals that only he, of all those at court, has any sensitivity to the tense undercurrents established in the opening scene. The dominance of Hamlet's point of view then increases as the action develops: soliloquy after soliloquy adds to the effect of the first; Polonius soon starts to perform the role of tedious old fool that Hamlet has conceived for him; Claudius is unmasked as the smiling, "damnèd" villain Hamlet took him to be. In the scene of the play-within-the-play the spectators watch "The Murder of Gonzago" less through their own eyes than through those of Hamlet. They heed only those parts of it that he underlines with choric comment; in response to his direction they focus not on the play but on the reactions of Gertrude and Claudius.

The decisive effect in this process is the change that takes place in Hamlet's nature. At the beginning of the play Shakespeare introduces his spectators to a hero whose most notable characteristic is a profound lack of integration. The first scene in which he appears presents not one Hamlet but three: the petulant nonconformist whose recalcitrance disrupts the even tenor of Claudius' court, the lonely sufferer who dares reveal only to himself the grief and disgust that tempt him to thoughts of suicide, and the active courtier who can greet his friends charmingly, convert his bitterness to witty jests, and eagerly look forward to the midnight rendezvous with the Ghost. Throughout the first half of the play Hamlet is so crippled by doubt and emotional confusion that he knows not who he is or what he should do. For this reason he constantly examines his motives; for this reason he can turn abruptly from the joyful anticipation of future accomplishment (end of II.ii) to the expression of utter despair (beginning of III.i). Already in Act III, however, the spectators begin to sense a change. Here Hamlet refuses for the first time to accept the evaluations that others make of him, even rejecting the right of Rosencrantz and Guildenstern to characterize him at all (III.ii.354–362). In the closet scene (III.iv) he reverses the roles of mother and son, becoming teacher to Gertrude the pupil and father-confessor to Gertrude the sinner. His letter to Claudius (IV.vii.43–47) manifests an attitude toward the king which he has never before displayed openly. He no longer conceals his hatred within an aside or behind a mask of madness or beneath an ironic comment on "The Murder of Gonzago." Nor is his hatred of Claudius any longer so excessive that it is in itself sufficient revenge. In the letter Hamlet's attitude is clear and open, but its tone is that of the mild ridicule epitomized in the phrases "High and Mighty" and "your kingly eyes."

When Hamlet returns in Act V, it is obvious that during his absence from Denmark the gradual change in his nature has taken complete effect. For one thing, his appearance is different. In Act I he wore the melancholy suit of mourning that visualized the tone and content of the first soliloquy. In Acts II through IV his clothing, judging from Ophelia's description of it (II.i.78–80), was in a state of disarray symbolic of his antic disposition. The text of the play does not specify what Hamlet wears when he enters the graveyard, but it should be simple, ordinary, and neat, in keeping with the new calm that possesses his soul.[5] This new calm is fully evident in his speech, especially when he exhibits an attitude toward death comparable to that of

[5] Cf. a similar analysis of Hamlet's costumes by Maynard Mack, "The World of *Hamlet*," in *Shakespeare: Modern Essays in Criticism*, ed. Leonard F. Dean (New York: Oxford University Press, 1957), p. 246.

the first gravedigger. Hamlet marvels at the clown's detachment, but he cannot quarrel with it because he now regards death in much the same way. He had originally felt it necessary to engage in an excessive display of mourning when the court had indifferently forgotten his father's death, and throughout he has both desired and feared his own; but here, in the graveyard, he shows that he has come to accept death for what it is. Death, he now knows, is not a fascinating horror but merely a universal fact: even Alexander may have become a stop for a bunghole; Caesar himself probably fills a chink in a wall. Hamlet's jests about the maggots consuming Polonius' body (IV.iii.20–31) were inspired by his awareness that all must die, but the thought then filled him with loathing. In the graveyard the loathing has dwindled into a scarcely perceptible aspect of a complex but generally contemplative response.

Throughout the act Hamlet's statements and behavior strengthen the spectators' realization of his change. While still in the graveyard he seems to deliberately reject his former, disintegrated nature with the firm announcement, "This is I, / Hamlet the Dane" (V.i.251–252). He has a new attitude toward his revenge: where before he oscillated between a need for instant action and a need to delay, where he felt his delay and sought motives for it, now he has passed beyond either inordinate haste or futile hesitation. He feels that it is "perfect conscience / To quit him [Claudius] with this arm" (V.ii.67–68). He will act when he has the appropriate opportunity, for he now holds control: "the interim is mine" (l. 73). The meeting with Osric, who in some ways resembles Polonius, indicates that Hamlet has rid himself of the petty commitment that allowed the old man to stir his nausea. Osric is not old, but like Polonius he is a tedious fool, and yet Hamlet can view him with little more than a tolerant smile and a raised eyebrow. Similarly, the genuine sincerity with which he pardons Laertes suggests that he is at last prepared to accept the conditions of "this harsh world" (l. 340). Particularly significant, finally, is the complete absence of soliloquies. In the earlier acts,

Hamlet had used the soliloquy as a sounding board to test the quality of his grief, his intentions, and his despair—above all to seek self-understanding. The absence of this device during Act V suggests the elimination of the needs that made it congenial.

As Hamlet becomes gradually more sure of himself and his proper role, the spectators cannot help increasing their tendency to equate their point of view with his. It is, however, the end result of Hamlet's change, his new mood of Act V, which is the decisive factor, for the serenity he here displays could only be the result of his conviction that he has attained a state of complete understanding. Whether or not he actually has attained valid understanding is irrelevant; he speaks and acts as if he has, and for the spectators, who already tend to see things as he sees them and who themselves desire understanding, the appearance is sufficient. Thus Hamlet's speeches in the fifth act have the force of expository statement, and thus the spectators must share with him his vision of a divine and beneficent order governing the affairs of men:

> Our indiscretion sometime serves us well,
> When our deep plots do pall; and that should learn us
> There's a divinity that shapes our ends,
> Rough-hew them how we will   [V.ii.8-11].

Heaven has been "ordinant" (l. 48), Hamlet insists, not only in his discovery of the sealed commission ordering his death but also in his having with him the means by which he could fashion a substitute commission. And, evidently, it will continue to be ordinant. For despite Horatio's warning, and even though he himself feels "a kind of gain-giving as would perhaps trouble a woman" (ll. 207–208), he will go to his last duel. He defies augury; he believes that his revenge and his own fate are in hands more powerful than his own: "There is a special providence in the fall of a sparrow. If it be now, 'tis not to come; if it be not to come, it will be now; if it be not now, yet it will come—the readiness is all" (ll. 211–215).

The spectators' tendency to accept these speeches as expository statement is strengthened by expository statement of a more conventional kind. Horatio has been throughout the play largely a functional figure, called upon to narrate exposition, define certain aspects of the Ghost, deliver necessary information, and act as Hamlet's confidant. His comments are generally authoritative. At the end of the play, after Hamlet has urged him to "report me and my cause aright / To the unsatisfied" (ll. 331–332), his eulogy restates for the spectators the reality of heaven and of Hamlet's role as its "scourge and minister":

> Now cracks a noble heart. Good night, sweet prince,
> And flights of angels sing thee to thy rest! [ll. 351–352].

Yet Horatio's suggestion that Hamlet has been welcomed by the divinity he had perceived in his ultimate wisdom merely reinforces an understanding that the spectators have acquired through Shakespeare's steady manipulation of them no less than of Hamlet until the attitudes of audience and of hero are virtually identical. The spectators retain enough detachment to perceive as well the possible validity of additional perspectives, and therefore they are able to experience the different interpretations of the action of depth asserted by other aspects of the play. But because they have learned of the existence of divinity from Hamlet's voice, these other interpretations cannot deny its validity. They must instead merge with it in an action of depth so complex that not even Hamlet can comprehend its entire substance.

All major characters have, no doubt, some capacity to impress their points of view on an audience. But Hamlet, as Henry James remarked, is "the most polished of possible mirrors of the subject." [6] His case is extremely rare. And apart from functional figures, or "central intelligences" like Hamlet, the dramatist has only his ordinary individualized characters with their varying degrees of perception. These are incapable of producing independ-

---

[6] *The Art of the Novel: Critical Prefaces* (New York: Scribner's, 1934), pp. 62, 70.

ent authoritative insights about the action of depth. Lacking the functional figure's detachment and motivated by the emotions that their meager experience has instilled in them, they can only grope blindly. Like those characters who interpret Hamlet, they usually tell the spectators far more about themselves than they do about the object they attempt to describe. Nevertheless, the dramatist can use their pronouncements to help shape his audience's understanding in at least two ways. One of these involves the function of exposition. The other depends on the organization of many statements into a valuable device of dramatic economy, reciprocal reflection.

The Function of Exposition

One of the few kinds of statements a spectator is likely to accept at face value consists of the various narrated reports of the unstaged portion of the plot, the past and intervening events that complete the story of the immediate action. These accounts—the exposition—fill in the details that, by clarifying character and situation, allow an enlightened appreciation of those events that are actually seen. But the primary function of exposition lies in the way it combines with the visible events to create for the spectators a point of view from which they may perceive one glimpse of the action of depth. This function of exposition is especially apparent in plays like Arthur Miller's *Death of a Salesman* and Eugene O'Neill's *The Emperor Jones*, which derive a great deal of their meaning from the dramatized collision between past events and present circumstances. But the function pertains as well to any play. To illustrate it, I shall re-examine the first half of the *Agamemnon*, which I discussed in the preceding chapter only for the method by which Aeschylus defines its titular character.[7]

[7] Most of the characters who introduce exposition in the *Agamemnon* happen to be functional figures, but that circumstance does not affect the point at issue. The examination in Chapter 8 of the structure of *Rosmers-*

The immediate action of the *Agamemnon* up to the symbolic treading on the carpet consists of the Watchman's expression of his feelings, the chorus' musings on the Trojan War and on the sacrifice of Iphigeneia, its mingled evocations of joy and sorrow, Clytaemestra's portrayal of a false innocence that tends to deceive the chorus but not the audience, the Herald's announcement of Agamemnon's imminent arrival, and the arrival itself. This action derives its greatest importance, however, from its references to selected events of the past and the distant, and particularly from the attitudes these references, as they accumulate, arouse in the audience. The spectators are especially interested in the interpretations of past events because of their own prior knowledge of the legend. They know of the curse that moves through and lays waste to the generation of Tantalus: how Atreus revenged himself on Thyestes, how Aegisthus, the remaining son of Thyestes, has joined with Clytaemestra for revenge against Agamemnon, and how Orestes will eventually achieve vengeance against his mother and her lover. When the spectators come to see the *Oresteia*, the legend is established in their consciousness as a chain of sin and retribution, and their foreknowledge constitutes the first effect providing them with a meaning that the past has for the present.

The title of the first play and the Watchman's opening monologue, with its emphasis on Agamemnon, focus the audience's attention on a specific link in the chain. Because of its prior knowledge, the audience already surpasses the Watchman in understanding, but he has much to contribute. His first words provide an extended image in which he unknowingly defines some of the significance of the action he introduces. Throughout his long vigil he has observed the passing "dynasties in their shining blazoned on the air, / these stars, upon their wane and when the rest arise" (ll. 6–7). The waning of old dynasties and the rise of

---

holm shows that this device works in much the same way when functional figures are unavailable.

new connote the defeat of King Agamemnon and the resulting triumphant rise of Tyrant Aegisthus. The continuous pattern of rise and fall suggested by the image re-creates the sense of the chain of sin and retribution with which the spectators already view the legend. More dimly, the image also foreshadows the divine and social alterations that will ultimately result from Agamemnon's murder: the completed rise of a new dynasty of gods under Zeus and the waning of an ancient order of retribution as it is replaced by a more humane code of justice.

But the Watchman's main contribution to exposition consists of the announcement of a particular subject and the introduction of an emotional attitude. His whole monologue emphasizes the Trojan War. Although he attempts no assessment of its significance, his very emphasis suggests the vital importance of Troy for the understanding of these events on the mainland of Greece. At the same time, his personal relationship to the action creates two conflicting emotions designed to influence the spectators' attitude toward the material he has introduced. The joy and hope with which he anticipates the homecoming of his lord contrast sharply with the fear and foreboding he associates with the palace, where, as the spectators know, Clytaemestra and Aegisthus wait. The Watchman fears the palace superstitiously, fears even to speak coherently of his fear (ll. 34–37). The conflicting emotions, which suggest that Agamemnon's homecoming must be seen as both good and evil, converge in the Watchman's vacillation from one emotion to the other: "I sing, / only to weep again the pity of this house" (ll. 16–17).

In its first ode the chorus echoes and intensifies the Watchman's emphasis on the Trojan War. The chorus' knowledge of the past is greater than the Watchman's but about equal to that of the audience, for whom the story of the war is an essential part of cultural experience. What the audience does not know is the significance that Troy has for the curse on the House of Atreus, and this it must learn from the chorus' oblique narration.

The chorus begins by defining the war itself, which it sees as an example of the gods' practice of driving "the Fury upon the transgressors":

> So drives Zeus the great guest god
> the Atreidae against Alexander:
> for one woman's promiscuous sake.
>
> . . . . .
>
>   The end will be destiny.
> You cannot burn flesh or pour unguents,
> not innocent cool tears,
> that will soften the gods' stiff anger   [ll. 59–62, 68–71].

The war was fought to do vengeance on Paris (Alexander), who had sinned. It was directed by the gods and waged by their agents, Menelaus and Agamemnon (the Atreidae). It is a clear-cut case of retribution, and it illustrates the justice of retribution as a punishment for sin.

The chorus also reinforces the emphasis that the Watchman has given to the conflicting emotions. Unable to comprehend why the silent Clytaemestra busies herself in sacrifice, why "to all the gods of the city . . . the altars blaze with oblations" (ll. 88–91), the chorus must evaluate the symbol according to its own attitudes, and it imagines hope to counter sorrow already deeply felt:

> Be healer to this perplexity
> that grows now into darkness of thought,
> while again sweet hope shining from the flames
> beats back the pitiless pondering
> of sorrow that eats my heart   [ll. 99–103].

Similarly, although the chorus now turns to the theme of the sacrifice of Iphigeneia, it punctuates its narration with the refrain, "Sing sorrow, sorrow: but good win out in the end" (ll. 121, 138, 159). And here also, woven into the account of the sacrifice, occur both the prayer to Zeus, with its concept of "wisdom through suffering" (ll. 160–183), and, despite the chorus' own sorrow and perplexity, its insistence that "All will come clear in the next dawn's sunlight" (l. 254).

The account of the sacrifice does more than reinforce the conflicting emotions, however, for although the chorus admits that the killing of Iphigeneia was necessary before Troy could be justly punished, it nevertheless regards the act as "sacrilegious, utterly infidel" (l. 220). In performing it, Agamemnon not only furthered the ultimate will of the gods but also warped his own. He, like Paris, became a sinner. At this point, however, the chorus' sure knowledge fails, and the spectators must achieve understanding by combining what the chorus has told them of past events with their own awareness of Clytaemestra's intentions. Throughout the ode the spectators can see the silent queen ever busy at her altar. They realize that her activity must constitute a thank offering to the gods for the safe return of her intended victim as well as a prayer seeking divine aid for carrying out her purpose. The words of the ode, stressing that Agememnon has sinned, merge with the visual effect of Clytaemestra's wordless activity to inform the spectators that Agamemnon the sinner is to receive retribution just as he brought retribution to Troy.

In the brief episode that follows the first choral ode, this implication is reinforced through the speech in which Clytaemestra describes the course of the flaming beacons from Ida to Argos. By evoking a vast range in space to accompany the range in time already evoked by the Watchman and the chorus, this speech helps dramatize the impression of scope and magnitude which encourages in a general way a recognition of the trilogy's social and metaphysical implications; like the chorus' prayer to Zeus, it insists that Agamemnon's personal tragedy must be seen in relation to all the events, both human and divine, which impinge on it. More specifically, the speech also restresses the relevance of Troy to the present situation and therefore of the interpretation the chorus has given the war: the law that crushed Troy evidently pertains to Argos as well. Both Clytaemestra's speech and the later arrival of the Herald emphasize a movement from Troy to Argos; both therefore suggest the symbolic passage to Agamemnon's homeland of Troy and all that it signifies.

As Clytaemestra goes on to provide additional exposition by picturing the destruction at Troy, Aeschylus implies that the connection between Troy's fall and Agamemnon's may be more than merely thematic. The agents of vengeance have won; yet, Clytaemestra warns, they must still be wary:

> if they reverence the gods who hold the city
> and all the holy temples of the captured land,
> they, the despoilers, might not be despoiled in turn
>
> [ll. 338–340].

If, however, they show irreverence, they are doomed; even though they may escape Troy and return home safely, "the anger of these slaughtered men / may never sleep" (ll. 346–347).

The chorus develops this new implication in its second ode. It reiterates the theme of the just retribution heaped on Troy—the rape of Helen was a sin, for which Zeus "wrung from Alexander such payment" (l. 363)—and this time it generalizes from the Trojan example to define the inevitability of retribution for sin as a universal law:

> There is not any armor
> in gold against perdition
> for him who spurns the high altar
> of Justice down to the darkness   [ll. 381–384].

From this point of view the war is just and necessary; from that of the citizens of Argos, however, whose sons have been carried home in burial urns, the war is an evil waste, "and all for some strange woman" (l. 448). The law of retribution therefore applies to Troy in another way as well, for "The curse of the people must be paid for" (l. 458). This conclusion prompts from the chorus a further generalization:

> The gods fail not to mark
> those who have killed many.
> The black Furies stalking the man
> fortunate beyond all right
> wrench back again the set of his life
> and drop him to darkness. There among
> the ciphers there is no more comfort
> in power. And the vaunt of high glory
> is bitterness; for God's thunderbolts
> crash on the towering mountains   [ll. 461–470].

The chorus does not name Agamemnon—as its deliberate vagueness suggests, it perhaps does not even allow itself to realize that it is he to whom these words refer. But its next lines make the application inescapable:

> Let me attain no envied wealth,
> let me not plunder cities,
> neither be taken in turn, and face
> life in the power of another   [ll. 471–474].

Once more the visual effect of Clytaemestra's presence merges with the import of the spoken lines to render the full meaning. Hers is "the power of another" that will strike down Agamemnon as he struck down Troy.

It is, however, the Herald, a symbol of the army that smashed Troy, who rounds off the developing implication. The Herald augments the recurring emphasis on the conflicting emotions when he recalls that "part of our fortune you could say held favorable, / but part we cursed again" (ll. 552–553); he also reinforces the idea that Priam's house has atoned for its sins (l. 537); and, in describing Agamemnon as "the man who has wrecked Ilium with the spade of Zeus / vindictive" (ll. 525–526), he is the first to formulate explicitly the growing awareness of Agamemnon's role as the gods' agent. But the Herald's most important contribution is to inform the spectators that the blasphemy Clytaemestra imagined might happen at Troy has actually taken place: "Gone are their altars, the sacred places of the gods / are gone" (ll. 527–528). Here, however, the Herald's direct contribution to the spectators' understanding ends, for he is unaware of the full significance of his statement. The spectators must add his information to their fear that this blasphemy might occur in order to realize that now Agamemnon can never escape. He has unleashed the forces of retribution not only through his sacrifice of Iphigeneia but also through his actions at Troy. In destroying Paris' city, he had been an agent of the gods effecting a just retribution, but the carrying out of this justice has made him as guilty as Paris. Consequently, the Herald's account of the great storm that wrecked the Greek fleet and carried off Menelaus also conveys more than its speaker intends: as seen from the point of view already established for the spectators, it suggests that the other Greeks have paid for their crimes in Troy. Agamemnon alone remains unpunished. And when the Herald calls Agamemnon "a man / fortunate to be honored far above all men / alive" (ll. 530–532), he unwittingly identifies him as "the man / fortunate beyond all right" (ll. 463–464) of the chorus' generalization, the man whom the black Furies stalk.

The realization that Agamemnon will deserve his coming death for his actions at Troy as well as for killing his daughter gives the spectators greater understanding of Clytaemestra's role. They knew from the beginning that she intended to murder her husband; during the first ode they learned her motive, a personal motive that did not decrease their antagonism, even though they can appreciate that her daughter's death must have deeply grieved her. The Herald's contribution complicates their feeling toward her by convincing them that in murdering her husband she will herself be acting as an agent of the gods. And like her husband, in performing an act of just retribution, she will also sin and be liable in turn.

The third ode of the chorus, which follows the Herald's report, has a function characteristic of several speeches in these opening moments of the *Agamemnon* and typical of the control of point of view in all drama. In this ode the intellectual pattern taking shape in the spectators' consciousness through the accumulation of statement and suggestion is suddenly and vividly articulated. The chorus, once more musing on the sin and punishment of Troy, declares:

> the act of evil
> breeds others to follow,
> young sins in its own likeness   [ll.758–760].

The effect of these lines is to assure the spectators of the validity of their growing awareness. They now realize that retribution creates a chain reaction, that, like the curse on the House of Atreus, it is unending: first Agamemnon, soon Clytaemestra, eventually Orestes. The spectators' attitude toward this awareness, shaped by their recognition of Agamemnon as a man both good and evil and by their new ambivalence toward Clytaemestra in her double role, takes the form of the mingled joy and sorrow stressed throughout the first half of the play.

Then Agamemnon enters. Just as his entrance lends confirmation to the previously established characterization of him, it also helps codify the play's larger implications. The visual splendor, which testifies to his magnificence, also serves to incriminate him further, for the plundered treasure of Troy provides a concrete referent for the chorus' words about "Righteousness":

> From high halls starred with gold by reeking hands
> she turns back
> with eyes that glance away to the simple in heart,
> spurning the strength of gold
> stamped false with flattery.
> And all things she steers to fulfillment   [ll. 776–781].

In announcing Agamemnon's approach, moreover, the chorus explicitly associates him with both the chain of retribution stemming from the sin and fall of Troy and the chain of retribution implicit in the history of the family curse:

> Behold, my king: sacker of Troy's citadel,
> own issue of Atreus   [ll. 783–784].

As the hero who has justly executed retribution and as the sinner who justly deserves it, Agamemnon visually symbolizes the complex understanding that Aeschylus has demanded for the retributive code of justice. Agamemnon is a magnificent figure; he has served the gods well; and for these reasons the spectators admire and respect him. They grieve that this man must die the death he enacts before their eyes by walking on the blood-colored carpet, and this response convinces them that the retributive code of justice is evil. But along with the doomed magnificence he also displays the *hybris* that epitomizes his guilt and that prompts them to condemn him. They are pleased that the sinner will be punished, and this response assures them that retribution is good.

The ambivalence toward Clytaemestra, which affects the spectators in much the same way, is more firmly established during this and the following scene. Her activity in the carpet scene illustrates her role as agent of the gods. Justice, she tells Agamemnon equivocally, shall lead him along the carpet to the palace (l. 911), and evidently she is right, for her ability to compel him to act against his will suggests that more than her personal force is brought to bear on him. The compulsion she exerts is the same power of necessity, the same working of the will of the gods that enabled her husband to crush Troy.[8] In the following episode she attempts unsuccessfully to force the unyielding Cassandra to enter the palace. The attempt, which brings out her hatred and jealousy of Cassandra, suggests that her husband's possession of a concubine gives her one more personal—and petty—motive for

[8] Cf. Robert F. Goheen, "Aspects of Dramatic Symbolism: Three Studies in the *Oresteia*," *American Journal of Philology*, LXXVI (1955), pp. 126, 131.

revenge. But by far the most important effect is the failure to make Cassandra yield, for Clytaemestra's ineffectuality here reinforces the impression that in manipulating Agamemnon she was strengthened by the power of divine justice. This simultaneous presentation of the dubious personal motive and the just impersonal motive solidifies the spectators' ambivalence toward her.

Cassandra's forevision of the murder, which now follows, will fill in the details of the second chain of retribution in which Agamemnon and Clytaemestra are involved—the family curse. And the murder itself, through the many conflicting responses it exacts from Cassandra, Clytaemestra, Aegisthus, and the chorus, will provide a new symbol of the complexity of retribution. Already, however, the ambivalence provoked by Agamemnon and Clytaemestra, who as victim and performer are the chief embodiments of retribution in the immediate action of the first play, has fixed for the spectators a specific understanding of the retributive code of justice. Retribution, they realize, indeed creates an inevitable succession, and though each act of vengeance may be just, it is also a new crime demanding further vengeance. The retributive code of justice, like its practitioners Agamemnon and Clytaemestra, is both good and evil. The spectators are never told this explicitly. Their understanding gradually takes shape as knowledge gained from the exposition merges with the concrete effects of the immediate action. The synthesis establishes the point of view from which they must see the images of Agamemnon and Clytaemestra and, through them, the concept of retribution.

The Central Referent

No device of drama demonstrates the ultimate inseparability of immediate action and action of depth more clearly than the process of reciprocal reflection, for this device, which groups several characters around a central referent, ordinarily illuminates both

THE IDIOM OF DRAMA

levels of action simultaneously. This device has been well described by Henry James in his critical prefaces, especially in the passage that discusses his original conception of *The Spoils of Poynton:*

The real centre, as I say, the citadel of the interest, with the fight waged round it, would have been the felt beauty and value of the prize of battle, the Things, always the splendid Things, placed in the middle light, figured and constituted, with each identity made vivid, each character discriminated, and their common consciousness of their great dramatic part established.[9]

As James's remarks indicate, the attitude that each character holds toward the central referent helps clarify his own nature, for the central referent discriminates the various characters by reflecting each as a mirror reflects the face of its viewer. But equally important is the reciprocal action. The "splendid Things" not only discriminate the characters who value them, but their own beauty and value are "felt," created through the attitudes of the characters who treasure them and thereby make them important. These characters thus resemble the "social occasions" of *The Awkward Age* as James conceived them in a diagram of the novel's structure: "a number of small rounds disposed at equal distance about a central object," representing "so many distinct lamps, . . . the function of each of which would be to light with all due intensity one of [the central object's] aspects." [10] In other words, the meaning that the central object —or referent—itself expresses is determined by a synthesis of all the available attitudes.

It is, of course, the second of these results which is of primary concern for my survey of expository references to the action of depth. The great value of the central referent to the dramatist is that since it acquires meaning only from the various assertions of those reflecting it, it validates these assertions, and

---

[9] *The Art of the Novel*, p. 126.   [10] *The Art of the Novel*, p. 110.

consequently it enables the dramatist to make full and convincing use of certain speeches by even his most limited characters.
When a number of assertions converge on a central referent, the
spectators cannot grant complete acceptance to a single assertion,
nor can they wholly reject another. They must instead merge all
the given assertions into one complex realization.

The central referent assumes many forms in drama. It may be
a character—like Hamlet, to the extent that his observers' evaluations take hold. Or it may be a concrete object, like James's furniture or the orphanage in Ibsen's *Ghosts;* an event, like the murder of Agamemnon or the binding of Prometheus; or even a concept, like the "true morality" of Shaw's *Major Barbara* or the
"honor" of *1 Henry IV*. Similarly, the central referent may be
concisely established within a few consecutive speeches, or it
may so pervade its play that it imparts form and meaning to the
entire action, as does Chekhov's cherry orchard, which illuminates most of the play's characters and, through the meanings
with which their attitudes endow it, comes to symbolize both the
idea of the past and all the personal pasts of the individuals it reflects. The scope of most central referents falls somewhere between these extremes, however; a relevant example, which will
serve to illustrate this device more fully, is the concept of political liberalism in *Rosmersholm*.

This central referent is first seen through the jaundiced eye of
Kroll, who reduces it to the current radical movement—for him
an element of unmitigated evil which seeks to overthrow sacred
traditions and which therefore provides an excuse for any actions
that may be necessary to ensure its defeat. Kroll's opinion is
heard often and inevitably takes some hold in the spectators' consciousness, but, like the Player Queen, he protests too much: as
always, the more adamant he is, the less likely he is to convince.
Kroll thus helps promote acceptance of the view held by Brendel, for whom social and political liberalism is a great and good
cause, almost a religious principle, to which he must dedicate

even the profound thoughts that he has until now selfishly reserved for his own private enjoyment. Yet Brendel is little better as an advocate than Kroll. Brendel's notion of liberalism, in keeping with his nature, is formless and fantastic, which suggests that the movement attracting him itself lacks a precise focus or, even worse, encourages frivolity.

Rosmer defends more successfully the excellence of the drive for political and social freedom. Although he tends to idealize, his view is more definite than Brendel's. He would grant to Kroll that the present strife is evil—but on both sides. His own aim is to unite all men "in the great world of truth and freedom" (I, p. 144):

I want to devote my life and all the strength I possess to this one thing—to create a true democracy in this country. . . . I shall show the democracy its true task . . . of making all the people of this country noblemen . . . as many as possible, at any rate . . . by freeing their minds and purifying their wills [p. 143].

Rosmer's intentions are appealing and prompt favor for a movement that can inspire such goals in men. But the validity of his view becomes suspect through its juxtaposition to Brendel's obvious impracticality, through Rosmer's own note of doubt in the "as many as possible," and through the intention of "purifying their wills," for the irony of this phrase underscores those aspects of his view that reflect his own nature. Rosmer declares himself publicly only under compulsion; he had thought he "could keep on living here as before, quiet, contented, happy": "I wanted to read and lose myself in all the works that had previously been closed books to me" (p. 144). Rosmer's tendency toward quiet retirement conflicts with his noble intentions. When his plans are changed and he must enter the world of action, he too is prepared to fight in his own way, but his conception of the cause he hopes to support reveals his inability to free himself completely from the past and from his previous mode of existence. Even his devotion to the new movement is clearly motivated by his links with tradition: "I think it's my imperative duty to bring a little light and joy here, where the Rosmer family has created gloom and oppression throughout all these long, long years" (II, p. 158). From the audience's point of view, Rosmer's reflection of the new spirit to which he has pledged his allegiance suggests that it lacks sufficient power to quell the opposing forces of tradition, that in fact it has already been infiltrated by the opposition.

A view of political liberalism that shows no influence from the past is that of Peter Mortensgaard, one of the radical leaders. Mortensgaard, an unyielding, unprincipled fighter who very much resembles Kroll, stresses, in his determination to help the movement succeed, its overwhelming necessity. Yet just as Kroll's belligerence tends to make the spectators favor the new movement, Mortensgaard's methods of operation prompt them to reject it. He is an opportunist, willing to lie, cheat, and wreck reputations in order to gain his ends. He wants Rosmer's aid, but not for the purpose of incorporating within the movement the idea of ennoblement. Rosmer has value because as *Pastor* Rosmer he represents to the world a quality the radical party vitally requires: "a Christian element—a thing that everyone has to respect. It is that which we have such great need of" (p. 162). If Rosmer openly declares his apostasy, as he feels he must, Mortensgaard wants nothing to do with him. Such scrupulosity betrays a devotion to ideals, and ideals have no place in Mortensgaard's conception of the movement.

Rebecca's view, which completes the revolving view of the central referent, is never specifically articulated. At first, indeed, her apparent view is amply indicated by her attitudes toward other characters: her distrust and ridicule of Kroll, her admiration for Brendel, her willingness to work with Mortensgaard, and her idealized love for Rosmer. The spectators perceive, however, that her apparent view alters as the action progresses. At first she evidently shares Rosmer's ideals. She seems content to listen to him dream; and their love, as she lets Rosmer believe, accords with his noble thoughts, for it is only a virtuous friendship, based on their "common faith in a pure comradeship between man and woman" (p. 171). Then, from the revelations of her long confession in Act III, the audience discovers that her view is really closer to Mortensgaard's. The motive she gives for sending Beata to her death assuredly emphasizes her belief in the necessity of the new movement, but it also reveals a rather obvious lack of scruple: "There was this gloomy, insurmountable barrier between you and total freedom. . . . I mean this, Rosmer, that you could not grow up into freedom without the bright sunshine —and here you were, ailing and drooping in the gloom of a marriage like that" (III, p. 191). Ultimately, when she completes her confession in the fourth act, the audience realizes that Rebecca has actually been more corrupt than Mortensgaard would ever dream of being. To the Rebecca there revealed the glorious movement for freedom has only the value of a weapon she can use to hack her way to Rosmer's heart. In such a view all ideals, all worth fade; the movement has importance only as it can be turned to personal advantage.

The spectators' multiple view of the central referent enriches their understanding of the entire action by defining for them some of the complexity in the opposition between tradition and progress which is probed throughout the play and of which the liberal movement is only one symbol. Their multiple view of the movement informs them that progress, which should be and is good, also has its evil aspects. Although it can improve man and his lot (as Rosmer passively hopes), it can also corrupt him (as Mortensgaard actively demonstrates), or even provide (as Rebecca's behavior shows) an instrument for fashioning the most hideous of evils. Equally important, the spectators' multiple view also assures them that the new is less likely to win than seemed probable at the beginning of the play, for it is, after all, strongly infiltrated by the old. Brendel is a figure from the romantic past attempting to foster the future but out of touch with the reality of the present. Rosmer's devotion to the new way of life betrays overtones that are more in keeping with the traditions of his family.

Kroll and Mortensgaard are blinded by party spirit. Brendel and Rosmer inhabit dream worlds of their own conceiving. Rebecca has let selfish passion warp her judgment. But because these characters all see a little, the spectators catch a glimpse of the universe of *Rosmersholm* which is as fully and convincingly enunciated as if it were reported by the *Agamemnon* chorus or by Hamlet in his new mood of Act V.

5. Stylistic Devices

> To proceed from the word to the image in its verse setting, and thence to trace the way in which a pattern of interdependent themes is gradually woven into the dramatic action, unifying and illuminating it, is the most fruitful approach— the most accurate and, if properly handled, the least subject to prejudice—to Shakespeare's art.
> —D. A. Traversi, *An Approach to Shakespeare*

The analysis of Hamlet's soliloquy in Chapter 3 illustrates a basic characteristic of dramatic speech: like any other literary construct, it contains more than its mere paraphrasable content. Its full content—what it really *says*—depends in the final analysis on its form, on the specific language that gives the paraphrasable content its particular shape. The distinction between content and style is, then, invalid metaphysically. But as an arbitrary critical tool, it is highly useful, for it enables us to see exactly what part is played in the formation of "content" by those devices of language which can be called elements of "style." The distinction is made, in other words, in order to demonstrate that content and style are equally meaningful. In Hamlet's soliloquy, for example, both create significant effects expressive of a single moment in his progress; and both establish points of contact with the rest of the play which clarify the soliloquy's function in helping to define the quality of his progress as a whole.

Every successful dramatic speech creates to some extent a similar multidimensional effect. A typical example, which Polonius provokes when he concludes his preparations for spying on Hamlet by making a hypocritical remark about our blameworthy tendency to conceal foul and sinful actions behind pious display, is Claudius' aside in Act III, scene i, of *Hamlet:*

> O, 'tis too true!
> How smart a lash that speech doth give my conscience!
> The harlot's cheek, beautied with plast'ring art,
> Is not more ugly to the thing that helps it
> Than is my deed to my most painted word.
> O heavy burden! [ll. 49–54].

This aside, Claudius' first admission of his guilt, fulfills the necessary plot function of confirming his guilt through his own lips. At the same time, it links for the spectators two previously established but incompatible points of view. Prior to the aside, the spectators have seen Claudius either through the eyes of Hamlet and the Ghost as a foul criminal or through his own public demeanor as a benign and forceful king very much concerned with the welfare of his nephew-stepson. Claudius' aside shows that both views are relevant, and the contrast between his "deed" and his "most painted word" precisely indicates one relationship between the two irreconcilable pictures: the first presents reality; the second is deceitful appearance. Shakespeare complicates this clear distinction, however, by allowing Claudius to view it with the guilt, shame, and self-disgust evident in his final phrase, "O heavy burden!" These responses suggest that Claudius is not so foul after all. He has certainly committed the crime, and therefore Hamlet and the Ghost are right; but he also feels remorse, and therefore the positive attitude demanded by his public behavior retains some validity. The speech, then, not only associates the two views but tends at the same time to fuse them into one.

The details I have so far considered, to make the arbitrary but useful separation, might be called the content of the speech. More important is its style, especially the image of the harlot's cheek. On the one hand, this image can be regarded as chosen by Claudius to indicate emotionally the disgust he himself assigns to his act. On the other hand, it is simultaneously chosen by Shakespeare as a means of establishing the point of view from which Claudius' act must be seen regardless of his own attitude toward it. Whatever Claudius may feel, the image suggests, his deed remains a foul and loathsome actuality, one that necessarily calls forth the responses normally elicited by cheap cosmetics, purchased sex, disease, and rotting flesh. The image's most meaningful contribution, however—also an aspect of its function in defining Claudius from Shakespeare's point of view—derives from its similarity to numerous other images introduced throughout the play. The relationship of cheek to "plast'ring art" is but one of many details connoting a breach between inner and outer, while the cheek itself, with its suggestions of decay and corruption, takes its place in a second dominant pattern of imagery evoking basic qualities of the world of *Hamlet*. The image is Claudius' and Shakespeare's at the same time. Claudius employs it in order to make a statement about his own situation, and he conveys perfectly valid information. Without realizing it, he also furthers Shakespeare's over-all purpose by helping to reveal larger meanings of which he is unaware. Claudius, concerned only with his own feelings, unknowingly establishes his crime and himself as primary examples, even sources, of the deceit and rottenness pervading the whole of Denmark.

It is this last aspect of Claudius' speech that has central importance for the present chapter. His aside illustrates how the dramatist uses dialogue to establish the action of depth even when the speaker himself has no conception of it. In this technique, understanding is conveyed not through conscious evaluations—like those of an omniscient chorus, a character specially endowed with authority, or the observers who interpret a central referent

—but through devices of speech that implicitly reveal a level of awareness beyond the speaker's own comprehension. By introducing changes of tone, images, allusions, ambiguous words, and variations in sound, or by constructing a speech from words, images, and symbols repeated or duplicated in other contexts, the dramatist breaks the barrier reared by the human limitations of his individualized characters. Through these devices he creates authoritative dramatic facts relevant to all the characters but ordinarily unperceived by any of them.

Sound Patterns

None of these stylistic devices functions independently, of course; they all acquire their significance from the general context of the action, which they in turn help to elucidate through their own contributions; each of them works jointly with other devices, of language and structure, in prompting the spectators to view the action as a whole in a certain perspective. This lack of autonomy is especially true of the sound pattern into which the dramatist shapes his individual words, that is, the pattern produced by variations in stress and pitch, differences in the placement and duration of pauses, the relationships between individual words or lines, the presence or absence of rhyme, and the contrast of one speaking voice with another.[1] While it is possible to isolate and describe this pattern, if only roughly, the resulting description can embody no specific meaning. The sound pattern may have only appropriateness—which means that the emotion articulated by the content of expressive words determines their

[1] Shaw, for example, "contrived his casts of characters . . . with an eye to vocal balance in addition to everything else" (Martin Meisel, *Shaw and the Nineteenth-Century Theater* [Princeton, N.J.: Princeton University Press, 1963], p. 48). Shaw insisted that the actors chosen for the four principal roles in any play "should be soprano, alto, tenor, and bass" ("Shaw's Rules for Directors," quoted by Meisel, p. 48).

arrangement. Nevertheless, in many instances devices of this category lead the spectator toward a clearer conception of the situation being presented. Stichomythia focuses more sharply the
clash of antithetical points of view. Rhyme, particularly in the
couplet of heroic tragedy, implies a special notion about the relationship of details in human experience. At best, the pattern of
sounds can establish a general impression that supports or confirms—and thus elucidates—the basic effect conveyed by words,
action, and physical picture.

This sort of contribution manifests itself with remarkable clarity in the first scene of *Hamlet*. As T. S. Eliot has noted, the
speeches of Bernardo, Francisco, Marcellus, and Horatio create
"a kind of musical design . . . which reinforces and is one with
the dramatic movement." [2] In this scene Shakespeare employs
contrasting effects of sound to compose his "musical design":
tension alternates with relaxation; short exclamatory speeches oppose more formal and elaborate rhetorical constructions. The
staccato outbursts in the opening lines—

> BER. Who's there?
> FRAN. Nay, answer me. Stand and unfold yourself.
> BER. Long live the King!
> FRAN. Bernardo?
> BER. He.

—corroborate the sense of confusion implied by Bernardo's mis-
challenge and prepare for the uneasiness expressed in Francisco's
"I am sick at heart" (l. 9). The voices of Marcellus and Horatio
then join the opening duet, and the resulting rapid alternation
from voice to voice cuts through the formal base of the blank-
verse line. This effect, reinforced by the sharp ejaculations of the
individual voices, increases the tension and emphasizes the confusion:

[2] *Poetry and Drama* (Cambridge, Mass.: Harvard University Press,
1951), p. 19.

MAR.   O, farewell, honest soldier!
  Who hath reliev'd you?
FRAN.   Bernardo hath my place.
  Give you good night.
MAR.   Holla, Bernardo!
BER.   Say—
  What, is Horatio there?
HOR.   A piece of him   [ll. 16–19].

The following speeches, in which the sense unit of the words conforms to the length of the verse line, point up the preceding tension through contrast. Indeed, the climax of this second movement is a speech by Bernardo that not only displays an especially careful ordering of its verbal components but even focuses on an image of order and recurrence:

> Last night of all,
> When yond same star that's westward from the pole
> Had made his course t' illume that part of heaven
> Where now it burns, Marcellus and myself,
> The bell then beating one— [ll. 35–39].

Yet this movement by no means provides an example of tension becoming harmony; Bernardo's speech turns out to be a false start, an abortive attempt to impose order where none exists; for Bernardo is abruptly silenced by the entrance of the Ghost. Shakespeare relaxes only to heighten.

The Ghost's entrance initiates a third movement. The next few lines (ll. 40–44) replace the long formal constructions with a series of short speeches, each of which corresponds to a single line of blank verse. Succeeding speeches continue this expression of controlled excitement by combining formality with minute distortions of the poetic rhythm. Lines made slightly uneven by the insertion of hypermetrical unaccented syllables—

> In which the majesty of buried Denmark
> Did sometimes march? By heaven I charge thee, speak!

—coexist with lines in which the absence of expected syllables or the failure to complete the established metrical unit produces choppy verse:

HOR. Stay! speak, speak! I charge thee, speak!
MAR. 'Tis gone, and will not answer   [ll. 48–52].

Once again Shakespeare varies the pattern by returning to longer, more carefully developed speeches, as Marcellus and Horatio discuss the current preparations for war and the general significance of omens. Once again the effect of balance and order, which the length and arrangement of these speeches establish, is destroyed by an entrance of the Ghost. When Horatio confronts it (ll. 127–139), the flow of his verse is interrupted in three places by long silences while he awaits a reply (ll. 129, 132, 135); in the final line of this speech the verse is twice broken by emphatic pauses. The whole movement is again one of increasing tension, and the climax occurs at the Ghost's exit with the cacophony of " 'Tis here!" " 'Tis here!" " 'Tis gone!" produced by the three contrasting voices of Bernardo, Horatio, and Marcellus, followed once more by a brief silence.

From here to the end of the scene (ll. 143–175), harmony predominates. The rhythm remains controlled; the content stresses images of peace and tranquility; the verse even approaches an exaggerated poetic effect with the conceits of Horatio's

But look, the morn, in russet mantle clad,
Walks o'er the dew of yon high eastward hill
[ll. 166–167].

The shift to harmony at the end of the scene suggests the possibility of resolution—or, because of the preceding movements, of even greater disturbance to follow. But more important is the stressing of the original tension through the prolonged contrast. Tension therefore remains the principal effect of the scene's sound pattern, and because of that pattern, Shakespeare introduces his spectators to the play from a point of view that compels them to apprehend a pervading imbalance. The sound pattern of the scene confirms the reaction that all four characters have shared; it makes their sense of confusion, uneasiness, and fear a valid mood for viewing the events that follow, despite any contrary impressions that subsequent scenes might convey.

The most significant aspect of the scene's sound pattern, however, is Shakespeare's application of it. The sense of imbalance is not just a vague mood. Shakespeare uses it to define in a preliminary way the basic quality of those elements of the total experience with which he is most concerned. Since each speaker reflects in his own way his recognition of the general tension, tension becomes a distinct part of his presented character: man's nature seems only a compound of fear, confusion, uneasiness, foreboding, and helplessness. Moreover—and this effect illustrates the inevitable dependence of one stylistic device upon another— along with the sound pattern Shakespeare establishes another pattern consisting of the repetition of related words and phrases. Line after line emphasizes the kingdom. From the pronouncement of the watchword—"Long live the King!"—to Horatio's detailed narration of old Hamlet's war with Fortinbras, Shakespeare stresses Denmark so emphatically that it soon shares importance with the idea of imbalance. When Horatio says of the Ghost, "This bodes some strange eruption to our state" (l. 69), the two combine. In the spectators' consciousness Denmark and imbalance are made synonymous.

Another stylistic device, the selection and phrasing of individual details, confirms the validity of the association between Denmark and imbalance and also suggests a further application of the tension embodied in the sound pattern. When Marcellus describes the preparations for war (ll. 70–79), he speaks calmly and smoothly, in long elaborate sentences, with one carefully arranged clause poised against another: the sense of imbalance is not in the rhythm. Nevertheless, it is suggested by two salient images: the "sore task" of the shipwrights "does not divide the Sunday from the week" (l. 76); and the general haste "doth make the night joint-labourer with the day" (l. 78). Both images focus on the elimination of the formal units of time and thus evoke disorder. These images, which clarify the nature of Denmark, anticipate and are later echoed by a lengthy series of images through which Horatio describes the similarity between the omens that foretold Julius Caesar's death and those now visible in Denmark (ll. 112–125). In this speech the imbalance already attributed to the individual and to the state extends to the universe itself. In fact, Horatio's images link the three realms. The "stars with trains of fire," the "dews of blood," and the "disasters in the sun" (ll. 117–118), all elements signifying universal disorder, have particular function, both in Rome and in Denmark, as indications of an evil threatening the state. The "moist star / Upon whose influence Neptune's empire stands" is "sick" (ll. 118–120), and this recalls Francisco's "sick at heart."

In the figure of the Ghost, the focal element of the scene, Shakespeare crystallizes and unifies the various suggestions of imbalance. The Ghost directly causes the dislocations in verbal rhythm. Its first entrance interrupts Bernardo's speech and turns apparent harmony into increased discord. Its presence provokes the tonal irregularities in Horatio's speeches to it, and the vain attempt to stop it from leaving results in the climactic expression of broken rhythm: " 'Tis here!' " " 'Tis here!' " " 'Tis gone!' " In its very nature the Ghost exemplifies the shared disorder that links the individual with the state and the universe. It was once a human being. It appears in armor and resembles the dead king; consequently, "it bodes some strange eruption to our state." Like "the sheeted dead" that "did squeak and gibber in the Roman streets" (ll. 115–116), its mere presence betokens a universe askew. Most important of all, the Ghost, as visual object, provides an extremely effective theatrical image of imbalance. The visual and verbal devices reinforce one another in such a way that the vague sense of disorder inherent in the sound pattern of the dialogue becomes a precise evocation of the exact state of all three levels of experience within the play. This is the multiple imbalance that Hamlet is called on to set right.

Hamlet and similar verse plays also contain another kind of sound pattern, one of larger scope. This type, which combines contrasts in word choice and in appropriate acting technique with those of sound, results from the dramatist's alternation between one style and another. Much of the drama in any Greek tragedy, for example, consists of the distinction between the way the chorus speaks and the way the protagonist speaks. In Shakespeare and Racine, this contrast stems from the differences in style that distinguish the hero from his confidant.[3] The most familiar version of the contrast between one style and another, and the one that lends itself most readily to analysis, is the alternation between verse and prose. T. S. Eliot cautions modern dramatists against this alternation, because, he says, the shift from one plane of reality to another jolts the audience into a distracting awareness of the medium. In discussing his own *Murder in the Cathedral,* however, Eliot points out that the "platform prose" of the knights, so different from the verse in which most of the play is cast, makes a legitimate contribution: it is designed "to shock the audience out of their complacency." [4] Eliot's "jolt" works thematically. The verse, though allowing more precision of meaning than prose, tends to distance the twelfth-century action, so that the modern spectator, accustomed in his visits to the theater to speech resembling his own, can comprehend and evaluate Becket's experience while ignoring its pertinence to himself and his own time. The sudden shift to prose in the knights' speeches not

[3] See Maynard Mack, "The Jacobean Shakespeare: Some Observations on the Construction of the Tragedies," in *Jacobean Theatre,* ed. John Russell Brown and Bernard Harris, Stratford-upon-Avon Studies, I (London: Edward Arnold, 1960).

[4] *Poetry and Drama,* pp. 13, 30.

only makes the historical event inescapably relevant; it also erases the apparent gap between then (Becket's era) and now (the realistic contemporary idiom of the knights' prose), and this erasure helps dramatize the concept of eternal recurrence also established by the equation of Becket with pagan nature deities and with Samson, St. Stephen, and—especially—Christ. Becket's martyrdom, the knights' prose affirms, is relevant now as then; it is the enactment in time of an event perpetually recurring in eternity which has been enacted before his era and must still be re-enacted today.

In Elizabethan drama the shift from one medium of expression to another is fairly constant and, if only in a general way, usually thematic.[5] Renaissance notions of decorum dictated that particular types of content—principally comic business, low-life situations, and madness—be presented in prose. Therefore the shift from verse to prose easily represents a deviation of some sort from an ideal and heroic norm, and the juxtaposition of the two mediums can be made to yield valuable effects of contrast. The most successful exploitation of this device is undoubtedly *1 Henry IV*, in which prose, used according to convention, helps fashion a unique world. The verse in this play is the property of the heroic domain inhabited by Henry IV, his court, and the rebels; the world of Falstaff, which provides the opposition, is a world of prose: low life, comedy, and nonheroic realism all combine to make the use of prose both a foregone conclusion and a significant expression of basic characteristics. But Shakespeare is not content with simple opposition alone; he employs the shift from one medium to another dramatically to stress Prince Hal's relation to the two worlds and the final relation of the two worlds to each other.

The first scene defines the heroic domain and its activity, while King Henry laments his son's willful exclusion from it. At

[5] See Milton Crane, *Shakespeare's Prose* (Chicago: University of Chicago Press, 1951).

once, in the second scene, the spectators meet Hal in Falstaff's milieu, and what is more, they hear him speaking Falstaff's idiom. But at the end of this scene, Hal informs them that his involvement with Falstaff is both incomplete and temporary; because he speaks his soliloquy in verse, the medium of the heroic world, his claim convinces. Hal also employs verse in a prose context when he frustrates Falstaff's Gadshill robbery (II.ii.100–106) and when he protects Falstaff from the sheriff (II.iv.488–506). The latter occasion well exemplifies his vacillation between the two worlds, for in action he defends Falstaff, but in speech he associates himself with a minor representative of the law and order that are the principal concern of the heroic domain. Already, however, Hal's vacillation, never emphasized as internal struggle, has just about ended. At his next appearance he joins forces with his father (III.ii), and the lengthy speeches in verse mark his full entry into his father's world. From this point on, Hal's use of prose considerably lessens. In Act III, scene iii, he dallies briefly with Falstaff but soon reintroduces verse and the theme of war. Act IV, scene ii, provides a brief prose exchange in which Hal meets Falstaff on the way to battle and ridicules the soldiers he has mustered. And this is Hal's last use of prose. By the beginning of Act V he has so fully committed himself to the heroic world that his verse, now customary, even assimilates his father's characteristic rhythm and rhetoric (V.i.3–6). His only meeting with Falstaff on the battlefield (V.iii.39–52) presents an utter contrast in views which Shakespeare heightens by giving Hal verse and Falstaff prose. Appropriately, even Hal's final eulogy to the supposedly dead Falstaff also takes the form of verse; the farewell is doubly final.

As Hal slowly rejects one domain in favor of the other, the one he chooses becomes the play's dominant world. This change also Shakespeare represents in part through the shift from verse to prose and back. In the early acts, scenes in verse and scenes in prose alternate with reasonable regularity. The first three acts contain a total of ten scenes, five in each medium. Act IV, by contrast, contains one brief scene in prose (76 lines) and three in verse (a total of 290 lines). Act V has no prose scenes whatever: Falstaff's speeches are intrusions, as foreign to the dominant mode as were Hal's verse lines in the earlier part of the play. Falstaff survives, but he survives in an alien world where verse and the values it represents have virtually ousted prose and its characteristic commitments. The heroic world has conquered, and Falstaff's is quite clearly doomed.

The distribution of prose and verse in *Hamlet* obviously lacks such a clear-cut thematic function; nevertheless, certain implications do emerge. In *Hamlet* the prose originates with the hero; it enters the play for the first time in Act II, scene ii, when Hamlet begins to bait Polonius, and until late in the fourth act no one speaks in prose unless Hamlet is present. Here the contrast does not embody a conflict between opposing worlds that exert their separate influences on the hero; rather, the alternation tends to represent the hero's own internal conflict, for his is the prose that is distinguished from his own impassioned verse. Throughout most of the play the prose stems from Hamlet's feigned or real madness (II.ii, III.i, III.ii, IV.ii, and IV.iii), or from the clearly genuine madness of Ophelia (IV.v); as a result, prose tends in itself to suggest effectively the presence and persistence of madness as one element of Denmark's rottenness. But even during these scenes prose begins to acquire a second connotation. When Hamlet chats with Rosencrantz, Guildenstern, and the players (II.ii), and when he delivers his advice on acting (III.i), prose associates not with madness but with informality, with a kind of everyday sane reasonableness. This mood represents an alternative possibility that is never fully realized until the final act, when two long scenes, one with the clowns (V.i), the other with Osric (V.ii), make it the primary content of prose. These comic scenes dissolve the recurring association of prose and madness and set in its place an impression of normality, sanity, and re-

laxed tension. Hamlet himself culminates this mood with his acceptance—in prose—that "there is a special providence in the fall
of a sparrow" (ll. 212–213).

Words

The conclusion of Act II of *Rosmersholm* beautifully demonstrates some of the many ways in which a dramatist can derive
effects from the relationship between a word's established significations and the context in which it occurs. Rosmer has just discovered, through information furnished by Kroll and Mortensgaard, that Beata had known about his loss of faith and about the
intellectual intimacy that had sprung up between him and Rebecca. He realizes that Beata's knowledge may have caused her
suicide, and the realization awakens feelings of guilt that threaten
to destroy his developing peace of mind and thus thwart his
plans to ennoble men by freeing their wills. Rebecca perceives
this threat and fights it by urging Rosmer to set up in opposition
to his doubts and suspicions a new positive relationship with the
world. His response endows her vague suggestion with concrete
form; he sees that the necessary relationship already potentially
exists in his friendship with Rebecca, and in order to actualize it,
he asks her to marry him. To his complete consternation, Rebecca, after a brief moment of joy, flatly refuses, even threatening to leave Rosmersholm or follow Beata should he ever ask her
again. The moment is typical of the excitement of an Ibsen curtain scene. The spectators are as shocked as Rosmer, for they
have witnessed throughout the first two acts Rebecca's obvious
personal interest in him. Ibsen has hinted at their intimacy in various ways, especially through Kroll, who has been wise enough
to notice it and has inferred the worst. This scene is the first moment in the play when the Rosmer-Rebecca relationship comes
into direct focus. The spectators are rightly shocked by Rebecca's reply because they would expect Rosmer's proposal to offer

her an opportunity to express openly the great love she undoubtedly feels for him. The situation, with its surprise, is extremely tense. But even greater tension arises from the language that embodies this situation.

When Rosmer describes their potential relationship as "a new, a living reality" (*en ny, en levende virkelighed*—II, p. 172), his words define that relationship as much more than a mere intimacy between man and woman. Both *ny* and *levende* have been repeated often before this speech, and in the process they have acquired particular associations. The flowers, which Rebecca has supplied, which Rosmer delights in, and which would have bewildered Beata, are *levende* (I, p. 123). Kroll explains his absence from Rosmersholm by saying he would have been a living (*levende*) reminder of the dead Beata (p. 128). In the scene under discussion Rosmer perceives that his feeling of guilt seems to restore Beata to some ghastly form of life (*uhyggelig levende* —II, p. 167). Rebecca then reminds him of his plans, which were to involve his embracing "living life—in the living life of today" (*levende liv,—i dagens levende liv*—p. 169). When, a few lines later, she repeats the phrase *levende liv*, she employs it as an antithesis to the white horses with their implications of imminent death (p. 170). Rosmer again places the word *levende* in opposition to Beata when he insists he shall not let his course in life be prescribed for him "either by the living or by—anyone else" (*hverken af levende eller af—nogen anden*—p. 171). Repetitions of *ny* give it similar associations with healthy, active vitality as well as additional connotations that spell out more concretely some of the implicit aspects of the full meaning of *levende*. Rosmer calls his emancipation "a new summer" and "a new youthful outlook" (*en ny sommer . . . et nyt ungdomssyn*—I, p. 142), and Kroll later refers to it as a "new way of thinking" (*nye retning*—II, p. 152). Mortensgaard is anxious to print the "momentous news" (*vigtig nyhed*) that Rosmer now supports the true cause (p. 161; compare his *store nyheden* of p. 166). Rosmer and

Rebecca had always spoken together of the "new things" (*nye ting*—p. 168), the advanced political and social ideas of the day, and Rosmer's intentions to ennoble mankind are "new life plans" (*nye livsplaner*—p. 169). Thus, when Ibsen has Rosmer speak of the potential relationship as a *ny, levende* reality, he endows it with the qualities both words have acquired through repetition. The marriage of Rebecca and Rosmer would be a thing of nature, like the flowers and the summer; it would uphold the cause of life in the conflict between life and the death represented by Beata and the white horse; it would embody all the ideals of freedom and ennoblement that the advanced political and social beliefs encompass. This potential marriage, Ibsen suggests, both epitomizes and completes that spirit of the new which wars with the past, with unnatural restriction, with superstition, and with death. This marriage, if brought to fulfillment, would mark the victory of the new.

But there are also other significant words in the scene which invite the spectators to see the Rosmer-Rebecca relationship in a quite different light. Instead of merely proposing marriage, Rosmer asks Rebecca to become his second wife, and thus the form of his request contains a reminder of Beata, whose death, as the spectators have come to realize, has somehow resulted from the relationship that now seeks to replace her forever. Other verbal details vastly increase the suspicion and doubt that this effect arouses. Rebecca speaks of their past relationship as a series of talks "in the twilight" (*i mørkningen*—p. 169), and her words take on ironic significance because their context includes the "gloom" (*mørke*—p. 158) that the Rosmer family has caused throughout many generations, the "evening during twilight" (*en kveld i mørkningen*—p. 165) when Mortensgaard received Beata's letter hinting at sinful doings at Rosmersholm, and the "darkness" (*i mørket*—p. 170) through which the white horses rush.

Even more damning is the effect of the word Ibsen uses to denote Rosmer and Rebecca's relationship: *forhold*. Similar in meaning to the English "intercourse," it is a term with a wide range of potential applications, not the least of which is its use to denote a sexual affair. The word *forhold* is often spoken during the first two acts, and in the process it picks up a variety of connotations. Kroll introduces it in a reference to Mortensgaard's "immoral [sexual] behavior" (*usædeligt forhold*—I, p. 132), and though Rebecca speaks of Rosmer's past association with Kroll as a "good relationship" (*godt forhold*—II, p. 149), later uses of the word consistently evoke negative implications similar to those that Kroll assigns to it. Its first application to the friendship between Rosmer and Rebecca occurs in a context in which Kroll questions the morality of Rosmer's present way of life (p. 156). A few minutes later Kroll adds further dubious associations to the word when he tells Rosmer, "I believe you no longer. Not on any point. In no respect [*forhold*] shall I believe you from now on" (p. 159). When it next appears, the term refers to Rosmer's past relationship with the church (p. 161), but Rosmer has already expressed regret about that, and immediately afterward Mortensgaard undercuts whatever positive associations the word might here acquire by using it in a sense that connotes shady, unethical scheming: he knows enough to suppress the news of Rosmer's separation from the church because he is "up on all the angles" (*inde i alle forholdene*). The next repetition, from Beata's letter to Mortensgaard, mentions the possibility of "sinful [sexual] behavior" (*syndigt forhold*) at Rosmersholm (p. 165). While Rosmer suggests marriage to Rebecca, Ibsen repeats the word six times in rapid succession (p. 171), with each occasion denoting either the new relationship with the world which she advises or the particular relationship between the two which Rosmer sees as fulfilling her meaning. The heavy emphasis indicates the great importance of their relationship, but at the same time the repetitions also tend to play on the word in such a way as to call up the whole meaning that Ibsen has built throughout the two acts, a meaning consisting almost entirely of negative associations that make ironic the hope that this relationship could possibly help Rosmer in any way.

Other examples of verbal irony also imply something highly questionable in the alliance. When Rebecca insists she can never marry him, Rosmer tries to convince her that their marriage would be quite natural: "Is there not already a *stænk af kærlighed* in our relationship?" (p. 172). The untranslated phrase presents considerable difficulty, and any attempt to render it adequately in English must meet with frustration. Rosmer's meaning is easy enough: he means "touch of love"; but in the original his words convey implications of which he is unaware. *Stænk* does mean "touch"; but it also means "stain." *Kærlighed* is but one possibility for denoting "love"—Rosmer has used *elske* in the preceding sentence—and therefore the chosen word echoes its earlier uses. The word has appeared twice before in the play, both times in this act and both times in emphatic contexts. Kroll introduces it when he implies that Rebecca and Rosmer, who indulge in free thought, must very likely yield with equal ease to "free love" (*fri kærlighed*—p. 157). The association with immorality is reinforced by an association with disgust when the word's second use conveys a sense of morbid, unbridled passion. Rosmer has already expressed his great distaste for Beata's "ungovernable, wild passionateness" (p. 153) during her last months; he now describes her behavior as "sick love" (*syge kærlighed*—p. 168). It is but a few minutes later that he speaks to Rebecca of the *stænk af kærlighed* in their friendship. He wants to say "touch of love," but because of ambiguity and preceding associations he also says "stain of morbid, immoral passion." In his next speech he once more refers to their relationship as a *forhold,* and here all the various implications coalesce. By his strategic manipulation of words Ibsen suggests that Beata's hint to Mortensgaard has validity. In actuality the Rebecca-Rosmer relationship is unimpeachable; symbolically, however, there is indeed *syndigt forhold* at Rosmersholm.

The scene contains one more significant example of word-play, one that sums up the double attitude Ibsen has established toward the potential marriage. Pressed by Rosmer's demand to know why she "cannot" marry him, Rebecca replies, "Dear friend—both for your sake and for mine—do not ask why" (p. 173). Her words complete the pattern asserting the symbolic evil in their relationship by suggesting that it might somehow destroy them. Moreover, her response also reveals that something lies hidden which makes their marriage an impossibility, and through verbal ambiguity Ibsen provides a suggestion of what this hidden factor might be. Rebecca's word for "sake" is *skyld*, which also means "guilt"; therefore she also says: We can pursue this question no further, "both because of your own guilt and because of mine." Rosmer looked on this marriage as a means of combating the "guilt" he has begun to feel (p. 167), as a means of once more achieving "guiltlessness" (*skyldfrihed*—p. 170). Rebecca first broached the necessity of his establishing a new relationship because it would remove from his mind the feeling she describes as mere "wild imaginings" (p. 170). Yet, ironically, further exploration of the possibility leads ultimately to the suggestion that the new relationship can never come into existence because their mutual guilt prohibits it. Rosmer sought security in an ideal union; he finds instead confusion and bewilderment that confirm his self-doubt and raise, for the first time, questions in his mind about Rebecca. But the implications of her words also restore the positive connotation of their potential marriage: if their guilt bars them from it, the marriage must surely be something ideal. The result is an impasse. As potentiality, their marriage promises salvation and victory. But for the promise to be fulfilled, the marriage must become an actuality, and this process would saturate it with all the guilt, sin, disgust, and evil symbolically implicit in their present relationship.

These examples of wordplay in *Rosmersholm* illustrate two basic devices commonly employed by the dramatist to establish meanings beyond the immediate action, meanings of which the speaker is unaware. *Stænk* and *skyld* both exemplify ambiguity, a device so prevalent in the literary use of language as to require little explanation here. In drama, which necessarily lacks the conscious ambiguity of a dominant narrative voice seeking utmost precision of expression, this device ordinarily takes only a single form, one in which a character selects a word having two or more senses, intends but one of these, and is betrayed by the context or sometimes simply by the audience's knowledge into saying more than he intends or even realizes.

As should be obvious, this kind of wordplay is especially prevalent in verse drama; a further example of it, Shakespeare's manipulation of "common" in the second scene of *Hamlet*, will illustrate a more complex use of the device than that in *Rosmersholm*. In this scene Gertrude, attempting to inspire in her son some of the good sense displayed by the rest of the court, points out why he should stop mourning his father's death: "Thou know'st 'tis common—all that lives must die" (I.ii.72). The tone of Hamlet's reply—"Ay, madam, it is common"—twists her word's meaning from "usual, and therefore to be unquestionably accepted" to "cheap and low." Hamlet then develops his redefinition as he insists that he "knows not seems": his woe is genuine; to ignore it because its cause is "common" in Gertrude's sense would make him "common" in his own. Hamlet's reply helps to fill out his characterization by demonstrating his awareness of multiple possibilities and of the slipperiness of words; unlike the others, he is incapable of reducing the complexity of experience to a series of conventional formulas. The by now well-established ambiguity makes its greatest contribution, however, when Claudius follows with a lengthy speech, expanding on his wife's theme and twice using her word in her sense alone:

> For what we know must be, and is as *common*
> As any the most vulgar thing to sense,
> Why should we in our peevish opposition

Take it to heart? Fie! 'tis a fault to heaven,
A fault against the dead, a fault to nature,
To reason most absurd; whose *common* theme
Is death of fathers   [ll. 98–104].[6]

Once again characterization is furthered, for Claudius exposes some deficiency in himself or in his relation to Hamlet by his failure to acknowledge and answer Hamlet's pun. But far more important is the similarity between Claudius' speech and the examples from Ibsen. By having the spectators listen to Claudius' speech with Hamlet's sense of "common" in mind, Shakespeare suggests that there is something cheap and low in the mindless acceptance of "what we know must be"—the implication is reinforced by "vulgar" in line 99—and that there is something equally cheap and low in the nature of existence itself if it contains no more than Claudius' "common theme." This ambiguity, stressed at the first appearance of Hamlet, effectively establishes a perspective that not only justifies but even demands his subsequent prolonged refusal to accept "what must be."

In this example from *Hamlet* repetition is of secondary importance; it merely ensures that both significations of the ambiguous word will become effectual. A different kind of wordplay, observable in Ibsen's handling of *ny, levende, forhold, mørke,* and *kærlighed,* depends entirely on the repetition of a single word during a large stretch of action or throughout a whole play. Sometimes the pattern of repetition involves a shift from one word to another—as in *Titus Andronicus,* where the sequence "honour" and related words (Act I), "blood" (Act II), "tears" and other words emphasizing grief (III.i), and "revenge" and its synonyms (III.i.271 ff.) records in the play's rhetorical structure the same action that is going forward in the plot and underlines the basic significance of each stage. Sometimes, in contrast, the same word is used throughout, while its denotation constantly

[6] My italics.

166

changes—as in O'Neill's *Desire under the Elms*, where the shifting application of the word "purty" (the characters' only verbal means of assigning value) traces the growth of Eben and Abbie as they progress from a search for value in material things to the discovery of it in a spiritual relationship from which all vestiges of the material have been purged. But perhaps the most typical use of verbal repetition is that which is evident in the examples from *Rosmersholm*, that in which the dramatist builds up a system of associations, enlarging and focusing the meaning of the word, until it soon becomes an extremely rich means of characterizing, briefly and incisively, any event or object brought into the accumulating system.

The *Oresteia* contains an especially noteworthy example of this use of verbal repetition. Early in the *Agamemnon*, in the prayer to Zeus, the chorus states directly a concept that the whole trilogy ultimately enacts, that of "wisdom through suffering" (*pathei mathos*—l. 177). Repetition at the end of this ode (*pathousin mathein*—l. 250) emphasizes both the concept and the words that embody it. From this point to the end of the trilogy Aeschylus skillfully weaves into his poetic text numerous repetitions of these two words, or variants of them, separately and in combination. The effect for the spectators is manifold. The repetitions, spoken by more than one character, reinforce the validity of the concept first expressed by the omniscient voice of the chorus. At the same time, the repetitions operate like a musical theme to link the original concept to every significant event or motif incorporated within the action: the destruction of Troy (*Agamemnon*, ll. 533, 545, 567, 584), the sinking of the Greek fleet (l. 669), Clytaemestra's professed longing for her husband (ll. 859, 893), Cassandra's desperate plight (ll. 1137, 1176), the family curse (ll. 1163, 1171), Agamemnon's murder (ll. 1564, 1658, 1661; *Libation Bearers*, ll. 7, 17, 21), Electra's discovery of her brother (*L.B*, ll. 165, 171, 173, 175), Orestes' decision (ll. 313–314), the killing of Clytaemestra (ll. 516, 547,

554, 930), Orestes' flight (l. 1009; *Eumenides*, l. 86), and his trial (*Eum.*, ll. 301, 420 ff.). This linking helps convey the idea of cause and effect, of the continuous and unending chain reaction that runs from Troy to Athens and from Atreus to Orestes. The linking also insists upon the relevance of the concept to each of these events: all are identified as examples of suffering from which wisdom will emerge. As the repetitions accumulate another result occurs: each new situation or event enlarges the meaning of the original words until they can accommodate all the versions of suffering, until they amazingly complicate and particularize the meaning that wisdom must ultimately assume. Finally, the device as Aeschylus employs it in the *Oresteia* also allows him to clarify the relationship of certain events or characters to the whole dramatized experience. This effect is best seen in relation to the Furies. They pursue Orestes; he and Apollo show an antagonism toward them that tends to place them outside the basic movement; they are monstrous and loathsome. But Aeschylus, by emphasizing through his language their participation in the suffering that encompasses all (*Eum.*, ll. 144, 497, 790, 837), shows that they are by no means to be regarded as the opposition that stands in the way of emerging wisdom. The Furies too must be included within the universal harmony achieved by Athene because they too have shared the universal misery.

Allusions

The words of a text, alone or in combination, also fulfill numerous additional functions that can best be dealt with in separate categories, the first of which consists of allusions to pre-existing contexts. Such allusions are constant in drama, as in all literature, and they stem from a wide variety of sources. In *Hamlet*, for example, historical personages mingle with classical deities, biblical figures, and popular conceptions like John-a-dreams and the hobbyhorse, while familiar ballads and English theatrical history, from the raging Herod to the War of the Theaters, are frequently alluded to as well.

Purely visual allusion is a fairly common device. Shaw, as Martin Meisel has shown, liked to design stage pictures that would evoke, for the purpose of contrast, conventional scenes in plays already well known to his audience: thus Dick Dudgeon of *The Devil's Disciple* stands alongside his gallows in a visual parody of the defiant stance with which numerous nineteenth-century stage heroes demonstrated their scorn of the guillotine.[7] And there are, of course, the abundant characters of American drama who find occasion (justifiably or not) to spread wide their arms in visual imitation of the Crucifixion.

When the allusion is made verbally, as is more common, a number of alternatives are available. *Hamlet* specializes in direct references that name the analogous figure or situation, but often a mere detail or two will establish an indirect though clear reference, as in the case of Hamlet's "special providence in the fall of a sparrow," which should remind its hearers of Matthew 10:29. Quotation and paraphrase provide additional tools for verbal allusion, especially—but not always—when the relevant parallels come from the Bible and familiar works of literature. Sometimes even parody achieves the desired result, as Sean O'Casey shows in the third act of *Juno and the Paycock*, which contains a bitter little poem utilizing the rhythm, diction, and imagery of Tennyson's "Locksley Hall" while rejecting its surface optimism.

Whatever the means of producing the allusion, it tends to have a twofold effect. Every allusion fulfills a particular function in its immediate context, usually by evoking a parallel of some kind, though as the examples from Shaw and O'Casey indicate, striking contrast is also normal. In addition—and more important—the separate allusions often combine to form implications that suggest specific qualities of the play's world. In *Hamlet*, for exam-

[7] *Shaw and the Nineteenth-Century Theater*, p. 199; cf. the illustration Meisel includes between p. 212 and p. 213.

THE IDIOM OF DRAMA

ple, although the eclectic texture of the allusions points to the absence of any emphatic general impression like that of eternal recurrence in *Murder in the Cathedral* or of legend in *Titus Andronicus*, a number of well-defined strands, each composed of a few related allusions, individually enrich the basic significance of the play.

One of these strands consists of a series of references to legendary and historical figures noted for decisive action; Shakespeare uses it to emphasize an important concern of the play and to suggest some appropriate conclusions. Julius Caesar is mentioned three times, and the effect is much the same in every case. Horatio, in speaking of Rome "a little ere the mightiest Julius fell" (I.i.114), juxtaposes Caesar's power with his destruction in such a way that the one acquires the qualities of the other. The implication anticipates the force of the second allusion, Polonius' "I did enact Julius Caesar; I was kill'd i' th' Capitol; Brutus kill'd me" (III.ii.100–101). Here the might that Caesar's name should connote is entirely obliterated by the focus upon his death, by the substitution of a world of theatrical make-believe for the world of actuality, and especially by the association of the role with the actor who performed it. In the final reference, during the graveyard scene, Caesar is not only dead but "turn'd to clay" (V.i.207); his onetime greatness, which "kept the world in awe," seems ludicrously irrelevant in the face of his present task of stopping "a hole to keep the wind away." Shakespeare makes the implication about Caesar doubly sure by coupling him at this point with Alexander the Great (ll. 192–206). The allusion ignores Alexander's accomplishments as if they had never been; all that matters is the absurd cycle that brought him to his current status: "Alexander died, Alexander was buried, Alexander returneth to dust; the dust is earth; of earth we make loam; and why of that loam whereto he was converted might they not stop a beer-barrel?"

These references to Caesar and Alexander serve in part to enhance Hamlet by placing him alongside standard examples of great men who suffered tragic falls. However, this function scarcely accounts for the sardonic tone that most of the references convey. That belongs more to the strand's major contribution, which other allusions make clear by suggesting additional, though equally negative, evaluations of decisive action. The long description of Pyrrhus in Act II, scene ii, emphasizes a definite accomplishment, but since Shakespeare sees Pyrrhus as "horridly trick'd / With blood of fathers, mothers, daughters, sons" (ll. 451–452) and making "malicious sport" (l. 507) "on the milky head / Of reverend Priam" (ll. 472–473), the effect is one of horror. Hamlet's allusion to Nero adds a condensed version of this impression by linking positive action with "unnatural" behavior (III.ii.383–385). Hercules first appears as a contrast to Hamlet, a means of emphasizing Hamlet's incapacity for achievement (I.ii.152–153), but the second allusion to the demigod focuses upon his most arduous task—his acting as a substitute for Atlas (II.ii.357)—and the third suggests his utter ineffectuality:

> Let Hercules himself do what he may,
> The cat will mew, and dog will have his day
>
> [V.i.285–286].

Since the play concerns itself with a man who must act but fails to do so, it is surely significant that the context includes a pattern of allusions that question the whole idea of action by stressing its hideousness, its basic ineffectuality, and its ultimate pointlessness.

Another strand of allusions in *Hamlet* links several references that suggest a Christian dimension. This group begins in the first scene when Marcellus speaks of "that season . . . / Wherein our Saviour's birth is celebrated" (I.i.158–159); it includes references to St. Patrick (I.v.136), to the baker's daughter who was punished for slighting Christ (IV.v.41), to the pelican, traditionally symbolic of Christ (IV.v.143), to Adam (V.i.31), and to Cain (V.i.77); and it concludes with Hamlet's echo of St. Matthew. These allusions add solidity to the many other aspects of the play that implicitly assume a Christian universe. J. A. Bryant, Jr., would argue that they contribute even more; in Bryant's view, Shakespeare not only writes from a fundamentally Christian standpoint but even utilizes the medieval principle of typological exegesis which interpreted events and characters of the Old Testament as sacramental prefigurements of Christ. From this point of view Claudius' allusions to the killing of Abel (I.ii.105 and III.iii.37–38) urge much more than a purely emotional response. According to medieval exegesis, Abel prefigured Christ, while Cain prefigured the Jews who were Christ's adversaries; since Claudius identifies himself with Cain, Hamlet becomes Christ, Abel's avenger. With this identification established, Shakespeare can then concentrate on his primary theme, the tragic discrepancy between divine perfection and human limitation, for Hamlet is "the human, fallible, blind, tragic counterpart of the Christ who was knowingly both the scourge of evil and the sacrificial victim who willingly took that evil upon himself." [8] Bryant's argument relies too heavily on a mere pair of allusions and an untested assumption about Shakespeare's processes of composition; nevertheless, he does point out a function of allusions valid for medieval drama and for the plays of T. S. Eliot, which consciously employ the principle of typology.[9] Moreover, even if Bryant's reasoning must be rejected, his argument retains the virtue of suggesting a concrete basis for the impression—conveyed by the entire sequence of episodes in the final scene—that Hamlet in cleansing Denmark of evil becomes a sort of sacrificial victim. At least part of this impression does stem from an allusion, for Hamlet gives the

[8] *Hippolyta's View: Some Christian Aspects of Shakespeare's Plays* (Lexington: University of Kentucky Press, 1961), pp. 10–17, 113–114, 118–121.

[9] Cf. William V. Spanos, "*Murder in the Cathedral:* The *Figura* as Mimetic Principle," *Drama Survey*, III (1963), 206–223.

whole Christian pattern pertinence to himself when, in the final reference of the strand, he makes Christ's words his own.

Modern prose drama finds allusions much less congenial to its technique. *Rosmersholm* has few, and most of these appear in the fantastic idiom of Ulrik Brendel. Yet because they occur in an otherwise bleak context they stand out with peculiar force. During his visit in the first act Brendel announces his plan "to put on a new man" (*nu vil jeg iføre mig et nyt menneske*—p. 138), which echoes, with variations, St. Paul (*iføre det nye menneske* —Eph. 4:24). Except that it blends with the other excesses of speech which characterize their user, the allusion seems relatively meaningless. Upon his return in Act IV, however, new allusions recall the first and suggest that it may have considerable significance after all. Here Brendel delivers a valedictory that sums up the wisdom he has acquired by venturing, like the Lady of Shalott, from the world of dream into the world of reality. One piece of advice is especially striking: "Don't build your castle on shifting sand" (p. 207). This speech, despite Brendel's characteristic alteration, draws on Christ's parable of the two houses, the one built on rock which withstood all storms, the other built on sand and thus a prey to the least wind (Matt. 7:26). Brendel borrows Christ's words once more at his exit when he says, "Peace be with you" (*Fred være med jer*—p. 207), a close echo of John 20:21 (*fred være med eder*). Like the allusion in the first act, these two speeches reflect Brendel's whimsical turn of mind; at the same time, however, they work with their context to project an evocative implication. It is just before his exit that Brendel insists upon the necessity for extreme physical sacrifice if Rosmer hopes to achieve victory in his great quest. Brendel's specifications, which involve self-mutilation by Rebecca, are ignored, but it is the spirit of his advice that Rosmer and Rebecca later act on when they leap from the bridge, even though they do not fully realize it. By having Brendel speak like Christ while laying the groundwork for the suicide, Ibsen throws light on its essential meaning. The device suggests that Rosmer and Rebecca, in taking their own lives, enact a purging self-sacrifice that wins them salvation. They are the ones who fulfill the intention Brendel voiced in the first act: by committing suicide, they put off the old worldly and sinful Adam and put on in its place the spiritual nature of St. Paul's new man. This is not to suggest, however, that Ibsen implies a specifically Christian ethic or Christian salvation: the means adopted make that rather obvious. He uses Christ and the Christian doctrine of salvation only as convenient metaphors to express the content of his own personal vision.

Although *Rosmersholm* shows the possibility of employing the evocative power of allusions in realistic drama, it shows as well a different use of them than that of Shakespearean tragedy, in which the allusion, directly established, sets up an independent analogy designed to contribute its own inherent implications to the character, event, or world that it parallels. All three of Brendel's verbal echoes have been altered just enough to make them appropriate to his character and compatible with the everyday surface of the play. Instead of a single function, moreover, they have two: primarily, they provide further evidence of Brendel's habit of filling his speech with excessively elegant phrases; secondarily—and unobtrusively—they comment on the action. Furthermore, Ibsen makes no attempt to suggest that this man, who is utterly crushed, going "downhill" (IV, p. 205), and heading into the "dark night" (p. 207), is himself Christ or even Christlike. In contrast to Shakespeare, Ibsen associates his character with Christ only for a single moment and only with reference to the character's role as the one who suggests a solution of great importance to the central characters. Hamlet is like Christ because the comparison illuminates his function as a cleansing scapegoat; Ulrik Brendel is like Christ only because this association allows Ibsen to alert his spectators to a special way of looking at an event in which Brendel himself takes no part.

Image Patterns

The most familiar of the verbal devices that enable the dramatist to record a clearly defined attitude within the dialogue of separate and limited characters is also one of the most impressive. Verse drama, especially, gains much of its control over an audience's understanding by the clusters or patterns of images with which the dramatist charges his text. Thanks to the pioneer efforts of Caroline Spurgeon and the increasing sophistication of her followers, the principles involved are abundantly clear. Like any other poet, the dramatist constantly calls on the image to clarify and evaluate a feeling, idea, situation, person, or object. Whether the image is a figure of speech, such as a metaphor or simile, or merely a vivid concrete detail makes little difference. What does matter is the effect that takes place when other images follow the first. When the individual vehicles of comparison or concreteness share a similarity of subject matter, they link their different contexts by what Reuben Brower calls a "network of connections." They weave a "key design" of many cognate details, all of which reflect or contribute to the formation of a "key metaphor," that is, "the basic analogy of which they are variants." [10] A play may have one such key design, or it may have several. Each succeeds in erecting an unbroken pattern of thought or feeling completely independent of the speakers who introduce the separate variants.

Some of these patterns, especially vivid or strikingly unusual, will impress themselves on the spectator's conscious awareness, and he can then work up a mental association between the experience presented and the implications of the key design. More often than not, however, the key design affects the spectator on a level beneath the threshold of consciousness so that, in the final

[10] *The Fields of Light* (New York: Oxford University Press, 1951), pp. 7, 91.

analysis, he can say how he has felt about what he has seen, but he may not be able to say why he has felt that way. Whether consciously perceived or not, these patterns make enormous contributions. If recurring imagery accomplishes nothing else toward the shaping of meaning, it at least "knits the play together," [11] and in doing so, it suggests a solid core of unity behind the apparent chaos of ordinary experience. But recurring imagery also has a more specific contribution, for the world examined within the play ultimately takes on the qualities inherent in the key metaphors that form one of its essential elements.

In the *Oresteia* a great many images denote physical exhaustion, pain, disease, wounds, mutilation, and poisoning. They often occur in conjunction with images of medicine, antidote, cure, and healing. The related pairs establish a powerful design —of which the key metaphors are sickness and health—that encompasses almost every detail of the action.

When, in the first line of the *Agamemnon*, the Watchman expresses "weariness," he uses a word (*ponōn*) that evokes not only drudgery and grief but also bodily exertion, pain, and sickness. The impression extends from the human being to his universe through the reference to the stars "upon their wane" (l. 7), for *phthinōsin* ("wane") carries with it a strong sense of physical decay. Aeschylus then makes this potential metaphor explicit. To keep awake, the Watchman has prescribed for himself the "medicine" (*akos*) of song (l. 17). It has worked; but for the more persistent and far-reaching sickness there is as yet no cure. The Watchman still awaits "redemption" (*apallagē*) from the "distress" (*ponōn* again) that unites him with the stars.

The illness intuited by the Watchman permeates Argos and the contiguous world. The chorus, aged and decrepit, propping its baby strength with artificial supports (ll. 72–75), epitomizes

[11] Una Ellis-Fermor, *The Frontiers of Drama* (London: Methuen, 1945), p. 83.

the physical weakness. It sees that Clytaemestra's blazing altars are "drugged [*pharmassomenē*] by the simple soft / persuasion of sacred unguents" (ll. 94–95), and it entreats her, though ironically, to "be healer [*paiōn*] to this perplexity" (l. 99), for "sorrow" (*lupēs*), which is also *pain*,[12] "eats my heart" (l. 103). The sacrifice of Iphigeneia, the chorus recalls, grew out of a similar illness. The winds that held back the Greek fleet brought "sick idleness" (l. 192) and "crumbled the flower and pride / of Argos" (ll. 197–198). Calchas the seer knew that only one "medicine" (*mēchar*—l. 199) could effect a cure, the killing of Agamemnon's innocent daughter. This did its particular job, but the suppression of the disease in one area served only to expose its presence in another, for the sacrifice, intended as medicine, appealed to "the sickening in men's minds" (l. 222), which, the chorus notes, is itself the primal cause of injury (*protopēmōn*— l. 223).

This imagery of an illness for which local cures are only temporary springs from the lips of all the characters in the *Agamemnon* and applies with remarkable consistency to every major event, whether narrated or presented.[13] Clytaemestra relates it to the fall of Troy (ll. 330, 346). The chorus observes that every "medicine" is vain against "designing Ruin" (ll. 386–387). The Herald felt "sickness" at Troy (l. 542; compare ll. 544, 567, 574); now he must tell of the "wound" (l. 640) inflicted on "the body of the people" by the sinking of the Greek fleet. Agamemnon knows how "envy's wicked poison . . . piles up the pain in one sick with unhappiness" (ll. 834–835), and therefore he realizes that, as king, he must become the state's physician:

[12] In this section italicized translations of the *Oresteia* represent alternatives to Lattimore's version.

[13] The cited images provide only a sampling of those available. Furthermore, though I later take up other image patterns in the *Oresteia*, my survey should by no means be regarded as an attempt to furnish a thorough study of the trilogy's imagery.

we must use medicine,
or burn, or amputate, with kind intention, take
all means at hand that might beat down corruption's pain
[*pēm' . . . nosou, the pain of illness*] [ll. 848–850].

Clytaemestra, again, would have her husband believe that news
of his "wounds" (l. 867) struck like a "fever" (l. 863). But Clytaemestra, Cassandra insists, intends a "stroke of atrocity" (or
pain: achos—l. 1102) "to beat down the beloved beyond hope
of healing" (l. 1103); "rescue [or *bodily strength: alka*] is far
away" (l. 1104). Cassandra's own fate, as both she and the chorus realize, will exemplify the general sickness (ll. 1165–1167,
1172, and *passim*). There is no medicine (*akos*—l. 1169) to relieve the present suffering.

The deathblows wielded against Agamemnon (ll. 1343–1344)
are the most immediately vivid details in the key design, and they
climax its development in this first part of the trilogy. The remaining images of this pattern in the *Agamemnon* attest to the
centrality of the murder, for all of them are inspired by it. The
chorus, stunned by the event, wishes that

without pain
and the slow bed of sickness
death could come to us now, death that forever
carries sleep without ending [ll. 1448–1451].

Clytaemestra, defending her act, warns the chorus not to blame
Helen alone for "the grief [or *pain: algos*] that is past all healing" (l. 1467). She speaks of "the spirit thrice glutted that lives
in this race" (l. 1477), which sees to it "that before / the old
wound dries, it bleeds again" (ll. 1479–1480). When Aegisthus
finally appears, he offers the verbally rebellious chorus "starvation
with its pain" (l. 1621) and advises, "Lash not at the goads for
fear you hit them, and be hurt" (l. 1624). Clytaemestra completes the pattern for this first play when she calls for an end to
the tension between Aegisthus and the Argive Elders: "There is
pain enough already" (l. 1656). Her speech sums up the whole

impression thus far conveyed by the key design, but it also falsely assumes a cure where none has yet appeared. Her act, like the sacrifice of Iphigeneia, has only applied a local and superficial remedy to a more wide-spread disease, of which her act itself is another symptom. The general disease remains and still awaits a really potent medicine.

This image pattern continues with equal emphasis and consistency throughout the remainder of the trilogy. It knits all three parts together in a way that insists on the ubiquity of the sickness that Clytaemestra's malpractice seriously aggravates. When Cassandra laments the absence of a medicine (*akos*) to save Troy from its suffering (*pathein*—ll. 1169–1171), her use of *pathein* articulates an important verbal relationship. For the imagery of sickness provides the spectators with a concrete version of the "suffering" phase of the "wisdom through suffering" formula expressed by the chorus and illustrated by the action. These images therefore enable Aeschylus to make an abstract concept continuously felt as an emotional fact. But the imagery also has a more purely intellectual function, and as Aeschylus completes the pattern in the final play, the intellectual function eventually outweighs the emotional.

In *The Eumenides*, though incidental applications of the pattern still occur, Aeschylus associates most of its images with either Apollo or the Furies. Apollo was a deity of many capacities, but in the *Oresteia* one of these looms larger than all the others. When he is first mentioned in the *Agamemnon*, it is in his role as *Paiana* (l. 146), the healer, physician of the gods. The Herald also refers to him in this capacity:

> Beside Scamandrus you were grim; be satisfied
> and turn to savior now and healer [*paiōnios*] of our hurts,
> my lord Apollo [ll. 511–513].

And so does Cassandra, who insists that Agamemnon cannot escape death because "there is no god of healing [*paiōn*] in this story" (l. 1248). Cassandra's speech is doubly ironic, for it was

Apollo who sent her to Argos to die, and as *The Eumenides* makes clear, Apollo as the god of healing has a most important place "in this story." In *The Eumenides*, Apollo actually appears, and throughout the play Aeschylus stresses his role as healer. Just before his entrance his priestess introduces him as

> Apollo Loxias, who is very strong
> and heals by divination [*iatromantis*]; reads portentous signs,
> and so clears out the houses others hold as well   [ll. 61–63].

The word for "clears out" is *katharsios*, which along with its basic meaning of religious purification also carries medical connotations. Variations of this word recur (ll. 277, 283, 449–450, 474, 578), each of them denoting the moral and medicinal cleansing Apollo has given Orestes. Apollo himself assures the Furies that despite their opposition he will "rescue" Orestes, and the word he chooses—*hrysomai*—also means *cure* (l. 232).

But if Apollo is the healer, it is the Furies who spread the disease. Present but unseen, they join the action at the end of *The Libation Bearers* when Orestes first begins to feel the *pains* (*pēmatōn*—l. 1060) they inflict upon the matricide. In *The Eumenides* they are visible. Apollo's priestess announces their presence by describing the physical weakness that seeing them has brought her: "I have no strength and cannot stand on springing / feet" (ll. 36–37). To her, they are *bdelyktropoi* ("utterly repulsive"—l. 52), which vaguely suggests a sense of physical decay. Aeschylus makes other similar though unemphatic applications of the key design to the Furies, but two passages more than any others stress their basic association with mutilation, pain, sickness, and poison. The first of these occurs as Apollo demands that they leave his sanctuary:

> This house is no right place for such as you to cling
> upon; but where, by judgment given, heads are lopped
> and eyes gouged out, throats cut, and by the spoil of sex

the glory of young boys is defeated, where mutilation
lives, and stoning, and the long moan of tortured men
spiked underneath the spine and stuck on pales   [ll. 185–190].

Later, with more detachment but equal awareness, Athene also
describes the primary nature of the Furies:

if this action so runs that they fail to win,
the venom of their resolution will return
to infect the soil, and sicken all my land to death.
Here is dilemma. Whether I let them stay or drive
them off, it is a hard course and will hurt   [ll. 477–481].

In the opposition between Apollo and the Furies, then, Aeschylus provides a nonverbal, theatrical counterpart of the verbal
imagery. The opposites that make up the key metaphor assume
physical proportions through the actor who plays Apollo and
through the chorus of the Furies. The device confirms preceding
implications that the sickness is cosmic as well as earthly. It also
recapitulates and explains all images that emphasized the supreme
difficulty of finding an adequate medicine, for Apollo, though divine, cannot by himself overcome the Furies or cure the plague
spread by their poison. He has cleansed Orestes, but vestiges of
the disease remain as long as the Furies pursue. Therefore he
sends Orestes to Athene, goddess of wisdom, and this event solidifies, on the level of action rather than words, the relationship between the pattern of sickness-health and the abstract formula of
"wisdom through suffering": images of sickness embody the
"suffering"; the only possible cure consists in the introduction of
"wisdom." From this point to the end of the play Athene, acting
for her father Zeus, administers the cure to man and his universe.
She sets up the court that tries Orestes, and she herself casts the
deciding vote in his favor. Divine wisdom has therefore cured
man by absolving him of guilt.

But even this medicine treats the part instead of the whole: as
long as the Furies remain, sickness continues in the universe.

Thwarted in their efforts to destroy Orestes, they threaten to infect the land:

> I, disinherited, suffering, heavy with anger
> shall let loose on the land
> the vindictive poison
> dripping deadly out of my heart upon the ground;
> this from itself shall breed
> cancer   [ll. 780–785; repeated, ll. 810–815].

Wisdom must once more act, and at last the disease is treated at
its heart. Athene expunges sickness from the universe by converting the Furies to blessed spirits, to Eumenides. That Aeschylus
regards this metamorphosis as a symbolic cure is beyond question. Once changed, the former Furies now pray on behalf of the
land: "Let no barren deadly sickness creep and kill" (l. 942). As
Eumenides they offer medicine instead of poison:

> Let them [the men of our city] render grace for grace.
> Let love be their common will;
> let them hate with single heart.
> Much wrong in the world thereby is healed   [ll. 984–987].

Their Greek for "healed" is *akos*, the same word with which the
Watchman first introduced the imagery of cure at the very beginning of the trilogy.

This image pattern has a kind of logical completeness that permits it to express its own statement about the meaning of action
in the *Oresteia*. As the pattern makes clear, everything and everyone on earth suffers from a symbolic illness that pervades the
entire universe. Man has tried to be his own physician, but he has
failed miserably. The true cure lies not on earth but only in the
heavens, to be dispensed by the cosmic physician, the divine wisdom that Athene personifies. Man cannot cure his radical illness
by the wholesale amputation that Agamemnon, Clytaemestra,
and Orestes practice. He must instead learn from the gods and
substitute for his own vindictiveness such earthly models of di-

vine wisdom as the court Athene has founded for his benefit—
and his cure.

Aeschylus' image pattern of sickness and health illustrates several potential characteristics of the device. One of these is its appeal to both intellectual and emotional responses. Another involves the arrangement given the numerous separate images. In
The Philosophy of Literary Form, Kenneth Burke added to the
study of thematic imagery his principle of "the *qualitative* importance of beginning, middle, and end." Much of the significance
of an image pattern, he suggests, derives from the manner in
which it affects "the situations on which the work opens and
closes, and the events by which the peripety, or reversal is
contrived." [14] In other words, the pattern's emergence at these
crucial moments is the factor that establishes its thematic value.
Aeschylus' pattern begins with the Watchman's opening monologue and comes to a full close at the very end of the trilogy.
The *Oresteia* has several peripeteia, particularly the two murders
and the trial, and each of these events symbolizes some relationship between sickness and cure. But the arrangement has other
values as well, and Aeschylus' pattern duplicates in its way the
growth that Reuben Brower has perceived in the key design of
The Tempest: "But if Shakespeare's total metaphor is in a sense
present everywhere, it is also a design that develops in close relation to the main dramatic movement of the play. . . . A particular metaphor will be varied to fit a new dramatic situation and so
serve to express the situation more fully and to anticipate the
next step in the development of the drama." [15] These qualities of
imagery are purely verbal, however; they might well be found in
any good poem or novel. What makes Aeschylus' imagery distinctly dramatic is his tendency, just perceptible with the *Agamemnon* chorus and inescapable throughout *The Eumenides*, to
translate the verbal imagery into a theatrical dimension. This,

[14] New York: Vintage Books, 1957, pp. 59–60.
[15] *The Fields of Light*, p. 116.

too, is a fundamental characteristic of the image pattern in drama, and Alan Downer has assembled many evocative examples of Shakespeare's supplementation of verbal images both by visual effects, such as the skulls in *Hamlet*, and by "symbolic action," such as the behavior on the battlefield in *1 Henry IV*.[16]

Perhaps the most impressive quality of the *Oresteia* imagery is its rich abundance, for the trilogy also contains several other key designs, each of which exhibits many of the same characteristics while adding its own specific contributions to meaning. Three of these patterns have already been isolated; in the introduction to his translation of the trilogy Richmond Lattimore defines as one of its central motifs "the idea of entanglement," a motif that occurs most frequently "through the symbol-complex of the net"; the other patterns, identified by Robert F. Goheen, link recurring images of "blood on the ground" and of light and its attributes.[17] These patterns are well worth examining, not only because of their importance in establishing the full meaning of the *Oresteia*, but also for what they reveal about the interrelationship of several key designs within a single drama.

The motif of entanglement, which centers on a victim trapped in a net, produces as well images of the curb, the bit, the yoke, and the snare of the huntsman. Associated with the destruction of Troy, the slaying of Iphigeneia, the helplessness of Cassandra, and the murder of Agamemnon, these images help clarify several centers of thematic importance. Agamemnon, yoked "in twofold power" (*zeugos*—l. 44) to Menelaus, and former yokefel-

[16] "The Life of Our Design: The Function of Imagery in the Poetic Drama," *Hudson Review*, II (1949), 242–260; for a fuller study of this sort, cf. Maurice Charney, *Shakespeare's Roman Plays* (Cambridge, Mass.: Harvard University Press, 1961).

[17] Introduction to the *Oresteia*, *The Complete Greek Tragedies*, ed. David Grene and Richmond Lattimore (Chicago: University of Chicago Press, 1959), I, 16; Goheen, "Aspects of Dramatic Symbolism: Three Studies in the *Oresteia*," *American Journal of Philology*, LXXVI (1955), pp. 116–124, 124–125.

low (*zeuchtheis*—l. 842) of Odysseus, soon emerges as the primary victim. Conversely, Clytaemestra appears in this first play as both the instrument and the artificer of entanglement. The chorus introduces her as "our Apian land's singlehearted protectress" (l. 257), but its word for "protectress" (*herkos*) also means *net*, and later Aegisthus so uses it to refer to the robes that trapped Agamemnon (l. 1611). In her vision Cassandra sees a "net of death" that she cannot distinguish from the one that wields it: "Or is the trap the woman there, the murderess?" (ll. 1115–1116). After the murder the chorus weeps for its king, "caught in this spider's web" (l. 1492). Aegisthus shares with Clytaemestra the role of artificer when he threatens the chorus with "chains" (l. 1621) and warns it that "the mutinous man shall feel the yoke / drag at his neck" (ll. 1639–1640). But in the second play both Clytaemestra and Aegisthus, as Orestes makes clear, fall victim to their own design: "by treachery tangled in the self same net / they too shall die" (*Libation Bearers*, ll. 557–558). The function of this key design is to associate these characters, some innocent, some guilty, as the prey of the same code of justice. The net, the yoke, and the curb connote the inextricable grip from which no one can escape, the abstract force of necessity that leads each to his doom and in that doom initiates the next movement in the sequence. The sense of entanglement arouses in the spectators a feeling of emotional claustrophobia that prompts them to view with distaste the retributive justice it images. Feeling the compulsion of retribution in their own consciousnesses, they naturally yearn for the freedom and release that the abolition of this kind of justice promises.

Like the pattern of sickness and health, this motif also assumes nonverbal manifestations. Cassandra, who wears "the slave's yoke" on her neck (l. 1226), visually represents all the victims, but another device provides an even more powerful theatrical symbol for the key design. When Clytaemestra appears after killing her husband, she proudly displays the robe that helped her entrap him. Her complex language at this point unalterably fuses the verbal imagery with the visual object, for in calling the garment an *amphiblēstron* (l. 1382), she makes it both robe and fishing net. This visual device recurs in *The Libation Bearers* when Orestes holds aloft the same robe as justification for the revenge he took against his mother. His description of the robe increases the spectators' hatred of the net and all its implications:

> And this thing: what shall I call it and be right, in all
> eloquence? Trap for an animal or winding sheet
> for dead man?
>
> . . . . .
>
> Some highwayman might own a thing like this, to catch
> the wayfarer and rob him of his money and
> so make a living. With a treacherous thing like this
> he could take many victims and go warm within
>
> [ll. 997–1004].

But Orestes himself must ultimately submit to entanglement, and Aeschylus expresses this aspect of his theme through symbolic action. The *Agamemnon* provides a physical enactment of the key design when Clytaemestra forces her husband to walk on the carpet against his will, but its principal translation into symbolic action occurs in the third play, *The Eumenides*. Once the Furies capture Orestes on the Acropolis, they give the motif of entanglement total theatrical expression in music, dance, and gesture through the binding song they sing as they secure their prey (ll. 307–396).

This ode places Orestes squarely in the sequences of crime that stem from Atreus and Troy. It arouses in the spectators compelling sympathy for the victim whose cause Aeschylus has induced them to adopt during *The Libation Bearers*. The creation of an entirely sympathetic victim completes the purpose of the key design by solidifying the spectators' growing desire for release. Orestes does get free, but not before Aeschylus has shown that entanglement, like sickness, is also cosmic, for the Furies remind Athene that "Zeus himself shackled elder Cronus, his own / father" (ll. 641–642). By equating Zeus with Clytaemestra and Aegisthus, the Furies stress the god's part in the cosmic version of the earthly cycle that now threatens Orestes. Entanglement is universal because the gods themselves are snarled in their own dynastic struggles; but because it is universal, only the gods can provide release. Fortunately, Zeus has a capacity not given to man, as Athene points out in her conclusive answer to the Furies: "Zeus could undo shackles" (l. 645). When Athene frees Orestes, she puts Zeus's potential capacity into effect, and her action therefore suggests the elimination of destructive compulsion from the entire universe. The freeing of Orestes from obligation shatters the sense of entanglement, and the relief felt by the spectators richly enhances their emotional understanding of the final harmony.

Images of blood appear everywhere in the *Agamemnon*, occurring in an especially dense cluster during Cassandra's prevision of the murder. In the carpet scene Aeschylus isolates a single strand of this complex to form the pattern of "blood on the ground." Although the first verbal description of blood on the ground does not occur until the ensuing choral ode (ll. 1018–1021), the pattern is initiated in this episode by means of a visual object, the carpet. Goheen has demonstrated that Aeschylus intended the carpet to be "almost certainly an ambiguous blood-color, probably the dark purplish red or deep reddish brown which blood takes on after it is exposed to the air—or when it forms stains in the dust." [18] Clytaemestra views the carpet as a symbol of justice (ll. 910–911), and the pattern it introduces thus provides another intellectual and emotional statement about retribution. This recurring image is a constant reminder of the great waste of human life involved in the recurring murders, and, as Goheen remarks, the pattern implies that "since blood

[18] "Aspects of Dramatic Symbolism," p. 116.

shed is irredeemable, bloodshed is not an adequate solution." [19]

Each of the murders in the trilogy physically enacts the verbal imagery, but two instances of activity in *The Libation Bearers* give the pattern unusual theatrical emphasis. Both of these examples of symbolic action help to clarify the full significance of the killing of Clytaemestra and Aegisthus, which Orestes, Electra, and the chorus of slaves represent as perfect justice. The first enactment occurs during the long kommos, in which Orestes, Electra, and the chorus pray for the vengeance they hope to exact. Electra pours libations on the grave of Agamemnon (ll. 149–150), seeking her dead father's aid in justly punishing the evil killers who destroyed him. In recalling the imagery it imitates, however, her act highlights an aspect of their plan that neither she nor Orestes acknowledges: no matter how just their intentions, they will nevertheless be shedding additional blood. The second enactment shows that this implication ultimately becomes the only one of consequence. At the end of the play the Furies—unseen but powerfully felt through Orestes' agonized speeches—follow the trail of blood that drips from his guilty hands. The hope of Orestes and Electra has proved illusory because blood still falls steadily to the ground.

In *The Eumenides*, Aeschylus uses this image as a further means of associating the ambivalence of human retribution with the conflict between succeeding dynasties of gods. The Furies, who thrive on the blood of their guilty victims, oppose Apollo and Athene. When thwarted, they threaten (in a passage already quoted) to pour poison on the ground. In the purification of Orestes at Apollo's shrine and Athene's sanctuary, the blood of guilt, the wasted blood of retribution, is cleansed from man. In the transformation of the Furies into Eumenides the bloodshed caused by generations of cosmic strife is finally brought to an end. Once more the culmination of an image pattern symbolizes both the abolition of retribution and the institution of universal harmony.

[19] "Aspects of Dramatic Symbolism," p. 120.

The principal symbol of universal harmony, however, occurs in the culmination of another key design, that which is formed by the pervasive images of light. This pattern is undoubtedly the richest of all, and Aeschylus uses several devices to make it intellectually perceptible. The Watchman weaves a verbal impression of darkness and then announces his eager expectation of light, his yearning for "the flare burning from the blackness in good augury" (l. 20). And then a light appears. The Greek outdoor, daylight staging probably precluded the actual showing of a distant beacon, but if, as is likely, the performance of this trilogy began at dawn,[20] there may well have been such a visual effect. At any rate, the Watchman's supreme joy at the discovery sufficiently conveys the sense of a sudden gleam of light in darkness. The chorus soon takes up the imagery, and Clytaemestra gives this particular key design unmistakable emphasis in her elaborate beacon speech (ll. 281–316), with its many repetitions of *lampron, selas, phryktos, pyros, panon, hēlios, phaos,* and *phlogos.* From here to the end of the trilogy images of light recur almost incessantly. But what is even more remarkable, Aeschylus strengthens the basic effect through frequent verbs and adjectives that convey the idea of making something clear by casting light on it and through his usual word for "man" (*phōs*), which in this context cannot avoid suggesting its near homophone *phōs,* one of the words for light.

The various images and references to light or its absence divide the key design into three interwoven strands. The Watchman's attitude toward the beacon flare prompts the spectators to respond with their habitual conception of light as symbolic of clarity, release from darkness, illumination of the mind, hope and satisfaction, beauty, peace, and harmony. In the first choral ode light images the wisdom that the chorus predicts will finally emerge from the present suffering: "All will come clear in the next dawn's sunlight" (l. 254). This original sense is the radical

[20] Roy C. Flickinger, *The Greek Theater and Its Drama* (3d ed.; Chicago: University of Chicago Press, 1926), p. 225.

meaning of light in the trilogy, the one that finds fulfillment at the end and the one from which the other meanings derive their significance. The second connotation of light is introduced verbally by Clytaemestra's beacon speech and visually by the altar she has lit in thankfulness for Agamemnon's safe return. Her use of light imagery suggests her vain belief that she has found the final wisdom, that in killing Agamemnon she will end the succession of crimes. In this and similar passages later in the trilogy light implies falseness, mistaken hope, and specious clarity that in reality brings more darkness. Closely interwoven with the recurring images of false light are images of darkness, forming the third strand in this key design, ironically exposing the mistaken hope and stressing the continuation of suffering. As a result, darkness becomes a new symbol of retribution, its connotations in the spectators' consciousness arousing an intense desire for the final coming of the true light sought by the chorus.

The constant darkness is imaged in the later plays of the trilogy by visual devices. In *The Libation Bearers* the chorus wears black robes of mourning. In *The Eumenides* the Furies are black, and Aeschylus reinforces this visual impression with the description of them by Apollo's priestess (l. 52) and with the numerous other verbal images of darkness that they provoke (ll. 72, 386–387, 394–396, 416). But Aeschylus also opposes to the Furies a living symbol of the true light, the golden Apollo, god of the sun. In this way the imagery of light and darkness is given the same theatrical extension as the imagery of sickness and health, and like all the key designs of the play, it provides a link between the human action and the divine. Both actions are resolved by Athene, "who was never fostered in the dark of the womb" (l. 665), and by the outcome of the trial, which, as Athene says, acts on "the luminous [*lampra*] evidence of Zeus" (l. 797). By changing the Furies to blessed spirits, Athene suffuses the darkness with light, for she promises them a new home deep underground which will have its own unique brightness (ll.

804–807). The Furies acknowledge their acceptance of their new destiny when they also adopt the dominant imagery:

> I speak this prayer for them
> that the sun's bright magnificence shall break out wave
> on wave of all the happiness
> life can give, across their land   [ll. 922–926].

Athene's creation of the court on the Hill of Ares physically enacts the giving of true light, and her elicitation of wisdom from the plights of the individual, the state, and the heavens acquires its own physical manifestation in the final triumphant chorus of the trilogy. The women of the city, pledged to guide the Eumenides to their new home, sing of the wisdom of Zeus and carry lighted torches as a final visual summation of the emergence of the true light that has brought metaphysical illumination to the characters of the *Oresteia* and to the spectators who have witnessed their destinies.

The imagery of the *Oresteia*, then, illustrates the possibility of a number of key designs augmenting the significance of a single action. Each design affirms the basic intellectual concept underlying the surface events and symbolizes one of its many aspects. All the designs jointly establish the arrival of relief through universal harmony. Finally, they also illustrate one more characteristic of dramatic imagery when it forms two or more key designs. Throughout the trilogy Aeschylus constantly links the various patterns, as when Orestes awaits the counting of the votes: "This is the end for me. The noose, or else the light" (l. 746). Significantly, through the final chorus that celebrates the emergence of true light, Aeschylus also concludes two of the other key designs. The robe that was a net to entangle Agamemnon has been replaced by the robes draping the bodies of the joyful women, and, as Goheen points out, these robes are of the same color as the carpet that first imaged blood on the ground.[21] The merging

---

[21] "Aspects of Dramatic Symbolism," pp. 122–124.

of these key designs in the visual appearance of the final chorus mirrors the merging of opposites in harmony recorded by the expository statement of the choral song: Zeus and destiny, mercy and justice, are now one.

The *Oresteia* key designs muster concrete detail to reinforce and complete the abstract meanings stated more directly by the *Agamemnon* chorus and the final choral ode and clearly enacted in the near-allegorical construction of *The Eumenides*. In contrast, the major recurring images of *Hamlet* independently create some of the meaning that underlies and illuminates the immediate action. The primary key design of *Hamlet* has been thoroughly studied by Caroline Spurgeon, Wolfgang Clemen, and others. It stresses the intrinsic rottenness and decay that seethe beneath the thin layer of normalcy in Hamlet's world, threatening to burst through and destroy that world momentarily. The key metaphor can be precisely described. From her compilation of the images Miss Spurgeon concludes that "the idea of an ulcer or tumour, as descriptive of the unwholesome condition of Denmark morally, is, on the whole, the dominating one." More exactly, "the state of things in Denmark which shocks, paralyses and finally overwhelms Hamlet, is as the foul tumour breaking inwardly and poisoning the whole body, while showing 'no cause without / Why the man dies' " [22] (IV.iv.27–28). Clemen shows that Shakespeare enlarges and varies the dominant idea of the cancerous ulcer through associated images of sickness, rottenness, decay, corruption, and—perhaps the most important—poisoning.[23]

The general sense of rottenness made vivid and real by the recurring imagery manifests itself in specific actions, such as Gertrude's hasty and incestuous second marriage, and in more uni-

[22] *Shakespeare's Imagery* (Cambridge: University Press, 1958), pp. 316, 318.
[23] *The Development of Shakespeare's Imagery* (London: Methuen, 1951), pp. 113–118.

versal and abstract conditions, such as the "time" that is out of joint. More consistently, the feeling and meaning established by the key design widen from the particular event and narrow from the universal condition to become a complex symbol of Claudius' Denmark. In so doing, they give concrete reality to the sense of imbalance first expressed by the visual effects, sound patterns, and repetitions in the opening scene of the play. Shakespeare unites the vague apprehension generated by the opening scene to the implications of the imagery by means of a single speech that has the quality of expository statement, Marcellus' "Something is rotten in the state of Denmark" (I.iv.90). The key design therefore exposes with full clarity a world where evil has driven out good and values have been undermined, a world, in short, whose utter chaos enrages, sickens, and bewilders the one person with adequate sensitivity and perception to recognize the imminent menace. In responding to the substance and connotations of the images, the spectators, consciously or not, understand Hamlet's situation and sympathetically participate in it. With him they seek a restoration of soundness and health to the Denmark that represents their own world.

In his article on dramatic imagery Alan Downer has shown how Shakespeare gives the key design theatrical extension in the visual effects of the graveyard and its skulls. But it receives its most emphatic nonverbal expression in events that symbolically enact the substance of the verbal imagery. During the fifth and seventh scenes of Act IV, for example, the period of Hamlet's absence from Denmark, Shakespeare presents three vignettes concretely illustrating the rottenness that feeds on the heart of the state. These scenes portray Ophelia's madness—which, as Claudius notes, results from "the poison of deep grief" (IV.v.72); the rebellion of Laertes—whose ear has been infected "with pestilent speeches of his father's death" (ll. 87–88); and the plotting against Hamlet—a weird epitome of the corruption in Claudius' court, in which the king conspires with the courtier to destroy the prince, while in the process both plotters take on the role of poisoner.

The motif of poisoning also receives physical enactment in other events of the immediate action. The dumb show that precedes "The Murder of Gonzago" is an elaborate theatrical image recapitulating the verbal narration of the Ghost. In the fifth act, as the ulcer finally ruptures, the poison spreads to almost every corner of the court. All the remaining characters of importance —Hamlet, Laertes, Claudius, and Gertrude—die from poisoning; the king, the original source of Denmark's rottenness, is doubly poisoned. Even Horatio nearly succumbs. But he is spared to help Fortinbras assume the throne and restore sanity, balance, and health to Denmark. Fortinbras' arrival therefore resolves the effect of the play's dominant key design. But Shakespeare has already culminated it in a manner thoroughly characteristic of drama: what began as a possibility hinted at verbally becomes, by the end of the play, the very essence of the visual action.[24]

Repetition of Ideas

Most of the poisonings that dominate the final scene of *Hamlet* are also symbolic enactments of another aspect of the play. This one Shakespeare presents by means of a further stylistic device, the repetition not of an image but of an idea.[25] In 1699, in one of the earliest critical comments on *Hamlet*, James Drake represented it as a tragedy of intrigue and irony: "The Criminals are not only brought to execution but they are taken in their own

[24] This account of imagery in *Hamlet* makes no attempt to provide a full treatment. See the works by Spurgeon and Clemen previously cited; see also Maynard Mack, "The World of *Hamlet*," in *Shakespeare: Modern Essays in Criticism*, ed. Leonard F. Dean (New York: Oxford University Press, 1957), pp. 237–257.

[25] Cf. the illuminating analysis of the repeated "aphoristic commonplaces" in Lope de Vega's *Fuente Ovejuna* by R. D. F. Pring-Mill, "Sententiousness in *Fuente Ovejuna*," *Tulane Drama Review*, VII (Fall 1962), 5–37.

Toyls, their own Stratagems recoyl upon 'em, and they are involved themselves in that mischief and ruine which they had projected for Hamlet." [26] Drake's interpretation obviously echoes a
famous speech by Hamlet, one in which he anticipates the plotting of Rosencrantz and Guildenstern with evident pleasure:

> Let it work;
> For 'tis the sport to have the engineer
> Hoist with his own petar; and't shall go hard
> But I will delve one yard below their mines
> And blow them at the moon   [III.iv.205–209].

Several features of this speech insistently assert its fundamental
importance, for it is spoken by Hamlet, it is phrased with imaginative vividness, it suggests the proverbial, and it forms a climax
to the tense scenes of Act III. But support for Drake's interpretation is not confined to a single statement. The killing of Rosencrantz and Guildenstern, the event predicted by Hamlet, re-establishes the force of his words and gives them the authority of
fulfillment. Furthermore, the prediction itself by no means stands
alone; a few lines earlier, for example, Hamlet has already told
his mother the story of another victim of self-hoisting:

> No, in despite of sense and secrecy,
> Unpeg the basket on the house's top,
> Let the birds fly, and, like the famous ape,
> To try conclusions, in the basket creep
> And break your own neck down   [ll. 192–196].

The emphasis resulting from the proximity of these two statements suggests that the principle they embody has more than
local significance. At the same time, the allusion to the ape is not
anchored to specific characters in the way that the engineer
image refers to Rosencrantz and Guildenstern; it indicates a more
abstract and therefore more inclusive application.

[26] Quoted by E. E. Stoll, *Art and Artifice in Shakespeare* (Cambridge:
University Press, 1933), p. 106.

The basic importance of these two speeches consists in their emphasizing a principle of ironic reversal which is repeated again and again by Hamlet and by other characters, and continually symbolized by enacted events. Hamlet's image of the engineer precisely renders his response to a single moment of action; but it functions additionally as the major formulation of a leitmotif that runs throughout the entire play.[27] Especially significant is Shakespeare's sequential arrangement of the various repetitions, for by Kenneth Burke's standard of "the *qualitative* importance of beginning, middle, and end," ironic reversal is genuinely thematic.

Shakespeare introduces this principle during the richly evocative opening scene that also initiates the sense of general uneasiness and suggests the presence of an evil threatening the apparent stability of Denmark. In explaining why Denmark fears a foreign invasion, Horatio narrates the story of old Fortinbras, who risked a portion of his territories in the expectation of augmenting them but, ironically, "Did forfeit, with his life, all those his lands / Which he stood seiz'd of, to the conqueror" (I.i.88–89). This speech, while establishing ironic reversal as one of the seeds from which the ensuing tragedy will grow, indicates the unlimited relevance of the principle for *Hamlet:* in the earliest and most remote of all the actions recognized within the play's universe, an individual's self-assertion brings him only self-destruction.

Between this opening and the peripety of the third act, the leitmotif receives only incidental expression, as when Hamlet observes that the "eyrie of children," in attacking the adult theater troupes, "exclaim against their own succession" (II.ii.343–347), and when his allusion to Jepthah (ll. 398–407) evokes a biblical example of a man hoist with his own petard. But in the climactic

[27] For a discussion of the conventional status of this motif in Elizabethan drama and the difference in Shakespeare's use of it, see Thomas F. Van Laan, "Ironic Reversal in *Hamlet,*" *Studies in English Literature,* VI (1966), 247–262.

scenes that include the exposure and sparing of Claudius, the killing of Polonius, and the scourging of Gertrude, ironic reversal
becomes an irremovable part of the dramatic texture. The Player
King, whose formal speeches generalize many of the themes implicitly developed in the basic action,[28] typically supplies an abstract version of the principle:

> Our wills and fates do so contrary run
> That our devices still are overthrown;
> Our thoughts are ours, their ends none of our own
> [III.ii.206–208].

Shakespeare translates this principle into action when Polonius,
whose devious ways and wily stratagems qualify him as "engineer" in one Elizabethan sense,[29] willfully selects concealment
behind the arras as his own particular petard. Seeking added
favor for himself, he wins instead both the unforeseen thrust
from Hamlet's sword and a highly appropriate epitaph:

> Thou wretched, rash, intruding fool, farewell!
> I took thee for thy better. Take thy fortune;
> Thou find'st to be too busy is some danger
> [III.iv.31–33].

The almost immediate echoing of this comment in the speeches
about the ape and the engineer focuses attention on the developing leitmotif; the actual fate of Polonius demonstrates that its significance is organic rather than purely verbal.

In the fourth act the principle once more finds only incidental

[28] See Francis Fergusson, *The Idea of a Theater* (Princeton, N.J.:
Princeton University Press, 1949), p. 124.

[29] According to the *Oxford English Dictionary*, "engineer" had two
primary meanings when *Hamlet* was written: (1) "one who contrives,
designs, or invents; an author, designer," or "inventor; a plotter, a layer
of snares"; (2) "one who designs and constructs military works for attack or defense." Thus the "engineer" of Hamlet's speech, less metaphorical in Shakespeare's time than it now seems, would explicitly denote the
tricksters of the play.

expression, but the repetitions are frequent and come from more than one speaker. In a speech that links ironic reversal to the recurring imagery of the play, Claudius compares himself to "the owner of a foul disease," who, wanting to keep it hidden, "let it feed / Even on the pith of life" (IV.i.21–23). In a later scene the usually imperceptive Gertrude receives inspiration from Ophelia's madness:

> So full of artless jealousy is guilt,
> It spills itself in fearing to be spilt   [IV.v.19–20].

Ophelia's madness contributes another example of ironic reversal in her Valentine's Day song about a maid who gives herself to a young man so that he will marry her and is then rejected because she is no longer chaste. Finally, Claudius again employs the motif in telling Laertes why he did not publicly expose Hamlet as Polonius' murderer; the people, he explains, so love their prince that

> my arrows,
> Too slightly timber'd for so loud a wind,
> Would have reverted to my bow again,
> But not where I have aim'd them   [IV.vii.21–24].

These minor repetitions, like those in Act II, touch on several different areas of human experience, and this effect reaffirms the pertinence of ironic reversal to every aspect of life known in the play's universe. But their major function is to recur like a musical theme in anticipation of the crescendo of the final act.

It is in the fifth act, especially at the end of the play, that the relevance of the leitmotif is most impressively established, for here repetitions of it provide explanations for the deaths of several major characters. The fate of Rosencrantz and Guildenstern is analogous to that of Polonius, and Hamlet dismisses them with equal serenity:

> Why, man, they did make love to this employment;
> They are not near my conscience; their defeat
> Does by their own insinuation grow   [V.ii.57–59].

The dying Laertes admits that the "engine" of the poisoned sword was his own invention, and to explain what has happened to him, he adopts the common Elizabethan proverbial expression of ironic reversal:

> Why, as a woodcock, to mine own springe, Osric;
> I am justly kill'd with mine own treachery [ll. 298–299].

After repeating the same confession in different imagery—"The foul practice / Hath turn'd itself on me" (ll. 309–310)—he articulates the significance of Hamlet's forcing Claudius to drink from the poisoned cup: "He is justly serv'd: / It is a poison temper'd by himself" (ll. 319–320).

Since so many of the play's deaths are defined as examples of ironic reversal, death tends to symbolize this principle even when it is not explicitly formulated. Gertrude dies at the same time as Claudius and Laertes, and, significantly, her death is the direct result of one of her few decisive acts in the play; Claudius warns her not to drink from the poisoned cup, but she deliberately disobeys him: "I will, my lord; I pray you pardon me" (l. 283). Ophelia, whose funeral in Act V, scene i, initiates this fifth-act emphasis on death, is even more passive than Gertrude; her self-assertions consist only of her devotion to her father and her love for Hamlet. But, as Laertes perceives, these commitments lead to her destruction:

> Nature is fine in love; and where 'tis fine
> It sends some precious instance of itself
> After the thing it loves [IV.v.158–160].

His perception is verified by the songs she sings in her madness: one on death and burial, suggesting the impact of the loss of her father, the other on sex, suggesting the perversion by madness of her feeling for Hamlet. Ophelia has passively sacrificed herself by seeking to create a stable individuality through reliance on others; she has split her own essence and invested the two halves.

She loses Hamlet, as her allusion to the baker's daughter implies (ll. 40–41), because of the excessive caution that obedience to her father has dictated. When she loses her father as well, her destruction is complete. Her investment has failed, and only the bankruptcy of madness and suicide can follow.

Shakespeare has organically woven ironic reversal into the pattern of tragedy. Introduced in the opening scene, it is sustained throughout the play by numerous repetitions that, like the engineer image, express ironic reversal in some kind of verbal formula, or, like the examples of old Fortinbras and the ape, testify to its effectuality. The principle asserts its thematic pertinence during the third act, and then, at the end of the play, as the various lines of action converge, its relevance is overwhelmingly established, not only through the many deaths that exemplify its scope but also through one of the final speeches, for in devoting almost one-third of his Seneca-like summary of the action to "purposes mistook / Fall'n on th' inventors' heads" (V.ii.376–377), Horatio identifies ironic reversal as a mainspring of the entire tragedy. While thus emphasizing the leitmotif, Shakespeare gives it a particular relation to the play's universe. The principle derives not from Hamlet's mind alone but is echoed by Horatio, Claudius, the Player King, and Laertes, and this agreement suggests that ironic reversal exists apart from the limited consciousnesses of the individuals who glimpse its reality either dimly or unknowingly. The actual fate of the majority of the characters confirms its existence not as a matter of human opinion but as an objective quality of the universe.

Helen Gardner, who has already pointed out in a much more general way this intensification of a "basic element in the revenge play," believes that Shakespeare's functional elaboration of the principle accounts for Hamlet's delay. Hamlet, she writes, conforms to the "conception of a hero who is committed to counter-action, and to response to events rather than to the creation of events." Through the working of the irony, the villain unwit-

tingly creates the opportunity for the hero, whose moral responsibility is to only stand and wait.[30] The difficulty of Miss Gardner's suggestion lies in her understanding of the principle. Her
discussion of it as it appears in *The Spanish Tragedy*, for example, centers upon Lorenzo's naively inviting Hieronimo to stage
the play that will make possible the final revenge, but in this interpretation the engineer, instead of being hoist with his own petard, merely permits his petard-bearing enemy to slip unnoticed
through the lines. Shakespeare is not satisfied with the somewhat
vague notion that the individual's conscious acts merely *allow* his
destruction; on the contrary, each expression of the principle in
Hamlet dramatizes a rationale of human existence in which the
individual's own self-seeking gesture, through a reflex action, becomes itself the weapon that destroys him. *Hamlet* indeed intensifies a basic revenge-tragedy theme, but it also particularizes the
theme's precise nature not as ironic outcome but as ironic reversal. This special conception of human action and of the universe
apparently determining it is what the leitmotif contributes to the
total meaning of the play.

From one point of view this conception might well reinforce
Hamlet's identification of Christian providence as the ultimate
universal reality. M. C. Bradbrook has asserted that the existence
of ironic reversal in revenge tragedy "depends on the conception
of an underlying pattern in [the lives of the characters], of a divinity shaping them." [31] From this point of view, Hamlet's
glimpse of a divinely ordered universe, which Miss Bradbrook
paraphrases, may be seen as a central statement of the developing
leitmotif:

> There's a divinity that shapes our ends,
> Rough-hew them how we will [V.ii.10–11].

[30] *The Business of Criticism* (Oxford: Clarendon Press, 1959), pp. 41–
45.

[31] *Themes and Conventions of Elizabethan Tragedy* (Cambridge: University Press, 1935), p. 33.

In this speech the notion of ironic reversal, which is fully evident in the distinction between intention and result, acquires obvious Christian implications. When man acts in accordance with the transcendent good—by serving it as scourge and minister, perhaps—what he initiates will prosper. But when man attempts to violate that order, he sins and consequently calls down his own punishment. The leitmotif's emphasis on personal responsibility ("*thy* fortune," "his *own* petar," "their *own* insinuation," "mine *own* springe," "poison temper'd *by himself*"—italics mine) suggests the responsibility that Christianity assigns to the individual, whose salvation or damnation is of his own making. Laertes' use of "justly" for both himself and Claudius tends to characterize their acts as sins meriting the punishment they provoke. The selfish motives of such "engineers" as old Fortinbras, the boy actors, and Claudius connote Pride, the chief of the Seven Deadly Sins. There is indeed much about the leitmotif, as Bertram Joseph has seen, that "makes us aware of the hand of Providence destroying evil." [32]

Nevertheless, the idea of guilt contained in Hamlet's primary image of the engineer is qualified by the allusion that immediately precedes it. Like the engineer, the ape destroys himself through a deliberate act intended to enhance his own situation. But unlike the engineer, the ape in no way threatens the welfare of others; his fate is not only ironic but, apparently, unjustified as well. This possibility of a nonmoral conception of ironic reversal is further developed throughout the presentation of the leitmotif by the Shakespearean habit of interrelating images. The pattern of creator and creation in Hamlet's engineer and petard recurs in Laertes' woodcock and springe. The Player King's ambiguous word "devices" connotes not only an end result but also the process of plot, plan, or intention which produces it. The process performed by engineer and woodcock finds further exemplifica-

[32] *Conscience and the King* (London: Chatto and Windus, 1953), p. 151.

tion in the ape's experimenting ("To try conclusions") and in Claudius' tempering poison. The idea of doing, of creating, which runs through these different expressions, is made explicit in Horatio's final "inventors." The entire cluster of related images, through which the Elizabethan concept of the "enginer" yields to the more modern one of the "engineer," connotes a particular kind of human endeavor: man's eternal attempt to impose order on his environment, to substitute his own act of creation for nature's. By deflecting attention from the idea of human guilt, these images suggest that the moral evaluation of ironic reversal is rooted only in the individual's attempt to domesticate the principle he has glimpsed. Hamlet's three different expressions of the principle further illustrate the subjectivity of the moral evaluation, for in them the principle remains unchanged; only his interpretation of it undergoes alteration. In his speech on divinity he sees the irony as characteristically Christian, but when he speaks of the ape there is far less certainty. His central image presents an even more complex evaluation; although it concerns what might readily be considered just punishment for immoral behavior, its tone stresses the sardonically humorous aspects of the principle; it is *the sport* to have the engineer hoist with his own petard. Since the victims of ironic reversal in this play range from the guilty through the neutral to the innocent, the conclusion must be that the universe of *Hamlet* negates all human activity, whether vicious or not.[33]

As Henri Bergson has well shown, the reversal of expectation is inherently comic: the convention of the "robber robbed" lends

[33] That the principle is not necessarily Christian is effectively confirmed by its popularity in pre-Christian literature. Similarly, in the twentieth century, Jean-Paul Sartre has discovered that the principle expresses a major tenet in his non-Christian existentialist philosophy. The hell of *No Exit* consists of the self-elected damnations of the individual sinners, a concept which, left implicit in that play, receives precise verbal formulation in *The Flies;* see *No Exit and Three Other Plays* (New York: Vintage Books, 1955), II.ii.

farcical overtones to scenes that do not otherwise provoke laughter.[34] The hoisting of Barabas is one of the effects that gives Marlowe's *Jew of Malta* its quality of tragic farce. The final scene of *The Atheist's Tragedy*, where the villainous D'Amville unintentionally knocks out his own brains, is, despite its explicit Christian message, unspeakably ludicrous. When tragic situations take the shape of a convention of farce, they of necessity create the impression of a universe essentially absurd and savage so far as human pretensions are concerned. The farcical, sadistic aspect of the leitmotif suits well the key metaphor of the cancerous ulcer. The two patterns, explicitly linked in Claudius' image of the foul disease that its owner ironically aggravated, combine to suggest a particular conception of the play's universe, one very much in keeping with the sardonic tone of Hamlet's "hoist" image and with the extreme fatalism of the Player King. As it fuses with the sense of ubiquitous evil, the leitmotif posits a universe that is the negation of the Christian world view, a universe that has order but an order essentially malevolent, a universe that allows man his puny self-assertions only in order that these may be the means of his self-destruction.

But what of Hamlet and ironic reversal? Only once does Shakespeare apply the leitmotif directly to him—through Claudius, who claims that Hamlet himself is responsible for his departure for England: "and he most violent author / Of his own just remove" (IV.v.77–78). Claudius here interprets an aspect of Hamlet's experience in terms of several elements of the theme: conscious and assertive action ("violent author"—which joins the imagery of man the creator), unexpected result (the "remove"), and inviolable order ("just"). Claudius' perception

---

[34] See "Laughter," in *Comedy*, ed. Wylie Sypher (Garden City, N.Y.: Doubleday, 1956), pp. 122–123; cf. W. G. Moore, *Molière: A New Criticism* (2d ed.; Garden City, N.Y.: Doubleday, 1962), p. 71: "Audiences have always been incited to laugh at 'le trompeur trompé,' at the schemer hoist with his own petard."

characterizes only a minor part of Hamlet's activity, however; the play contains no explicit formulation, like those summing up Polonius, Laertes, and Claudius, to indicate its total meaning. But Hamlet's association with the other characters suggests that he is governed by the same laws, and his inclusion among the victims of ironic reversal is further indicated by a minor motif deriving from the basic leitmotif. In a universe apparently awaiting man's efforts with sinister anticipation, the most practical advice that one can offer consists of warnings. The play abounds in warnings, as character after character advises his fellows to follow a course of inaction. But none of these warnings is heeded, and the result is self-destruction. Laertes ultimately ignores his father's cautious advice, Rosencrantz and Guildenstern pay no attention to Hamlet's assurance that "though you can fret me, yet you cannot play upon me" (III.ii.362–363), and Gertrude drinks despite her husband's plea. Ophelia's case is more complicated: she obeys Polonius' insistence that she be "something scanter of [her] maiden presence" (I.iii.121), but she disregards the tacit warning to forget Hamlet altogether, and her failure to do so contributes to her madness. Hamlet himself twice rejects attempts to limit his activity. In Act I, scene iv, Horatio begs him not to follow the Ghost because the experience might lead to madness. Expecting to obtain relief through the clarification of his doubts and suspicions, Hamlet ignores Horatio. But his willfulness ironically yields him only the increased sense of chaos that is symbolized by his antic disposition. Horatio's second warning occurs during the final scene of the play in response to the slight "gain-giving" with which Hamlet anticipates the duel: "If your mind dislike anything, obey it" (V.ii.209). This time Hamlet's failure to heed advice costs him his life. For the second time he consciously substitutes an assertion of his will for caution; on both occasions the action turns against him.

Hamlet's vulnerability to ironic reversal affords the spectators one way of seeing his whole tragic experience. Learning that his uncle is the apparent source of the evil of which he is almost morbidly conscious, Hamlet converts awareness of evil into a desire to eliminate it. But the compulsion to act conflicts with another kind of awareness, for as his allusions to ape and engineer show, he at least dimly perceives a universe seemingly sadistic and destructive, eager to anticipate any overt action on the part of man. This dim awareness gives him pause; it prompts the inaction that almost nullifies the pledge to the Ghost and to himself. Nevertheless, in a universe that permits no challenge to its own absolute sovereignty, the pledge itself is a sufficient assertion of his will; it takes him directly and inevitably to his death from Laertes' poisoned sword. Like Claudius, Hamlet drinks "a poison temper'd by himself."

Both this leitmotif and the imagery of rottenness express for the spectators of *Hamlet* aspects of the play's universe, the action of depth within which the immediate action is performed. Each pattern influences the spectators' emotional responses by its mere existence, but Shakespeare also conveys the substance of each pattern through symbolic action so that it can influence the spectators' intellectual responses as well. Moreover, even as the physical enactment of image or concept serves to give it theatrical extension, the enactment also confirms the validity of the meaning asserted verbally. Ophelia's madness exemplifies the rottenness of Denmark and is caused by it. Polonius' death is both illustration and result of the law of ironic reversal.

Symbols

The drama of formal realism, exploiting everyday conversation, provides few opportunities for thematic imagery or the repetition of ideas. *Rosmersholm* contains only a limited number of conspicuous images, most of which express the relevance to the play's action of the realm of nature. Rosmer tells Kroll that his emancipation from the church has brought a "new summer" into his mind (I, p. 142). Rebecca's origin in Finmark and her love of flowers indicate her close association with nature, and she explains her destruction of Beata by saying that Rosmer, whom she found sickening in the gloom of his marriage, could not "wax" (*vokse*) without the bright sunshine (III, p. 191). These sparse images suggest that Rosmer's adoption of the new way of life has the validity and the innate virtue of natural growth. In leaving the church he has rejected the institutions imposed by men and embraced a higher reality, the spontaneous flow of life. Rebecca supplies the germinating force that will help him grow. But Ibsen recognizes that nature has more than one dimension: as in the case of Rebecca and the Rosmer marriage, creation vies with destruction. Therefore Ibsen introduces the image of a storm. During his first visit to Rosmer Brendel speaks of the "storm-tossed solstice time" in which they live (I, p. 138). This seems only one of his extravagant metaphors until, at the end of the first act, storm imagery gains significance. Here Rebecca predicts a "severe storm," even though, as Madam Helseth helpfully observes, there is no cloud to be seen in the sky (pp. 146–147). The storm becomes even more pertinent when Kroll warns Rosmer that he does not suspect "how violent a storm will come over" him (II, p. 158). Eventually Ibsen reveals that the storm is nothing but Rebecca's destructive passion. Kroll implies this when he accuses her of possessing a "cold heart" (III, p. 184), but in the final act Ibsen makes the identification explicit through Rebecca's own realization: "It came over me like a storm from the sea. It was like one of the storms we have up north in the winter time" (IV, p. 201). Rebecca, who brings with her the potentiality of nature's peacefulness—she recalls as well the "stillness . . . on a fowling cliff under the midnight sun up at home" (p. 202)—brings also its violence. She, the embodiment of nature, is both an "attractive mermaid" (Brendel's phrase—p. 207) and, in her own ultimate self-view, "a sea troll who clings to the ship and hampers it" (p. 211). In accepting the influence of nature, Rosmer unavoidably surrenders himself to both its aspects; while finding freedom, he also finds anarchy. This pattern of imagery, which develops the allusions to nature in the first-act setting, clearly has much significance for the play, but it just as clearly lacks the emphasis that Aeschylus and Shakespeare give their key designs.

Another important difference involves the repetition of ideas. The characters of *Rosmersholm* often generalize, but they lack the sort of agreement the characters in *Hamlet* have about the law of ironic reversal. Indeed, Ibsen builds his surface action out of the conflicts that arise between differing interpretations of reality. Any spoken generalization, therefore, tends to be nothing more than the assumption of the speaker who voices it, and for the most part it will be opposed at once by someone who holds a contrasting belief: Kroll may argue that the past is potent and authoritative, but the others remain skeptical. Equally significant is a character's tendency to alter his own generalizations when his knowledge of the immediate situation changes: Kroll insists often on the necessity of each man's taking an active part in life—until, that is, he learns that Rosmer, whom he has been trying to convince, belongs to the other side.

But if Ibsen's realistic mode cuts him off from the advantages of recurrent imagery and repetition of ideas, he does have recourse to a different stylistic device, the symbol. Since a symbol is in essence any concrete detail, verbal or visual, that serves as the perceptible edge of a larger but otherwise impalpable abstraction, it would be true to say that such devices as Shakespeare's Ghost or the key designs in both the *Oresteia* and *Hamlet* acquire symbolic status. There is a difference, however, in Ibsen's technique. Like Aeschylus and Shakespeare, he constantly exploits the tendency of all art to make a person, object, or event be both itself and the means of expressing equally real though less tangible aspects of experience. But unlike Aeschylus and Shakespeare, he also creates more conspicuous symbols that attract attention because of their very oddity. Of this sort are his "ghosts," his wild duck, his towers, and his white horses, which, instead of arising naturally from the story material, seem to be imposed on it for the particular illumination they can provide. These symbols, because they stand out in the texture of the immediate action, are directly experienced as indices of meaning, and their intrinsic associations combine with others assigned by the characters who discuss them to form patterns of implication similar to those established through key designs. *Rosmersholm* contains two such symbols: one—the white horse—is a repeated reference; the other—the setting—is primarily visual.

The value Ibsen placed on the verbal symbol of the white horse is indicated by his giving an early draft of *Rosmersholm* the title "White Horses." He also establishes its importance within the text of the final version. Introduced in the first minutes of the play, it recurs at every significant turn in the action: when Kroll breaks with Rosmer, when Kroll reveals Beata's accusations about Rosmer and Rebecca, when Rebecca makes her startling confession, and, finally, when she and Rosmer go together to their deaths.

Ibsen stresses at once the association between the white horse and the past. Madam Helseth, one of the fixtures of Rosmersholm, the house of tradition, superstitiously accepts the white horse as an awe-provoking reality. Rebecca, who represents the new, is skeptically amused. Moreover, the white horse suggests death and is specifically linked to Beata's death (II, p. 155), a past event whose influence extends into and threatens to destroy the present. As a product of superstition and an image of death, the symbol arouses in the spectators an unfavorable attitude toward the forces of the past and toward those who believe in the efficacy of ghostly white horses.

As the action progresses, however, the symbol acquires further significance. To Madam Helseth's despair, Rebecca can still make fun of the superstition at the end of Act I, this time with reference to the angry Kroll: "Let's hope he doesn't meet the white horse. For I'm afraid we shall soon be hearing from some spook of that sort" (p. 147). But her jest has pungency: her realization that she and Rosmer are now subject to the white horse's influence makes of it something more than a mere omen warning of a physical death in the family. In qualifying her remark with greater seriousness, she assures Madam Helseth that "there are so many kinds of white horses in this world." Rebecca's later references to the symbol continue to expand its significance until it characterizes the power of the past to hold on to its own while foretelling the death of innovations that endanger its dominance. Rosmer's "quiet, joyful guiltlessness" is continuously disturbed by the "wild imaginings" that fill his mind with thoughts of Beata, and Rebecca compares these crippling fantasies to "the white horse of Rosmersholm" (II, p. 170). While thus obsessed, Rosmer fears that his love for Rebecca drove Beata to her death; he is therefore certain that he cannot realize his idealistic hopes: "Victory is never won for a cause that has its origin in guilt." Rebecca protests "in an outburst": "Oh, these are the doubts of your family—the anxieties of your family—the scruples of your family. They chatter hereabouts that the dead come back as rushing white horses. I think that this is something of that sort" (III, p. 182). Her equation of the symbol with the scruples of his heritage receives confirmation even as she presents it: Rosmer expects failure because his personal past, the mysterious suicide of Beata, is upon him, holding him in check.

The most important aspect of Rebecca's expanding definition of the symbol is the way in which her own attitude toward the white horse changes. When, at first, it meant no more to her than a local superstition foretelling an imminent death, she could treat it as a joke. But as she forms in her mind the larger meanings of the symbol, she begins to believe that white horses really exist. Ultimately, she reveals both her complete faith in their reality and her acceptance of their dominating influence. When she has lost her struggle with the past over the possession of Rosmer and must leave his house in the aftermath of her first confession, she perceives that the force that has never let Rosmer free has also conquered her. To Madam Helseth, for whom she had originally expressed her skepticism, she now passionately acknowledges her faith: "I think I saw something like a glimpse of white horses" (III, p. 195). Now it is Madam Helseth who listens skeptically.

Like Aeschylus and Shakespeare, Ibsen links the verbal device to a visual effect. His use of Rebecca's white shawl suggests the reliability of her later understanding of the horse symbol. Even when she had dismissed the white horse, the spectators could see her busily folding up her shawl (I, p. 122) and therefore suspected that she was not really untouched by the symbol's implications. As she expresses her more perceptive interpretations of the symbol and finally admits her own capitulation to it, the spectators see her become more and more preoccupied with her shawl (I, p. 147; III, pp. 174, 177; IV, p. 196). When she and Rosmer prepare to go to the bridge and their deaths, she pauses; perhaps, she suggests, his desire to accompany her is only a delusion, only "one of these white horses of Rosmersholm." "It could well be," Rosmer agrees: "For we do not get away from them—we of this house" (p. 212). Then Rebecca, her white shawl draped over her head and about her body (stage direction, p. 210), takes his hand and they go out together. The shawl, as visual representation of the verbal symbol, implies that the act which Rosmer and Rebecca view as victory may be in reality more of a defeat. In the final speech of the play Madam Helseth strengthens this implication. Through the window she sees Rebecca and Rosmer on the bridge; she also sees "that white thing there—!" (p. 212). What she sees is Rebecca's shawl, but it is obvious that she thinks she sees the white horse that brings death to Rosmersholm. Through the ambiguity of her speech Ibsen suggests that the white horse, like the dead wife, "has taken" Rosmer and Rebecca. Family scruples, the forces of the past, and the personal pasts of Rosmer and Rebecca have apparently destroyed those who tried to free themselves.

The play's dominant visual symbol, the setting, establishes a pattern of meaning closely related to that evoked by the references to the white horse. The first-act setting, as Chapter 2 shows, visualizes the underlying conflict between old and new. In this original picture the vibrant tokens of the new dominate the lifeless relics of the past, and the past seems both powerless in its stagnancy and evil in its persistence. But the alterations Ibsen makes in the setting slowly reveal that the impotency, at any rate, is deceptive.

The setting of Act II, Rosmer's study, is devoid of Rebecca's flowers and the tranquil glow of twilight, nor is there any open door or window to admit the influences of the outside world where the new spirit rages most vehemently: this setting defines the continued force of the past in all its pristine power and omnipresence.[35] The implication is clear enough from the stage picture, yet like most dramatists, Ibsen not only supplements his verbal effects through visual objects and symbolic action, he also tends to re-express the significance of his primarily visual symbols in words. Consequently, within this setting he has Kroll verbally stress the force that is visually symbolized:

Rosmersholm has since time immemorial been like a dwelling place for discipline and order—for respectful deference to everything that is time-honored and approved by the best people in society. The whole area has taken its stamp from Rosmersholm. It will bring about a baleful, an irreparable confusion if it is reported that you yourself have broken with what I shall call the Rosmer family ideal [p.158].

In Acts III and IV the setting is once more the original sitting room, but changes in its appearance indicate ultimate victory for the "family ideal" that Kroll describes. At the beginning of Act

[35] Cf. John Northam, *Ibsen's Dramatic Method* (London: Faber and Faber, 1953), p. 118.

III, Rebecca "stands by the window, watering and arranging the flowers" (p. 174), and her action calls attention to the weakness and impermanence of one of the principal symbols of the new in the house of the old. Appropriately, in this act and its sequel references stressing the traditional and oppressive aspects of the setting become more frequent. Madam Helseth recalls that "little children don't cry at Rosmersholm," and that "when they grow up they never laugh" (p. 177); in fact, such power has the house to "infect" its surroundings that in the whole region no one ever laughs (p. 178). Kroll, as in the first act, emphasizes the significance of the portraits that visualize Rosmer's heritage, and this time Rebecca reluctantly agrees that "Johannes Rosmer has exceedingly deep roots in his race" (p. 185). Kroll, shocked by Rebecca's first confession, once more looks round at the portraits: "Ah—those who are gone—if they could only see now" (p. 194).

In the fourth act the flowers have vanished. The night is dark, but the lamp, which had been Rebecca's weapon against darkness in Act I, is now muted by a shade (p. 196). In this act the only one to enter from the outside world is Brendel; and he brings with him only further proof that the forces of tradition have won. Rebecca, who ultimately came to see the reality of the white horse, also perceives that the house of Rosmer and the spirit it embodies have thwarted her efforts to negate their influence. She who sought to conquer the house is conquered by it: "Rosmersholm has struck me powerless. I've had my courageous will clipped here. And murdered! The time is gone for me when I dared risk whatever might be necessary. I've lost the ability to act" (p. 201). When Brendel has come and gone, and no hope remains, Rebecca feels as if the walls of the house were closing in to suffocate her: "Oh, how close and stuffy it is here!" (p. 207). She opens the window in a last feeble attempt to reduce the potency of the forces that menace her. It is, of course, useless: outside there is now only the dark night and the millrace calling to her and Rosmer. The white horse awaits them.

6. Structural Devices

> The total structural unity of a work does not yield itself to a simple description, but only to a quite lengthy analysis of the complex interrelationships of all major elements.
> —Dorothy Van Ghent, *The English Novel: Form and Function*

The language of a play helps reveal the action of depth in more than one way. Through such devices as expository statement, patterns of sound and rhythm, repetition, and key designs, the language directly and concretely embodies various aspects of the action of depth. At the same time, language also makes a more indirect contribution; alongside such momentous effects as Aeschylus' "wisdom through suffering" formula and Shakespeare's repetition of ironic reversal, other verbal effects, less conspicuous but equally concrete, work in conjunction with each other and with nonverbal devices of sight and sound to produce intermediate impressions whose implications establish nonconcrete and nonverbal revelations of the action of depth. These intermediate impressions are elements of structure. Every character and episode, both in itself and in relation to other structural components of the same order, has a particular significance which, though not concretely embodied in any specific verbal device, is the product of language, and which must be perceived if the whole import of the play is to be experienced. Agamemnon, for example, is not only a particular figure involved in a distinct action but also, as agent and victim, a symbol of retributive justice. This function of his role is never expressed in so many words or epitomized by any single verbal device, but his behavior, appearance, and speech, and the reactions of others all imply it. Furthermore, recognition of this symbolic dimension is crucial to an appreciation of the study of retribution that occupies the action of depth in the *Oresteia*. In this respect Agamemnon typifies all characters in drama. Similarly, a specific scene, such as the opening of *Hamlet*, is not only a happening or an occurrence but also a well-ordered event bristling with significance. Every character and every scene, like the individual image or the carefully chosen word, is both a fact and a meaningful sign.

Character in the Action of Depth

Agamemnon's dual role exemplifies a basic attribute of all fictional characters, especially in drama. On the level of the immediate action the character, as portrayed by actor or actress, is a distinct individual. On this level, in other words, the character consists of a cluster of impressions suggesting a fairly unique combination of recognizable human personality traits. But on the level of the action of depth the same character loses its concrete uniqueness to symbolize an abstract concept such as a generalized human type, an institution, an emotion, an idea, or a universal force. A number of examples have already been suggested in preceding chapters. The *Oresteia* has Clytaemestra as well as Agamemnon to convey its evaluation of retribution. Apollo and the Furies, the deities who eventually involve themselves in human affairs, represent light and darkness, cure and disease, old and new. Athene acts for Zeus in resolving the impasse in the human action; she is also, by virtue of her nature, the wisdom that emerges from and puts an end to the continual suffering dominant until her appearance. In Ibsen's *Rosmersholm*, Kroll and Rebecca respectively project the opposing forces of tradition and progress, conservatism and revolt, that each of them personally upholds.

Almost any play can furnish additional examples. The symbolic or allegorical function of character is especially obvious in a morality like *Everyman,* in which the emphasis on abstract meaning almost squeezes out any human focus. *Everyman* does offer, of course, some psychological examination of human nature. The episodes in which the hero fruitlessly seeks a companion neatly dramatize the way people quickly qualify and rationalize their vows to help, once they discover the potential danger for themselves. Even more attention falls on the anguish of the abandoned sufferer. But this human focus soon yields to a level that emphasizes general ideas, especially since the hero and his adversaries bear names—like Fellowship, Kindred, Cousin, and Goods—which designate abstractions rather than human beings. In character as well as other elements of this play, the action of depth predominates. Moreover, in keeping with the medieval tendency to exploit four levels of meaning—the literal, allegorical, moral, and anagogical—the characters of *Everyman* have more than one symbolic dimension. Everyman's adversaries, allegorically considered, represent the various relationships and concepts expressed by their names. Morally, as the details of their speeches make clear, they stand for man's traditional enemies, the Seven Deadly Sins.[1] Ultimately and anagogically, they embody the evil of the universe that opposes the beatific vision Everyman hopes to attain in heaven.

Shaw stands at a great distance from the author of *Everyman,* both in time and in doctrine, but his development of character, except that it lacks multiple symbolic dimensions, is basically the same. In *Saint Joan,* for example, Shaw pits Joan against such adversaries as Cauchon and Warwick and invites the spectator to witness the conflicts arising from opposed attitudes and commitments. But in the action of depth, which in Shaw is the level

[1] See Thomas F. Van Laan, "*Everyman:* A Structural Analysis," *PMLA,* LXXVIII (1963), 465–475.

where ideas interact, a more abstract and universal drama takes place. As the fourth scene of the play insists, these characters are less important as individuals than as representatives of various institutions and types. Cauchon's every word shows that he acts in the interest of, and therefore represents, the medieval church; he wants to destroy Joan because she threatens the meaning and existence of the institution that has absorbed, both actually and dramatically, almost all his individuality. A comment by Warwick makes Cauchon's personification of the Church explicit and simultaneously opposes to it his own representation of Feudalism: "My lord: pray get The Church out of your head for a moment; and remember that there are temporal institutions in the world as well as spiritual ones. I and my peers represent the feudal aristocracy as you represent The Church. We are the temporal power." Despite their differences, both recognize Joan as the "common enemy," and in doing so they define the spirit she represents. To Warwick, Joan's behavior manifests "the protest of the individual soul against the interference of priest or peer between the private man and his God. I should call it Protestantism if I had to find a name for it." [2] On the literal level Joan may be a version of the historical Maid of Orléans, but on the more important level of the action of depth, she, like her adversaries, is a personification. She is Shaw's notion of the Saint, that supreme individualist who encompasses and transcends all temporary institutions and who by direct contact with his God—the Life Force —absorbs the courage and compulsion that enable him to introduce progress into the torpid affairs of his more conservative fellow men. The other characters in *Saint Joan* have less important roles, but all of them are as allegorically conceived as Cauchon, Warwick, and Joan. A good example is De Stogumber the chaplain, who represents the fanatic patriot and loathes Joan not because she is a nationalist but because she is French.

But the symbolic dimension of character is not always so general as the examples from *Everyman* and *Saint Joan* suggest.

[2] *Saint Joan* (Baltimore: Penguin Books, 1951), scene iv.

Shakespeare's John of Gaunt (in *Richard II*), whose nature demonstrates a similar dramatic technique, projects a more specific allegorical conception. Gaunt, like the characters in *Saint Joan*, has a double role. On the level of history as recorded fact, of events occurring in time, he is a particularized individual whose affiliations to the major characters play an important part in the plot. Gaunt is Richard's uncle, but Richard slights the relationship; to him Gaunt has more meaning as the possessor of "plate, coin, revenues, and moveables" (II.i.161), which he can use to finance his Irish wars. Thus, he prays for Gaunt's death (I.iii.59–64), and when Gaunt dies, he seizes his property. This act proves to be one of Richard's fatal mistakes, however, since Gaunt is also the father of Bolingbroke. The seizure prompts the son to seek his individual rights through force, and this counteraction, once begun, ends only with the deposition of Richard. But the conflict between king and usurper has also a larger significance, for it embodies a transformation from one kind of world to another, and this transformation provides the title character with a meaningful tragic setting.[3] It is in this dimension of the play that Gaunt's second, more symbolic role fulfills its purpose.

The England of this play, as Gaunt points out in a key speech, has undergone a change for the worse. In Gaunt's eyes, England, abstractly considered, symbolizes divine fertility:

> This royal throne of kings, this scept'red isle,
> This earth of majesty, this seat of Mars,
> This other Eden, demi-paradise.
>
> . . . . .
>
> This blessed plot, this earth, this realm, this England,
> This nurse, this teeming womb of royal kings [II.i.40–51].

[3] Cf. E. M. W. Tillyard, *Shakespeare's History Plays* (New York: Collier Books, 1962), p. 295. Tillyard quite rightly stresses the theme of transformation, which he sees as involving a shift from the "world of medieval refinement" to "the more familiar world of the present," but he errs in giving too little attention to the function of this transformation as the source of Richard's tragic suffering.

This realm, as Gaunt describes it, provided an appropriate setting for its preceding king, Edward III, whose own aura of divine fertility is witnessed by the fact that his seven sons "were as seven vials of his sacred blood, / Or seven fair branches springing from one root" (I.ii.12–13). But Gaunt's "demi-paradise" no longer exists; he makes his speech about England not to glorify it in its present state but to emphasize how much Richard has debased it. The England of Gaunt's vision, a "fortress built by Nature for herself / Against infection" (II.i.43–44), is now diseased. Under Richard's management the England that was once a "little world" (l. 45) has been "leas'd out . . . like to a tenement or pelting farm" (ll. 59–60). Similarly, Edward III is dead, replaced by his grandson, who, as York maintains in a speech contrasting Richard with his father, resembles his forebears only in physical appearance (ll. 176–183).

Gaunt's place in the dramatic situation, which is partly suggested by his glorification of England as it used to be, is even more fully indicated by another key speech. When the Duchess of Gloucester pleads with him to avenge Richard's murder of her husband, Gaunt disappoints her, even though the Duke was his own brother, and despite the threat to himself implicit in the Duke's fate:

> God's is the quarrel; for God's substitute,
> His deputy anointed in His sight,
> Hath caus'd his death; the which if wrongfully,
> Let heaven revenge; for I may never lift
> An angry arm against His minister [I.ii.37–41].

Gaunt's absolute allegiance to the principle that the king as God's representative on earth is answerable only to God demonstrates his adherence to the past, to a medieval way of life, for he upholds a doctrine that the present king abuses and that the future king must ignore if he is, in fact, ever to become king. Lacking Edward's magnificence, Richard makes a mockery of the medieval view of kingship. Although he insists on the sacred character of his office, he observes only the empty form; his neglect of his responsibilities violates the inner substance and renders it meaningless. Richard is therefore a fitting symbol of the England he has debased. Gaunt, preserving the traditional view of kingship and speaking in behalf of an older, dearer England, is one of the two remaining direct survivors of Edward III. He represents England as it was at the height of its glory.

On the level of history as meaningful pattern, then, Gaunt embodies England's heroic, idealized past, the England whose divine fertility was ensured by a great king serving as God's agent in fact as well as form. Because Gaunt possesses this allegorical dimension, his sickness and death carry more than literal significance. Gaunt himself, through the speech in which he puns on his name, associates his physical condition with England's debasement:

> O, how that name befits my composition!
> Old Gaunt, indeed; and gaunt in being old.
> Within me grief hath kept a tedious fast;
> And who abstains from meat that is not gaunt?
> For sleeping England long time have I watch'd;
> Watching breeds leanness, leanness is all gaunt
>
> [II.i.73–78].

Just as his sickness provides a powerful dramatic metaphor for England's decline, his death, occurring at the beginning of Act II, indicates the elimination from the present world of the last trace of its glorious past:

> This land of such dear souls, this dear dear land,
> Dear for her reputation through the world,
> Is now leas'd out—I die pronouncing it—
> Like to a tenement or pelting farm   [ll. 57–60].

But Gaunt's death marks a beginning as well as an end. If it means the passing of the old England, it also signifies the emergence of the new. For the announcement of Gaunt's death

(l. 147) is almost immediately followed by the first report of Bolingbroke's rebellion (l. 270). Two lines epitomize the point of transformation:

NORTHUMBERLAND. Well, lords, the Duke of Lancaster is dead.
Ross. And living too; for now his son is Duke [ll. 224–225].[4]

Richard II has two other characters whose functions reveal that the allegorical dimension of character need not always project a conceptual abstraction. The Duchess of Gloucester, who shares Act I, scene ii, with Gaunt, personifies no particular idea or institution. Her function in the action of depth derives from her expression of grief and her desire for vengeance. Her presence, which helps Shakespeare stress the horror of Richard's crimes, suggests how justly he deserves any punishment he may receive. The Duchess of Gloucester then disappears from the action, but Shakespeare parallels her one appearance early in the play with the brief introduction, toward the end, of another duchess, York's wife. The only other woman in the play except for Richard's queen and her attendant, she dominates Act V, scene ii. She also derives most of her importance from the feelings she expresses, but the effect she has on the audience differs considerably from that of the Duchess of Gloucester. Where the first duchess evoked condemnation of Richard, her successor demands pity for the now deposed monarch as she pictures "that sad stop . . . / Where rude misgoverned hands from windows' tops / Threw dust and rubbish on King Richard's head" (V.ii.4–6). Furthermore, in trying to stop her husband from revealing their son's treachery to the new king, Henry IV, she gives voice to a

----

[4] A glance at the probable sources of *Richard II* indicates how deliberately Shakespeare conceived Gaunt's symbolic dimension, for Shakespeare's duke is notably different from the "turbulent and self-seeking magnate" of Holinshed; see Peter Ure, Introduction to *King Richard II*, New Arden Shakespeare (Cambridge, Mass.: Harvard University Press, 1956), p. xxxiv. Similarly, Holinshed makes no mention of Gaunt's last illness, though Shakespeare may have taken it from Froissart.

fear that is as moving as the Duchess of Gloucester's grief, but now the source of the painful emotion is Bolingbroke rather than Richard. Since Shakespeare develops the transformation from one world to another in order to examine its ramifications, especially as they affect and expose the natures of the men involved in it, these women are extremely useful to him. Their historical identities and human individuality subserve a higher dimension consisting not of personified ideas but of projected attitudes.

Despite this distinction, Shakespeare's duchesses, like John of Gaunt, belong to the same breed as Shaw's Joan and the Fellowship of *Everyman*. Each of these has a double level of significance and therefore exemplifies the fictional character in general. Yet, obviously, Fellowship and Joan or Everyman and Gaunt are scarcely twins; neither pair would fit comfortably in the same play. The difference is not one of kind, however, but one of degree. It is not that some of these characters are allegorical and others literal; on the contrary, the difference lies in the relative emphasis given the two levels. In *Everyman* the immediate action, while definitely there, seems almost invisible; it leaves the impression of being a by-product of the allegory in the action of depth. Shaw, in contrast, ordinarily appears to be writing two plays, or a single play with two concurrent actions, the one a witty comedy, presenting unusual characters and cleverly inverting the standard theatrical clichés, the other a rational argument, sorting and evaluating various ideas and reaching intelligent conclusions. Shaw's characters live a full life in the immediate action, while those of *Everyman* do not; at the same time, however, as ideas and institutions they also live another equally full life in the action of depth. Their symbolic function does not, then, supersede their literal significance, but the importance of their symbolic function is clearly evident, especially in the way it often dictates the behavior and speech of the immediate action: Warwick's self-consciousness, for example, allows the allegory to show through rather ingenuously. Shakespeare's Gaunt differs from the typical Shavian character because he has much more integrity as a particularized individual. His allegorical dimension does not show through, as does Warwick's, because it cannot: it is exactly equivalent to what he is as a man; Gaunt symbolizes England's dying heroic past because his age, family ties, character, and physical condition all imply it. Furthermore, while in Shaw the allegorical dimension tends to dictate the nature of the character embodying it, in the kind of characterization exemplified by Gaunt the particularized individuality of the character dictates the nature of his allegorical dimension. This quality gives the Shakespearean character and those similarly constructed the capacity to evoke varying resonances as the action in which they are placed changes its nature. Such characters, though related to those of Shaw, are ultimately less allegorical than symbolic.

Shakespeare's handling of character is largely the product of a particular kind of thinking that he shares with his age: like most Renaissance artists, he perceives objects sacramentally. For Shakespeare, in other words, each object, while remaining a unique entity, simultaneously projects one or more of the entities to which it corresponds by virtue of its participation in a universal structure. The most familiar of these correspondences is the equivalence between the microcosm and the macrocosm, an equivalence that allows Shakespeare so to portray his heroes that they seem to embody all mankind. Similarly, this equivalence, and the convention of referring to the monarch by the name of his country, give his kings the power to symbolize the larger worlds they head. Lear provides the best example because his inner turmoil also represents the disorder in his family, the civil war in his state, and the storm in the universe, just as these in turn represent his own suffering. But all Shakespeare's monarchs epitomize in their individual conditions the circumstances of their kingdoms: hence Richard II's clinging to forms that no longer have inner meaning, Henry IV's physical ailments and sleeplessness, and Henry V's ultimate success in all enterprises.

Cleopatra is "Egypt" and therefore embodies in herself the realm of the imagination that Egypt symbolizes. Throughout most of *Hamlet*, Claudius is "the Dane"—and rightly so: the discrepancy in him between an external appearance of calm, order, and control and an inner reality filled with evil and agony matches exactly the nature of Denmark as defined by the imagery of a cancerous ulcer festering beneath a smooth, seemingly healthy surface.

Claudius is but one of many characters in *Hamlet*, however, and his embodiment of Denmark's condition acquires even more significance through its juxtaposition to the symbolic dimensions of the others. It would be inadequate, therefore, to stress the contribution of individual figures while ignoring the more meaningful fact that each character constitutes a single point in an elaborate pattern that includes all the characters in the same play. The design resulting from the grouping of characters is, indeed, one of the most important elements of a play's structure. Sometimes, as in much Restoration drama, this design forms the central substance of the play.[5] Elsewhere it is less crucial, but in any play this design, and its individual segments, establish basic constituents of the action of depth.

The most obvious effect of character grouping is the emphasis that results from simple opposition and contrast. The symbolic dimensions of such characters as Apollo, the Furies, Kroll, Rebecca, Joan, and her adversaries are meaningful in themselves, but their chief functions in defining the universes of their respective plays derive from the oppositions in which they participate. Despite the importance of John of Gaunt to *Richard II*, the main burden of the motif of transformation is carried by the contrast that opposes Richard's nature and fortune to those of Boling-

---

[5] This point about Restoration drama is expanded in Chapter 7. For the concept of character grouping I am indebted to Una Ellis-Fermor, *Shakespeare the Dramatist*, ed. Kenneth Muir (London: Methuen, 1961), pp. 79 ff.

broke. One of the primary themes in *Hamlet*, as its hero points out, is the duel between "mighty opposites" (V.ii.62). Claudius, in epitomizing Denmark, symbolizes the discrepancy between appearance and reality and between fact and value. Hamlet his opponent is the supersensitive individual who possesses enough insight to perceive the discrepancy and enough moral judgment to wish it abolished. Although Hamlet's perception merely bewilders him throughout most of the play, when he returns from the sea, his mind made up, the duel is virtually over. His statement, "This is I, / Hamlet the Dane" (V.i.251–252), announces the end of Claudius' reign. Since Hamlet's newfound certainty itself realigns fact and value, it suggests that Denmark has *already* regained the healthy condition that will be finally affirmed by the succession of Fortinbras. Therefore it is Hamlet who now fittingly becomes "the Dane," the microcosm of the state.

Character grouping also involves other kinds of meaningful relationships. The end of Shaw's *Major Barbara*, which presents a coalition of Barbara, Cusins, and Undershaft, or spirit, intellect, and practical will, stresses harmony rather than opposition, though this coalition obviously rejects the faulty approaches to reality represented by such characters as Lady Britomart and Stephen. The relationship between Brendel and Rosmer suggests yet another result of character grouping, the effect of resemblance. Before Brendel's entrance in Act I, Ibsen has already used Rosmer's involvement with both Kroll and Rebecca to suggest his position at the center of the conflict between tradition and revolt. Brendel's arrival gives Ibsen the opportunity to define his hero's emancipation more precisely. Brendel had been Rosmer's tutor; it was he, as Kroll reminds Rosmer, who "went and crammed your head full of revolutionary ideas" (p. 135). During his visit Brendel unconsciously renews the old relationship, this time teaching by example rather than precept, for Brendel's determination to participate in the radical movement finally prompts Rosmer to confess freely his emancipation from family tradition. The dedication of both Brendel and Rosmer to the same cause and the suggestion that one has influenced the ideas of the other establish a close resemblance between the two, at least insofar as revolt is concerned. But Brendel, tramp and sponger, former member of a traveling theater company and former inmate of a workhouse, is an irresponsible buffoon. His contribution to the great cause can consist only of the "golden dreams" that "sank down" over him and "intoxicated" him. His store contains only the "new, giddy far-reaching thoughts" that uplifted him on "soaring wings," thoughts that he has turned into "poems, visions, and pictures—only in the rough outlines, you understand" (p. 138). Brendel thus stands to Rosmer as an ironic caricature of his emancipation. And when, a few minutes later, Rosmer tells Kroll that "a new summer" and "a new youthful outlook" have come into his mind (p. 142), he cannot help sounding like a feeble echo of his former tutor. For once the spectators must heed Kroll when he quietly underlines Ibsen's point: "You are a dreamer, Rosmer" (p. 143).

In those designs that embrace almost every character of a play, the resulting effect depends less on individual symbolic dimensions or pairings than on the cumulative force of a whole series of character relationships. A large design of this sort, which like the Brendel-Rosmer relationship utilizes the principle of resemblance, helps Shakespeare establish one of his major evaluations of Hamlet's Denmark.

After the first scene dramatizes the imbalance disturbing the universe, the state, and the individual, Shakespeare provides a close examination of the state and some of its leading citizens. The result is a more precise definition of the pervading imbalance. Scene ii opens with a powerful visual symbol of alienation: Hamlet separates himself from the rest of the court by his costume and presumably by his placement as well. Shakespeare adds to this initial impression by stressing the presence of alienation in relationships that would ideally exclude it. Although there is obvious harmony between the king and his court, between Polonius and Laertes, and between Claudius and Gertrude, the major focus of the scene is the tension between Hamlet and his mother and—with even greater emphasis—Hamlet's quite evident hostility toward the man who is his uncle, his stepfather, and his king. In the following soliloquy, Hamlet makes even more explicit the agony that is the current result of his relationship with his mother, and his bitter tone in speaking of her reveals more fully the alienation that divides them.

Up to this point Shakespeare has dwelt on the existence of tension in what should be harmonious human relationships. The conclusion of Hamlet's soliloquy introduces a new aspect of the as yet scarcely perceptible design. To Hamlet the marriage of Gertrude and Claudius is "incestuous"—partly because of his profound emotion but also because, as he perceives it, this marriage differs so drastically from the pure relationship between old Hamlet and Gertrude which it has replaced. The new marriage therefore represents to Hamlet a corrupted version of a potentially ideal human union. The presentation of this motif helps ensure the relevance of the following scene, which presents a carefully delineated family portrait. The emphasis here is not on alienation but on indifference, for there is little evidence of any sincere affection linking Ophelia, Laertes, and Polonius. Both the brother and the father regard Ophelia less as a human being deserving their love than as an ignorant pupil who needs to be lectured, and Polonius sees his son in the same light. Both the brother and the father do their best to put an end to another kind of intimate human relationship, that which Hamlet and Ophelia would share as lovers. Significantly, in the central speech of this scene, a speech emphasizing distrust, Polonius warns Laertes against close human ties in general.

The existence of this scene, which stresses familial and other relationships, suggests that Shakespeare is concerned with his characters not only as individuals but also as sons, mothers, uncles, fathers, lovers, and so forth. The most important expression of this pattern is the Ghost's revelation of Claudius' crime, for this murder of a king is also the murder of a brother and "hath the primal eldest curse upon't" (III.iii.37); it presents in their extreme forms both the alienation and the corruption that scar most of the human relationships dramatized within the play. But Shakespeare has not yet completed his over-all design. Act II, scene i, provides further evidence of debasement of the bond between father and son, and in sending Reynaldo to spy on Laertes, Polonius extends the corruption to include one more basic human relationship, that between servant and master. In the second scene of this act, two more spies appear; these are, of course, Rosencrantz and Guildenstern, former friends of Hamlet who have decided to sacrifice friendship to self-interest.

Although Shakespeare ordinarily gives a great deal of attention to intimate human associations, none of his other plays introduces so many different types. Those individuals who are not close kin are attached to each other, at least formally, by such bonds as marriage, love, friendship, or allegiance. This wide spectrum results in a complex design that acquires meaning as constant repetition produces ever increasing clarity. Each of the characters is more impressive in isolation as a distinct individual than as an embodiment of such qualities as fatherhood or friendship, but as character follows character and each reveals his involvement in a corrupted version of an essential human tie, the abstract pattern of resemblance ultimately assumes independent dramatic validity.

Moreover, on several occasions this implicit structural design becomes explicit in the language of the play. Claudius opens Act I, scene ii, in which the implicit pattern originates, by speaking of "our dear brother's death." Subsequently, for such a relatively brief episode (128 lines), there occur an amazing number of references to sisters, brothers, fathers, uncles, nephews, cousins, sons, and mothers. Some of these references already suggest the corruption that further action will emphasize. Claudius addresses

Gertrude as "our sometime sister, now our queen" (l. 8), a phrase that underscores the instability of relationships when transformation occurs so easily. Hamlet's punning remark to Claudius—"I am too much in the sun" (l. 67)—stresses both the falsity of the relationship that has been forced upon him and his refusal to fulfill its obligations. This verbal emphasis continues well beyond Act I, scene ii. In speaking to Rosencrantz and Guildenstern, for example, Hamlet shows his fascination with the strange hybrids of "uncle-father and aunt-mother" (II.ii.371–372), and the speech reveals his deep concern about the corruption that destroys familial relationships. But the real culmination of this verbal pattern occurs when Hamlet, after failing to re-establish an ideal association with Gertrude, bitterly salutes Claudius as "dear mother" (IV.iii.49).

This decisive thrust suddenly lays bare the whole point of the structural design—that human relationships are essentially meaningless in Hamlet's world. All those that the play presents—or almost all, for Horatio's fidelity is a norm that highlights the abundant failures—reveal tension or corruption or are deliberately suppressed. Through this structural design embracing almost every character in the play, Shakespeare exposes Denmark as an utterly chaotic and disordered land in which, evidently, human ties have no hope of prospering.

The Scene

In drama a scene is any narrative unit that, having its own beginning, middle, and end, stands out in the over-all pattern of action as a self-contained sequence of incidents. Frequently the limits of a particular scene are determined by a change of locale or by the temporary clearing of the stage. But this is not always the case. In Greek tragedy those narrative units that precede the entrance of the chorus or that occur between choral odes normally constitute separate scenes. In later drama a shift in focus often indicates a new scene; Act I, scene ii, of *Hamlet*, for example, consists of three closely related yet nevertheless distinct scenes: the gathering of the full court, Hamlet's soliloquy, and the conversation of Hamlet, Horatio, and Marcellus. Similarly, an event that noticeably alters the course of the dramatic development, such as the arrival of Ulrik Brendel, marks the beginning of a new scene. In fact, though the events that make up the first act of *Rosmersholm* follow one upon another without a pause or a shift in location, this act really contains six scenes. In the "prologue" Madam Helseth and Rebecca introduce most of the significant motifs of the play and anticipate the arrivals of both Kroll and Rosmer. The second scene begins with the exit of Madam Helseth and the entrance of Kroll; it focuses on the relationship between Kroll and Rebecca and suggests their representation of the opposites in the conflict between tradition and revolt. When Rosmer enters, a new scene begins, one in which Kroll and Rebecca battle for possession of Rosmer's soul. The fourth scene consists of the interruption in which Brendel demonstrates *his* willingness to place a contribution on the altar of emancipation, and the fifth then presents Rosmer's response as, in colloquy with Kroll, he confesses his own altered views. Finally, the sixth scene, beginning with the return of Rebecca, acts as an epilogue that examines the reactions evoked by Rosmer's announcement and suggests new difficulties to follow.

The opening scene of *Hamlet* fully indicates the importance of the individual episode as a structural unit, for as the analysis in the preceding chapter shows, this scene possesses a double dimension. On one hand, its sequence of unique incidents tells the specific story of what happened when Horatio visited the guard platform at Elsinore to investigate reports that a ghost had been seen there. On the other hand, this same sequence of incidents and the way Shakespeare has fashioned it suggest a vast imbalance permeating the entire universe but centering on Denmark. This scene, in other words, is not only literal narrative but also metaphor. Nor is the opening of *Hamlet* unusual: every scene in drama, like each character and like a play as a whole, has both a literal significance and a symbolic dimension, though the major contribution of a scene's metaphoric content lies in the implications that arise from its relationships to other parts of the play. This structural effect is most easily perceived in the relationship between two contiguous scenes, as is evident, for example, in the way that the impact of the first scene of *Hamlet* completely alters the apparent significance of the second.

Except for the visual symbol of alienation, scene ii begins with a persuasive impression of order and control. Claudius speaks at great length, quietly, calmly, and formally; the sense of order rings out in every element of his speech, from the fluid rhythm to the elaborate sentences with their carefully arranged balances and antitheses. The speech as a whole is deliberately patterned. It consists of three sections, one on the orderly disposition of the state following the death of the "dear brother," one on the threat posed by Fortinbras, and one celebrating the quick competence with which Claudius has disposed of this threat. Each section is brought to a formal conclusion (ll. 16, 25, 41), and each new section is initiated by a transitional "Now" (ll. 17, 26). The general impression abundantly suggests Claudius' capable management of the affairs of state. This impression continues when Claudius turns to domestic business and the familiar transition echoes once more: "And now, Laertes" (l. 42). Not until the next such transition—"But now, my cousin Hamlet, and my son" (l. 64)—does the disharmony established by visual effect interrupt the verbal harmony of the scene. With Hamlet's bitter reply his recalcitrance usurps the major point of focus. As seen from the perspective provided by Claudius' speeches, Hamlet's behavior looks like a willful and culpable refusal to adapt himself to a healthy order that everyone else gladly accepts. If there is any disorder in Denmark, it all stems, evidently, from Hamlet's unjustified revolt.

But for the spectator who has witnessed the opening scene of the play, this conclusion is impossible. No matter how much Claudius may wish to impress it on his court, Shakespeare has insulated the audience from it by establishing a prior perspective. As the first scene insists, Denmark and disorder are synonymous; the imbalance is ubiquitous, even cosmic. As a result, Claudius' carefully controlled speech rings very strangely indeed, especially when he scoffs at the possibility that to Fortinbras "our state" might seem "disjoint and out of frame." Since the disorder is inescapably real, either Claudius is unaware of it, or he deliberately conceals its existence: the man who would present himself as remarkably competent seems on the contrary either grossly insensitive or suspiciously deceptive. The same prior perspective amply justifies Hamlet's attitudes, for in contrast to the other characters, who so patently ignore the existing disorder, he perceives nothing else, and it is not until his soliloquy, with its heavy spondees, jerky phrasing, exclamations, and outcries, that the discordant rhythms characteristic of the opening scene are heard within this new setting. Hamlet's constant, deeply felt sense of disorder corroborates his claim that he knows not "seems" (l. 76); it is Claudius and the rest of his court who ignore reality and subscribe to appearance. While they expose their superficiality, Hamlet alone reveals any capacity to penetrate beneath the surface and see the rottenness at Denmark's heart. Hamlet does not yet understand the full nature of the disorder he has perceived, he is confused by his agony, and he may be unnecessarily antagonistic. But because of the juxtaposition of these two scenes the spectators know that he is the only member of Claudius' court whose voice has any ultimate authority.

Scene as Microcosmic Reflector. The complex relationship between an individual scene and its context makes possible a wide variety of structural effects. In one of the more unusual of these effects the scene serves as a microcosmic reflection of the entire play in which it occurs. Marlowe, for example, has epitomized most of the ramifications of *Doctor Faustus* in the few lines that record Faustus' signing of the pact with Mephostophilis (II.i.29–80).[6] The irony that permeates this scene begins almost at once. Faustus knows he is binding his soul "that at some certain day / Great Lucifer may claim it as his own" (ll. 48–49), yet he believes that this act will make him "as great as Lucifer" (l. 50); moreover, in the Christian context of this play, to be as great as Lucifer is to inherit eternal pain. Before he can sign, however, Faustus' blood congeals. This detail suggests on a psychological level the hesitancy that Faustus also expresses in his soliloquies and in his debates with the good and evil angels, but on a metaphysical level the congealing of the blood represents God's intervention as He gives Faustus a last opportunity to escape his doom. As a result, the fire that Mephostophilis fetches in order to make the blood flow freely is symbolic of the hell that has already won Faustus' soul; through the fire's efficacy Faustus can indeed "make an end immediately" (l. 70). The phrase that signifies this twofold ending—"*Consummatum est*"—echoes precisely the last words of Christ, the savior Faustus has hereby abjured. Consciously a sign of revolt, the phrase ironically emphasizes his damnation, for Faustus uses it to surrender to the devil one of the prizes that Christ had wrested from him when speaking these words originally. Faustus, who will not "fly" from the danger (l. 79), can never fly again in any sense, as he discovers when at the end of his twenty-four years he vainly desires to "leap up to my God!" (V.ii.149). But the major irony of the scene emerges from Mephostophilis' asides: "What will not I do to obtain his soul!" (II.i.71); "I'll fetch him somewhat to delight his mind" (l. 80). These asides reveal conclusively that the man who sought conscious control of his own destiny has merely been hoodwinked by the devil's empty shows. Appropriately, the scene ends with the presentation to Faustus of the first of the utterly

[6] Citations are to the text established by W. W. Greg, as reprinted in *The Genius of the Early English Theater,* ed. Sylvan Barnet *et al.* (New York: New American Library, 1962).

worthless gifts he has won by bartering his soul: "Enter devils giving crowns and rich apparel to Faustus: they dance and then depart."

This scene provides a condensation of the whole tragedy of Faustus. Here, as throughout, the desire to be omniscient mixes incongruously with the perverse refusal to see the truth clearly delineated before his eyes; here, as in the entire movement of the action, the urge for omnipotence brings him only eternal bondage. Above all, this scene, as an epitome of its play, stresses what might be called the tragic absurdity of the human condition: that man, who has the capacity to conceive of and desire godhead, can never escape his human limitations. And because all this is conveyed by the scene in which Faustus signs his pact, the spectators are made to see with unusual clarity the indissoluble link that connects an act to its ultimate consequences.

1 Henry IV contains a famous scene in which Hal, pretending to be his father, the king of England, vows to banish Falstaff, who, in the role of the prince, fruitlessly begs to keep "plump Jack" as a permanent member of "Harry's company" (II.iv.460–464). Because this episode portrays a rejection of *Falstaff*, it obviously foreshadows the ending of *2 Henry IV*; but the real object of banishment here, since Falstaff is taking the role of the prince, is the *fusion* of Hal and Falstaff, and therefore the vow epitomizes an operation that goes on continuously throughout both parts of the play. This scene, then, fulfills a function much like that of the pact-signing in *Doctor Faustus*. The two scenes, furthermore, have another characteristic in common. Both of them have special importance in the narrative lines of their respective plays, and therefore they command close attention: their peculiar contributions are not likely to be missed. At the same time, however, each of them epitomizes an action that is not yet complete; its full significance can become clear only in retrospect, when the audience has seen the conclusion of the entire play. A microcosmic reflector of this sort tends to have an anticipatory function: it prepares the audience to understand more fully the whole design of which it constitutes a single part.

A slightly different use of this structural device appears in the *Oresteia*. Aeschylus makes his microcosmic reflector, the highly theatrical trial scene (*Eumenides*, ll. 566-753), immediately significant by placing it near the end of the trilogy, where it both summarizes and culminates the long sequence of events that it brings to a close. This episode easily enlists the full involvement of the spectators. Its theatrical effectiveness—which the long history of trial scenes in drama attests to—still holds any audience in its grip, but for the Athenians who first saw it, it had an additional value: it dramatized the kind of *agon*—their word for lawsuit—they could readily comprehend. The Greek citizens, who personally defended their own rights, had almost all participated in similar trials; for them this scene would have the quality of familiar ritual, and Aeschylus reinforces the effect through such details as Athene's address to the herald, the trumpet call, the orderly placing of the principals, the formal speeches, and the ritualistic voting. In effect, the members of the theatrical audience became spectators at a real trial.

This participation ensured their thorough response to the thematic implications that the metaphorical function of the scene defines so sharply. By its very nature the trial calls attention to the central question of the trilogy, the problem of justice. As a contest between two diametrically opposed points of view, the trial schematizes the sense of conflict that Aeschylus has established throughout, principally in the incongruity between the desire for justice and the continued injustices perpetrated by the code of retribution. Furthermore, this trial, ostensibly an attempt to determine Orestes' guilt or innocence, involves much more than the fate of a single individual. Apollo and the Furies become the opposing advocates, and this opposition indicates that the defendant's suffering has cosmic as well as human relevance. In the actual conduct of the trial, in fact, the importance of Orestes' fate recedes before a more vital issue, the evidently irreconcilable antagonism between the old gods, represented by the Furies, and the new dynasty of Zeus, so vigorously defended by Apollo. The change in focus confirms an assumption previously voiced by the *Agamemnon* chorus, that the universe as a whole still awaits its final ordering: Orestes' suffering, ultimately, merely reflects the greater disorder in the heavens, and both wounds must be healed together. As the trial further suggests, the final dispensation will affect not only the individual and the gods but one more plane of existence as well, for this trial inaugurates a new source of earthly justice, the Areopagus, whose twelve jurors represent not the individual but the state—man as a collective group. Through these jurors Aeschylus at last reveals the full relevance of the impassioned involvement that has been shown throughout the trilogy by such peripheral figures as the Watchman, the Argive Elders, the captured slave women, and the nurse Cilissa.

In addition to summarizing the effect of all that has preceded it, the trial scene also epitomizes the whole trilogy by suggesting an inevitable outcome. The individual, Aeschylus implies, can overcome his suffering only by submitting himself to a higher wisdom. The shift in focus from Orestes to the gods de-emphasizes the importance of the individual and therefore suggests a logical conclusion to the prolonged examination of the utterly destructive futility of personal revenge. The individual is further de-emphasized by Athene's creation of the Areopagus: from this moment on, the state will decide all those legal issues that hitherto have depended on individual initiative. Yet above the state and its court stands an even higher power, the divinity that provides sanctions for all human institutions. At the end of the trial the state too is de-emphasized, for the voting produces an impasse. Only Athene, divine wisdom herself, can make the ultimate decision, because absolute justice depends, finally, on divine order. In breaking this impasse, Athene triumphantly closes a richly evocative scene that in its whole effect simultaneously recapitulates and resolves the manifold issues and ramifications of the entire trilogy.

Scene-to-Scene Relationships. The scene that can clarify basic implications by epitomizing a complete action is obviously rare. More commonly, meaning arises from the relationship one scene acquires to another, whether through immediate juxtaposition, as with the first two scenes of *Hamlet,* or through some similarity that prompts the spectators to associate episodes from different parts of the same play. These structural effects utilize the basic principles of analogy, the principles of likeness in difference and difference in likeness.

The third act of *1 Henry IV* demonstrates the result of intrinsic likeness in a series of successive but apparently unrelated episodes. Its first scene presents the quarrel between Hotspur and Glendower and the relatively ineffectual attempts of Mortimer and Worcester to calm the antagonists. The second scene enacts the reconciliation between the king and his son. The third and final scene of the act contains several events that center on Falstaff: his badgering of Bardolph, his quarrel with Mistress Quickly, and his falling-out with Hal, whom he accuses of picking his pocket. Each of these scenes utilizes different material, different locales, and—except for Hal's presence in scenes ii and iii—different characters. Yet each focuses upon the same motif —harmony—and through their contiguity the three scenes reflect one upon another to summarize the entire play. The disharmony in the rebel camp heightens the contrasting harmony between king and prince and indicates that the rebels cannot win: they will be crushed by a united defense. Hal's congenial reconciliation with his father differs sharply from his subsequent meeting with Falstaff, who tries to dominate him but fails, with the failure all the more evident because of its juxtaposition to Falstaff's victories over Bardolph and Mistress Quickly. This final scene of the act evokes the same sense of discord as the first, and therefore it suggests Hal's ultimate defeat not only of the rebels but of Falstaff as well. In short, the act's contrast between harmony and disharmony implies both the victory at Shrewsbury and the rejection of Falstaff that concludes *2 Henry IV*.

The third act of *Hamlet* has much more external unity. All four of its scenes center on the play's hero, and all occur within the walls of Elsinore; scenes ii through iv even shape a recognizably continuous movement. But in each of these four scenes Hamlet—who quarrels with Ophelia, produces a play, avoids killing Claudius, and lectures his mother—is involved in actions with seemingly little relation to those he performs in the other three, and each scene creates its own distinctive mood: hence the superficial differences. Through their juxtaposition, however, these four scenes reveal a unity more basic than that of plot. Each scene establishes an implication that in itself has little significance, but since these implications occur in rapid succession, they accumulate to form a major assessment of Hamlet's present situation.

The first scene of the act develops the image of alienation by pitting the isolated Hamlet against the hostile world that surrounds him. In this scene Hamlet has no one with whom he can find rapport, with whom he can share his feelings. All the other characters—Claudius, Polonius, Rosencrantz, Guildenstern, Gertrude, and Ophelia—are engaged, willingly or not, in a plot to spy on him. His soliloquy especially emphasizes the alienation, for in a rather unusual dramatic effect he delivers it while Ophelia is in full view of the audience and while Claudius and Polonius wait just behind the arras: even in the midst of the others, then, Hamlet is profoundly alone. The content of the soliloquy makes explicit Hamlet's sense of a hostile world. Opposing him he perceives "the slings and arrows of outrageous fortune," "a sea of troubles," and "the heart-ache and the thousand natural shocks / That flesh is heir to." Since the oppressions he catalogues (ll. 70–74) are all general, and since few of them apply directly to his own situation, he seems to have moved beyond personal agony to a more settled conviction about the "calamity" of "weary life." The way in which this soliloquy recalls, with one significant alteration, his first soliloquy, in Act I, scene ii, confirms the implication. There also he contemplated suicide, but then he easily suppressed the thought with the assurance that "the Everlasting had . . . fix'd / His canon 'gainst self-slaughter" (I.ii.131–132). Now the only consideration that makes him hesitate is "the dread of something after death." Nor does he here cry out to God as he had on the earlier occasion. Hamlet evidently faces, therefore, a universe in which he can no longer find any traces of divinity.

This attitude contradicts the zestful sense of future accomplishment with which Hamlet, anticipating the exposure of Claudius, concluded Act II. But in the general context of the play it is not surprising. It is a natural consequence of a sensitive mind confronting a world like that of Denmark, where, as the preceding scenes have already established, utter corruption nullifies those primary human relationships that form the basis of personal, social, and political order. Hamlet's conversation with Ophelia reveals how completely he has accepted the attitude implied by his soliloquy. His treatment of her embodies his response to the whole world that has alienated him, for in lashing out against her, he really attacks his mother, Claudius, Polonius, and himself as well. He cynically insists that "the power of beauty will sooner transform honesty from what it is to a bawd than the force of honesty can translate beauty into his likeness" (III.i.111–113), and thus he reveals his concern with the distortion of human values. Value has become so ambiguous for him that "nunnery" can interchangeably denote either a religious institution or a brothel. Reality itself no longer possesses fixed contours in his eyes: "I did love you once" (l. 115) alters without transition to "I loved you not" (l. 119). Existence has lost all meaning, and Hamlet asks, "What should such fellows as I do crawling between earth and heaven?" (l. 128). In this scene as a whole Hamlet looks more deeply into the universe than ever before, and his reward is a vision of chaos from which God and the stability He imposes have disappeared.

The beginning of Act III, scene ii, in which Hamlet advises the players, presents a different mood, somewhat reminiscent of that which Hamlet felt at the end of the second act. Here he speaks with certainty and without the agony of the preceding scene. His words are calm as he lectures his audience on the proper way of performing "The Murder of Gonzago" and all plays, and as he offers his opinions about the use of theatrical art. But the new mood has close links with that of Act III, scene i: Hamlet has not forgotten his glimpse of void; he now acts on it. The advice to the players is an attempt, however minor, to impose some kind of order somewhere. This prologue to the major activity of scene ii suggests the real function of Hamlet's play-within-the-play. Although he has not written it, he has chosen it and is, in effect, its producer; like Shakespeare himself, Hamlet uses art as an exploration of reality, as a means of discovering order in the midst of apparent chaos. And if the play proves successful, he will have filled the void around him with at least one absolute, the guilt of Claudius. Hamlet's behavior throughout this scene, as he comments upon and interprets the players' work, continually evokes his seeming desire to translate reality into art so that he may stand outside it, controlling it with a steady hand. As he tells Ophelia, "I could interpret between you and your love, if I could see the puppets dallying" (ll. 240–242).

Once the play-within-the-play has shown Hamlet his ability to exert some measure of control over his surroundings, his attempt to impose order becomes more cosmic and more eschatological. He spares Claudius in the next scene because mere earthly revenge no longer satisfies him. He wishes instead to catch Claudius engaged in

> some act
> That has no relish of salvation in't—
>
> .   .   .   .   .

> . . . that his heels may kick at heaven,
> And that his soul may be as damn'd and black
> As hell, whereto it goes [III.iii.91–95].

This clearly expressed intention of determining Claudius' damnation accentuates the major impression of the following scene, in which Hamlet bends all his efforts to making his mother realize the evil he sees in her soul. When he bids her "for love of grace" (III.iv.144) to confess herself to heaven, "repent what's past; avoid what is to come" (ll. 149–150), his purpose is made obvious. She must "throw away the worser part" of her heart "and live the purer with the other half" (ll. 157–158). Hamlet wishes, in other words, to purge his mother of sin so that her soul may be saved.

The juxtaposition of these two scenes heightens the significance of each; as a result, Hamlet's desire to control the destinies of the two characters with whom he is most involved takes on major importance. In the scene with his mother the purpose of this heightening becomes explicit. When Hamlet kills Polonius, he mockingly advises the corpse, "Take thy fortune" (III.iv.32). Hamlet, who saw himself as fortune's victim at the beginning of the act, now behaves instead as if he were its controlling agent. For Hamlet has changed. He absolves himself of killing Polonius by saying that heaven has been pleased to make him its "scourge and minister" (l. 175), and this speech completes the thread of meaning that has been woven throughout the act by the juxtaposition of separate scenes. Hamlet has reacted to the recognition of chaos by playing God; unable to find any order in the universe around him, he has sought to restore order by arrogating to himself the function of deity.

This thread of meaning does not exist in a vacuum, however, and several major effects of these last two scenes throw an ironic light on Hamlet's attempt to fill the void left by the disappearance of God. His arrogant assumption that he can determine Claudius' destiny contrasts rather pointedly with his inability to perceive that Claudius by no means enjoys the state of grace implied by his kneeling position: the god is only mortal after all; like any human being he can be deceived by appearance. While enacting his new role, Hamlet thoughtlessly kills Polonius, and this connection between mood and deed suggests that the one has caused the other. The entrance of the Ghost later in the scene reminds the spectators that Hamlet, who would control, is himself controlled to some extent by an external force. Finally, Hamlet's ambivalence about himself is a major factor in the irony. Unable to determine finally how he should view his killing of Polonius, he vacillates between glee and repentance, and even when insisting that heaven has given him his mandate, he assumes that it is punishment as well as justification (III.iv.172–174). These qualifications complete the central meaning delineated by the accumulation of scenes in Act III. In seeking to replace God, Hamlet undertakes the impossible; moreover, in doing so, he performs his most vicious and most fatal act.

The linking of successive scenes by the principle of likeness in apparent difference is also a major structural device of plays in which the separate scenes are less clearly demarcated than in Shakespearean drama. Act II of *Rosmersholm* presents a continuous development within a single setting. It has even greater narrative unity than the third act of *Hamlet*, yet it works in much the same way as the examples from Shakespeare. Despite its continuity this act really consists of a brief prologue followed by three distinct scenes, in which Rosmer talks first with Kroll, then with Mortensgaard, and finally with Rebecca. In each case the conversation takes its theme from Rosmer's particular relationship to the character who shares the scene with him. Here, far more than in *1 Henry IV*, or even in *Hamlet*, the significance of the sequence depends on the narrative progression from one scene to another. But that progression becomes meaningful only through the intrinsic similarity that makes each of the separate scenes a variation on the same pattern. The focus throughout is on Rosmer, and the similarity of pattern that links the successive episodes defines with precision one result of his emancipation.

In the prologue to this act Rebecca and Rosmer discuss the main event of the preceding evening. By confessing his altered beliefs Rosmer has seriously strained the relationship with his old friend Kroll, but the clearing of his conscience has made him more "light-hearted" than he has been able to feel for a long time (p. 148). Furthermore, he cheerfully believes that a single meeting with Kroll will restore the harmony that once united them. With these emphases, the prologue presents the condition in which Rosmer begins the act. His feeling of well-being, confidence, and security forms the high point that is to be undermined by the scenes that follow.

In the first of these Kroll soon lets it be known that he does not share Rosmer's optimism. He lays down without equivocation the conditions that Rosmer must observe if he plans to remain in peace. Since Rosmer will not join Kroll and his friends in their great cause, he must in any case "hush up the change of mind—the distressing apostasy" that, as Kroll puts it, Rebecca has led him into (p. 157). But Rosmer cannot keep silent; to do so, he feels, would cripple him. Therefore Kroll threatens him with the repercussions of a "violent storm" (p. 158), and when Mortensgaard arrives, Kroll, assuming that Rosmer has summoned him, angrily leaves, promising that "now it means a war with knives": "We shall see, however, if we can't make you harmless" (p. 159). Kroll's exit epitomizes their complete break. Rosmer has lost a close friend and part of his security.

The second scene offers, in Mortensgaard, a possible replacement. Although he has not been Rosmer's friend, Ibsen has already established his importance in the act's prologue. There, in response to Rosmer's desire to avoid Mortensgaard, Rebecca had pointed out how much he might be needed: "You can't be really secure now—since this has come between you and your friends" (p. 149). The loss of Kroll makes the necessity for Mortensgaard all the more acute, and he should have much to offer. Since the two are united in their liberal ideas, Mortensgaard should be able to give Rosmer the moral support he seems to require as well as specific aid in implementing his scheme to ennoble mankind. But Mortensgaard will not fill the void left by the loss of Kroll. He welcomes Rosmer as an ally, but he is disturbed by Rosmer's separation from the church, and he soon convinces Rosmer that he will have nothing to do with him if he openly confesses it. Like Kroll, Mortensgaard wants to use Rosmer for his own purposes and will help him only if Rosmer has already sacrificed his personal integrity. This scene contains no open break, but it does reveal that a possible avenue of support is in reality a blind alley. Mortensgaard's exit, in which he announces his intention of printing only as much of Rosmer's emancipation as "the people have occasion to know" (p. 166), is therefore as expressive as Kroll's.

The losses represented by these exits are accompanied by a further loss of a different sort. The information that Kroll and Mortensgaard have brought about Beata convinces Rosmer that he has somehow helped cause her death. As a result, he can no longer feel the contentment that his sense of innocence gave him. Ibsen stresses his new state of mind by having Rebecca recall how happy he had become before the events of the present act: "You should have begun to live by now, Rosmer. You *had* already begun. You had gotten completely free—on all sides. You felt so joyful and so light" (p. 169). But Rosmer interrupts her. The painful incongruity of her remarks merely increases his despair: "I will never again be able to revel in that which makes life such a wonderful delight to live . . . quiet, joyful guiltlessness" (p. 170).

Deserted by his friends, betrayed by those with whose cause he sympathizes, and shaken in his own self-confidence, Rosmer at last turns to the only support now left him—Rebecca. Her supreme value for him at this moment is unmistakable: "I don't think I've ever before needed you this much" (p. 167). This speech sums up the seriousness of the losses he has already sustained, and since Rebecca is all that remains, it looks forward to an even more consequential loss. For Rebecca also disappoints him. In this final scene of the act Rosmer's desperation is evident in the intensity with which he pursues their relationship. Kroll and Mortensgaard came to him, but now Rosmer takes the initiative. His marriage proposal is virtually a plea for help (p. 172). But even here he meets nothing but frustration: Rebecca not only refuses him; she also vows that if he repeats his request she will leave him forever. The significance of her response is made visual by her exit, which repeats those of Kroll and Mortensgaard. Rebecca, too, has deserted him; Rosmer, "staring like a lost soul" (stage direction, p. 173), can only cry out, "What—is —this?"

Each of these scenes begins with expectation and ends in disillusionment. Each brings Rosmer a significant loss. The similarity of pattern links the three scenes in such a way that they trace the decline of his fortunes. Throughout the act he is relentlessly stripped of those forces, both external and internal, which have given him the stability and security he needs to face the world. But the sequence also establishes an additional effect. Since Rebecca duplicates the actions of Kroll and Mortensgaard in their desertion of Rosmer, she seems to resemble them as well in a further respect. Both men have shown interest in Rosmer only as long as they believed they could use him for their own purposes. Rebecca has never as yet revealed such self-interest in her relationship with him, but by placing her desertion in a pattern that links her to Kroll and Mortensgaard, Ibsen suggests that she, too, possesses some ulterior motive. This implication, which heightens the audience's already developing suspicion of her, joins with her mysterious refusal of marriage in bringing the act to its highly charged conclusion.

In utilizing the reverse effect of analogy—the principle of

difference in likeness—a dramatist presents a speech, event, or entire scene which parallels in some way an earlier moment in his play. The parallel reminds the spectators of this earlier moment, and their memory of it becomes superimposed on their view of the present action. The value of this device lies in the great emphasis it lends to the most meaningful aspect of the relationship, the differences that distinguish the new moment from its predecessor. As has been suggested, this device can be used to establish the significance of individual speeches and brief actions—or even single words; but its most impressive effects emerge from the paralleling of whole scenes.

One instance of this device appears in the *Oresteia*, in the deliberate parallel between the murder of Agamemnon and the murder of Clytaemestra. In addition to the natural similarity that makes two murders alike, several specific effects cause the second scene to closely resemble the first. Each scene forms the climax of its respective play, the *Agamemnon* or *The Libation Bearers*. Each occurs offstage—conventional in Greek tragedy—and is revealed to the spectators when the doors of the palace open, disclosing the slaughtered victims. Standing over the corpses, each murderer—first Clytaemestra, then Orestes—holds a robe aloft and delivers a long speech of justification to an audience consisting of the chorus. During his defense Orestes heightens the association between the two murder scenes by making specific reference to the first. The point of the parallelism lies, of course, in the intrinsic differences that prevent Orestes' act from merely repeating Clytaemestra's. Orestes' motives are pure, while those of Clytaemestra and Aegisthus were not: he acts only to avenge his father and in obedience to a command by Apollo. Clytaemestra had also carried out the will of the gods, but she was unaware of this aspect of her crime, and Aeschylus further de-emphasized it by keeping it a matter of implication; Orestes, in contrast, has clearly subordinated himself to a higher authority. Furthermore, Orestes' procedure differs considerably from that of Clytaemes-

tra and Aegisthus. The spectators did not witness the actual killing of Agamemnon, but they know that Clytaemestra treacher-
ously lured her husband into his bath and "caught him fast" in
the "deadly abundance of rich robes" before striking him with
the sword (*Agamemnon*, l. 1383). Orestes also employs decep-
tion, but only against Aegisthus, who deserves no better (*Libation Bearers*, ll. 989–990). His mother is allowed to foresee the
fate that awaits her and therefore has an opportunity to defend
her behavior and plead for her life, an opportunity she denied
her husband. These differences, which help justify Orestes'
vengeance, are crucial factors in the presentation of him as the
first entirely sympathetic agent of retribution.

The linking of scenes through the principle of difference in
likeness need not depend, however, on such an obvious resemblance as that which connects these two murders. An example of
paralleling produced by the repetition of pageantry and spectacle
occurs in *Hamlet*, in the three instances of the assembling of the
full Danish court (I.ii, III.ii, and V.ii). In this case the likeness is
largely a matter of the trumpet flourish that introduces each
scene and of the visual tableau of Claudius, his queen, and his
courtiers, with Hamlet's definite separation from the others indicated by costume (at least in I.ii and III.ii), pose, and manner.

In the first of these scenes Claudius and his court and the beliefs they uphold have pre-eminence. From his position in the
center of the stage Claudius dominates the action with his deft
summary of the events that made him king, his skillful disposition of the foreign situation, his magnanimous granting of
Laertes' requests, and his easy suppression of Hamlet's incipient
revolt. Placed in sharp contrast to the colorful, almost festive
costuming of the king, queen, and courtiers is Hamlet in his
"customary suits of solemn black," obviously not a part of this
harmonious group. In the eyes of the court Hamlet's failure to
conform merely signifies his own regrettable and abnormal morbidity: his opposition in no way reflects on the harmony he

chooses to reject. Having witnessed the first scene of the play, the spectators know of the ubiquitous disorder and realize that Hamlet's opposition has impersonal justification. They know that the serene surface that Claudius projects ignores the entire story. Nevertheless, his show of strength is impressive; he arouses suspicion, but he holds the reins and seemingly has everything under his control. Hamlet's greater sensitivity to the disorder beneath the surface is admirable, but there is little he can do. He cannot even fully reveal his emotions except in the privacy of soliloquy.

When the court meets again in Act III, scene ii, Ophelia has replaced Laertes, while Rosencrantz and Guildenstern have been added. The basic division of Act I, scene ii, is still evident, however. The king and his court remain united, this time in their attempt to humor Hamlet, whose morbidity, as most of them think, has developed into insanity. Once again Hamlet's alienation is partly indicated through visual effect, for now he wears the costume called for by his antic disposition, and partly by his contemptuous remarks. This time, however, Hamlet is not utterly alone; near him waits Horatio. The addition is significant, for it points to the principal difference that places this scene in contrast to the first gathering of the court. In Act I, scene ii, the court met at Claudius' request for the purpose of conducting state business. Now it meets at Hamlet's request, ostensibly to be entertained but in reality so that Hamlet can catch the conscience of its king. In Act III, scene ii, therefore, it is Hamlet who dominates. He chooses the activity of the scene, comments on it throughout, and constantly holds the center of attention. Claudius' corresponding loss of control is fully indicated by his cautious questions: "Have you heard the argument? Is there no offence in't?" (ll. 227–228). He gives the command that causes the exit of his courtiers, as he did in Act I, scene ii, but this time he acts only because Hamlet has forced his hand. And he is visibly shaken. His disturbance and the brief turmoil that it provokes introduce disorder into the court itself. The serene surface that Claudius used as a shield in Act I, scene ii, has cracked. Even though Hamlet cannot yet act openly, and even though Claudius retains the trappings of authority, the scene as a whole symbolically portrays the transferral of control from king to prince.

In the final gathering of the full court (V.ii), symbol becomes reality. The disorder that at one time remained hidden is now everywhere visible. Ophelia, Rosencrantz, and Guildenstern have fallen victims to it. Polonius, the valued courtier, is missed, and Osric, who fills his position in the tableau, manifests all Polonius' worst traits without showing any quality that might make him useful to a king. Laertes has returned; but where before he only sought permission to go to Paris, he now helps Claudius carry out a treacherous murder. Claudius still occupies his throne, and his verse has resumed the formal polish and superficial flow that characterized it in the play's second scene, but other aspects of his situation belie this desperately maintained appearance. Gertrude, once his "sometime sister," is now almost his sometime wife, for she has drawn away from him. His position is as weak as Hamlet's was before Act III, scene ii, for now he also must employ the ruse of entertainment to mask a far different purpose that he dare not make public. The backfiring of his plan reveals that Claudius no longer has any control whatever. Before the scene ends, his whole world and he with it are destroyed. The rottenness of Denmark, momentarily visible in Act III, scene ii, at last breaks through the thin, superficial outer shell of apparent serenity.

Hamlet, whom the opposed court had once seen as the sole abnormality in its normal world, now clearly emerges as an element of health in the midst of disease. No longer flaunting his difference from the others by costume or manner, he even participates freely in the supposed entertainment. His distinctness from the rest of the court now depends not on exterior manifestations but on the greater importance he has earned in the eyes of the spectators. In his battle with Claudius for dominance he has obviously won, as his killing of the king and his bequeathing of the crown to Fortinbras indicate. But even though Hamlet has conquered Claudius, his command of the situation as a whole is far from absolute. He has come to the duel without knowing its real purpose, and this ignorance is an ironic measure of his own lack of full control. Similarly, he also falls victim to the spreading poison that destroys Denmark's court. Thus the battle for control, which has been a major feature of this whole sequence of scenes, ends with the implication that true control lies beyond the grasp of any individual. Hamlet defeats Claudius, but he does not win. He, too, must submit to a superior force, be it divinity, fate, circumstances, or a pattern of evil that, though originating with a willful human act, soon acquires a strength of its own too powerful for any human being to defeat.

The parallel linking these three scenes provides a recurring norm against which the spectators can more readily perceive both the increasing chaos in Denmark and the shifting balance in Hamlet's conflict with Claudius; therefore, by placing an assembly of the full court at the beginning, middle, and end of the play, Shakespeare has immeasurably assisted his spectators in comprehending the main contours of a rich and varied action. A comparable use of difference in likeness appears in *Rosmersholm*, in the parallel established by the two visits of Ulrik Brendel. These visits, in Act I and Act IV, unite the end of the play with its beginning and thus heighten the spectators' awareness of the exact nature of all that has occurred.

Brendel's first visit injects a bit of comic relief into the tense situation in which Kroll and Rebecca vie to determine a course of action for Rosmer. In part the comic tone reflects ironically upon Brendel himself, for it stems from his own absurdity, and since Brendel serves Ibsen as a caricature of Rosmer, it also throws into question Rosmer's whole character and particularly the nature of his involvement with progressive ideas. Nevertheless, it is the positive implications of this comic tone which tend to dominate. Though ill-equipped, Brendel is at any rate a living symbol of that which Rebecca has already made admirable. His break with tradition augments the other testimony asserting that the past is evil, just as his great desire to at last do something reveals the contagious effect of the new spirit that pervades the land. Brendel's own contribution will undoubtedly prove negligible, but his presence is the external manifestation of an irresistible force that seems assured of victory. And even though Brendel may be useless in himself, he at least inspires Rosmer to emulate him by making his own revolt public. Through Brendel's influence, Rosmer finally dissolves the last ties that bind him to the past and can consequently march forward boldly as he guides the spirit of progress along the paths of moral excellence. Or so it looks at this point.

When Brendel returns in Act IV, he enters a greatly altered situation. Rosmer's world has crumbled around him. Now it is Rosmer who desperately urges another to act: he needs proof of Rebecca's belief in him if his world is to retain any meaning at all. The changes in Brendel reflect the collapse of Rosmer's hopes. Once again the mood Brendel evokes carries significance, but this time it contributes to the spreading gloom of physical and emotional darkness. In the first act Brendel was heading into town, into life and conflict; he intended to "step upward" (I, p. 138). Now he goes "downhill," back into "the great nothingness" (IV, p. 205). Like Rosmer, he is "a deposed king amid the ashes of my burned-out palace" (p. 206). Earlier he sought a loan of money and clothes because he saw a future before him; now he begs only "a couple of cast-off ideals." Having looked into the treasure chest of ideas on which he based his hopes, he, like Rosmer, has found only his own bankruptcy: "There was *nichts* and nothing in the whole show."

Where Brendel's first visit seemed to assure a victory for progress, his return, with its impression of utter defeat, suggests rather the insuperability of the past, a force that has never wholly let Rosmer free and has ultimately conquered even Rebecca, the living symbol of the new. In keeping with this emphasis, Brendel also reinforces one implication of Rebecca's confession by providing additional evidence that the new is far less attractive than it originally seemed. During his first visit he expressed his contempt for Mortensgaard but was nevertheless willing to work with him because the association promised success for the cause of progress. Now, although he has come to admire Mortensgaard's capacity for action, he realizes that Mortensgaard is a Machiavellian demagogue who by spurning ideals will become the "lord and master of the future" (p. 206)—that, in other words, he is as oppressive as the forces he opposes. It is, however, more than anything else the result of Brendel's second visit that most incisively reflects the changed alignment in the opposition between tradition and revolt. Once again he suggests a course of action for others to emulate. In the first act his example compelled Rosmer to strike a blow for the new; now his recommendation of Rebecca's sacrifice prompts both Rosmer and Rebecca to give themselves over to the white horse and the millrace, symbols of the irrepressible power of the past.[7]

These examples from *Hamlet* and *Rosmersholm* may have created a false emphasis, for they both show the principle of difference in likeness being used to focus the shifting contours of an entire action. The *Oresteia* murder sequence, on the other hand, serves its purpose by helping to illuminate a single event, the killing of Clytaemestra. This more limited scope, which is quite common, can be seen again in a final example of the device, one that links single moments rather than whole scenes. The famous speech that Polonius delivers to Laertes in Act I, scene iii, of *Hamlet* may be the highlight of its particular scene, but it is even more impressive as the second of three occurrences in

---

[7] This reading obviously reaches a conclusion far different from that based on Brendel's allusions, in Chapter 5. Both readings are valid; in Chapter 8, I establish their relationship.

which a "father" gives "advice" to his "son." In the first of these, which precedes Polonius' speech, Claudius lectures his "chiefest courtier, cousin, and . . . son" on the facts of human existence, pointing out how foolish and how reprehensible it is to oppose "what we know must be" (I.ii.87–117). Polonius is followed in scene v by a third father, the Ghost, whose "advice" to his son Hamlet consists of the call for revenge. The linking of these three colloquies evokes numerous implications as each incident ironically reflects the others. The result is a more complex understanding not of the entire action but of the situation from which it springs.

The Auxiliary Scene. The relationship between the Polonius-Laertes incident and the rest of the sequence also exemplifies the one basic function of scene-context interplay which still requires consideration. If all plays consisted of a single, tightly woven action concentrating without digressions on the fortunes of one character or the interrelations of a small group, no further discussion would be necessary. But most dramatists complicate their central actions by developing one or more subordinate areas of concern. *Hamlet* is the obvious text here. Its core, unified by the single hero and given form through the contest between king and prince, is the main plot that comprises Hamlet's conflicts with others, himself, and his surroundings. But Shakespeare has supplemented this basic action in a variety of ways. Curving beneath it is a subplot that traces the fortunes of the Polonius family. Another subplot, more accurately described as a "side plot" because of its function in the play, combines occasional references to the activity of Fortinbras. In addition, the main action is also interrupted by a number of dramatic adjuncts that qualify as digressions since they do not materially advance the narrative. Hamlet's advice to the players, the scene between the two gravediggers, and the interlude with Osric all belong to this category. Similarly, though the recitation of the Pyrrhus speech is relevant to the plot, its content is not, and even the play-within-the-play, an essential part of the story line, contains speeches that have no narrative function. This fragmentation of the action of *Hamlet* into its several components shows that the play's unity does not derive from a single hero or a single narrative line. It consists, rather, in the organic interrelationship of an infinite number of implications from many different sources. The fragmentation also shows that several of these sources—the subplots and digressions—have a special place in the interrelationship. Because these interruptions of the main narrative introduce seemingly irrelevant issues, their content acquires a peculiar emphasis. This effect makes them extremely useful for establishing and developing implications of great consequence to the entire play. And *Hamlet* is by no means the only play that utilizes this structural device: it appears regularly in drama, especially in plays whose construction approximates the Shakespearean model.

The most familiar version of this structural device is the subplot, a staple of English drama from the Middle Ages to the eighteenth century. In one of its forms it appears as a distinct underplot, usually comic though sometimes serious, running concurrently with the main action but presenting different characters and different events. Standard examples of this type include Middleton and Rowley's *The Changeling*, Heywood's *A Woman Killed with Kindness*, and Otway's *Venice Preserved*. The second type of subplot, the more common of the two, portrays additional events in the lives of characters who also participate in the main action. A constant feature of Shakespeare's plays, this type is exemplified by the plot line in *King Lear* which dramatizes the activity of Gloucester and his two sons. Despite the distinction, both kinds of subplot utilize the principle of likeness in apparent difference. The first type, as M. C. Bradbrook describes it, "was contrasted and not interwoven with the main action: it reflected upon it, either as a criticism or a contrast, or a parallel illustration of the same moral worked out in

another manner, a kind of echo or metaphor of the tragedy." [8]
The second type is more fully integrated into the narrative design of its play, but it has similar interpretive functions. As Miss
Bradbrook's comment indicates, one result of this structural device in either of its forms is the effect produced by the relation
between a *complete* subplot and the action it accompanies. But
since the subplot usually appears in the form of separate episodes,
it also provides numerous opportunities for purely local commentary.[9]

Both the over-all and the local relations are illustrated in *Hamlet* by the narrative line involving Polonius and his family, the sequence that Francis Fergusson has called a "comic-pathetic subplot, with many ironic parallels to the story of Hamlet and his father's Ghost." [10] The complete Polonius subplot, an example of
the second type, reflects the main action by its emphasis on a father's relations with his children and, especially, by establishing
two different reactions toward a father's death, both of which
contrast sharply with that of Hamlet. Moreover, this subplot,
which furnishes three of the play's victims, helps Shakespeare
portray more convincingly the far-reaching consequences of the
evil in Hamlet's world. It is unlikely, however, that this narrative
line is perceived as a distinct plot; by the end of the play at least,
it has become fully absorbed into the main action, and the deaths
of Polonius, Ophelia, and Laertes, though significant in themselves, are more significant as they affect Hamlet and his struggle

---

[8] *Themes and Conventions of Elizabethan Tragedy* (Cambridge: University Press, 1935), p. 46.

[9] On this structural device in general—also called the double plot—see
William Empson, "Double Plots," in *English Pastoral Poetry* (New
York: Norton, 1938), pp. 27–68; for a superb analysis of one example,
see Jonas A. Barish, "The Double Plot in *Volpone*," *Modern Philology*,
LI (1953), 83–92.

[10] *The Idea of a Theater* (Princeton, N.J.: Princeton University Press,
1949), p. 102.

with Claudius. Furthermore, in the theater this subplot is first perceived as a number of individual episodes that interrupt the main action to explore issues with less immediate narrative interest. Consequently, this subplot's most valuable contribution is the creation of a number of auxiliary scenes (I.iii, II.i, IV.v, and IV.vii) much like those that I have labeled "digressions." What still requires examination is the wide range of structural effects such auxiliary scenes make possible.

The brief but pithy episode between Polonius and Reynaldo (II.i.1–73) neatly illustrates several functions of the auxiliary scene. This episode immediately follows a major turning point in Hamlet's story. He has just heard the Ghost's report, sworn vengeance on Claudius, warned Horatio that he might adopt an antic disposition, and lamented his new responsibilities. The spectators naturally wonder what he will do next, but Shakespeare rewards their curiosity with this obvious digression. Its narrative contribution to the main plot is slim indeed; apart from further characterizing Polonius, one of Hamlet's adversaries, it merely suggests that a considerable amount of time has elapsed since Hamlet saw the Ghost. The scene's primary interest lies elsewhere, therefore—in its implicit associations with the main plot.

In the first place, it offers a parody of two aspects of the preceding scene. By sending Reynaldo on his questionable mission, Polonius imitates the Ghost: he is haunting his son, trying to control his life even though they are physically separated. Nor does the resemblance stop here, for Polonius is also imitating the Ghost when he commands another to carry out a plan of action that must necessarily affect his moral character. The second parody stems from the philosophy that lies behind this plan of action, and here Hamlet is the target, for Polonius' use of "indirections" to "find directions out" reflects ironically on Hamlet's intention to feign madness. Both Polonius' comic fumbling and the insidious nature of his scheme are pertinent. They are, in fact, essential elements of the double parody: by juxtaposing this scene to the one that precedes it, Shakespeare not only deflates the heroic proportions of the call to revenge; he also questions its ultimate goodness.

In the process of qualifying the earlier impression, the scene also looks forward. Whatever Polonius' intentions may be, his accomplishment is clear: he orders Reynaldo to spy on his son. This emphasis on spying alerts the spectators to a dominant motif of the succeeding scenes, where spying becomes a commonplace activity. In the next scene Polonius, Rosencrantz, and Guildenstern all spy on Hamlet. In Act III, scene i, Polonius and Claudius hide behind the arras. In Act III, scene ii, Hamlet uses the play-within-the-play to spy on Claudius. This sequence, which eventually includes even Ophelia, Horatio, and Gertrude in subordinate roles, ends only when Polonius, in a new effort at spying, loses his life. The Polonius-Reynaldo scene introduces the motif of spying in a context where it cannot be obscured by other issues. It thus focuses attention on an important and recurring metaphor that adds to the delineation of evil in Denmark by stressing the mutual distrust and hostility of its inhabitants.

But even this effect does not exhaust the scene's contributions. Polonius' scheme also increases both the weight and the applicability of another basic implication. As I have already shown earlier in this chapter, Polonius' manipulation of Reynaldo adds one more example to a lengthy catalogue illustrating the corruption of fundamental human relationships in Hamlet's Denmark. Moreover, since it is a servant that Polonius infects, he extends the corruption to a new level of society: no longer does the rottenness of Denmark concern only the soldiers and the aristocracy. Nor, for that matter, does it any longer concern only Denmark. The evil has begun to spread. By sending Reynaldo to spy on Laertes, Polonius unwittingly makes sure that it will pursue his son even into France.

Through its multiple relations with its context the Polonius-Reynaldo episode reveals most of the structural effects typical of the auxiliary scene. Two basic functions are observable. In the first of these the auxiliary scene indirectly influences the spectators' understanding of the play as a whole by examining an aspect of the main action in a new perspective. The auxiliary scene can alter an impression by parody, contrast, or heightening; it can confirm the validity of an impression by adducing new evidence; or, by applying the emphasis that comes through isolation, it can focus on an impression and thus ensure that it will not be ignored. In its second basic function the auxiliary scene influences the spectators' understanding of the whole play more directly by conveying impressions of its own which, instead of interpreting those of the main action, supplement them. Closely related to focusing is amplification, which consists of the introduction of new examples designed to increase the weight of an impression already abundantly clear. Amplification is also one source of another effect—universalizing, a process in which the dramatist explores the activity of minor characters in an effort to show that the implications he develops have pertinence far beyond the necessarily narrow range of the main action. Finally, in fulfilling the second basic function, the auxiliary scene can also introduce impressions that appear nowhere else in the play.[11] The examples that follow, which explore these structural effects in more detail, demonstrate that, though the Polonius-Reynaldo episode enriches its context in several ways, more often than not a single auxiliary scene is much less extensive in its contributions to meaning.

The Pyrrhus speech in *Hamlet* (II.ii.446–512) amply illustrates this point; as an auxiliary scene, its only function is to alter a prominent impression of the main action. The speech itself, as an event, has considerable narrative relevance because it provokes in Hamlet the passionate outburst that begins the soliloquy with which he concludes the scene. But the content of this

[11] The structural effects described in this paragraph can also be produced by a subplot as a whole when it is felt as a distinct unit.

speech is not determined by its dramatic occasion: in creating something for the player to recite, Shakespeare could have chosen any episode of equal force and intensity. He evidently chose this one because of its peculiar relevance. As Chapter 5 points out, in the section on allusions, the whole speech presents an indictment of heroic action; Pyrrhus' brutal slaughter of his noble and helpless victim can only inspire unmitigated horror. Especially pertinent here, however, is the type of action that Pyrrhus performs, and Shakespeare makes it explicit. Pyrrhus hesitates only once; then, as the speech relates, "a roused vengeance sets him new a-work" (l. 482). Pyrrhus, that is, has more than patriotic zeal to stir him on: he is Achilles' son, Achilles was struck down by a Trojan, and the crushing of Priam completes one phase in Pyrrhus' act of revenge. Because of his purpose, this brutal monster, "horridly trick'd / With blood of fathers, mothers, daughters, sons" (ll. 451–452), parallels Hamlet, who also seeks to avenge a father's death. Furthermore, Pyrrhus' "sable arms" are as "black as his purpose" (ll. 446–447); like Hamlet, he wears emblems of mourning. Through these parallels the speech offers a shocking view of Hamlet's situation: if he is Pyrrhus, then Claudius is the helpless Priam and Gertrude the grief-stricken, pitiful Hecuba.

Since Hamlet himself has recalled and requested this particular speech, the horror it evokes may very well reflect his own attitude toward the task he has been assigned. This implication is adequately confirmed, for it occurs at a time when Hamlet does nothing to complete his task, and it echoes the regret already expressed in "The time is out of joint. O cursed spite, / That ever I was born to set it right!" (I.v.189–190). The Pyrrhus speech has great significance, therefore, as one of the few indications in the whole play of how Hamlet regards his responsibility. But more important is the effect this speech, as auxiliary scene, has on the spectators' understanding of the responsibility itself. The Ghost's command and Hamlet's instantaneous acceptance of it in the first act made revenge seem a matter of course. Once the villain has been singled out and the Ghost has clearly identified him, the hero need only give him his just deserts. Hamlet, when he berates himself for inaction, shows that, consciously at least, he accepts the validity of this assumption, as do all those critics who accuse Hamlet of delay. But through Pyrrhus' action and the explicit evaluation of his "black purpose" this assumption is seriously questioned. Shakespeare will later pursue the matter more fully when he presents the similar behavior of Laertes and the much different action of Fortinbras—both of whom have lost a father—but the Pyrrhus speech provides the first inkling in the play that revenge, far from being simple, is an extremely complex issue with many enigmatic overtones. In this manner the Pyrrhus speech duplicates the accomplishment of the double parody in the Polonius-Reynaldo episode: it alters an impression put forth by the main action. But where that episode qualified the spectators' response to a contiguous event, this one alters a more general impression conveyed by the main action as a whole.

Act I, scene iii, of *Hamlet,* a scene that introduces the spectators to the family circle of Polonius in the privacy of his home, illustrates the process by which the auxiliary scene confirms a previous implication. The narrative links between this episode and the preceding action are few and minor: Hamlet, as Ophelia's suitor, provides a prominent topic of conversation, and Polonius' children show their father a respect emulating that implied by Claudius' tribute to his value (I.ii.47–49). But Laertes' departure for France is the immediate occasion, and since it has nothing to do with the awaited meeting between Hamlet and the Ghost, the scene rather frustratingly digresses from the main action. At the same time, however, two fundamental underlying links emerge. First, as I have shown in the section on the symbolic dimension of character, this scene amplifies the portrayal of corruption in basic human relationships. Second, and of particular interest here, it mimics the first episode of the scene that precedes it. Polonius, Ophelia, and Laertes have met together to conduct family business, both foreign and domestic, just as Claudius and his court had met to deal with affairs of state. To the Elizabethans the family, as a social unit, mirrored the macrocosm of the state, with the father taking the place of the king. Polonius, moreover, in his conduct of family affairs and especially in giving advice to his son, closely resembles Claudius. These parallels prompt the spectators to recall the first gathering of the court; what they learn here enables them to understand it more fully.

To begin with, Laertes' sketch of Hamlet rings false. Hamlet, he professes to believe, is "trifling" with Ophelia; a prince can hardly choose his consort so recklessly, "for on his choice depends / The sanity and health of this whole state" (I.iii.20–21). To this charge of superficiality of feeling, Laertes adds another: since Hamlet does pursue his sister, it can only mean that he intends to seduce her, and her innocence, Laertes fears, will provide the key to open her "chaste treasure." This confusion of Hamlet with Lothario lacks authority. The spectators have come to know Hamlet too well during the preceding scene; having experienced the intensity and sincerity of his emotional involvements with Claudius, Gertrude, Horatio, and the memory of his father, they naturally assume that any affection he has shown Ophelia must be genuine, and Ophelia, who shares their assumptions, soon offers support for this point of view (ll. 110–114). Instead of being convinced of Hamlet's superficiality and insincerity, then, the spectators perceive that it is not Hamlet but Laertes who looks suspicious. His emphasis on the political role rather than the human role, which suggests that he does not really know Hamlet, causes the charge of superficiality to recoil upon himself.

When, a few minutes later, Polonius repeats with little variation his son's warning, Laertes' superficiality seems all the more apparent. Father and son evidently think and act alike. One of them, and Shakespeare makes no attempt to say which, is merely a carbon copy of the other. But if the repetition increases the sense of Laertes' shallowness, it also indicts Polonius under the same charge, and in doing so, it merely confirms what the basic texture of his speech of advice has already implied. Despite the air of common sense that pervades the speech, Polonius' "few precepts" fail to offer a program that really comes to grips with the complexities of human experience. One sign of this failure is the abundance of negative forms; words like "no," "not," "nor," and "neither" occur eight times in the twenty-three lines, while other words, such as "beware," "few," and "reserve," intensify the basic idea of the speech—which is that experience is to be carefully avoided. Furthermore, most of Polonius' precepts have to do with the keeping up of a good appearance in the eyes of others, and it is undoubtedly this excessive concern with surface values that motivates both the length and the climactic placing of the disquisition on proper dress. After such emphasis, Polonius' conclusion—"to thine own self be true"—seems a rather ludicrous *non sequitur*.

The links between this scene and the first episode of Act I, scene ii, suggest that the superficiality so evident in Laertes and Polonius must have a wider application. Shakespeare thus uses Act I, scene iii, to comment on the first gathering of the full court. Polonius and Laertes were then introduced as members of this court and in perfect harmony with their king. In making their shallowness obvious, Shakespeare provides his spectators with a closer look at two of those who have concurred in Claudius' advancement to the throne and in his questionable marriage, and who, speaking through Claudius and Gertrude, belittled Hamlet's preoccupation with his father's death. Act I, scene iii, therefore helps confirm an implication already advanced by the juxtaposition of the first two scenes in the play. The impressive surface smoothness that made everything seem so admirably managed was merely slick superficiality. The members of the court had freely gone along with Claudius' accession not because he guaranteed a stable transition but because of their own inability to perceive reality. This first digression from the main action has more than one relationship to its context, but by far the most important is its confirmation of the shallow optimism that makes most of the play's characters blind not only to the real issues of the central conflict but even to the doom that threatens them personally.

The process of focusing is well illustrated by one of the few auxiliary scenes of the *Oresteia*, the long episode in the *Agamemnon* in which Cassandra and the chorus hold the stage alone. It is here that Cassandra recapitulates the history of the family curse and prophesies its latest result, the murder of her master. Tightly interwoven with these motifs, however, are the threads of her own story, which Aeschylus gives considerable emphasis. For some minutes Cassandra is completely absorbed with the god Apollo; her first words evoke his name in a cry of anguish, and this cry occurs twice more in refrain-like repetition. Finally, she clarifies her preoccupation by assigning him responsibility for her plight:

> Lord of the ways, my ruin.
> You have undone me once again, and utterly
> [ll. 1081–1082].

The chorus' comment, "I think she will be prophetic of her own disaster" (l. 1083), suggests that the god's responsibility extends even to her approaching death at the hands of Clytaemestra, and Cassandra confirms this suggestion; Apollo has sent her to Argos to die:

> Why have you brought me here in all unhappiness?
> Why, why? Except to die with him? What else could be?
> [ll. 1138–1139].

In presenting this story, Aeschylus drew on his spectators' prior knowledge of the sin of Cassandra. Apollo had been her lover and had given her the divine gift of prophecy. She then violated her vow by spurning him, and in revenge he caused her prophetic voice to go unheeded. Her story was common knowledge, and Aeschylus refreshed his spectators' memory of it by the answers that the chorus' persistent questions elicit from the victim (ll. 1198–1212). But, Aeschylus suggests, Apollo remained dissatisfied; seeking further revenge, he sent her to Argos in Agamemnon's train to be murdered by Clytaemestra in just retribution for her crime against a god:

> And now the seer has done with me, his prophetess,
> and led me into such a place as this, to die   [ll. 1275–1276].

Cassandra realizes that she cannot escape (ll. 1299, 1301); she knows that the will of Apollo must be her destiny. So she is ready to die. Yet, as a prophetess, she also knows that someday her master's son will return to Argos to strike down the murderess, himself an avenger dealing just retribution (ll. 1279–1285). She prays to Apollo, as she enters the palace to her death, that when the avengers destroy Clytaemestra and Aegisthus, "they avenge as well / one simple slave who died, a small thing, lightly killed" (ll. 1325–1326).

Cassandra's story is therefore completely rendered, and though it seems to digress from the central action of the play, it has considerable relevance. Up to this point the play has centered on Agamemnon. Aeschylus has stressed his greatness and his smallness, his heroic, regal magnificence and his all too human guilt. Dramatically, he looms as a figure of gigantic proportions, and it is this colossus who will soon pathetically fall. Cassandra's story interrupts this development. It dramatizes the theme of retribution in material entirely unrelated to Agamemnon,[12] and therefore it directs attention away from the personal tragedy. The inclusion of her story assures the spectators that this play examines

[12] The importance of Cassandra as an additional victim of retribution is pointed out by H. D. F. Kitto, in *Form and Meaning in Drama* (London: Methuen, 1956), pp. 28–29.

retributive justice as a general principle rather than merely as a minor motif in the death of a hero.

While thus keeping the spectators' attention focused on his basic theme, Aeschylus also reiterates some of its primary aspects. Cassandra, for her sin, deserves to die; her death fulfills the will of the gods, and the importance that Apollo has in her story makes the gods' involvement in all cases of retribution especially clear. In killing Cassandra, as in killing her husband, Clytaemestra serves as an agent of divine will. But in this case, too, her pure motive is complicated by a personal concern: she hates Cassandra because she is her husband's concubine. Once more justice and crime hopelessly intermix. The outcome, as in the major chain of retribution dramatized by the whole trilogy, can take only one form. The "outlaw and wanderer" foreseen by Cassandra (l. 1282) will return to Argos. The slave, like her master, will have vengeance. And in the process, of course, the avenger, like those who preceded him, will trigger a new attempt to render justice once and for all.

In fulfilling its primary task, the Cassandra episode also illustrates one effect of the second basic function of the auxiliary scene, for her case helps universalize the issues that Aeschylus develops in the main action. Indeed, most subplots and auxiliary scenes that introduce subordinate characters have this purpose as a secondary goal even when some other desired effect is uppermost. In *Rosmersholm*, for example, Ibsen uses Ulrik Brendel primarily to alter responses to the central story line, but Brendel is at the same time one more individual who in seeking to encourage progress has precipitated his own destruction, and this represents universalizing because it suggests that Rosmer's failure is not merely personal. Universalizing is only incidental in these examples, however; as a primary effect the process is best illustrated by the Fortinbras episodes in *Hamlet*. These episodes, of crucial importance to the play's meaning, illustrate, in fact, all three effects characteristic of the second basic function of the auxiliary scene. Shakespeare employs them to amplify, to universalize, and to establish an effect found nowhere else.

Although Fortinbras appears just twice in the play, his story, given in skeletal form, runs concurrently with the main action. First mentioned in the all-important opening scene, Fortinbras is assigned a role of great importance. Since, as Horatio explains, he seeks "to recover of us, by strong hand / And terms compulsatory, those foresaid lands / So by his father lost" (I.i.102–104), Fortinbras has instigated the preparations for war that constitute one sign of the turmoil in Denmark. He first takes on, therefore, a significance second only to that of the Ghost. In the next scene, however, the threat he poses seems far less ominous; to Claudius, who reduces him to the status of a "pest" (I.ii.22), his demands, provoked by false assumptions of Denmark's weakness, offer no difficulties that skillful diplomacy cannot forestall. The next reference to Fortinbras, in Act II, scene ii, suggests that Claudius was correct. Chastised by his uncle, Fortinbras has abandoned his plan to invade Denmark; no longer demanding return of the territories lost by his father, he now humbly requests nothing more than permission to cross Claudius' lands on his way to a skirmish in Poland. For Polonius, "This business is well ended" (l. 85). As it turns out, however, Polonius' complacency is just one more sign of the blindness that besets Claudius' court. Far from ended, the business resumes in Act IV, scene iv, where Fortinbras' importance assumes the added dimension of concreteness. Here, for the first time, he appears in his own person, present in Denmark, a definite force in the action even though Poland still remains his acknowledged destination. Shakespeare never indicates Fortinbras' exact intentions. The attack on Poland may be his primary interest, or it may be only a smoke screen. At any rate, it gives him the proximity that allows him to take immediate advantage, in the last scene of the play, of Hamlet's prophecy that "th' election lights / On Fortinbras" (V.ii.347–348). In embracing the fortune that now lies open to him, Fortinbras at last attains the full significance promised for him in the opening scene of the play. The Fortinbras sequence provides one episode with direct bearing on the main plot of *Hamlet*. His appearance in Act IV, scene iv, presents the contrast between action and inaction which Hamlet notes and then generalizes into the soliloquy "How all occasions do inform against me" (ll. 30–66). But it is as a complete unit that the Fortinbras plot makes its most significant contributions to meaning.

The story of Fortinbras, like those of Hamlet, Laertes, and Pyrrhus, describes the program of action adopted by a son who has lost his father. In this way the Fortinbras plot amplifies a basic theme of the play and subjects it to the analysis made possible by the difference between Fortinbras' approach and those of the others. This amplification also involves the additional process of universalizing a central theme, but Fortinbras' activity produces another example of universalizing of much greater consequence. Even more than the Polonius subplot, the inclusion of Fortinbras extends the play's focus beyond the narrow range established by the affairs that concern the small group of characters participating in the main action. By remaining always present, if only subliminally, Fortinbras guarantees the spectators' continued retention of the all-inclusive perspective established by the opening scene. The presence of Fortinbras offers little insight into Hamlet and even less into Claudius and the others. His concern is not the duel between mighty opposites but the area in which the duel is fought; oblivious to what transpires in Denmark, he cares only for the state itself. Without Fortinbras, *Hamlet* would still be a complex revenge tragedy; with him, it becomes much more. Through continual reminders of his place in the action more than through any other device, Shakespeare ensures that Denmark itself, whose significance he has emphasized through imagery and other effects, will assume its proper rank in the hierarchy of dramatic issues. Fortinbras' concern with Denmark removes it from the level of mere setting and exalts it to a position of vast importance. His presence converts the conflict fought *in* Denmark into a conflict fought *for* Denmark. Only the universalizing achieved by the inclusion of Fortinbras makes Hamlet's act of sacrifice wholly meaningful.

Yet, until the end of the play, Fortinbras' role remains ambiguous, and through this aspect of his plot it fulfills its final function, the introduction of a motif established in no other way. At first view Fortinbras presents a threat aimed directly at the welfare of Denmark. Evidently discouraged, he directs his attention elsewhere, but his intervention continues to be a distinct possibility. At the same time, through the respect with which Hamlet speaks of him in Act IV, scene iv, he comes to inspire admiration rather than fear. These shifting impressions, along with the sketchiness of his role, endow Fortinbras with a peculiar quality. To spectators absorbed in the main action he exists as an external force poised somewhere on the periphery: he may strike and he may not; he may prove catastrophic to Denmark and he may guarantee its salvation. This effect is especially meaningful in a play that from the beginning has suggested the close relationship between human action and the mysterious forces of the universe. Only through the ambiguity of Fortinbras do these forces acquire a full dramatic embodiment, one that expresses both their imminence and their inscrutability. The end of the play seems to resolve, of course, the questions that enshroud Fortinbras' full significance. He does finally enter the heart of the action, and his arrival will evidently prove beneficial to Denmark. This ending does not occur, however, until Hamlet, in completing his sacrificial act of purgation, has made it possible.

A Note on Tempo

Act II, scene ii, of *Hamlet* is, writes Harley Granville-Barker, "the play's longest, and it advances the action not a jot. But its dramatic significance lies just in this; in the casual (or so seeming) encounters and the evasively irrelevant talk, diluted at last into topical gossip of theatrical affairs—the smallest of small beer!—silenced only to hear a strolling actor declaim an old-fashioned speech about the burning of Troy." In one detail of this scene at least—the theatrical gossip—Shakespeare lowers "the emotional tension to as near zero point as may be." [13] The "dramatic significance" that Granville-Barker finds in this lowering of the emotional tension and its accompanying retardation of action is, in part, the result of tempo. This element of drama, easily overlooked and difficult to define, has unquestionable importance. No examination of structural devices, however thoroughly it explored the functions of characters and individual scenes or subplots, would be complete without some consideration of the characteristic pace that every unit of action assumes in performance.

The individual scene, such as that which Granville-Barker describes, may be fast or slow; its movement may involve acceleration or deceleration; or it may combine varying speeds in a complex pattern. But to be played at all, the scene must take on a definite and distinctive pace. A play as a whole therefore consists, from one point of view at any rate, of the design formed by the modulation or alternation from one tempo to another as scene follows scene throughout the action. Its special quality makes tempo most readily discernible in performance, but it is already inherent in the text as an inseparable dimension of the dramatic material. Nor is this element of drama a concern only of the play's director: "Tempo," as J. L. Styan notes, "always exists to evoke meaning." [14] The scene from *Hamlet* tends to confirm his generalization. Its leisurely pace helps make concrete the complete lack of purposeful activity that characterizes the hero at

[13] *Prefaces to Shakespeare*, I (Princeton, N.J.: Princeton University Press, 1946), 69.

[14] *The Elements of Drama* (Cambridge: University Press, 1960), p. 142.

this point in the play and that he will himself explicitly mention in the soliloquy concluding the scene. One reason that Hamlet's inaction becomes a valid dramatic motif is that tempo has given it actuality.

The role of this element of structure in the whole dramatic experience requires more precise definition, however, for several factors severely limit its capacity to affect understanding independently. To begin with, tempo depends entirely on the intrinsic nature of the material that determines its character; like the sound pattern of spoken dialogue, it provides only a secondary indication of meaning: it reinforces instead of establishes. In the scene from *Hamlet* tempo merely embodies that which the existence of so much talk and so little action has already implicitly rendered. Furthermore, tempo is a relative concept. If all of *Hamlet* moved at the same leisurely pace, the tempo of Act II, scene ii, would possess no significance whatever. It is only the experience of the earlier scenes, with their contrasting richness of overt action and their more rapid pace, that makes the relaxed tempo of Act II, scene ii, a realized dramatic fact. Once established, however, tempo furnishes a formal expression of the scene's specific dramatic intensity, and it serves as a vehicle by which this intensity can transfer from stage to audience. By alternately creating and relaxing tension, tempo continually adjusts the spectators' emotional relationship to the experience of which the play consists. But tempo does not perform even this limited function without assistance. The soliloquy concluding Act II, scene ii, demonstrates that increased tension need not always depend on a change of pace. The tempo of this soliloquy remains the same as that of the activity that precedes it; the greater dramatic intensity is the product not of theatrical timing but of Hamlet's language. This factor especially discloses the problematic nature of tempo. It suggests that the truly meaningful structural element is not tempo itself but rather the relative dramatic intensity of which tempo is merely one available sign. I

have already dealt with this aspect of drama, somewhat obliquely, in the analysis of the first scene of *Hamlet* in Chapter 5.
But the focus in that analysis was on a stylistic effect, the way in
which the variations in the sound pattern of spoken dialogue can
produce a single coherent impression. As a structural element of
much importance and difficulty, relative dramatic intensity requires its own independent consideration.

The nature and function of this structural element are well illustrated by the sequence of events that fills out the last half of
The Eumenides. Here, in rapid succession, occur the trial and
freeing of Orestes, the vindictive outburst of the disappointed
Furies, their conversion by Athene, and the final chorus of
"maidens, wives, elder women, in processional" (l. 1027), bless-
ing the newly created Eumenides and praising Zeus, whose meeting with Destiny has inaugurated eternal peace. The intellectual
significance of these events is abundantly clear. The individual,
as represented by Orestes, has been released from his personal,
self-destructive responsibility in the administration of justice and
has surrendered it to a new and higher authority, the institution
of public law. Through this act, then, the community now super-
sedes the individual, and its emergence establishes harmony on
earth, not only within the single polis but also, as Orestes' vow of
perpetual friendship between Argos and Athens suggests, among
all men (ll. 762–774). Thus forever cease all those conflicts between and within individuals which made suffering a necessary
attribute of existence. Moreover, since the new communal authority actualizes Athene's divine will, its creation suggests that
man and his gods have also at last been reconciled. The Furies'
outburst points to the one rift that still prevents universal harmony, but Athene's conversion of them to blessed spirits links
even the old gods and the new. Quite rightly, therefore, the final
chorus celebrates both peace between men and the gods and
union in the heavens.

This sequence has more than purely intellectual significance, however. The dramatic movement, with its shifts in intensity, secures also full emotional understanding and participation. The trial scene is ritual, but it is a ritual of conflict. It builds to a high level of tension that reflects the anxiety of Orestes and elicits a corresponding emotion in the spectators. The trial's outcome therefore brings release and satisfaction. Orestes' speech acknowledging his escape, with its orderly iambics and focus on peace, relaxes the tempo. His exit, at the end of the speech, creates one of those dramatic moments in which, as Granville-Barker puts it, the emotional tension approaches zero point. It evokes a sense of finality, of calm ultimately attained. But Orestes' release is merely the eye of the storm. Immediately the Furies re-establish the former tension. Their anger mocks the previous moment of calm. Frenzy, irrationality, and violence are implicit in the heightened tempo. Their verse form, in sharp contrast to Orestes' speech and Athene's attempts to restore reason, is relatively free, lyrical, suggestive of great emotion. Athene's words go unheeded as the Furies, maddened by frustration, repeat whole stanzas verbatim (ll. 778–792, 808–822; 837–847, 870–880). A tremendous discord results, suggesting a breach in the very fabric of the universe.

This restoration of anxiety after the arousing of false hope at the end of the trial makes the final harmony, once Athene has persuaded the Furies to accept their new role, especially satisfying and therefore emotionally convincing. As a result, the attainment of full harmony, the most important event in the entire trilogy, rings dramatically true. Furthermore, Aeschylus establishes it not only through intellectual signification but also through another and decidedly final shift in dramatic intensity. With Athene's victory, the tempo again abates. Celebration succeeds conflict. As before, the effect is partly due to metrics: the Furies first indicate their willingness to yield by adopting the iambics that Orestes and Athene had employed (ll. 892 ff.); then, though the Furies' speeches become lyrical once more (ll. 916 ff.), this time

Athene shares their freer rhythm, and consequently the lyricism here suggests joy and exaltation. But the most dramatically impressive aspect of this quiet ending is the final chorus that gathers to sing the concluding lines and to escort the Eumenides to their new home. This "new home" is an actual shrine, already dedicated to the Eumenides and situated "a few hundred yards northwest of the theatre"; [15] the chorus of Athenian women is not only performing the final action of a play; it is also imitating an annual procession. Through this chorus, then, the trilogy draws to a close in an act of ritual celebration that implants in each spectator a sense of participation in the life of his community. The familiar procession evokes, moreover, a sense of ceremonial timelessness which adds unusual force to the idea of eternal peace with which the play ends. In this sequence as a whole, then, intellectual awareness is transcended by higher understanding. The total elimination of all tension—the product of content, metrical variation, tempo, and especially ritual involvement—makes the realization of finally attained universal order a completely felt experience.

[15] William Chase Greene, *Moira: Fate, Good, and Evil in Greek Thought* (New York: Harper and Row, 1963), p. 136.

7. The Whole Structure

Plot, indeed, whether simple or complex, single or multiple, may be said to have two aspects, the spatial, which is concerned with character-grouping, and the temporal, which has regard to the order and relation of events.

—Una Ellis-Fermor, *Shakespeare the Dramatist*

The full impact produced by the elimination of tension at the close of the *Oresteia* is the result not only of the immediately preceding action but also, and inevitably, of the trilogy in its entirety. With respect to relative dramatic intensity, as in its content and imagery, the final chorus of *The Eumenides* rounds off a design originally begun by the Watchman in his prologue to the *Agamemnon*. Structurally meaningful in itself, this chorus acquires further significance as the finishing touch to a fully articulated form. In like fashion, all the various elements of structure examined in Chapter 6 for their independent creation of meaning function additionally as parts of a larger whole, the complete structure that they combine to produce. This aspect of a play is ontologically inseparable from its individual impressions, because, after all, the whole structure is merely the arrangement that the dramatist has given them; nevertheless, for the spectator who witnesses the play, the shape that it takes is perceptible as a further, more complex impression helping to define the quality of the action that it orders. No spectator can fully perceive the whole structure of a given play until the performance has ended, but it does not therefore suddenly emerge. Form, especially in a medium like drama, is in part a process of accumulation. The spectator in the theater is aware of a constant growth, a continual burgeoning into many parts. But the relationship that these parts hold to one another implies an ultimate unity whose nature stands fully revealed when the play has reached its conclusion. Thus a play's whole structure, though only an abstraction and not even a completed abstraction until the end, operates from the beginning to order the individual impressions and to control the spectators' manner of perceiving them.

In all art, ordinarily, form and content interfuse so perfectly that form is perceived, if at all, only as the expression of content; it becomes known through its effects rather than its substance. For the most part, therefore, the mere mention of form requires an arbitrary critical distinction. But in some plays what I have called the whole structure is so deliberately articulated that it tends to assume the proportions of an independent agent. It is in such plays that the importance of the concept is most evident.

The deceptively simple and seemingly naturalistic action of Synge's *Riders to the Sea* is confined to the submission of Maurya, the play's heroine, who, in what is carefully established as the climax of a long series of like capitulations, helplessly yields to the antagonist that has relentlessly opposed her. This antagonist, the play's motivating force, is usually identified as the sea, because it is in the sea that her husband and children have been drowned, and it is the sea that during the present action takes Bartley, her only remaining son. Whatever archetypal significance the sea may have for mankind, however, this identification seems scarcely adequate to explain the intense emotion that the play excites, especially since the sea here exists only as a verbal reference somehow affecting a visible and consequently more immediate action. Synge himself, describing in another work the keen with which the Aran Islanders voice their response to death, provides a far more convincing identification: "In this cry of pain the inner consciousness of the people seems to lay itself bare for an instant, and to reveal the mood of beings who feel their isolation in the face of a universe that wars on them with winds and seas." [1] Here, then, is a concept large enough to account for the play's emotional force, a concept that evokes a realm at once including the sea and yet vaster, at once manifesting itself in concretions like the sea yet also suggesting something intangible that transcends them. But Synge's concept is only an abstraction, while Maurya's antagonist, though unseen and never explicitly defined, seems actually present. Through Synge's art, it is. For the islanders, and for Synge who shared their experience, mention of the sea and the wind would adequately call up the sense of a warring universe. But to convey this feeling to his spectators Synge had to create a metaphor more in keeping with the characteristics of the theater. It is not, then, the few verbal references to wind and sea that make the warring universe effectively felt but rather the complex form with which Synge has endowed his otherwise simple action.

Through Synge's constant violation of the naturalistic perspective, several features of the play's form are so palpable as to suggest deliberate emphasis. The unusual brevity, noticeable in itself, is all the more conspicuous because Synge has created such a clear disparity between the actual playing time and the time demanded by his offstage events. As in the final soliloquy of *Doctor Faustus*, where shrinking time forms a trap from which the hero cannot escape, the disparity defines the strikingly *non*natural swiftness with which the events occur. And in this play the events are especially crucial. For Synge, as if to preserve the swiftness of his action, has carefully restricted its development. The steady movement toward the ultimate conclusion rarely

---

[1] *The Aran Islands*, in *The Complete Works of John M. Synge* (New York: Random House, 1935), p. 346. All citations to Synge's writings are to this edition.

pauses to dwell on specific details; those that are introduced merely intensify the increasing momentum, as, for example, the new boards leaning against the wall, which come to represent not only the coffin of Michael (the most recent victim) but also that of Bartley and of those who died long before the present action. As in almost no other play, it is the bare sequence of events that expresses the basic meaning.

Another formal characteristic, the frequent epitomizing scenes, reinforces this emphasis on the sequence of events. The action as a whole traces the cornering and defeat of Maurya by her antagonist; the separate moments that lead up to this outcome—principally, Maurya's futile struggles with her daughters and with Bartley—continually reveal her ineffectuality against *any* opposition. These epitomizing scenes therefore provide Synge with additional structural means to convey the point of his main design. Moreover, they also help establish a further characteristic of the play's form, the unquestionable inevitability of the outcome. This feature of the play, which confronts the spectator almost at once, is especially developed with reference to Bartley, whose death Synge anticipates so thoroughly that it becomes a foregone conclusion before it actually takes place.

A more striking feature of the play's form than any of these, however, is the manner in which the various characters tend to dissolve into one another. The play begins with a search for the missing, probably dead, Michael; it ends with the discovery and return of the body, but the body is Bartley's. For Maurya, who learns of both drownings simultaneously, one death cannot be distinguished from the other. For the spectators the two become inseparably linked when Maurya, after Bartley's body has been brought in, "drops Michael's clothes across Bartley's feet" (stage direction, p. 96). The central speeches in which Maurya sums up all her losses (pp. 93–94) introduce further parallels. The linking of Michael and Bartley is echoed in her pairing of Stephen and Shawn. When she recounts the loss of "Sheamus and his father, and his own father again," the doubling has become a tripling. Her speeches eventually dissolve them all into one blurred group, a process that is heightened by her reaction to the announcement of death—"Is it Patch, or Michael, or what is it at all?" (p. 94)—and by an onlooker's remark about "all the coffins she's seen made already" (p. 97). This multiplication of victims ultimately assumes even greater importance: by the end of the play it includes all men everywhere. From the first Synge has suggested that others, outside the family group, are involved in Bartley's fate. The sign denoting Michael's death (his shirt) has for its signification "many another man" as well (p. 90). The relevance of these others acquires dramatic embodiment when the women and men begin to enter in groups. The ritual quality of their mourning indicates that it is recurrent, not isolated, a general lament for all their dead, not a particular grief for Maurya's loss. Synge completes his universalizing of the victim from the individual to the family to man in general when Maurya expands the account of her own loss so that it may accommodate all loss: "There does be a power of young men floating round in the sea, and what way would they know if it was Michael they had, or another man like him, for when a man is nine days in the sea, and the wind blowing, it's hard set his own mother would be to say what man was it" (p. 95). That Maurya's defeat by her antagonist is somehow the defeat of us all Synge shows through the inclusiveness of the play's final line: "*No man at all* can be living for ever, and *we* must be satisfied" (p. 97).[2]

Each of the characteristics of the play's form is individually significant because each helps Synge define the nature of the otherwise inexpressible antagonist. The swiftness, inevitability, and consistency of the action all testify to the antagonist's supernatural and irresistible power and its unrelenting, malevolent pur-

---

[2] Italics added. I have developed these characteristics of the play's structure more fully in "Form as Agent in Synge's *Riders to the Sea*," *Drama Survey*, III (1964), 352–366.

suit of its human victims. The elimination of human individuality that results from the dissolving of one character into another reveals the same power, but more obliquely—by focusing on the universal abject helplessness of those who would attempt to resist it. One of the epitome scenes, Maurya's struggle with Bartley, especially illustrates this tendency to define through form. In this scene Bartley, a visible presence, assumes the role of the antagonist. His aloofness, his utter disregard for Maurya's feelings, and his apparent indifference to her very existence allow Synge to present in the concrete terms of the theater some of the distinctive attributes of a force that must necessarily remain invisible.

Much more important than any of the individual elements of the form, however, is its primary characteristic, the felt complexity that results from the fusion of them all. Synge makes the experience of his islanders truly universal by creating a whole structure so carefully emphasized that it conveys the impression of independent reality. The various formal characteristics not only define; in uniting they establish a living essence that dominates the characters to become the leading actor of the play. The peculiar intensity of *Riders to the Sea* results therefore from Synge's successful rendering of that which is necessarily abstract and intangible in a presence as immediate as the more obviously tangible and visible elements of the theater. Just as an actor provides the living reality that converts the verbal and visual impressions of character into a single coherent image, the play's complex form provides an autonomous vehicle fully adequate to embody that invisible but omnipotent force, the warring universe whose victim is human life.

Synge's achievement in *Riders to the Sea* is, admittedly, rather unusual. The history of drama offers few other examples apart from farce in which the whole structure has been so deliberately emphasized as to become a felt part of the dramatic experience. Many of the examples that do occur—the school of Scribe and similar mistakes—betray the obvious difficulties that such an emphasis on form can unfortunately produce. But additional respectable examples suggest themselves nonetheless. Each of the two that follow illustrates not only a further use of the whole structure as a thing in itself but also a different kind of use.

William Chase Greene quite rightly and with proper esteem calls Sophocles' *Oedipus the King* "a triumph of manipulation." [3] The *Oedipus* was, of course, Aristotle's favorite play, primarily because it fulfilled so completely his conception of tragic form. Although it has the right kind of hero, the right sort of reversal and recognition, and the proper fusion of both, it was probably its fulfillment of another formal ideal which most impressed Aristotle. Both the reversal and the recognition, he wrote, "should arise from the internal structure of the plot, so that what follows should be the necessary or probable result of the preceding action." [4] No spectator of Sophocles' play can remain unaware of the admirable logical development by which not only the reversal but every episode of the play fits into a beautifully calculated movement that ultimately leads the hero to his full, tragic awareness. In contrast to other Greek plays, which seem hopelessly episodic beside the *Oedipus*, Sophocles' play well exemplifies what Aristotle meant by beginning, middle, and end. This inescapable tightness of form makes the play's whole structure one of its most conspicuous elements, and in this respect it resembles *Riders to the Sea*. But unlike the whole structure of *Riders to the Sea*, which forms a single, static vehicle capable of suggesting the constant presence of Maurya's unseen antagonist, that of the *Oedipus* manifests itself as a pattern of action developing inevitably toward an ultimate goal.

Despite this predominance of action, however, it would be improper to conclude that Sophocles, who also composed the much

[3] *Moira: Fate, Good, and Evil in Greek Thought* (New York: Harper and Row, 1963), p. 154.
[4] *The Poetics*, X.3, trans. S. H. Butcher.

looser *Oedipus at Colonnus,* necessarily shared Aristotle's faith in the abstract principle that character ought to be subordinate to plot. On the contrary, this structural effect is especially appropriate to its context: it defines much of the tragedy that Oedipus experiences. The action dominates only because this is a play about the supremacy of action in the highest human meaning of the term, the pattern of events that constitutes a man's life. Oedipus, believing himself capable of controlling action, sets in motion a sequence of events that soon begins to operate with complete independence, carrying him to the terrifying discovery that the steps he had taken in the past to avoid the action prophesied for him by the oracles were the direct cause of its fulfillment. The *Oedipus* is therefore a play that convinces its protagonist that character, motive, and intention matter less than result, which is the final indisputable fact and thus the only truth. It is a play in which the protagonist learns that there is in action itself an order over which he, its performer, cannot possibly exercise full, conscious control.

Racine's *Phèdre* is almost as celebrated as the *Oedipus* for excellence of form. Here, however, it is not action but *interaction* that dominates. The play's title suggests that the tragic focus is Phèdre herself, that Racine examines the suffering of a woman who knows the right course but is compelled to choose incorrectly and must nevertheless accept responsibility for her acts. Yet a spectator's experience of the play also includes the suffering of two other central figures: Hippolyte, the relatively innocent victim, whose refusal to incriminate Phèdre costs him his life, and Thésée, who realizes too late that his moral blindness has brought about the death of his son. All three figures, though clearly differentiated, are necessary to the whole effect. What unites them, however, is something other than the subtle principle of analogy characteristic of Euripides and Shakespeare. Racine is not examining a tragic theme that all three reflect in varying ways. He is concerned, rather, with the result that the natures, personal involvements, and independent actions of all three protagonists combine to produce.

All three are necessary to the play because with any of them missing the tragic situation would not materialize. Tragedy occurs because all three are as they are and do what they do. Phèdre may initiate the sequence of events by allowing Oenone to persuade her that she can safely yield to her desire for Hippolyte, but she does so only because Thésée's prolonged absence has encouraged the rumor of his death. The confession of her love fills her with the intense shame that motivates her further acts, but the primary cause of this shame is the response of Hippolyte, whose love for Aricie necessitates his rejection of Phèdre, and even then the shame would have little consequence were it not for the sudden and unexpected return of Thésée. Confronted by her husband, Phèdre once again feels the necessity to act. She momentarily hesitates between two alternatives, for she can preserve her reputation and safeguard her children's future by blaming Hippolyte, or she can protect the innocent Hippolyte by freely admitting her guilt. She chooses the latter course and would abide by her decision except that she then learns for the first time of Hippolyte's love for Aricie, and the discovery occasions an attack of jealousy that compels her to follow the first course. But even her accusation does not in itself cause the destruction of Hippolyte which is the primary source of tragic suffering—that event requires as well the impetuosity and monomaniac heroism of Thésée, who believes Phèdre at once and consequently forgets his love for his son, whom he now regards as one more monster deserving elimination. What matters in this play, then, is not the separate natures of the characters or their analogical connections with each other but their direct interaction. The real focus in *Phèdre*, its most impressive feature, is not Phèdre herself but the whole structure, which in this case results from and is characterized by the remarkable coherence with which the play's various parts fit together. In *Phèdre*, which typifies Racine's art, the unity produced by interaction dominates. It does so because Racine envisions this unity as the primary source of tragedy.

The Spatial Dimension

Even in plays such as *Riders to the Sea, Oedipus the King,* and *Phèdre,* in which the whole structure tends to constitute a separate entity, a further characteristic is also evident. As the discussion of *Riders to the Sea* has shown, Synge constructs his play on the basis of a central conflict between Maurya and her antagonist. It is in this respect that *Riders to the Sea* most clearly resembles the majority of plays, for in these, where form and content interfuse, the whole structure is perceived not as a distinct entity but as an expression of the relationship between two or more focal points. Various attempts have been made to define this aspect of the whole structure. Marvin Rosenberg, for instance, has asserted that "the form of conventional drama is linear—that, while it takes place in a continuing present, it moves as it were from left to right, from a beginning through a chain of chronological sequences toward an end." [5] Rosenberg's assertion is obviously accurate for most drama; it errs only in omission, in its focus on one aspect of the structure to the exclusion of another. As G. Wilson Knight has written with reference to Shakespeare:

One must be prepared to see the whole play in space as well as in time. It is natural in analysis to pursue the steps of the tale in sequence, noticing the logic that connects them, regarding those essentials that Aristotle noted: the beginning, middle, and end. But by giving supreme attention to this temporal nature of drama we omit what, in Shakespeare, is at least of equivalent importance. A Shake-

[5] "A Metaphor for Dramatic Form," in John Gassner, *Directions in Modern Theatre and Drama* (New York: Holt, Rinehart, and Winston, 1965), pp. 341–342.

spearian tragedy is set spatially as well as temporally in the mind. By
this I mean that there are throughout the play a set of correspondences which relate to each other independently of the time-sequence
which is the story. . . . This I have sometimes called the play's "atmosphere."

The Shakespearean play is, in other words, "a space-time unity."
But, Knight adds, it "is yet only to be properly known as a unity
in so far as it has first been accepted as a duality." [6]

Knight speaks only of Shakespearean tragedy, but his notion
of the space-time unity has relevance for all drama. Almost every
play, Shakespearean or otherwise, establishes some kind of spatial
dimension. When Knight equates the Shakespearean spatial setting with "atmosphere" or describes it as "the omnipresent and
mysterious reality brooding motionless over and within the play's
movement," he is calling attention to that union between immediate action and action of depth which I am tracing throughout
this book as a general characteristic of drama. But a play's spatial
dimension also appears in the form of a more specific design that
itself creates one aspect of the action of depth. In many plays this
more specific design is of a "horizontal" nature: it expresses a
contrast or conflict—sometimes a parallel—between two or more
distinct elements of the basic situation. Knight illustrates this
kind of spatial design when he insists that interpretation of
Othello must treat the "essential relation, abstracted from the
story, existing between the Othello, Desdemona, and Iago
conceptions." [7] In other words, the "horizontal" version of the
spatial dimension includes all those character groupings I have
described in the preceding chapter, and the examples cited there
—such as the oppositions between Apollo and the Furies, Kroll
and Rebecca, and St. Joan and her adversaries—are also relevant
here.

[6] *The Wheel of Fire* (4th ed.; New York: Meridian Books, 1957),
pp. 3, x.
[7] *The Wheel of Fire*, pp. 4–5, 3.

But this form of the spatial dimension is not merely a matter of character relationships. Aeschylus supplements the confrontation of Apollo and the Furies with images of light opposing darkness, beauty opposing monstrosity, and health opposing disease. The conflict in *Rosmersholm,* which subtends the opposition dividing Kroll and Rebecca, also manifests itself in numerous other features of the play, including the nature of the house, the frequently evoked superstitions, the flowers, and Rosmer's own divided soul. Sometimes, indeed, this form of the spatial dimension is developed without recourse to a clear-cut character relationship. Knight also cites the juxtaposition in *Timon of Athens* of "two areas of human experience": "on the one side a glittering world, rich garments, feasting, luxury and love; on the other, nakedness and hatred, a desert cave and the muffled thunder of the breaking seas." [8] As these references should indicate, some kind of "horizontal" spatial design, whether developed through character grouping or not, is an intrinsic element of almost every existing play. Further exemplification would therefore be superfluous: a complete list of examples would constitute a virtual history of drama, ranging in scope from the ironic contrast between intention and achievement which pervades *Oedipus the King* to the destructive opposition between people and material objects which characterizes the world of Ionesco's *The Chairs.*

Although the horizontal design is the most consistent, other forms of the spatial dimension also appear. Plays with a double plot, like Middleton and Rowley's *The Changeling,* contain horizontal designs in both the main plot and the subplot and further complicate the whole structure by adding another spatial design consisting of the "vertical" relationship that links them. *King Lear* is even more complicated in form. It begins, like *The Changeling,* with main plot and subplot, each with its own conflict between good and evil characters and its own opposition between the blind assumptions of the central character and intractable ex-

[8] *The Christian Renaissance* (New York: Norton, 1963), p. 10.

THE IDIOM OF DRAMA

perience. The two plots parallel each other and in the process offer mutual illumination. But by the third act realignment has occurred. Edgar and Gloucester have joined Lear, the Fool, and Kent. Albany remains with Goneril, but—mentally and morally at least—he has shifted allegiance to Lear. Edmund has combined forces with Cornwall, and it is not Edmund but Lear's adversaries—Cornwall, Goneril, and Regan—who carry out the blinding of Gloucester. What begins as a vertical design becomes entirely horizontal, and in *this* process the two conflicts separate. The opposition between good and evil now becomes the dominant quality of the *Lear* universe; the other conflict—the opposition between assumptions and experience—can thus finally achieve its tragic resolution.

In making a statement about a play's universe, the spatial design functions as one of the most important devices for establishing the action of depth. Its significance for the understanding of most plays is therefore sufficiently clear. But this concept has additional significance, because although drama tends to present a space-time unity, some plays are so constructed that the spatial organization dominates. In these plays, whatever lineal pattern might result as a by-product of temporal presentation is deliberately nullified; it is subsumed by the spatial dimension and loses its significance. This kind of play is thus seen not as an action extending from a beginning to an end but as a static whole containing many interrelating parts. Its conclusion is not the ultimate goal toward which all has been leading but rather the finishing touch, something comparable to the final brush stroke in a painting.

Joseph Frank has already shown that modern literature tends to be spatial in form. In poems such as *The Waste Land* or Pound's *Cantos*, he writes, "syntactical sequence is given up for a structure depending on the perception of relationships between disconnected word-groups. To be properly understood, these word-groups must be juxtaposed with one another and perceived simultaneously . . . for while they follow one another in time, their meaning does not depend on this temporal relationship." The language of modern poetry is, instead, "reflexive"; the poem "asks its readers to suspend the process of individual reference temporarily until the entire pattern of internal references can be apprehended as a unity." The novel presents Frank with greater difficulty because of the obvious temporal nature of most fiction. But, as he points out, this does not prevent the spatial development of individual scenes, and in some cases even the over-all sequence becomes suspended. Proust, for example, "does not follow any of his characters through the whole course of the novel: they appear and re-appear, in various stages of their lives, but hundreds of pages sometimes go by between the time they are last seen and the time they re-appear; and when they do turn up again, the passage of time has invariably changed them in some decisive way." Through this means, then, through "the discontinuous presentation of character, Proust forces the readers to juxtapose disparate images of his characters spatially." Because of this technique in which the writer deliberately neglects sequential progression, modern poetry and fiction can "be properly understood only when their units of meaning are apprehended reflexively, in an instant of time." [9]

Frank does not discuss modern drama, but Rosenberg distinguishes what he calls a "contextual" form, in which "the tensions of context, rather than direction, of . . . depth, rather than . . . movement, become important." Contextual drama "seeks to surround and exhibit." It tries "to convey the content of experience before a form has been impressed on it by thought." In this variety of modern drama, "many perspectives of the same perception are brought together; many intense, momentary chorded experiences poise side by side in tension; and

[9] "Spatial Form in Modern Literature," in *Critiques and Essays in Criticism, 1920–1948*, ed. Robert Wooster Stallman (New York: Ronald Press, 1949), pp. 321, 327–328, 323.

the dynamic context conveys a sense of the ever-dissolving gestalts of existence." One of Rosenberg's key examples is Strindberg's *The Dream Play*—"a montage of scenes that follow each other without progressing, rich in symbol and association, meaningful not in sequence or suspense, but in the reflection of a discontinuous psychic activity." [10] Like Frank, Rosenberg sees the greater emphasis on the spatial dimension to be the result of a dismissal of those connections that establish lineal sequence. For Rosenberg, this phenomenon is peculiarly modern, a departure from "conventional drama." But to accept this distinction would necessitate ignoring a large group of plays—essentially a specific age of drama—which are equally spatial in nature though they acquire this emphasis in a somewhat different fashion.

Restoration comedy is more dominantly spatial than any drama that has succeeded it. The world that it presents, as Dale Underwood has persuasively argued, is "in large part the product of two broadly opposing sets of traditions: on the one hand Christianity and Christian humanism, the 'heroic' tradition, the honest-man tradition, and the tradition of courtly love; on the other, philosophic and moral libertinism, Machiavellian and Hobbesian concepts as to the nature of man, and Machiavellian ethics. The form and meaning of the plays reflect the juxtaposition of these two sets of traditions and the oppositions and conflicts which ensue." In the plays of Etherege, which Underwood examines in detail, "the immediate as well as ultimate comedy . . . is the comedy of one set of assumptions concerning reality and value playing out its merits, defects, inconsistencies, and equivocalities within a frame of other conflicting sets of assumptions." Underwood's analysis of the plays indicates that

---

[10] "A Metaphor for Dramatic Form," pp. 347, 350, 351. I have omitted, in the first passage, the words "horizontal" and "vertical" because their inclusion would confuse my own prior use of the terms. Also, fuller study would reveal, I believe, that the absence of lineal progression is not as evident in Pirandello, Ionesco, and Genet as Rosenberg suggests.

the formal oppositions assume complex proportions, that it is not merely a matter of a single focal point opposing another. In *The Man of Mode*, for example, the comic action consists of "the hero's conflict with and ultimate conquest of several contrasting 'worlds' within the total world of the play." The individual scenes do not really lead anywhere. Instead, they set up these various "worlds"—the aggressive pride of Dorimant, the unchecked passion of Mrs. Loveit, the honor and insistence on value of Young Bellair and Emilia, the old-fashioned tradition of Bellair's father and Lady Woodvil, and the affected novelty of Sir Fopling Flutter—and then juxtapose them in infinite fruitful combinations. The outcome of the play—the marriages and failures to marry—is less the end of an action than the final example in a demonstration. This spatial focus even affects the language of Restoration comedy. It is, as Underwood shows, prevailingly substantive in nature, with verbs having little or no importance —a language of *being* rather than *becoming*. Neither sensuous nor concrete, it "deliberately abstracts [the immediate and concrete surfaces of experience] into generalized classes and categories." [11] Its rhetoric, which contains a good deal of formal balance and antithesis, seeks primarily to establish relationships among these categories, usually by erecting oppositions.

What Underwood has shown about Restoration comedy equally applies to the serious drama of the same age, particularly the heroic play, whose essentially spatial nature is well suggested by John Dryden's essay "Of Heroic Plays." In this essay Dryden pontificates on several of his genre's requirements, including theme—"An heroic play ought to be an imitation, in little, of an heroic poem; and, consequently . . . love and valour ought to be the subject of it"—verse form, characters, and even the necessity of introducing the supernatural and scenes of spectacle. The most interesting aspect of this essay, however, is Dryden's failure

[11] *Etherege and the Seventeenth-Century Comedy of Manners* (New Haven, Conn.: Yale University Press, 1957), pp. 8, 108, 73, 94.

to treat a topic almost obligatory in discussions of drama—plot. Dryden mentions plot only twice, once in a noncommittal reference to the "common drama," and once in a highly significant statement indicating that he saw plot in spatial terms. This passage occurs in his brief account of the origin of the heroic play in the work of Davenant, whose *Siege of Rhodes* had not quite perfected the genre: "There wanted the fulness of a plot, and the variety of characters to form it as it ought." In another statement on the same page he adds that *The Siege of Rhodes* lacked "design and variety of characters." [12] These remarks and the whole tenor of the essay—with its neglect of plot and its emphasis on character and theme—suggest that when Dryden thought of the heroic play, he thought of a drama that was basically static, deriving its organization not from a forward movement but from character grouping and "design." His actual practice amply confirms the essay's implications.

Aureng-Zebe, a late heroic play, might well have motivated Harley Granville-Barker's inspired question about Wycherley's *Love in a Wood:* "How could an audience both be clever enough to understand the story and stupid enough to be interested by it when they did?" [13] *Aureng-Zebe* has, in fact, two plot strands, concurrent and interrelated, evidently corresponding to Dryden's yoking of love and valor. The valor belongs to a military-political intrigue that Dryden has conceived on an epic scale. The scene is Agra, in the year 1660, and the empire nears chaos. Custom has it that when the emperor shall be succeeded by his oldest son, "the younger sons are doomed to die" (I.i.), and since the emperor is old and his death may occur at any time, all four sons, suppported by huge armies, are fighting desperately

[12] *John Dryden* (*Three Plays*), ed. George Saintsbury (New York: Hill and Wang, n.d.), p. 8. All citations to Dryden are to this volume.

[13] *On Dramatic Method* (New York: Hill and Wang, 1956), p. 121. I have not selected *Aureng-Zebe* because it is the best possible example of the spatial nature of the heroic play; *The Conquest of Granada* holds that distinction, but it is, after all, twice as long.

for control and consequently for preservation of life. When the play begins, Aureng-Zebe, the favorite son, has just defeated his two older brothers and now returns to the palace to share his victory with his father, claim his prize—the captive queen Indamora —and prevent a coup d'etat by the fourth son, his stepbrother Morat, only descendant of Nourmahal, the emperor's second wife. Aureng-Zebe is a man of honor, loyal and dutiful, concerned only with defending the interests of his father and preserving his safety. Morat, in contrast, exhibits a completely Hobbesian nature; envious and self-centered, he seeks glory and power. His victory, clearly, would mean destruction for the emperor, for Aureng-Zebe, and for the empire itself. Fortunately, Aureng-Zebe manages to withstand Morat's attack, and all would be well were it not that the emperor, in his dotage, has taken a fancy to Indamora. Since Aureng-Zebe refuses to yield her, to sacrifice love and honor for the sake of a crown, the emperor angrily decides to bestow his authority on Morat. Thus ends the second act.

In the third act Morat enters in state, cordially welcomed by his father, who surrenders to him the "drudgery of power," retaining only the fort "for my security" (III.i). Aureng-Zebe then announces that the two older brothers still threaten. He offers to fight one if Morat will fight the other and thereby prove his concern for the empire's welfare. But the emperor and Morat regard this plea as a trick; this ends the discussion, and the two brothers are never heard of again. The stage is then occupied with other business until late in the fourth act when a minor character rushes in to announce that a traitor has betrayed "the citadel" (the emperor's fort) to Morat. Since this coup endangers the life of all, Aureng-Zebe once more goes to his father's defense. In Act V, Morat returns to declare his victory, and someone else announces the death of Aureng-Zebe. But by this time Morat has discovered true love, and therefore the loss of his brother grieves him. Furthermore, when he learns shortly that a new faction has gathered against him and that his men retreat before it, he gladly goes to meet his fate. The new faction, it turns out, is headed by his mother Nourmahal, who has decided to seize the power from her now delinquent son. Her victory is accomplished within a few minutes, but her reign is equally short. When a new messenger enters to report that the citadel has revolted back to the emperor, she exits, seeking poison. Morat, meanwhile, has lost his life while saving Indamora from his mother, and the emperor now decides, finally, that Aureng-Zebe —who was not really dead—deserves the woman he loves. With their enemies eliminated, the emperor, Aureng-Zebe, and Indamora can look forward to a long reign of peace and quiet.

There can be no doubt that the political strand in *Aureng-Zebe* has sufficient material for a plot; here is, indeed, God's plenty. At the same time, it cannot be taken seriously. The loose end, which leaves the two older brothers still alive and gathering strength, indicates Dryden's own lack of interest, and he has done almost nothing to arouse that of his audience. Most of the elaborate complications occur offstage and become known only through the brief reports of functional figures. All the revolutions and counterrevolutions of the last act and a half can be meaningful only if the audience has attended to and remembered the two lines in which the emperor announces his retention of the fort. But even if the plot were followed with sufficient care, the interest it would generate hardly conforms to any idea of sequential motion. What movement there is resembles the standard seesaw pattern of all heroic plays, the exemplar of which is the continuous shift in allegiance by Almanzor in *The Conquest of Granada*. The political plot of *Aureng-Zebe*, in short, well fulfills the description of dramatic action contained in its epilogue: "The passions raised, and calm by just degrees, / As tides are swelled, and then retire to seas."

Much of the inadequacy of the political plot is doubtless due to Dryden's greater interest in the love theme. While the political events occur mostly offstage, the onstage action is devoted almost entirely to the weaving of all the characters into one gigantic love knot. Aureng-Zebe loves Indamora, but so does his father, the husband of Nourmahal; nor can Arimant, the governor of Agra and Indamora's jailer, resist her charms. In the third act Nourmahal, who had always done whatever she could to thwart Aureng-Zebe, suddenly confesses her passionate love for him. Before this act is over, Morat, married to the supremely devoted Melesinda, sees Indamora for the first time and at once loses his heart. Throughout the play Dryden constantly introduces scenes of love, of declarations of love, of rejection, of conflict between rivals, and of hatred motivated by jealousy.

Despite its greater prominence, however, the love plot is no more pertinent than the political. Even here sequential movement is minimal, for only two events create any sense of progression. In one of these the emperor finally controls his desire for Indamora and surrenders her to his son, but this change has little significance because it merely represents the victory of one side of the emperor's nature over the other and because it is a necessary device for bringing about the play's conclusion. As a result, only the transformation of Morat under the softening influence of his love for Indamora, a change that contributes to his death, stands out as a valid instance of an effect expressing temporal sequence. The rest of the play clearly reveals that Dryden cared little for logical, cause-and-effect progression in which each event stems from the one that precedes it and motivates the next. A highlight of Act IV is the violent scene of jealousy and pride which places Aureng-Zebe and Indamora in conflict. Although this scene is motivated by the interest that Morat has shown in Indamora, it leads nowhere; once it has played itself out, the two are suddenly in each other's arms, vowing eternal affection, and nothing that follows is in any logical manner influenced by the fact that they have quarreled. As little as this scene conforms to any concept of sequential action, however, for sheer irrelevance it cannot com-

pete with a scene in the fifth act, in which Aureng-Zebe and Indamora repeat the entire process. The repetition seems motivated
only by Dryden's satisfaction with the first version and a desire
to duplicate his success.

The love plot also presents, therefore, an essentially static situation. The various declarations of love could be introduced almost anywhere in the play. Arimant makes his love known in
Act II, and Act III reveals the passion of Nourmahal for Aureng-Zebe and the wifely devotion of Melesinda for Morat, but
in all three cases the declaration merely amounts to the sudden
exposure of a pre-existing state. In addition, though the events of
the love plot take place onstage, the narrative quality of the political plot carries over into its companion. In the love plot it is not
functional figures who announce what has happened but the participants themselves, yet the result is the same: the falling in love
is in each case a given factor, as if, like the events of the political
plot, it had occurred elsewhere. Every happening in the play
merits the comment with which Melesinda greets the news of
Morat's political success: "A change so unexpected must surprise" (III.i). The "story" in *Aureng-Zebe* therefore seems irrelevant, something to be quickly disposed of in a summary statement here and there. The events surprise as events because, ultimately, they are only devices. The framework of action merely
provides a means to set up the individual scenes that the several
events, political or passionate, make possible.

Dryden's interest, then, is not in plot but in the individual
scenes that plot allows him to bring onto the stage: the numerous
set pieces of lamentation or joy, such as Aureng-Zebe's famous
description of life as a "cheat" (IV.i), and the even more numerous extended debates between characters of contrasting persua-
sions. This irrelevance of plot was well known to Dryden's con-
temporaries, and one of them offered a witty and convincing explanation for it. In *The Rehearsal*, which burlesques the heroic
play, Smith, one of the onstage spectators, complains that the

plot of the play he is watching "stands still." Bayes the dramatist, a caricature of Dryden, provides the obvious reply: "Plot stand still! why, what a devil is the plot good for but to bring in fine things?"[14] This is not to say, however, that *Aureng-Zebe* is formless. What it lacks in plot, in sequential action, is more than compensated for by intricacy of spatial design.

For despite their failure to relate to one another sequentially, the separate scenes are tightly interwoven. Act II begins with a brief episode in which Arimant, declaring his love, is quickly restrained by Indamora, who can accept him only as a friend. Passive in nature, he is soon tamed, willing to become her hopeless slave. Immediately thereafter the emperor enters to advance his own claims, and since Indamora can no more accept his love than she could Arimant's, the basic situation is still that of the preceding scene. But where Arimant was timid, passive, and yielding, the emperor is direct, demanding, and persistent. Thus an obvious contrast emerges. The next episode, which opposes the emperor to Nourmahal, once again centers on a debate between pursuer and pursued, but this time it is the emperor who refuses to yield, thereby assuming Indamora's role, and Nourmahal who is the seemingly insistent pursuer. Moreover, while the two preceding scenes emphasized the loved one's refusal to reciprocate, this one focuses on the jealousy of the rejected lover. This sequence is not unusual. Its technique, in which each succeeding scene echoes with variations its predecessors, is evident throughout the play.

The real intricacy of design appears, however, not in the combining of two or three scenes but in the way that all of them eventually merge into one simultaneous whole. The fourth episode of Act II contains the quarrel between Aureng-Zebe and his father, which concludes with the decision to cede the power to

---

[14] George Villiers *et al.*, *The Rehearsal* (III.i), in *Plays of the Restoration and Eighteenth Century*, ed. Dougald MacMillan and Howard Mumford Jones (New York: Holt, Rinehart, and Winston, 1959).

Morat. Except that Aureng-Zebe lectures the emperor on the subject of the responsibilities attached to his role as a father, thus echoing Nourmahal's attempt to remind him of his husbandly obligations, this scene does not immediately reveal its formal relationship to those that precede it. Not until Act IV, which virtually repeats the same episodes in the same order, is its meticulous placing evident. The first episode of Act IV presents Nourmahal's insistent declaration of love for Aureng-Zebe and his rejection of her: it repeats the first two scenes of Act II, reversing the roles of male and female. The next episode opposes Melesinda's jealousy to Morat's contempt, and this repeats the second-act scene between Nourmahal and the emperor—though this time the wife is meek rather than shrewish. The following episode has the same place in the new sequence that the debate between Aureng-Zebe and the emperor had in the first. Appropriately, this episode also contains a quarrel between father and son over Indamora and ends with the father's wish to give the crown to his other son. But here the quarreling son is Morat; the son, not the father, has the power; and the desired outcome cannot be translated into action.

The repetition of the second-act sequence in the episodes of Act IV fully reveals Dryden's development of a spatial design rather than a temporal progression. As I have shown in the preceding chapter, Aeschylus, Shakespeare, and Ibsen also employ the device of seemingly repeating whole scenes. But where they use it to underscore the extent of the change that intervening events have wrought, Dryden repeats scenes in order to cancel any suggestion of motion. The repeated scene merely examines another facet of the generally static situation. His technique therefore differs from that which Joseph Frank ascribes to modern poetry and fiction. Dryden does not completely do away with temporal connections; instead, he nullifies them by putting greater emphasis on the parallels that tend to link scenes in nonnarrative fashion. In effect, he removes each scene from its place in the lineal pattern and juxtaposes it simultaneously to almost every other scene in the play.

Juxtaposition is also the key to the other principal element of the spatial design in *Aureng-Zebe*, the "variety of characters." Dryden's abstract diction and his habit of seeing his characters as "patterns" [15] produce dramatic figures who possess a few clearly defined general traits. Type characters, whose qualities are few and fixed, lend themselves readily to comparison and contrast, and Dryden exploits these possibilities to the limit. He constantly associates his characters, either through emphatic contrast, as with the repeated distinction between Aureng-Zebe and Morat, or through a parallel designed to highlight a significant difference, as when Nourmahal declares that Indamora matches her in beauty but owns a soul filled with "rubbish" (V.i). Ultimately, all the characters take their place in a single arrangement. The contrast between Aureng-Zebe, who upholds honor, duty, law, and custom, and Morat, who would be more at home in wild nature, is the most obvious segment of this arrangement. But an identical contrast exists among the female characters, in the opposition between Nourmahal, who is Morat's mother and pledges a similar allegiance to "natural" law (IV.i), and Indamora, Aureng-Zebe's beloved, who agrees with him that personal desire ought to yield to the claims of honor and duty. The presence of Melesinda, whom Dryden in his dedication to the Earl of Mulgrave admits creating as a contrast to Nourmahal, converts this character antithesis into a triad. Like Indamora, Melesinda believes in the supremacy of external authority, but while Indamora can be pushed only so far, while she refuses to give in to the demands of the emperor or endure the jealous accusations of her lover, Melesinda is completely passive: her self-elected death on her husband's funeral pyre makes this abundantly clear. Mele-

---

[15] Cf. his remark in "Of Heroic Plays" about Almanzor's status as a "perfect pattern of heroic virtue" (*Three Plays*, p. 11) and Indamora's description of Aureng-Zebe as "the blameless pattern of a son" (I.i).

sinda's place among the male characters is filled by Arimant, whose love for Indamora is also passive and who dies in order to save Aureng-Zebe, the man Indamora prefers: thus an identical triad emerges among the male characters. The only major figure not accounted for by these two triads is the emperor, who has a place distinctly his own. He, the husband of Nourmahal and would-be lover of Indamora, the father of the two contrasting sons, is the only character in the play who vacillates between one set of values and another. At the end, when he surrenders both his crown and the woman he loves, he even comes to resemble the wholly unselfish Melesinda and Arimant.

No single character or scene in *Aureng-Zebe* has much complexity in itself. But no character or scene can be perceived in isolation. By means of his spatial design Dryden manages to combine an almost unlimited series of partial perspectives into a unified whole. Shade after shade of love, jealousy, hatred, pride, and meekness takes its place in a continually shifting spectrum, and each shade is seen only in relation to the other shades that it serves to set off. The scenes of jealousy between Indamora and Aureng-Zebe are irrelevant from the point of view of temporal sequence, but they add a further touch to the multifarious portrait. The transformation of Morat, already noted as the only aspect of the play indicating temporal movement, is, in the final analysis, essentially static in effect: it merely dramatizes a quality of love unlike any other that the play presents. *Aureng-Zebe* is, then, not as empty as it seems if regarded as an example of lineal progression. Its meaning is the design, with all its many ramifications, and when the play is seen spatially, as it was meant to be seen, it has a richly interesting meaning indeed.

The Temporal Dimension

Despite Restoration drama and certain modern experiments, plays with a dominant spatial form are not typical. Ordinarily both aspects of the space-time unity receive more or less full development. This fact is quite apparent in drama with a well-defined beginning, middle, and end, but even in those plays that through variety of characters and intricacy of design seem to vie with *Aureng-Zebe*—the plays of Shakespeare, O'Casey, and Brecht, to suggest a few—the spatial dimension evolves along a clear temporal line. In most drama, therefore, the whole structure also projects a second meaningful dimension, the temporal. This dimension is established not by the relationship of simultaneous disparate focal points but by the sequential movement from one point to another through an entire action as it is performed in time. The obvious manifestation of this dimension is the narrative vehicle, what G. Wilson Knight calls "the plot-chain of event following event." [16] More important, however, is the underlying lineal pattern for which the "plot-chain" serves as metaphor. Through its expressive conformation this pattern offers an additional comment on the experience that it helps to organize.

The *Oresteia* has a fully realized spatial dimension, not only in Knight's sense of atmosphere but in other respects as well. Much of the tension in the *Agamemnon* stems from the growing conflict between the Argive Elders and Clytaemestra. Each of the first two plays pits a murderer against his victim, and each also introduces a secondary victim who provides a parallel to the first. Throughout, the various acts of violence are seen to have a double character: from one point of view the act rights a balance upset by a prior act; from the other, it causes a disturbance that demands a new attempt to restore equilibrium. In the third play this continuous duality becomes fully explicit in the carefully detailed and systematic opposition between Apollo and the Furies. Nevertheless, the trilogy is predominantly temporal in form. The three plays present a developing action that stresses both the cause-and-effect relationship of the separate events and the

[16] *The Wheel of Fire*, p. 4.

lengthy time span in which they occur. The plot chain of this action includes the narrated accounts of the sacrifice of Iphigeneia and the fall of Troy, Clytaemestra's murder of Agamemnon, Orestes' revenge on his mother and Aegisthus, and the trial at Athens. Underlying this sequence is the lineal pattern that traces the transformation from an unstable world, dominated by natural catastrophes, war, human sacrifice, crime, and revenge, to a peaceful universe, founded on the harmonious fellowship of men and gods. Two parallel movements supplement this basic pattern: in the first a seemingly endless cycle of eternal repetition is established and then finally eliminated; in the second the role of the gods becomes increasingly evident.

The trilogy form, with its three separate though connected plays, helps create the first of these movements. As Greene points out, there is an intrinsic relationship between Aeschylus' "frequent if not invariable custom of presenting trilogies" and "his conviction that the doom of an individual is only a moment in a longer process." [17] In the *Oresteia*, Aeschylus has given this "longer process" definite shape through his arrangement of the separate plays. The first two, each of which consists of four clearly defined sections, are almost exactly identical in form. Section one of each play is a brief prologue consisting of a single speech which acts as a focusing scene to anticipate, directly or indirectly, the play's major event, a murder. Section two, which comprises the first three choral odes and the two episodes they bracket, is devoted to an examination of the past in order to explain why the murder must occur. The major characters who appear (Clytaemestra in the first play, Orestes and Electra in the second) are those who plan to commit the murder, and their part in the action consists of preparation for this event. The third section, which begins with the entrance of the primary victim, centers more directly on the murder itself. In the odes of this section the chorus, dismissing the past, now focuses on the coming event. The first of the section's two episodes emphasizes the primary

[17] *Moira*, p. 106.

victim, who here unwittingly performs the act or acts that seal his fate—Agamemnon finally consents to walk on the carpet; Clytaemestra admits Orestes to the palace and sends Cilissa the nurse to bring Aegisthus—while the second emphasizes the subordinate victim (Cassandra or Aegisthus) and explores more fully the ramifications of the murder. This section ends with the announcement of the completed act and the chorus' attempt to assess the immediate implications. The fourth section presents the murder's aftermath. Here the murderer tries to justify his deed and expresses his hope that it has ended the sequence of crime and retribution. But he must confront a chorus which insists that more violence will inevitably follow.

The two plays dramatize distinct actions, clearly separated in time, but since each takes the same form, the resulting effect is one of cyclic repetition, the apparent endlessness of which is especially stressed in the way that both plays, which began by emphasizing the past, conclude without resolution, looking toward the future. In the final lines of *The Libation Bearers* the chorus reviews the entire sequence and wonders when it will ever end:

> Here on this house of the kings the third
> storm has broken, with wind
> from the inward race, and gone its course.
> The children were eaten: there was the first
> affliction, the curse of Thyestes.
> Next came the royal death, when a man
> and lord of Achaean armies went down
> killed in the bath. Third
> is for the savior. He came. Shall I call
> it that, or death? Where
> is the end? Where shall the fury of fate
> be stilled to sleep, be done with?   [ll. 1065–1076].

The third play of the trilogy somewhat resembles the other two in form. It begins with a prologue as focusing scene, inspects the past, leads up to a single significant event, and then closes with a long aftermath. Much more striking, however, are the basic alterations that Aeschylus has made in the parallel form. Orestes is the intended victim in this play, but he is present from the beginning, and the only other major character who appears during the first section is not his adversary but his champion, the god Apollo. At the point where the victims Agamemnon and Clytaemestra were introduced in the first two plays, Athene the goddess of wisdom enters in the third. Like her human predecessors she performs an act that makes possible the play's major event, but she is fully conscious of what she is doing, and instead of a third murder she provides for an entirely different kind of outcome, the trial that will remove from potentially guilty hands the necessity of securing justice. Because of her intervention it is the declaration of Orestes' acquittal which parallels the prior announcements of murder. This event also provokes an aftermath, and once again a chorus prophesies new violence, but under Athene's persuasion it finally agrees to a beneficial settlement. In this play, then, the action comes to a full conclusion; unlike the first two plays, whose open endings suggested eternal recurrence, *The Eumenides* is brought to a close with a choral ode celebrating a newly realized order. These changes, all of which substitute gods for the human agents of the first two plays, complete the lineal pattern by giving it a harmonious resolution, one that is especially meaningful because of the fully felt sequence of crime and retribution that has preceded it.

The presence of the gods in *The Eumenides* climaxes the second movement supplementing the basic lineal pattern, a movement that records the increasing relevance of the supernatural. This movement is in part expressed by the growing sense of the influence of the dead. Agamemnon must die because of his responsibility for the deaths that have preceded his, those of Aegisthus' brothers, of the Trojans, and—particularly—of Iphigeneia. Despite the importance of these prior dead, they are introduced only obliquely; the spectators hear of them through narrative alone, and their influence consists only in their supplying the living characters with motives for revenge. The murder in *The Libation Bearers* is also motivated by a prior death, that of Agamemnon, but in this case, through the prayers that Electra, Orestes, and the chorus address to Agamemnon's grave, the one whose death demands retribution seems not only immediately present but also directly involved in the planned vengeance. Aeschylus completes this movement in *The Eumenides* when the ghost of Clytaemestra actually appears onstage, urging the sleeping Furies to resume their pursuit of the son who has murdered her.

The primary manifestation of this second movement, however, is the increasing participation of the gods, for their role in the major sequence that runs from Atreus to Orestes is only gradually revealed.[18] The Watchman introduces the gods in the first line of the *Agamemnon*, and the chorus, through its prayer (ll. 160–183) and its odes, frequently asserts the involvement of Zeus in all human action. From the beginning the gods, individually and as a group, are constantly mentioned and supplicated, but before the murder of Agamemnon has actually taken place, no one states that his death will somehow fulfill divine purpose. Aeschylus thoroughly implies that in killing him Clytaemestra serves as an agent of the gods—as I have shown in Chapter 4—but until the play is nearly over the gods are explicitly associated only with other, related events: the sacrifice, the fall of Troy, and Cassandra's punishment. It is not until Clytaemestra returns to justify her deed that a change in this pattern occurs. At first she claims to be motivated only by the death of her daughter, but the chorus eventually perceives that the daimon that afflicts the House of Atreus has worked through her, and this perception in-

[18] In this account of the gods' increasing emergence I am partially indebted to the analysis of the *Oresteia* by Philip Wheelwright, in *The Burning Fountain* (Bloomington: Indiana University Press, 1954), pp. 243, 255.

spires an awareness of the involvement of Zeus: "For what thing without Zeus is done among mortals?" (l. 1487). Clytaemestra then extends the chorus' perception to full realization:

> Can you claim I have done this?
> Speak of me never
> more as wife of Agamemnon.
> In the shadow of this corpse's queen
> the old stark avenger
> of Atreus for his revel of hate
> struck down this man,
> last blood for the slaughtered children
>
> [ll. 1497–1504].

At this stage of the development the second play, *The Libation Bearers*, begins. Orestes speaks the prologue, praying to Zeus to "grant me vengeance for my father's / murder" (ll. 17–18), and this opening prayer is echoed throughout the play by Orestes, Electra, and the chorus. Moreover, Orestes soon declares that he undertakes his revenge at the command of Apollo (ll. 269–296), and after the killing he repeats this claim in order to justify himself (ll. 1029–1031). But the play does not remain at this stage; as at the end of the *Agamemnon*, a new revelation is achieved. Up to this point Aeschylus has established the gods' involvement only through the declarations made by his human characters. At the end of *The Libation Bearers*, however, Orestes is suddenly confronted by the Furies, though they are as yet seen only by him. This insistence that the gods are actually present effects a smooth transition to *The Eumenides*, where the gods—Apollo, the Furies, and Athene—become literally part of the action, visible and audible on the same stage with Orestes himself. And when the trial has ended and Orestes has gone, it is only the gods who remain.

This whole development is epitomized by the three prologues. The Watchman makes his brief mention of "the gods," but after that he is entirely concerned with human joys and fears. At the beginning of *The Libation Bearers*, Orestes invokes two gods by name, Hermes and Zeus, asking for their assistance in a human action. The Priestess who opens *The Eumenides* carries this sequence to its logical end. Her formal prayer honors several deities, from Earth to Zeus, and the only human activity she cites is that of worship.

These two movements—the cycle of unending repetition and the gradual emergence of the gods—together embody the basic significance of the trilogy's action. The universe as Aeschylus depicts it in the *Oresteia* is one in which all actions, earthly and cosmic, are tightly interwoven. The more closely human action is scrutinized, the more it reveals the involvement of the gods. And since the human and the divine are so inseparably linked, the welfare of the one depends on the compassionate intervention of the other. Human experience without divine participation can only form a meaningless sequence going nowhere. But once the gods choose to intervene directly and to make their intervention the occasion for ordering the entire universe, human experience can at last be rid of suffering, pain, and guilt so that peace, justice, and wisdom may reign in their stead. The ultimate priority of divine order must finally be realized, and therefore the gods alone occupy the stage just before the trilogy ends. But once this priority has been recognized, the specifically human focus again becomes relevant. Thus, in the concluding chorus, human beings, now representing mankind generally, return to take their part in the newly established harmony.

A number of interesting contrasts to the temporal dimension of the *Oresteia* are provided by that of *Hamlet*. The lineal pattern it forms has a different shape, and therefore it offers a comment of another kind. Unlike the *Oresteia*, in which the lineal pattern reflects the temporal development of a continuing situation, in *Hamlet* it derives its structure primarily from the progress of a single character, the play's hero. With its several plot strands, its multiple character oppositions and parallels, and its shifting perspectives in which "the action of the drama as a whole is presented only as each character in turn actualizes it in his story and according to his lights," [19] *Hamlet* is much more heavily spatial than the *Oresteia*. As a result, the lineal pattern of *Hamlet* is both less clearly defined and less crucial for understanding. To ignore it, however, would be to neglect an important area of the play's significance.

The lineal pattern of *Hamlet* has its origin in the opening scene, where Denmark, threatened by war and haunted by the dead, is shown to suffer an unspecified but pervading disorder. With Hamlet's entrance in Act I, scene ii, the pattern transfers to him. Hamlet senses the malady, laments it, and consequently dramatizes it. From here to the end of the play the basic movement traces his changing responses to the disturbing situation that confronts him. His progress, which moves through three distinct phases, gives his near defeat and eventual tragic victory a form expressive of his function in the play.

The first phase, continuing through Act III, scene i, describes a falling action in which Hamlet becomes increasingly aware of the extent of the detected evil and increasingly unable to combat it effectively. When first seen, he is contemplating suicide. Believing himself tainted by his mother's frailty and the "wicked speed" with which she has entered into a second, "incestuous" marriage, he finds life distasteful; the world around him has become "an unweeded garden." News of his father's ghost animates him, and he eagerly seeks a meeting with it, but this apparent reversal in his mood is merely a prelude to its intensification. The Ghost's presence nourishes his suspicion that "all is not well" (I.ii.254), and when he sees it, he learns that his own sense of disorder has more than enough objective validity: the king of Denmark is a murderer. This revelation and the Ghost's accompanying command awaken in Hamlet signs that betoken incipi-

[19] Francis Fergusson, *The Idea of a Theater* (Princeton, N.J.: Princeton University Press, 1949), p. 104.

ent madness. He himself realizes that he is "distracted" (I.v.97). His "wild and whirling words" to Horatio and Marcellus (l. 133) suggest that his prophesied "antic disposition" may be less feigned than he imagines. Nor is this the only effect of his meeting with the Ghost, for though he at first unhesitatingly welcomes the call to revenge, he soon regrets that the burden of correcting disjointed time has been assigned to him.

Both of these effects remain evident in the second act, in which madness and inaction are the dominant motifs. Hamlet, who has done nothing in the intervening weeks, now confines himself almost exclusively to fostering his observers' belief that he has lost his sanity. His moments of complete lucidity and the inadmissibility of his observers' testimony thoroughly support his claim to Rosencrantz and Guildenstern that he is "but mad north-north-west" (II.ii.374); but if it is unreal, the projected madness is nonetheless an effective metaphor for representing his great incapacity to cope with the evil that surrounds him. Moreover, other impressions of Act II help delineate a further aspect of the falling action. Hamlet already knows he cannot trust Claudius, his mother, or Polonius. The second act offers additional proof that he has only himself to rely on. Ophelia's account, in Act II, scene i, of his visit to her chamber suggests that he had hoped to make her an ally but had realized the uselessness of his effort. When Rosencrantz and Guildenstern arrive, he has no doubt that these supposed friends "were sent for" (II.ii.291). These discoveries lead to new expressions of discontent. Denmark, and the whole world, are now like prisons to him. He can no longer find any delight in earth, air, or man, all of which once seemed so excellent. The worst discovery still awaits him, however. The arrival of the players temporarily arrests his descent into further despair, as did the news of his father's ghost in Act I, scene ii, but once again apparent reversal produces greater intensification. Listening to the player's recitation acquaints Hamlet with the most treacherous betrayal of them all. He, who had only himself to rely on, has failed himself; hence the helpless turbulence of the soliloquy with which he ends the act.

The opening scene of Act III brings the first phase of Hamlet's progress to its climax. The spying of Claudius and Polonius and the soliloquy in the presence of other characters succinctly epitomize both the world that surrounds him and his helpless isolation in the midst of it. Here, as at the beginning of this phase, he thinks of suicide, but now there is no mention of an "Everlasting" who disapproves. The extent of Hamlet's fall is clearly indicated by the bitter frustration that prompts him to torture Ophelia and by his savage indictment of himself as one too evil to be "crawling between earth and heaven." Significantly, this picture is almost immediately followed by Ophelia's idealized account of what he had been in the past. In the second act Polonius describes Hamlet as having fallen

> into a sadness, then into a fast,
> Thence to a watch, thence into a weakness,
> Thence to a lightness, and, by this declension,
> Into the madness wherein now he raves
> And all we mourn for   [II.ii.146–150].

The substance of Polonius' speech consists of conventional Renaissance love clichés exaggerated for comic effect. But its *form* provides a strikingly accurate summary of Hamlet's progress through the first two acts of the play.

In Act III, scene ii, Hamlet begins the second phase of his progress. His experience has persuaded him that the universe is a void and that to give it meaning he must himself replace the God he can no longer discern. This effort, as I have shown in the preceding chapter, proves fruitless, and it also occasions the killing of Polonius, an act that will eventually cost Hamlet his life. But the killing of Polonius has more immediate consequences as well. It is shortly thereafter that Hamlet, in his speech on the engineer hoist with his own petard, pronounces his most sardonic assessment of the universe. The display of madness that then follows in the early scenes of Act IV seems highly convincing; at any rate, it reveals that Hamlet is more desperate than ever before. And he has good reason to be. The killing of Polonius has helped Claudius determine that Hamlet's trip to England is now an unavoidable necessity and that he must be put to death there. Because of this trip Hamlet hears of Fortinbras' intentions against Poland and once again is made to feel his own inadequacy. Furthermore, though he concludes the contrast between Fortinbras and himself by vowing that "from this time forth, / My thoughts be bloody, or be nothing worth," he is in reality under guard, being led away from Denmark to his appointed execution. In one sense, then, the action of this second phase, which begins hopefully, imitates on a larger scale the ironic pattern in which apparent reversal precipitates further decline, and therefore the second phase could be conceived of as an extension of the first. Yet there is one significant difference. The trip to England does not yield the result that Claudius intends; on the contrary, it allows Hamlet to encounter the experience that prepares him for the third and final phase of his progress.

This phase, a rising action, traces Hamlet's return from the depth to which he has fallen. Its first indication is the new tone of command, certainty, and detachment which characterizes his letters to Horatio and Claudius and his dialogue with the clown in the graveyard. Then comes his outburst beside Ophelia's grave. Its intensity is the one sign in all Act V which suggests the old Hamlet. Yet, in contrast to his responses of the preceding acts, this one scarcely displays excess. The shock of discovering Ophelia's death and the violence of Laertes' attack, which Hamlet considers unjust, fully motivate the shift from the calm and confident "This is I, / Hamlet the Dane" (V.i.251–252) to the hyperbolic speeches that follow. More important, this episode has much the same function in its context as did Hamlet's responses to the news of the Ghost and the arrival of the players in theirs: just as these earlier events led to a further decline, this one prompts a corresponding rise. In the next scene, while speaking to Horatio, Hamlet regrets

> That to Laertes I forgot myself;
> For by the image of my cause I see
> The portraiture of his   [V.ii.76–78].

The speech could not be more important. Hamlet, who always saw the disorder in his world only in personal or purely abstract terms, now realizes that others as well suffer from its evil effects. The sympathy he here expresses also indicates a major change because it shows that his alienation has begun to yield to a sense of kinship with his fellow beings. Hamlet can, as a result, now do what he would not have done before: he asks Laertes' pardon (ll. 218–236). And here more than anywhere else, in blaming his madness and in speaking of it as a thing of the past, he makes explicit the transformation he has undergone.

The major sign of this transformation is, of course, his restored faith in "divinity," "heaven," and a "special providence." This allows him to accept his task without qualms and to speak of his determination without any trace of the irony that accompanied his vow in Act IV, scene iv. He is now confident that he will kill Claudius when the occasion arises. It is this new-found faith that convinces Hamlet he serves a higher power and that sends him to the duel, even though he fears some danger for himself. Although Hamlet cannot foreknow it—and this in itself shows that he now abets the workings of an external force of some kind— the duel provides the occasion he has awaited, and he finally carries out the Ghost's command. This act purges Denmark of its evil. It also completes Hamlet's own purgation. Having paid for his crime with a fatal wound, Hamlet then receives earthly pardon from Laertes. Horatio's eulogy—"And flights of angels sing thee to thy rest"—suggests that the divinity that used Hamlet for its instrument was a benevolent providence and that now he can expect pardon in heaven as well. For Hamlet, as he approaches death, the only other concerns still requiring attention are the welfare of the state and his own posthumous reputation. He attends to the first by giving his "dying voice" to Fortinbras, and Fortinbras, when he enters, attends to the second with his tribute to Hamlet's royal nature. The rising pattern is complete. Hamlet is fully exalted in death.[20]

Although Hamlet's progress forms the basic lineal pattern of the play, it is paralleled by another that records the changing condition of Denmark. This pattern, partly conveyed by Hamlet's growing awareness of external disorder, also finds other means of expression, particularly the deaths that occur at spaced intervals. These deaths, like that of Gaunt in *Richard II*, are both directly symbolic and contextually significant, and each marks a new development in the growth and waning of the evil afflicting the kingdom. The first death that Shakespeare emphasizes is that of Hamlet's father. Although he is already dead when the play begins and appears only as the Ghost whose presence helps indicate the existing disorder, his memory persists as a living force in the action. Horatio recalls his heroic exploits against Norway and Poland. Hamlet, dissatisfied with the situation that confronts him, passionately insists on his eminent superiority to Claudius, the present king. The Ghost's own report that he has been murdered by Claudius lends confirmation to Hamlet's contrast and also fixes the regicide as the source of the evil that now threatens. Hamlet's father, though his ghost is fully conscious of his sins, is consistently idealized, and since there is no living reality to refute the verbal portrait, the idealization is persuasive. These effects characterize the current situation as a falling off, a decline from a

---

[20] I have discussed Hamlet's rise in the final act as if the play were particularly Christian in tone only because the lineal pattern of Hamlet's progress conveys this impression. As my earlier remarks on the play's universe have shown, I find the Christian interpretation an inadequate accounting of the play's many implications. I return to this problem in the final chapter.

former state of glory. Denmark, which once boasted a godlike, victorious king, is now governed by a "smiling, damned villain" primarily concerned with preserving his own evil life.

The death of Polonius, which occurs in Act III, scene iv, culminates the falling action dramatized by the first half of the play. Up to this point the evil in Denmark has been established by report, by Hamlet's expressions of malaise, or by such minor signs of discord as mutual alienation and reciprocal spying. Similarly, Claudius' response to the play-within-the-play has corroborated his villainy, but only with regard to the initial act of evil. The death of Polonius greatly intensifies the impression of disorder. It makes murder—the most incisive sign of Denmark's malady—an immediate and concrete reality, it unleashes, in the events that conclude Act IV, the fullest display of corruption which the play contains, and—most important of all—it shows that Hamlet, the only one with sufficient vision to right Denmark's imbalance, now contributes to its further downfall. Yet Polonius' death has also other, more hopeful implications. Since he has always been the chief embodiment of the court's moral blindness, his death suggests that evil will no longer be blinked away or concealed by a fatuous and hasty speculation. Moreover, his death, like the later elimination of Rosencrantz and Guildenstern, represents a lessening in the court of the sycophantic earnestness that gave Claudius the unwitting allies needed to strengthen his position of relative security. Claudius can still plot, as he does in the final scenes of Act IV, but now he must do so openly, giving his new ally full knowledge of his schemes. With Polonius gone, he must now enlist the aid of a more sensitive and volatile and therefore more dangerous ally, the impassioned Laertes.

The remaining deaths complete the movement that the death of Polonius has initiated. That of Ophelia, which climaxes the turbulence concluding Act IV, is in many respects the most significant in the play. Her own progress from innocence through madness to destruction mirrors and thus helps define that of Denmark up to the time of her burial. She is, moreover, a completely guiltless and helpless victim, who has contributed to Denmark's disorder only as a result of the best possible intentions; no crime can be attributed to her except that of passivity. Her death therefore strikingly discloses the extent to which the original evil has grown. No one, it now appears, can escape its influence. What was originally the crime of one man has become, like Adam's sin, what Hamlet calls "this canker of our nature" (V.ii.69), and, as Ophelia's death suggests, only a mass purgation can now cleanse the state. But also, insofar as her madness embodies the helpless perplexity that colors every attempt to cope with the spreading evil, her death, which puts an end to her madness, indicates a corresponding elimination of the greater madness in the macrocosm: significantly, Hamlet at once returns and exhibits his transformation. With the disorder in the state now fully manifest and with Hamlet at last capable of effective action, the evil has run its course. The many deaths occurring at the end of the play constitute the necessary purgation. All those who have been in any way tainted are destroyed. Denmark itself is virtually annihilated, but it is therefore purified. It stands ready to begin afresh with a new reign of order. When Fortinbras arrives and carries out the orderly disposition that completes the play, the new reign is inaugurated.

The patterns enacted by Hamlet and Denmark are almost identical. Fully anticipated by the magnificent opening scene in its movement from initial darkness and confusion, through full-scale turbulence, to the peace that comes with the advent of dawn, these patterns give the play its temporal form. Together they characterize the dramatic experience as an action of descent and ascent, of the fall to a nadir that at first promises imminent destruction but ultimately occasions the rise to a new state as great as, or greater than, the original.

The primary significance of this temporal design lies in the fact that the play's action has this shape and no other, and to this extent, the temporal design of *Hamlet* is like that of the *Oresteia*. But even here an important difference arises: unlike the *Oresteia*'s temporal design, which functions only in a reflexive manner —as a means of defining the nature of the action it orders—that of *Hamlet*, by virtue of its specific shape, performs an additional service. As a pattern of descent and ascent it establishes a complex nonverbal allusion to a whole series of mythic, religious, and literary narratives that formally embody the archetype of death and resurrection. Denmark consequently assumes in some measure the quality of an ailing "topocosm" that can be restored to health only through the sacrifice of a god-hero. Hamlet becomes, however faintly, the savior figure whose descent into and return from the abyss guarantees both his own purification and that of his land. When seen structurally, therefore, the play's images of death and rebirth take on considerable significance. Ophelia's death symbolically represents the moment of almost total collapse in the health of Denmark, but the possibility of rebirth is suggested in Laertes' hope that "from her fair and unpolluted flesh / May violets spring!" (V.i.233–234). Hamlet, when he returns to Denmark to complete its purgation, passes through a graveyard and then looks back on his dead past. These images, emphasized by the play's temporal design, reinforce its allusion to the basic archetype. But there are two lineal patterns here, not one, and no matter how closely they resemble each other, one primary difference prevents total similarity. Denmark, though severely afflicted, seemingly achieves full purgation and the promise of renewal. Hamlet, in contrast, receives his exaltation only in death. His fate therefore expresses not only his own tragedy but also the tragic cost of Denmark's rebirth.

The temporal design of *Hamlet* has also a special emotional significance. What gives the mythic archetype of death and rebirth its inexhaustible fascination and expressiveness is its psychological validity. It objectifies a familiar and fundamentally satisfying emotional rhythm, the sequence that leads from frustration to transcendence, the human "night journey." One of man's most common inner experiences, this rhythm appears in a whole variety of forms, ranging from the most minute and inconsequential incident of everyday life to the complex and important process of human individuation.[21] Since a play is primarily an experience that its spectators undergo, the temporal dimension of *Hamlet* makes it a new embodiment of the familiar rhythm. And in the achieved feeling of transcendence following frustration, the ending of *Hamlet* evokes a quality of joy and exultation which it shares with all genuine tragedy.

Any attempt to analyze Ibsen's *Rosmersholm* in the same way is bound to encounter difficulty. The play obviously has a fully realized temporal dimension, yet its action forms no coherent lineal designs similar to those in the *Oresteia* and *Hamlet*. The first two acts focus on Rosmer, and the second, as I have noted in the preceding chapter, establishes a pattern of attrition. But unlike *Hamlet*, this play does not consistently trace the progress of a single hero; in the third act the focus shifts to Rebecca, and another design begins. This shift, and the subsequent concern with both characters' somewhat differing experiences, also prevent the formation of a meaningful pattern deriving from the changing contours of a general situation. Further complications stem from Ibsen's use of the retrospective method. In *Hamlet* and the *Oresteia* every change in the basic situation is a distinct step forward, a movement away from an original condition toward a future goal. But in *Rosmersholm* almost every step forward results from and is accompanied by a step backward into the past, toward fuller understanding of the basic situation as it was originally consti-

[21] Cf. Maud Bodkin's discussion of Coleridge's *Rime of the Ancient Mariner*, in chapter ii of *Archetypal Patterns in Poetry* (New York: Vintage Books, 1958).

tuted. This is not to say, however, that the temporal dimension of *Rosmersholm* lacks significance; on the contrary, it is as vital for meaning as are those of *Hamlet* and the *Oresteia*. But since it functions in a different manner, it cannot be discussed in the same terms. Its analysis properly belongs to the final chapter.

Part IV: The Final Fusion

8. Modes of Combination

The process of becoming acquainted with a play is like that of becoming acquainted with a person. It is an empirical and inductive process; it starts with the observable facts; but it instinctively aims at a grasp of the very life of the machine which is both deeper and, oddly enough, more immediate than the surface appearances offer.

—Francis Fergusson, *The Idea of a Theater*

The preceding chapters have been concerned with individual devices and, consequently, with individual aspects of the unity that is a play; even the whole structure, despite its seeming inclusiveness, is but one expression of a complex design, one source of a rich significance that has numerous other sources as well. These chapters, then, have offered a number of fragmentary answers to the basic question with which I began: How can the dramatist, working in such an apparently objective medium, manage to control his spectators' responses so that they ultimately see his play as he sees it himself? A complete answer to this question requires a shift in focus from the individual device and the individual aspect of the play to the play as a whole.

Since the dramatist works in a medium that denies him the use of a controlling, interpretive voice, dramatic point of view is located not in the group of signs presented directly on the stage but in the consciousness of the audience that perceives them. If the dramatist has not sufficiently mastered his form—a difficulty that seems to have beset Pirandello momentarily in *Each in His Own Way*—or if his theatrical collaborators distort his creation by omitting, altering, or adding individual signs, then this point of view will to some extent be formed without his control. Under ideal circumstances, however, this point of view is one that the dramatist has himself determined, one that essentially corresponds to his own way of seeing the experience his signs embody. Explanation of the manner in which he exerts this control necessitates, first of all, a brief review. The preceding chapters discuss several kinds of devices—aural, visual, and structural, as well as verbal—but, in the final analysis, the dramatist has only one tool at his disposal, his command of language; his text can consist only of individual speeches interspersed with occasional stage directions. The following recapitulation is designed, therefore, not only to provide a quick restatement of the different kinds of effects characteristic of drama, but also to show that all these effects, however they might be categorized, result from the dramatist's successful employment of language.

Five kinds of effects can be distinguished. My arrangement of them, which is based on a scale of decreasing explicitness and directness and of increasing complexity, is intended to suggest not the actual but the logical steps by means of which the spectator, responding to the impressions that language creates, can be said to move from the outside in, from the surface to the center, from the immediate facts to "the very life of the machine."

Effects of the first type comprise all those more or less direct and overt statements formed by the explicit meaning of individual speeches, by the implications they immediately evoke, or—as in most cases—by both. Hamlet says, "there is a special providence in the fall of a sparrow," and at once the spectator has two impressions to record. The first of these is an assertion about the play's universe, and while fully explicit, it is nevertheless conditional; acceptance of it depends on two additional factors: the reliability of the speaker, and its credibility in the light of other statements or impressions relevant to the same subject. Simultaneously, however, Hamlet's sentence also makes a further statement that, while less explicit, is more immediately acceptable in itself. For Hamlet's sentence also reveals his current state of mind; whether or not his assertion has any objective validity, there can be no doubt that its speaker at this moment professes to believe it.

The effects of the second type are also specifically verbal, but since the "statements" they make are less explicitly articulated, they represent a more indirect means of communication. This type is formed by the stylistic features of language—its sound patterns, verbal ambiguities, allusions, image patterns, and the like—and it includes effects that arise not only from individual speeches but also from the stylistic similarities linking two or more speeches in a single design. Hamlet's sentence illustrates both of these processes. As an isolated effect, it establishes a powerful allusion that helps define exactly the sort of universe he has in mind and suggests the Christlike certainty with which he regards it. At the same time, because the speech is in prose, stylistically it also joins and extends the other prose passages of the fifth act which imply the elimination of madness both from the world of Denmark and from Hamlet himself.

In addition to performing specifically verbal functions, the language of drama acts as the source of effects that are themselves nonverbal in character. The same words that form the kinds of statements I have just described also determine—sometimes with the aid of stage directions—a third group of effects, the concrete aural and visual signs that accompany the spoken dialogue. The spectator who listens to Hamlet's sentence hears it pronounced in a particular tone by a speaker who adopts a particular facial expression and physical attitude and who employs a particular gesture or sequence of gestures. Thus the spectator intuits additional "statements," which, though they derive their existence and nature from the language that warrants them, act as independent means of communication. These visual and aural effects serve several purposes; those accompanying Hamlet's sentence tend to corroborate the implication about his state of mind, but nonverbal effects can also negate or modify the import of the spoken dialogue, or even provide entirely separate impressions. All effects of this category are concrete and immediate, but many of them—such as patterns of movement, vocal contrasts, the general appearance and manner of the actor, and the physical setting—are far more elaborate, complex, and lasting than those that derive from a single speech. These more complex nonverbal effects also take their character from language, but less directly: they are determined by detailed stage directions, by numerous individual speeches, by the union of several nonverbal signs, and even by the nature of the whole play.

The other two types of effects both result from the linking of separate speeches and other signs. It is, first of all, through combinations of this sort that the dramatist fixes the limits of character and event and establishes tempo. In this way he creates those intermediate and extraverbal aspects of the dramatic experience which the spectators perceive as elements of structure. These in turn project or help form the symbolic dimensions of character and scene, the structural juxtapositions, and the spatial and temporal designs which make up the effects of the fourth category. The relationship of Hamlet's sentence to two other speeches well illustrates how this kind of effect is determined by language. In his first soliloquy Hamlet directly indicates his belief in some kind of deity, but the "to be or not to be" soliloquy suggests just the opposite. His mention of a "special providence" is therefore both a third independent statement and also an effect that places the other two in perspective. Together the three statements form a structural design epitomizing the lineal pattern I traced in the preceding chapter, the progress in which Hamlet enacts his descent and return.

The effects of the fifth type are the least explicit in nature and the least open to precise definition. Every play contains countless impressions that seem to exist independent of the kinds of effects I have so far described. Hamlet's transformation is a valid and important fact of the play, but it is not directly established by any specific verbal, visual, or structural device. The spectator realizes it only because he has noted and understood numerous separate effects of every kind, including all those arising from the speech mentioning a "special providence." All such complexly formed impressions—the effects of the fifth category—are the product of the ultimate function of language. They occur because the dramatist, by making a number of individual statements, both direct and indirect, and by establishing various nonverbal and extraverbal signs, ultimately carves out, from the infinite possibilities that human experience makes available, the single impression he wishes to assert. By using his separate devices to select, group, and emphasize, he directs attention one way rather than another; he posits a particular cluster of sensations and insulates the spectators from all those that might have been posited instead.

To experience the complex impression that manifests Hamlet's transformation, the spectator must first realize the significance of each of several minor signs, all of which belong to the first four categories. Not every effect of the fifth category works in the same way, however. The act of selection always results from a combination of several statements, expressed or implied, but frequently the facts it presents seem as direct and immediate as the literal content of the simplest speech. What the spectators attend to is not the various individual statements but the otherwise unexpressed impression that they etch out. The selected fact, while never made explicit in so many words, is nonetheless as vivid as if it were. An aspect of *Hamlet* illustrating this kind of effect and its importance is the implied setting. The symbolic nature of the Elizabethan stage gave the dramatist complete freedom in choosing his setting; since specific locality—or the lack of it—was determined not by physical representation but only by the implications conveyed by individual scenes, nothing prevented the dramatist from having, as Sir Philip Sidney put it, "Asia of the one side, and Affricke of the other, and so manie other under Kingdomes, that the Player when he comes in, must ever begin with telling where he is, or else the tale will not be conceived." [1] *Hamlet* is unusual in this respect, however, because although much of relevance to the play's plot occurs outside Denmark—especially Hamlet's experiences at sea—Shakespeare rigorously excludes this material from his stage. In contrast to his usual practice in such plays as *Macbeth* and *King Lear*, which range freely from place to place, the setting of *Hamlet* is always Denmark and—with the exception of a single scene—Elsinore itself. Since no one acquaints the spectators with this fact of the play, it exists only as an effect of the fifth category; nevertheless, it is not only inescapable but it also has considerable influence on the spectators' relationship to the action. The constant focus on a single, limited area gives the action much of its sense of restriction and confinement: because of this limitation Hamlet truly inhabits a prison. Since it is Denmark that constitutes this single setting, the kingdom itself ultimately becomes synonymous with the evil that the individual scenes constantly expose. Most important of all, it is this aspect of the play—in conjunction with the presence of Fortinbras—which gives Denmark its special importance as a crucial factor in the experience it localizes.

Through these five kinds of effects the dramatist shapes his play. From them he creates a unified immediate action consisting of intelligible characters engaged in intelligible events, out of which emerges a coherent and potentially satisfying arrangement —the plot, or story. Simultaneously, the same effects and others like them—individually and in combination—establish an action of depth consisting of the accumulated implications that raise the

[1] *The Prose Works of Sir Philip Sidney*, ed. Albert Feuillerat (Cambridge: University Press, 1962), III, 38.

experience above the level of the purely literal. Together, as each interfuses the other, the immediate action and the action of depth weave a final fusion expressing an import that is both the play and its meaning. This import is the product not of a few basic impressions but of a countless number of separate effects, each serving to delineate a single aspect of an elaborate central referent, and from this feature of the play's make-up arises the "tension" described in the second chapter. The import of a play is nothing less than the precise texture of its internal organization as it relates to external experience, and therefore every play provides a unique, original, and complex experience that can be adequately represented only through extensive detailed analysis.

Since the exact quality of a play's import is, however, in part determined by the nature of the final fusion itself, one general aspect of drama still requires examination. The final fusion, as I have pointed out, is the combination of all the separate effects that the dramatist's devices have established. What the final fusion itself adds to these separate effects is the manner in which they are combined. Every play's specific organization is unique, but the act producing it necessitates the employment of some general mode of combination. This is the device through which the dramatist gives the whole play its unity, and therefore this device is itself an index to meaning. The mode of combination is that element of a play which corresponds to the focus of narration in fiction or the control of the camera angle in film. By determining what shall be included and what relationship each included detail shall have to all the others, it establishes the perspective or perspectives in which the audience must view the play as a whole. In the process it expresses the fundamental conception of reality at the play's heart. There are innumerable plays, and each has its own specific organization, but the modes of combination for fashioning a play's specific organization are few in number. The following analyses of the *Oresteia, Hamlet,* and *Rosmersholm* treat these plays as complete experiences; their purpose is to clarify this concept of the mode of combination and to illustrate the various modes that are available.

The Single View—*The Libation Bearers*

In the *Agamemnon*, the first play of the *Oresteia* trilogy, Aeschylus presents a chaotic universe. Conflict reigns in the heavens and turmoil on earth. Disharmony separates man from his gods. Until men sin the gods seem to take no notice of them; once they sin, however, punishment swiftly follows. The gods use men as the instruments of their will, but they feel no compassion for them. Nor, on their part, do men deserve it. They serve the gods because they cannot avoid doing so, but they remain ignorant of their function and of the divine guidance that leads them. In all that they perform, culpable personal motives intervene, and these brand every human act with the stigma of evil. The chief manifestation of the universal disorder is the series of crimes that perpetuate the curse of Atreus. Man senses the chaos they reveal and seeks to impose order by restoring the balance they have upset. With his limitations, however, he can address himself to but one wrongdoing at a time, and the only weapon he can forge is personal violence. Every crime eventually provokes its punishment, but crime itself continues unchecked. The effort to impose order merely prolongs disorder.

Because of the universal disorder everything in the play is equivocal. Zeus remains so inscrutable that the chorus cannot even be sure of his identity. Apollo acts justly in punishing Cassandra, but it is his victim who merits and wins the spectators' sympathy. Man naïvely hopes that all will turn out for the best, but he has no way of realizing what the gods have planned for him. Of the human beings who appear in the first play, only Cassandra has the capacity to see beyond immediate circumstances, and she is the traditional image of the prophetess whom no one can believe. The equivocality of earthly things is even more pronounced. Clytaemestra wears a mask of innocence behind which she conceals her evil intentions. Agamemnon is magnificent, heroic, admirable; but he deserves to die in payment for his crimes. Retribution, man's only means of imposing order, is a confused blend of good and evil. What the world of the *Agamemnon* lacks is a firm moral center, and without it order cannot possibly evolve. The spectators realize all this, for it is inescapable; but the equivocality of the play enters even their own relationship to the action. Intellectually, they perceive the disorder and the need for some kind of absolute. Intellectually, they realize the ultimate unworkability of retribution, man's pitiful substitute for justice. But their emotional participation betrays them. At the conclusion of the *Agamemnon* they seek punishment for Clytaemestra and Aegisthus. They look forward not to the elimination of retribution but to its persistence.

The Libation Bearers, by repeating the structure of the *Agamemnon*, dramatizes a prolongation of the basic disorder, but the way in which the situation is seen has been profoundly changed. The differences between the killing of Clytaemestra and that of Agamemnon, as I have shown in Chapter 6, compel the spectators to adopt a new point of view toward the agent of retribution, and this effect merely climaxes their participation in the entire play, all of which is so constructed that the change in attitude becomes inevitable. The equivocality characterizing the *Agamemnon* ends with that play; in *The Libation Bearers*, Aeschylus exchanges his mode of combination for one that rejects everything inscrutable, ambiguous, or contradictory. Until the killing of Clytaemestra at least, almost every detail in the play points to a single, uncomplicated conclusion—that Orestes is wholly justified in carrying out his revenge.

The Libation Bearers opens with Orestes, who speaks the prologue, and thus the spectators, whose relationship to the *Agamemnon* was initially established by the remote point of view of the Watchman, must first observe the action through the eyes of its hero. The effect is much like that of an Elizabethan soliloquy, for the spectators become intimately involved with Orestes and tend to accept his point of view as authoritative; by his side, moreover, stands Pylades, whose silent but constant presence seems to reinforce whatever he has to say. Orestes expresses happiness at having finally returned home, but his primary concern is his grief for his dead father: "I was not by, my father, to mourn for your death / nor stretched my hand out when they took your corpse away" (ll. 8–9). As Orestes' tone clearly indicates, only the admirable qualities of Agamemnon have any validity for him, and this makes his own course of action easy to determine. Revenge, he feels, is both necessary and proper, and so he prays, "Zeus, Zeus, grant me vengeance for my father's / murder. Stand and fight beside me, of your grace" (ll. 17–18). Orestes' attitudes, to be sure, are not unlike those of Clytaemestra in the first play, but his are authoritative where hers were not because it is through his eyes that the action is being seen. Whatever doubts the spectators might retain about the acceptability of Orestes' point of view are eliminated when he later reveals that he acts at the command of Apollo (ll. 269–305). This suggests that his intentions are wholly commendable. Unlike the characters of the *Agamemnon*, he has somehow managed to achieve a harmonious relation with the gods. He knows that in carrying out his revenge he will be fulfilling divine law. He also knows his other motives for the act, and he can easily subordinate those that are strictly personal:

> Here numerous desires converge to drive me on:
> the god's urgency and my father's passion, and
> with these the loss of my estates wears hard on me
>
> [ll. 299–301].

Once Orestes' attitudes have been established as the primary source of the play's values, Aeschylus makes sure that nothing shall interfere to complicate them. The chorus enters to recite its first ode when Orestes has finished speaking the prologue, but this chorus, in contrast to the Argive Elders, lacks omniscience. The Argive Elders were able to place themselves between the audience and the action by narrating past events and codifying timeless laws, but these slave women are concerned only with the present and their own intolerable lot under Aegisthus' regime: "This is my life: to feed the heart on hard-drawn breath" (ll. 24–26).[2] Whatever authority their role as chorus confers on them thus works entirely to Orestes' advantage. They know but one law and they formulate it in its simplest terms: "May you not hurt your enemy, when he struck first?" (l. 123). All their odes concentrate on the single fact of Agamemnon's death and the necessity of destroying his murderers. Once they hear what Orestes plans, they pray to the "Almighty Destinies" that he may succeed "in the turning of Justice": "blood stroke for the stroke of blood / shall be paid" (ll. 306–313). They even believe that Orestes' act, which they characterize as an "innocent murder" (l. 830), can end the continual slaughter:

> Zeus, Zeus, make him who is now
> in the house stand above those who
> hate. . . .
>
> . . . . .
>
> For things done in time past
> wash out the blood in fair-spoken verdict.
> Let the old murder in
> the house breed no more   [ll. 789–791, 803–806].

The surest sign of this group's lack of omniscience is its performance of a function rare for a Greek chorus, and even here it au-

---

[2] Cf. H. D. F. Kitto, *Greek Tragedy: A Literary Study* (2d, rev. ed.; Garden City, N.Y.: Doubleday, 1955), pp. 84–85, on the role of this chorus: "Their part, far from enveloping the action, is to be subordinate to it, in that they are continually presenting one point of view to Orestes."

thenticates Orestes' point of view: by reversing Clytaemestra's command that Aegisthus bring his bodyguard (ll. 770–773), it deliberately interferes with the action to alter its course so that the revenge can be carried out without impediment.

Electra enters with the chorus, thereby helping to reduce its potential omniscience and suggesting her similar acceptance of Orestes' point of view. Her speech and activity confirm this implication: like Orestes, she prays to her father's spirit for aid against his murderers; to supplement the idealized image of Agamemnon, she offers a view of Clytaemestra that stresses only her worst aspects, for she describes her mother as "no mother in her heart / which has assumed God's hate and hates her children" (ll. 190–191). Electra's main contribution, however, is the increased stature that her enthusiasm lends to Orestes himself. Before she sees him, she describes him as "the best beloved / of men to me" (ll. 193–194); when he appears, she welcomes him with a burst of passionate joy (ll. 235–238). In her eyes Orestes represents "salvation" (l. 236).

What gives this continual insistence on the reliability of a single point of view its energizing emotional force is the long kommos, the prayer of invocation over Agamemnon's grave (ll.315–478), in which Orestes, the chorus, Electra, and the spectators merge into a single consciousness. In this kommos Aeschylus draws on the full resources of his theater. In keeping with the attitudes already evoked, the words of the prayer idealize Agamemnon as the good man and great king, cruelly and unjustly murdered by the stroke of cowardice, his body savagely mutilated. For once, however, the words seem less important than the effects accompanying them. The kommos communicates its basic significance not through its verbal content but through the unity of attitude manifested by the three alternating voices, through the spectacle of the kneeling figures, and above all through the music that blends all these effects into a single powerful appeal. It is the totality of the kommos which signifies that from this moment of prayer will arise an instance of retribution that is wholly just. For the spectators this kommos forms the emotional center of the entire trilogy; once its impact has solidified their tendency to adopt Orestes' point of view, they can no longer experience the detachment that during the *Agamemnon* allowed them to view the agent of retribution objectively, as someone who in acting deservedly provokes his own future punishment.

In the scenes that follow the kommos Aeschylus helps preserve the emotional union between the spectators and Orestes by completely discrediting his hero's intended victim. The next choral ode, which precedes Clytaemestra's entrance, dwells on "the female force," "the guile" and "treacheries of the woman's heart" (ll. 599, 626). In this ode the chorus recalls the actions of some of the most evil women of legend, by implication transferring the loathing their names evoke to their present counterpart. Clytaemestra's own behavior upon entering verifies the justness of this imputation. Her first words ironically condemn her: the "comforts" she offers the supposed travelers Orestes and Pylades consist of "hot baths, and beds," and these images epitomize her roles as Agamemnon's murderess and Aegisthus' paramour. She exhibits grief upon hearing the false report of Orestes' death, but this only discredits her further, for it suggests the hypocrisy she utilized so skillfully in the first play of the trilogy. Moreover, as soon as Clytaemestra exits, Aeschylus replaces her with Cilissa, Orestes' old nurse, whose genuine display of grief provides an emphatic contrast. Cilissa, like the chorus, is more an individualized character than a functional figure, but she is this play's version of the conventional messenger, and therefore her words take on some of the authority of expository statement. As a result, she is able to make Clytaemestra's true feelings fully clear:

> She put a sad face on
> before the servants, to hide the smile inside her eyes
> over this work that has been done so happily
> for her   [ll. 737–740].

By this point, only one aspect of Orestes' purpose—the fact that his intended victim is his mother—could in any way make doubtful his full justification. This fact Aeschylus could not change. He does, however, mitigate its influence by deflecting from Clytaemestra to Cilissa the attitude that the fact of motherhood properly evokes. It is Cilissa, not Clytaemestra, who mourns Orestes. It is Cilissa who has truly felt maternal love: "I wore out my life / for him. I took him from his mother, brought him up" (ll. 749–750). And in the murder scene, when Clytaemestra at last knows that it is Orestes who threatens her, she is the first to nullify their relationship. For her, at this moment, Orestes is only an enemy she must kill in order to protect herself:

> We have been won with the treachery by which we slew.
> Bring me quick, somebody, an ax to kill a man [ll. 888–889].

The murder scene is, of course, the crucial scene of the play, and even here Aeschylus continues his justification of Orestes. Clytaemestra soon recovers from her original response in order to try an appeal to her son's filial instincts. Her plea is useless, however; she has already exposed her true character in the immediately preceding cry, "Beloved, strong Aegisthus, are you dead indeed?" (l. 893). Nevertheless, her appeal does occasion two highly significant effects. In the first of these, Orestes hesitates. The act suggests, perhaps, compassion; it certainly indicates his desire to be sure that he is entirely right. In doubt, he turns to Pylades for counsel and thus prompts the second effect, the most important aural sign of the whole play. Orestes' faithful companion has been by his side throughout, a constant visual confirmation of the justness of Orestes' revenge; but he has never spoken. Now, for the first time, the spectators hear his voice:

> What then becomes thereafter of the oracles
> declared by Loxias at Pytho? What of sworn oaths?
> Count all men hateful to you rather than the gods
>
> [ll. 900–903].

These words establish a causal link between universal order and Orestes' revenge: should Orestes fail, order would be impossible. More important than what Pylades has to say, however, is his sudden acquisition of the power of speech. It is as if Orestes had been granted omniscient sanction: "The effect is like a thunderclap." [3]

Throughout *The Libation Bearers*, from the prologue through the murder scene, Orestes' point of view dominates; the action can be seen only as Orestes himself sees it, and his values determine the attitudes that the spectators must assume. To this extent, then, *The Libation Bearers* exemplifies a standard means of organizing the many effects of an entire play, one that welds them into a monolithic whole having a univocal import. This mode of combination restricts the spectators to a single, narrow perspective from which all other possible perspectives are rigorously excluded; it offers a view of reality in which the complexities of experience have been reduced to an unequivocal scheme.

The mode of combination exemplified by *The Libation Bearers* is characteristic of many different kinds of drama, including plays with mere entertainment value as well as more ambitious works such as didactic thesis plays and religious moralities. In *The Libation Bearers*, however, this mode of combination is brilliantly adapted to control a single moment in the larger scheme of the whole trilogy, for Aeschylus uses it not to define the entire experience of the *Oresteia* but merely to present Orestes in a particular light. By identifying Orestes as the necessary moral center that the trilogy has previously lacked, this mode of combination lays the groundwork for an eventual solution. Orestes acts only because he must, because universal order depends on his

---

[3] Kitto, *Form and Meaning in Drama* (London: Methuen, 1956), p. 53; cf. John H. Finley, Jr., *Pindar and Aeschylus* (Cambridge, Mass.: Harvard University Press, 1955), p. 272: "This is the turning-point of the trilogy, the moment when the divine illumination enters mortal action."

successful effort; he deserves compassion and therefore he makes compassion a valid quality of the universe. Heretofore the gods have remained aloof, but now that Orestes has given them a reason to intervene, their intervention is inevitable. Furthermore, the effect this mode of combination has on the emotional responses of the spectators is considerable. Since Aeschylus has forced them to sympathize with Orestes throughout, at the end of the play, when the Furies begin their relentless pursuit, the spectators can desire only his salvation and with it the universal harmony that will free him. They are compelled not only to accept but also to demand the bold *deus ex machina* of the final play.

The Double View—*The Eumenides*

The sequence from *The Libation Bearers* which I have just examined contains two effects that momentarily relate this action to the larger context it modifies. Electra's pouring of libations on the grave of her father suggests, as I have shown in Chapter 5, the image pattern of blood spilled on the ground, and consequently her act characterizes the coming murder as one more link in the unending chain. Similarly, at the height of the persuasive kommos, Orestes suddenly speaks of his mission in terms that recall the equivocality of the *Agamemnon*: "Warstrength shall collide with warstrength; right with right" (l. 461).[4] Until Orestes has accomplished his revenge, Aeschylus does not allow these implications to have any real influence on the spectators' point of view, but when Clytaemestra lies dead and Orestes enters to defend himself, the situation acquires a complexity that only the inclusiveness of his momentary perception can adequately assess.

Here Aeschylus once again alters the spectators' relationship to the action. After Orestes has completed his defense, the chorus,

---

[4] In the Greek the "collision" literally occurs in the words that express it: *Arēs Arei xymbalei, Dika Dika.*

addressing Clytaemestra's corpse, reverses the attitude with which it had anticipated his act:

> Ah, but the pitiful work.
> Dismal the death that was your ending.
> He is left alive; pain flowers for him   [ll. 1007–1009].

Orestes himself must then admit: "I have won; but my victory is soiled, and has no pride" (l. 1017). Since the whole play has asserted the reliability of these speakers, the spectators are now invited to view the situation in a new perspective. The arrival of the Furies, which changes the setting from the human to the cosmic, completes the transformation from one perspective to another. Orestes is now seen against the background of the entire trilogy. His act has been wholly just, but it has not negated universal law: the act of retribution is evil, no matter how justified its performer. By killing his mother, Orestes has become infected with the disease that cripples his world: "pain flowers for him." He has done only what he had to do, but his pursuers have justice on their side. At the end of *The Libation Bearers*, then, Aeschylus again alters his mode of combination, returning to that of the *Agamemnon*, in which, by acknowledging the equal validity of conflicting opposites, he had established a double view. It is this mode of combination that is employed throughout *The Eumenides*.

The play's prologue, spoken by the priestess of Apollo, helps mold the spectators' acceptance of the double view by detaching them from Orestes and directing their attention outward from the individual to his cosmos. The first part of her prologue, an elaborate prayer describing the history of Apollo's shrine at Delphi, unites within a single framework "the various cults which have successfully occupied and ousted one another from the shrine." [5] The prayer thus acts as a focusing scene to indicate the essentially religious basis of the following action and to antic-

[5] E. T. Owen, *The Harmony of Aeschylus* (Toronto: Clarke, Irwin, 1952), p. 110.

ipate the ultimate resolution of opposites which Athene will effect. In the second part of her prologue the Priestess introduces the opposites themselves; recoiling from the temple in horror, she returns to describe the "things terrible to tell and for the eye to see / terrible" (ll. 34–35) which she has found within. One of these terrible things is "a man with god's / defilement on him" (ll. 40–41); the others—the Furies—are "black and utterly / repulsive" (ll. 52–53). These initial descriptions evoke rather complicated attitudes. Orestes has previously won the audience's full sympathy, but when he is seen objectively, only his guilt is evident. The Furies serve the cause of justice, but they are loathsome and disgusting. In the scenes that follow, the opposites here suggested are more thoroughly developed through the contest between Apollo and the Furies.

Apollo, as Orestes' advocate, is this play's spokesman for the values that Orestes had himself affirmed in *The Libation Bearers;* through Apollo the point of view there established remains in force. Apollo does more than merely sanction Orestes' act, however; he completely absolves him of all responsibility by taking it upon himself: "it was I who made you strike your mother down" (l. 84). This statement, since Apollo is a god, indicates that the justness of Orestes' revenge is an actual quality of the universe in which he lives and that Apollo is its embodiment. Moreover, Apollo—and through him the principle he embodies—is highly attractive to the spectators. By supporting Orestes, he translates into action attitudes that the spectators have already formed. As I have shown in Chapter 5, he inherits the positive aspects of the play's various image patterns. Above all, the radiant golden costume his function as sun-god requires him to wear suggests the light that all the characters have sought so passionately. Nevertheless, Apollo cannot win full approval. In keeping with his youth—he is one of Zeus's new gods—he is brash and irreverent. Much of his defense of Orestes during the trial takes the form of the scurrilous insults and petty threats he hurls at the Furies. His only substantial argument is that Orestes cannot be held guilty of matricide because the mother, far from being related to the son, is merely the "nurse of the new-planted seed / that grows" (ll. 659–660). This argument, as Greene puts it, is "astonishing." [6] Apollo's notion was, he concedes, "widely held in ancient Greece," but in this context it must confront the far more deeply felt conviction that murder, especially of a parent, is an unadulterated evil.[7]

One other aspect of the play helps prevent full acceptance of Apollo and his position. Orestes' attitudes gave the spectators their point of view in *The Libation Bearers* because no other attitudes were asserted; in *The Eumenides*, however, attitudes contradicting those of Apollo are put forth by the Furies, and Aeschylus makes these attitudes equally persuasive. The Furies, like Apollo, are divine; they too represent an actual force in the universe. They are, moreover, this play's chorus, and therefore their attitudes elicit at least some of the respect that the audience has learned to accord the views expressed by the Argive Elders and the slave women of the second play. The Furies' role as chorus also equips them with a powerful weapon—their choral odes— and the length and beauty of these odes give the Furies ample opportunity to emphasize and enhance the legitimacy of their pursuit of Orestes. They never let the audience forget that a "mother's blood spilled on the ground / can not come back again" (ll. 261–262). While they sing their binding song over Orestes, they chant the principle by which they act, their "privilege primeval," which "has been ordained, / granted and given by destiny / and god, absolute" (ll. 391–393); if a man is innocent, they let him alone, but they cannot allow the guilty to escape. Within the episodes Aeschylus uses other means to reinforce this

[6] William Chase Greene, *Moira: Fate, Good, and Evil in Greek Thought* (New York: Harper and Row, 1963), p. 135.

[7] For this conviction in fifth-century Athens, see C. M. Bowra, *Sophoclean Tragedy* (Oxford: Clarendon Press, 1944), p. 169.

insistence on the validity of the Furies' attitudes. Early in the play he introduces the ghost of Orestes' victim, who reminds the spectators that even though her own deeds have brought disgrace upon her, she "suffered too, horribly, and from those most dear": "I was slaughtered, and by matricidal hands. / Look at these gashes in my heart, think where they came / from" (ll. 99–104). Later, Orestes himself provides one of the most persuasive reinforcements of the Furies' position when during the trial he must admit that he performed the act with which they charge him. Yet, like Apollo, no matter how persuasive the Furies are, they cannot entirely win the spectators' approval. They stand between Orestes and the freedom that the spectators desire for him. As Apollo has inherited the positive aspects of the various image patterns, the Furies inherit the corresponding negative aspects, especially the suggestion of monstrosity that enters speech after speech in the first two plays of the trilogy. Ultimately, it is the terror and repulsion inspired by their hideousness which make complete acceptance of them a sheer impossibility.[8]

Neither the Furies nor Apollo can secure the spectators' full approval. Nor can either of the opposing positions that they advocate be altogether rejected. Because of the mode of combination that Aeschylus has employed, the spectators must give equal credence to both. This mode of combination, also a standard form of organization in drama, compels the spectators to adopt a double view of the action as a whole; it compels them to see reality as a tension between conflicting opposites, each of which can justly claim validity. This mode of combination enables Aeschylus to relate the human action of the first two plays more precisely to its cosmic background, for the double view dramatizes in itself the basic rift in the universe that makes human suffering

[8] Legend has it that the Furies so terrified their original audience that "children died and women suffered miscarriage" ("Bios Aischylou," trans. John J. Walsh, S.J., in *A Source Book in Theatrical History,* ed. A. M. Nagler [New York: Dover Publications, 1959], p. 5).

a necessity. Moreover, this implication becomes explicitly formulated. The conflict between Apollo and the Furies involves much more than the quarrel over Orestes; it stems from and dramatizes that struggle between opposing dynasties of gods first hinted by the chorus of the *Agamemnon*. To the Furies, Apollo's defense of Orestes typifies the evil practice of the dynasty to which Apollo belongs:

> Such are the actions of the younger gods. These hold
> by unconditional force, beyond all right, a throne
> that runs reeking blood,
> blood at the feet, blood at the head   [ll. 162–165].

True right, the Furies claim, is theirs by ancient dispensation, but Zeus the usurper "has ruled our blood dripping company / outcast, nor will deal with us" (ll. 365–366). As the imagery of these speeches suggests, this conflict of cosmic forces provides the real source of the spilled blood that symbolizes human misery.

But Orestes has made universal harmony desirable and necessary, and therefore the double view as Aeschylus develops it in *The Eumenides* also includes the possibility of resolution. What is needed is the wisdom that emerges through suffering, and in the person of Athene this wisdom takes an active part in the drama. Athene mends the rift that splits the universe and thereby creates the harmony that reconciles the gods with each other and with mankind. This solution is dramatically convincing because it is emotionally satisfying. For the original spectators, it was achieved by "their own goddess, the wisdom and majesty of Athens itself," [9] and it led to the exaltation of their own city. But for any audience this solution is eminently satisfying, because it is true to the complexity of the whole trilogy. Aeschylus slights neither of the opposites; instead, he brings them into delicate balance. Athene's first speech indicates her realization of their equal validity, for, as she tells Orestes, "I respect your rights. / Yet

[9] Owen, *The Harmony of Aeschylus*, p. 117.

these, too, have their work" (ll. 475–476). Nor does the ultimate reconciliation in any way belie the position expressed in her
initial statement. Orestes is guilty, but he deserves freedom:
through the suffering brought to him by the Furies' pursuit he is
punished, and through the intervention of Athene at his trial he
is saved. The retributive code of justice is good, but it is also evil:
in the transferral of vengeance from the individual to society, the
guilty can still be punished, but the agent of justice no longer in-
curs guilt of his own. Both sets of gods, the old and the new,
have right on their side, and in the transformation of the Furies
into beneficent spirits performing their function for a now all-
powerful Zeus, the ancient sanctity and righteousness of the old
gods coalesce with the power and mercy of the new. The concluding lines, which tell how "Zeus the all seeing / met with Destiny" (ll. 1045–1046), sum up the nature of the ultimate solution. On the one hand they suggest the meeting of two separate
forces and consequently the act of reconciliation. But on the
other hand, Zeus and Destiny are now identical, and therefore
these final lines also celebrate the reconciliation itself.

The Multiple View—*Hamlet*

Neither of the modes of combination described above could
produce a texture as rich as that of Shakespeare's *Hamlet*. Full response to the experience it dramatizes demands more than the single view of *The Libation Bearers* or even the double view of
The Eumenides. As H. T. Price observes, "Shakespeare, like
Marlowe, makes multiplicity the basis of all his art.
. . . Shakespeare's art is polyphonic, or it would, perhaps,
be better to say prismatic; he decomposes his truth into many
shades of color." [10] By adding that "each of his numerous characters reflects the idea in his own special way," Price reveals his

[10] *Construction in Shakespeare* (Ann Arbor: University of Michigan
Press, 1951), p. 36.

greater concern with method of presentation than with the "truth" this method presents. The two are, however, inseparable: the nature of a play's import depends on the nature of the method used to establish it. Shakespeare, in writing *Hamlet*, employs a mode of combination that unites a myriad of distinct points of view, and therefore the import he creates is itself multiple. Throughout *Hamlet* the spectators must view the action in a wide variety of different perspectives, none of which is wholly authoritative and none of which can be finally dismissed. What the spectators must ultimately see, then, is a conception of reality that embraces an infinite number of disparate and conflicting possibilities. The result is not, however, the absence of meaning; it is the presence of multivalence.

Almost any moment of the play would serve as an example of its essential multiplicity, for each illustrates the way in which Shakespeare constantly exacts simultaneous and conflicting responses from his spectators. A typical moment is the prayer scene (III.iii), the scene in which Hamlet finds and lets slip his best opportunity for killing Claudius.

As the scene begins, Claudius, who has just experienced the shock of the play-within-the-play, expresses what seems to be his present attitude toward Hamlet: "I like him not; nor stands it safe with us / To let his madness range" (ll. 1-2). This speech, which concludes with a reiteration of the scheme to send Hamlet to England, modifies the spectators' attitudes toward both Hamlet and Claudius in a number of ways. The speech reintroduces the theme of Hamlet's madness, and thus it faintly helps validate one possible way of viewing him. The speech also stresses another aspect of Hamlet, the threat he poses, and thus it provides external verification for the impression conveyed by Hamlet's tone in the soliloquy that has just concluded the preceding scene: "Now could I drink hot blood, / And do such bitter business as the day / Would quake to look on" (III.ii.380-382). More important, however, is the reflection the speech casts on Claudius himself. In Act III, scene i, Claudius had refused to call Hamlet's behavior madness; now, for the first time, he does so—even though the preceding scene has shown him how specious this madness may be. Claudius' remark, the spectators realize, is designed to conceal his guilt from his listeners, Rosencrantz and Guildenstern, but mixed with this hypocrisy is a touch of genuine fear, and this arouses sympathy. Moreover, since this speech immediately follows the performance of "The Murder of Gonzago," in which Claudius saw his own crime paralleled, both the hypocrisy and the fear connote increased perception. Claudius now knows exactly where he stands with Hamlet, and as the rest of his speech shows, he has the capacity to do what Hamlet cannot, to convert knowledge into action at once; even in his fear he remains the shrewd, skilled strategist of the play's second scene. In the face of such opposition, Hamlet's dangerousness seems far less consequential.

The next few speeches complicate the spectators' attitudes toward Claudius even further. Rosencrantz and Guildenstern reassure him of their unswerving loyalty by immediately acquiescing to his command to accompany Hamlet to England, and Rosencrantz then develops at length the abstract principle necessitating Hamlet's exile:

> The cease of majesty
> Dies not alone, but like a gulf doth draw
> What's near it with it. It is a massy wheel,
> Fix'd on the summit of the highest mount,
> To whose huge spokes ten thousand lesser things
> Are mortis'd and adjoin'd; which when it falls,
> Each small annexment, petty consequence,
> Attends the boist'rous ruin. Never alone
> Did the king sigh, but with a general groan
>
> [III.iii.15–23].

This speech views Claudius in relation to his office. Shakespeare reminds the spectators that whatever else Claudius may be, he is the king and that as such he inherits the importance that kingship automatically bestows: a threat against him endangers the stability of the whole kingdom. At the same time, however, other aspects of the speech call for quite different responses. Despite the credibility of this principle for a Renaissance audience, here it cannot help acquiring some of the superficiality of the fawning courtier who expresses it. By equating Claudius with his kingdom Shakespeare focuses on Claudius' role as a symbol for Denmark and thereby once more suggests the evil that is his basic attribute. Worst of all, so far as Claudius is concerned, whatever success the speech has in enhancing him must also serve to make his evil more acutely felt: in becoming king, Claudius has himself killed one.

Shakespeare augments and modifies these last two responses to Rosencrantz' speech almost immediately afterward. When the two courtiers have left and Polonius, on his way to spy on Hamlet in his mother's chamber, has received Claudius' thanks, Claudius begins the soliloquy that contains his first explicit admission of the crime with which he has been charged:

> O, my offence is rank, it smells to heaven;
> It hath the primal eldest curse upon't—
> A brother's murder!   [ll. 36–38].

This admission comes as no surprise, but in drawing on the central imagery of rottenness and in linking Claudius with Cain, it produces an equivalent impact. The perspective that views Claudius as unadulterated evil and the source of all that troubles Denmark here receives its principal authorization. Nevertheless, the admission cannot be separated from the effects it introduces and from the wholly different responses these additional effects elicit. Claudius the villain feels remorse and tries to pray for purification. Moreover, since his desire to repent is stymied by his inability to surrender the fruits of his sin, he experiences an intense suffering that is humanly compelling, and he becomes, for once, an object of compassion.

At this point Hamlet enters. The complex responses that Shakespeare has elicited from his spectators, both before this scene and during it, make them ambivalent toward Hamlet's opportune arrival, and this ambivalence soon affects their present view of Hamlet himself.

One aspect of this present view results from their prior relationship to him. Hamlet has been the play's most important and most interesting character, the one whose intense responses have done most toward making the action humanly relevant and whose attitudes have had the greatest influence on determining how it should be understood. He is the one with whom the spectators are most involved, and each of his entrances automatically re-establishes their general esteem and concern for him as a valid perspective for viewing the action.

Hamlet now enters, however, a special context that complicates this general attitude by evoking other, more specific attitudes of equal relevance. He gets his first real opportunity to carry out his revenge only after Shakespeare has greatly reduced its intellectual and emotional acceptability. The Pyrrhus speech questioned the idea of revenge in general; this scene, by stressing Claudius' office as king and by portraying his agony as sinner, has tended to invalidate the particular revenge that Hamlet seeks. The spectators' compassion for Claudius especially makes them regret that Hamlet must demand revenge and that he is now in a position to achieve it. This compassion has also a further effect. The spectators had been accustomed, before this scene, to view Claudius through Hamlet's eyes as a "damned villain." Now, after Claudius has been momentarily seen through his own eyes, Hamlet's repeated use of "villain" in speaking of him (ll. 76, 77) seems far too perverse, too much like Claudius' use of "madness" at the beginning of the scene to describe Hamlet. Nevertheless, this scene has also emphasized Claudius' guilt, and now Hamlet magnifies it by recalling how Claudius had endangered his father's soul:

'A took my father grossly, full of bread,
With all his crimes broad blown, as flush as May
[ll. 80–81].

From the point of view that these lines help to authenticate, Claudius clearly deserves his punishment.

Hamlet fails to take advantage of his opportunity; instead of killing Claudius he resheathes his sword. Insofar as the spectators discountenance the revenge, the failure must please them, especially as it contrasts him with Claudius, who with much less moral justification felt no qualms about taking a human life. At the same time, however, the spectators also want Hamlet to act, and his failure to do so disappoints them. It serves as one more indication of his general inability to cope with the demands of his situation, one more sign of the crippling paralysis that both symbolizes and causes his descent to the nadir of helplessness. These responses are but momentary, however; they are soon superseded by others provoked by Hamlet's explanation of his failure. He hesitates now, he says, in order to await

a more horrid hent.
When he is drunk asleep, or in his rage;
Or in th' incestuous pleasure of his bed;
At game, a-swearing, or about some act
That has no relish of salvation in't—
Then trip him, that his heels may kick at heaven,
And that his soul may be as damn'd and black
As hell, whereto, it goes   [ll. 88–95].

To such a fate, Hamlet thinks, Claudius assigned his father—but not, certainly, with such cold-blooded calculation. The speech creates an impression of vicious savagery that likens Hamlet to Pyrrhus, and the contrast between this impression and the impression of piteous suffering visually evoked by Claudius' attempt to pray upsets the simple balance that distinguishes the villain from the hero; it is almost as if the roles of the two characters had been suddenly reversed. Nor is this the only result of Hamlet's expressed reason for the present delay; in suggesting that he now arrogates to himself the prerogative of God, the speech also provides the first explicit clarification of a set of implications that has been developing throughout the act. But even the disapproval provoked by this aspect of the revelation is not unmixed, for it reminds the spectators of the intense agony that has compelled Hamlet to perceive his universe as a void he must himself endow with meaning.

Hamlet's next words—"my mother stays" (l. 95)—are more startling than any yet spoken in the scene. As part of the speech in which Hamlet explains his present delay, they suggest another, perhaps deeper reason. The order of this speech recalls that of his last soliloquy, in which he also moved from a savage outburst ("Now could I drink hot blood") to a statement of his intention to see his mother. Polonius' brief appearance in the present scene has kept that intention in focus for the spectators. Hamlet's restatement of the intention therefore climaxes a sequence of impressions which suddenly places the scene with Claudius in an entirely different perspective. What seemed to be a crucial phase in the prolonged duel between mighty opposites now looks more like a digression, a temporary interruption of Hamlet's real purpose—which is not to destroy Claudius but to save his mother. In this new perspective all the responses the scene had previously elicited seem to lose their importance. The complex truth that had been expressed with such care seems to become insignificant in relation to a truth of greater immediacy.

The last three lines of the scene, however, reinvoke the previous responses and draw them together. Hamlet concludes his speech by saying, "This physic but prolongs thy sickly days" (l. 96). His words are both a promise of further delay and an indication that he fully intends to carry out his task eventually, for he sees himself as a physician assigned to cure Denmark's disease. The "sickly," which once more links Claudius to the dominant imagery of the play, is ambiguous. Hamlet, it is obvious, means it as a characterization of Claudius' evil nature; but it suggests instead that Claudius is less a villain than a victim, and if so, Hamlet's attitudes are again shown to be inappropriate to the occasion. When Hamlet has left, the process of integrating the many responses already elicited is completed by Claudius' final ironic couplet:

> My words fly up, my thoughts remain below.
> Words without thoughts never to heaven go
>
> [ll. 97–98].

As a statement about its speaker this couplet stresses both his guilt and the frustration caused by his inability to repent: it therefore reinstates the ambivalence that is now the proper response to him. At the same time, the couplet also emphasizes both Hamlet's failure to act and the vicious explanation he gave for it by indicating that they were utterly needless. The main effect, however, is the rich irony that mocks Hamlet's assumptions about his own relationship to the situation. He who would play God cannot even perceive the reality before his very eyes.

Much of the complexity of this typical moment in the play results from Shakespeare's constant modification of the impressions conveyed by individual characters. In this respect the scene is but a microcosm of the whole play, for the individual character, like the individual scene, is symptomatic of the play's basic multiplicity. This is especially true of the character of Hamlet. The first scene in which he appears, as I have shown in Chapter 4, presents not one Hamlet but three, while subsequent scenes add innumerable and not always consistent details to these original impressions, as Hamlet is seen from a variety of separate points of view, including those embodied in the characters who try to classify him. One of the principal components of the resulting image, and a chief sign of its multiplicity, is the madness that exists as a dominant motif in the three central acts of the play.

From one point of view the madness is mere sham. Hamlet prepares the spectators for this point of view when he warns Horatio and Marcellus that he "perchance hereafter shall think meet / To put an antic disposition on" (I.v.171–172), and in the second act he tells Rosencrantz and Guildenstern that he is "but mad north-north-west": "When the wind is southerly I know a hawk from a handsaw" (II.ii.373–375). Throughout this act and the second scene of the third, Hamlet displays madness only when it suits him. Here, indeed, he obviously toys with Polonius and the others, deriving great pleasure from convincing them that their own mistaken opinions are valid. From this first point of view, therefore, the many comments about Hamlet's "lunacy," "madness," and "ecstacy" reveal only the thoroughness with which his adversaries have been taken in.

Nevertheless, another point of view is also firmly established. Even before Hamlet's warning, Horatio, whose original role as narrator has endowed his words with authority, foresees that madness is a likely possibility, for on the guard platform he cautions Hamlet that the Ghost "might deprive your sovereignty of reason / And draw you into madness" (I.iv.73–74), and when Hamlet breaks away from him and Marcellus, Horatio fears that he "waxes desperate with imagination" (l. 87). Later, after Hamlet has seen the Ghost, it is Horatio who quickly characterizes his odd pronouncements as "wild and whirling words" (I.v.133). The spectators' greater knowledge of the situation reduces the potential impact of Horatio's fear. Hamlet's prophecy and his behavior in the second act reduce it still more. But in Act III, scene i, and Act III, scene iv, when Hamlet treats Ophelia and his mother with a passionate bitterness far in excess of the provocation they have given him, the suggestion that the madness might be genuine returns with new force. The first few scenes of the fourth act seem designed to convert this suggestion into a certainty. This act begins with Gertrude's assertion to Claudius that her son is as "mad as the sea and wind, when both contend / Which is the mightier" (IV.i.7–8). Her speech is excessive as an account of Hamlet's behavior in her chamber, as if she were trying to mislead Claudius, but as an anticipation of the subsequent action it could not be better, for here Hamlet's behavior reaches its extreme. The game of "hide fox, and all after" (IV.ii.30), the concealment of Polonius' body and the peculiar comments about it, the morbid jests that he fires at the king—all tend to corroborate Gertrude's assessment. In the final act, moreover, when apologizing to Laertes, Hamlet declares, "What I have done . . . I here proclaim was madness" (V.ii.222–224). This speech, which follows his transformation, provides the most convincing assertion that he actually had been mad, for by now Hamlet's words have acquired much of the authority of expository statement.

The incompatibility of the opposing points of view cannot be entirely resolved by assigning the actual madness to a later stage of his descent. The view that seems more valid later is the first to be introduced, and the two alternate during the scenes of the third act. Even in Act IV, moreover, the display of madness is not unequivocal; although Rosencrantz and Claudius take Hamlet's speeches for the ravings of a mad man, a few of them contain some of his most incisive observations. Significantly, when Hamlet himself describes his past behavior as madness, he is referring specifically to the scene in which he had expressed his most insistent declaration of his complete rationality (III.iv.139–146). The impossibility of resolving the two conflicting views occasions the formation of a third, that Hamlet is sane and mad simultaneously. This view is not explicitly articulated in the play, for it demands a level of understanding beyond that of any of the characters, but Shakespeare hints at it in Polonius' "Though this be madness, yet there is method in't" (II.ii.203–204), and later one of the gravediggers shrewdly observes that Hamlet's madness will be unimportant once he gets to England, where all "the men are as mad as he" (V.i.150). It is, however, the significance that the madness acquires from its context which most effectively substantiates the third view. If Hamlet is in fact mad, it is also true that the madness is both a metaphor enabling Shakespeare to represent his character's inability to cope with his situation, and an instrument enabling Hamlet to make some kind of attempt. Furthermore, whether that which looks like madness should be accorded the response appropriate to madness depends on the point of view from which the madness is seen. From the point of view of those characters who show the least hesitation in classifying Hamlet, his behavior is unaccountable and therefore genuinely abnormal; no term other than "madness" could possibly describe it with sufficient accuracy. But the very inadequacy of this point of view and the ingrained superficiality it betrays make Hamlet's madness both a necessity and the only satisfactory response.

The prayer scene and the image that Hamlet projects are, however, merely parts of a larger whole. It is therefore the general significance of this larger whole which must finally be scrutinized, and it is here that the basic multiplicity of *Hamlet* most emphatically reveals itself.

The universe within which the events of *Hamlet* occur and from which they derive their fullest significance lacks the lucid schematization that Aeschylus has given the universe of the *Oresteia*. Unlike Aeschylus, who employs such clear allegorical representations of cosmic forces as Apollo and the Furies, Shakespeare embodies the universe of *Hamlet* only in the Ghost and, more obliquely, in Fortinbras, and these figures evoke conflicting or equivocal responses; both suggest a universe that is essentially ambiguous. Other elements of the play particularize this ambiguity by asserting three separate and incompatible possibilities. One of these, the one most frequently accepted in current criticism of the play, is that which Hamlet expresses in the final act. This view distinguishes a universal order, divine and perfect, governed by a benevolent providence, which manifests its influence even in such a seemingly trivial incident as the fall of a sparrow and which ensures that all human actions, however intended, will contribute to an ultimate good. This view occurs late in the play, however. It is preceded by another that sees the universe as orderless and irrational but permeated with evil. This universe is one in which nothing thrives except corruption. Here brother kills brother, wife betrays husband, the lover tortures his beloved, and friends blithely lead each other to their deaths. In this universe contentment betokens superficiality, innocence is naïveté, and moral sensitivity produces only paralysis, despair, and further evil. Ultimately, all ordinary distinctions tend to become irrelevant as everyone in this universe helps exemplify the workings of the ubiquitous evil. Those who do not foster it experience its effects; some exemplify it in both ways. Hamlet suffers, but so does Claudius, the putative cause of Hamlet's suffering. Claudius, performing a willful murder for the basest motives, brings disorder to his kingdom. Hamlet, seeking an honorable revenge, increases it. In this universe death is the chief sign of evil, and it shows no discrimination in choosing its victims; the ideally good, the innocent, the guilty, the morally ambiguous, the ignorant—all meet the same fate. These deaths also serve to illustrate the third view, one that seems to combine the other two. This view, which I developed extensively in Chapter 5, also pictures a universal order, but according to this view the order is malevolent. Like Hamlet's providence, it shapes the ends that man rough-hews, but it does so in order to punish him. It regards every human action, however intended, as an unwarranted self-assertion, and consequently it transforms every action into an instrument of self-destruction. All three of these views are thoroughly established in the play. Each is perceived, with varying degrees of preciseness, by Hamlet, and each is also given objective verification through action, imagery, or the repetition of ideas.

The multiplicity of his universe is what incapacitates Hamlet. Claudius, evidently, acts always from expediency: if an action, such as killing his brother or plotting Hamlet's assassination, will serve his immediate ends, he performs it; only later, as in the prayer scene, does he reflect on its larger consequences. Hamlet, in contrast, cannot perform an act so extreme as the taking of a human life—his own or Claudius'—until he has examined all its implications and satisfied himself that it is fully justified: hence his soliloquies on suicide and his staging of the play-within-the-play. Hamlet inhabits, however, a universe that lacks a single, clearly defined absolute, and this ambiguity makes moral certainty impossible. As a result, he does not act at all until, in his despair, he substitutes his own consciousness for the missing absolute. What he then performs, though closely reasoned, turns out to have been a mistake; thinking he has caught Claudius "about some act / That has no relish of salvation in't," he discovers instead that he has stabbed Polonius. This discovery makes the uncertainty, and the madness reflecting it, more substantial than ever before.

Hamlet's problem has only one acceptable solution. If he is ever to fulfill his assigned task, he must somehow discern a firm basis for action. Since his universe lacks the necessary absolute, he must reduce its multiplicity to more manageable proportions; from the available possibilities he must choose one that will allow him to act with the kind of sureness he perceives in the conduct of Fortinbras. The fortuitous happenings that take place on his trip to England simplify his decision: not only do they allow him to return to Denmark; they also allow him to return there believing in the benevolent divinity. In Act I, scene iii, Laertes insists that Hamlet cannot select his own wife, "for on his choice depends / The sanity and health of this whole state" (ll. 20–21). Later events give Laertes' remark far more significance than he suspects; detached from its immediate context, it sums up the whole action. Hamlet's choice of the benevolent divinity is the single most important occurrence in the entire play, for it resolves the stalemate in the action. It gives Hamlet the certainty he needs in order to accept his situation with equanimity and prepare himself to complete his task when circumstances permit. Because Hamlet has chosen, the principal carriers of the evil in Denmark can at last be destroyed. And since in drama *post hoc* does tend to mean *propter hoc*, Hamlet's choice also provides for the timely arrival of Fortinbras.

Although Hamlet's choice permits the action to reach its conclusion, it does not cancel out the basic multiplicity in the significance of this action. Like almost everything else in the play, Hamlet's choice demands an ambivalent response. Since it occasions such obvious benefits, and since it has been honestly and painfully extracted from actual experience, it is highly satisfying. Nevertheless, it is also distressing, and it is made so by one of the very qualities that allow it to elicit satisfaction. Unwilling to accept any conclusion not verified by the test of experience, Hamlet has placed himself at its mercy, and though experience is creative, it can also be destructive. Hamlet's has included not only the trip to England but also the killing of Polonius, and this act has provoked others to seek his life. Thus, even though Hamlet's choice equips him to act successfully for the first time, it also unavoidably puts him in a situation that guarantees his death.

Furthermore, Hamlet's choice cannot in itself resolve the ambiguity of his universe. It constitutes the most convincing assertion of one possible view, but it does not therefore nullify the others. Hamlet's belief in the benevolent divinity is an abstraction from reality rather than reality itself, and like all abstractions, it ignores rather than negates those aspects of reality that do not conform to its pattern. As a result, Hamlet's choice and the ensuing events can be legitimately viewed in three different perspectives.

In the perspective that Hamlet has himself adopted, his choice represents both his discovery of the true nature of reality and his acceptance of its workings. Once committed, he waits patiently for the opportunity that providence will create, and when, in the form of the proposed duel, this opportunity finally arrives, he goes to fulfill his role as scourge and minister; he becomes the human sacrifice that ensures the return to order and stability after the interregnum of evil's anarchy. Hamlet's death is, moreover, unavoidable, for this perspective also entails the conviction that the sinner must pay for his transgressions, and although in the final act Hamlet speaks with a conscience quite free from guilt, he cannot escape the fact that he has killed Polonius and promised to "answer well / The death I gave him" (III.iv.176–177).

The perspective that views the universe as orderless evil provides an entirely different evaluation. In this perspective Hamlet's choice necessarily becomes tainted with the evil that contaminates all human action. He fulfills his assigned task, but in doing so he unleashes the most severe outburst of death and destruction in the whole play. He purges Denmark only by eradicating its very life.

Finally, in the third perspective, that which views the universe as the domain of purposeful malevolence, Hamlet's choice is just one more human self-assertion, triggering its own ironic reversal and providing the occasion for others to fall victim to the same principle.

If these last two interpretations of the ending of *Hamlet* seem less convincing than the first, they do so only because they lack its familiarity and its comforting reassurance. These qualities may enhance the credibility of the first perspective, but this perspective by no means nullifies the other two. Shakespeare's mode of combination prevents that. Embracing multiplicity, it makes the clash of conflicting perspectives a fundamental aspect of the play. From this clash *Hamlet* acquires its essential fidelity to experience and thereby its genuinely tragic quality.

The Shifting View—*Rosmersholm*

In defending Ibsen's tendency to present exposition continually throughout the entire length of a play, Arthur Miller has praised this technique for its ability to ensure that "the present [will] be comprehended with wholeness, as a moment in a flow of time, and not—as with so many modern plays—as a situation without roots." [11] In most of Ibsen's later plays and especially in *Rosmersholm*, the retrospective method has even greater importance; not only does it help give the play its structure, but—and herein lies its primary value—it is also the major factor in determining the spectators' relationship to the action. Because of the retrospective method the basic facts of the dramatic situation emerge gradually and individually rather than all at once. Each new fact produces two effects: it forces the characters who do not already know it to readjust their positions, and it provides the spectators with increased understanding of a situation they had previously seen in a different light. Both effects necessarily cause a change in the spectators' intellectual and emotional participation. Since the facts that produce these changes emerge gradually, the perspective in which the action must be seen undergoes constant alteration.

The first act of *Rosmersholm* carefully establishes a clearly defined situation. It erects a conflict between old and new, between tradition and revolt, and it specifies the attitudes this conflict ought to evoke. Embodied by Kroll and closely associated with death, the past and its traditions are seen as inflexible and stifling. They foster oppression, decay, and gloom. The new, finding its embodiment in Rebecca, connotes, in contrast, life, vitality, and freshness. It promises enlightenment, ennoblement, freedom, and happiness. As indicated by the ease with which Rebecca overcomes Kroll, both before and during the struggle for Rosmer, the conflict seems to admit but one possible outcome: the old in its weakness must fall, while the new must prevail. In addition to defining this conflict and its likely result, the act also singles out the characters who will carry the burden of the action. The first of these is Rosmer. He has belonged to the past, and he still

[11] Introduction to *Arthur Miller's Collected Plays* (New York: Viking Press, 1957), p. 21.

shows his submission to it in his quiet nature and his fear of the footbridge. Despite these and other ties, he has managed a hesitant and tentative emancipation; given the necessary strength, he will free others from oppression and gloom by ennobling their minds. Second in importance only to Rosmer is Rebecca, whose support and encouragement will give him the strength he needs. For this reason, as well as because of her perfect embodiment of the new, Rebecca wins the spectators' approval and affection; her confidence and excellence guarantee the values they have been asked to accept. Nevertheless, their acceptance is not entirely free from doubt. Brendel's oddness tends to discredit both Rosmer and the course he pursues. Beata has died mysteriously in the millrace. Rebecca's role at Rosmersholm invites closer scrutiny.

As the first act ends, Ibsen summarizes what it has already established. Kroll, now knowing where Rosmer stands but believing that he and his fellow conservatives can force him to capitulate, says, "You're not the man to hold out standing alone" (p. 145). Rosmer replies, "I shall not be so entirely alone after all. There are two of us here to bear the loneliness." Kroll's reaction, in keeping with the kind of emphasis that similar hints have received, is abrupt, brief, enigmatic, and unfinished: "That too! Beata's words—!" But he refuses to explain what he means.

The events of Act II cast new light on the opening situation and vastly increase the spectators' tentative doubts. Kroll's renewed attempt to subdue Rosmer shows that he and the forces he upholds possess more strength than was previously realized. The sly, unprincipled Mortensgaard reveals that the spirit of revolt has qualities less admirable than those that Rosmer and Rebecca have ascribed to it. Far more important than the responses Kroll and Morgensgaard evoke through their behavior, however, is the information they contribute, for it develops the implication of Kroll's brief remark about Beata. This information, which convinces Rosmer that Beata must have killed herself because she had known of his changed views, is devastating for him. It deprives him of his feeling of "guiltlessness"—in other words, of his freedom from guilt—and thus it eliminates much of his emancipation. He now wonders how he can ever escape from "all the nagging memories—from the whole melancholy past" (p. 171).

Since Rebecca is both the chief embodiment of the new and the key to Rosmer's emancipation, the most important revelations of this act concern her. Kroll asks Rosmer if he knows "the really decisive reason why Beata ended her life" (p. 153), and Rosmer reminds him that she was "unfortunate, sick, irresponsible." One sign of this irresponsibility, he adds, was "her baseless, consuming self-reproaches." But these reflect adversely on Rebecca when Kroll recalls that there were at that time "books in the house dealing with the purpose of marriage—according to the advanced views of our time," and Rosmer must admit that they came from the library Rebecca's foster father had left her. Far more damning for Rebecca, however, is Kroll's account of two visits Beata paid him shortly before her death. During the first she had revealed that she knew of Rosmer's imminent apostasy—and Rebecca was the only one besides Rosmer who had reason to expect it. During the second visit, two days before her suicide, Beata had suddenly announced that her husband "must marry Rebecca at once" (p. 155). Kroll himself develops the implications of this disclosure when a short time later he adds his insinuation "that there is no gaping chasm between free thought . . . and free love" (p. 157). Mortensgaard then helps substantiate what Kroll has implied by relating the contents of a letter he had received from Beata. This letter's repetitious denial of "sinful things" and "sinful behavior" at Rosmersholm (p. 165), a defense preceding any accusation, suggests Beata's belief in their actuality.

These revelations call both the Rosmer-Rebecca alliance and Rebecca's character into question. But even more suspicious than anything said of her in this act is what Rebecca herself does. Rosmer learns that she has been eavesdropping during his interview with Kroll, and his disappointment suggests the kind of response Ibsen intends her act to elicit. Later, when Rosmer dwells inordinately on Beata's fate, Rebecca displays unmistakable fear: "Oh, don't talk about Beata! Don't think of Beata anymore!" (p. 167). She then unconditionally refuses to marry Rosmer, vowing that if he repeats his offer she will leave Rosmersholm, even, if necessary, "go the way Beata went" (p. 173). She had first acknowledged his proposal with obvious joy and excitement, and her apparent attitude toward him would seem to make acceptance inevitable; her refusal is therefore totally unexpected. It is partially explained, however, by her mention of Beata, which suggests that a guilty conscience holds her back, and this suggestion reduces belief in both her excellence of character and her utter freedom from the influence of the past. Significantly, when she returns at the beginning of Act III, she talks with Madam Helseth of Beata, at the same time picking up her crochet work (p. 177), the symbol of her partial capitulation to the things of the past. It is then but a few minutes later that Kroll amusedly forces her to admit that her emancipation may be only superficial, that "it has not got into [her] blood" (p. 188).

The interview producing this admission renews the struggle of the first act, but to some extent the roles have been reversed, and the outcome is completely different. Kroll is as inconsiderate and persistent as ever, but now his attitudes and opinions, if not his methods, seem less perverse. He begins the meeting by articulating the suspicions that have accrued to Rebecca in the preceding act. She has the power, he observes, to "bewitch" whomever she chooses (p. 184). He, however, now sees through her, now realizes that she had bewitched Beata, that she had deliberately wormed her way into Rosmersholm in order to gain some advantage for herself. Rebecca, he now knows, is a cold-hearted, calculating Machiavellian, and her innate immorality stems from a fact he has just discovered. Here Kroll releases his bombshell, and the spectators are given another significant revelation. Rebecca is immoral, Kroll points out, because she is illegitimate: her "foster father," with whom she lived after the death of her mother, was in reality her true father. The significant effect of this revelation is not, of course, what Kroll says but the response it provokes from Rebecca. Her outraged denial of his charge seems out of character, and her attempts to refute him embroil her in further difficulties; even Kroll perceives that more lies hidden than he has been able to uncover. Her response here and her admission to Rosmer in Act IV that she still has a secret in her past more appalling than anything she has yet confessed suggest incest. At any rate, whatever it is, the spectators now realize that she has a past to which she is shackled by bonds of guilt far more definitely and insolubly than Rosmer is to his.

The different outcome of this second struggle occurs as a result of what Rebecca now feels herself obligated to do. Before Kroll arrived she had learned from Rosmer how necessary to the fulfillment of his mission in life he regards gladness and the guiltlessness that instills it. Kroll's revelation has taught her how it feels to be crippled by guilt. She decides, therefore, that the only way she can free Rosmer is by confessing that it was she "who lured—who came to lure Beata into the labyrinthine ways . . . that led to the millrace" (III, p. 192). This shocking revelation tends to effect a tenuous balance in the spectators' attitude toward her, as their rapidly increasing disapproval here matches in force their diminishing admiration. The act of confessing demonstrates anew both her courage and her compassion for Rosmer. Her original deed, as she describes it, was inspired by the best of intentions: to free him completely, to give him the pure sunlight he needed, she had to release him from the gloom of his marriage. The deed itself rightly evokes, however, the horror and disgust it elicits from Rosmer; to achieve her noble ends she has willfully destroyed a human life.

This confession and its results also considerably readjust the spectators' relationship to the more abstract dimension of the action, the clash between the old and the new. Both in her original deed, with its design to bring light to Rosmer, and in her confession, with its design to restore this light, Rebecca works in behalf of the spirit of revolt. She affirms its urgency and its will to win at all costs; and she has, after all, made Rosmer "free from guilt" (p. 192). But her effort backfires, for she has also shown the disregard for basic human values which characterizes her cause. Furthermore, her confession costs her what little she had already gained. In his horror Rosmer now speaks of her in the third person (p. 192); as the act ends, he leaves the house with Kroll; neither of them bids her farewell or acknowledges her existence in any manner. For the first time in the play Kroll and his values seem not only more admirable but also more powerful. Since Rosmer and Rebecca have been defeated, they now merit the pitying epithet "poor" (*stakkers*) that Madam Helseth attaches to their names (III, p. 195, IV, p. 196). Before this it had been reserved for Beata.

When Rosmer and Rebecca meet for the last time, in Act IV, the signs of utter defeat are even more unmistakable. She is leaving Rosmersholm, returning to the north, going back "home" to the land from which she had come with such great expectations. She has abandoned all hope of achieving what she had set out to do. Rosmersholm, which she had planned to conquer, has "snapped [her] to bits" (p. 198) and "struck [her] powerless" (p. 201); she has had her "old courageous will clipped. And murdered." The Rosmer family view of life "has infected [her] will . . . and made it sick" (pp. 202–203), so that she no longer has the power to act. Rosmer too has been beaten, for the past has recaptured him. While he was gone he made his peace with Kroll, who, along with their other friends, has convinced him that the task of ennobling minds is not for him. Besides, he now realizes, the task itself is a hopeless one. He will attempt it no more. For the first time in the play Rebecca listens to his expressions of defeat in silence.

In his despair Rosmer accuses her of never having believed in him; he is convinced that she merely used him in fulfilling her own plans. His accusation prompts Rebecca to make her final confession, and through it emerges the last significant revelation of the retrospective action. As Kroll suspected, she had originally come to Rosmersholm with purely selfish motives; she wanted to "try my luck here" (p.200). Contact with Rosmer awakened in her a "wild, unconquerable desire" for him, and it was this, and this only, which inspired her to destroy Beata. Her revelation, which strips from her all pretense of noble purpose, fully exposes her unmitigated evil. The effect could scarcely be more horrifying, but for Rosmer its horror is compounded by the resemblance between her true motive and the "ungovernable, wild" sexuality that, as he has told Kroll, so disgusted him in Beata (II, p. 153). The increase in Rosmer's horror can only intensify the spectators' own response to Rebecca.

Rebecca's confession virtually completes the process begun in the opening act. It makes the original situation fully clear for the first time in the play. As a result, what Rebecca says and the effect her words have on Rosmer produce the last major adjustment in the point of view. The spectators are now invited to see the action in a perspective almost exactly opposite that which they had been compelled to assume at the beginning. This shift in perspective, which has taken place gradually through the entire play, results primarily from the retrospective method. But the process has also been intensified by other evolving patterns resulting from the examination of the liberal movement, from Rebecca's changing responses to the white horse, and from the alterations in the setting. When Brendel returns, the contrast between this visit and his prior visit will help solidify the new perspective's validity. The values asserted in the first act have evidently given way to their opposites. What then seemed admirable, powerful, and assured of success has now revealed its evil and its impotency.

The mode of combination Ibsen uses to organize the individual effects of *Rosmersholm* is, then, one that compels the audience to accept a constantly shifting, gradually evolving relationship to the dramatic action. If defines reality as a surface of deceptive appearances behind which lie other possibilities of greater validity and, often, of greater complexity. This mode of combination, with or without the retrospective method, easily lends itself to purely didactic purposes, to the discrediting of outworn attitudes or the substitution of one attitude for another, and something of this sort occurs frequently in the early plays of Shaw. Other dramatists, such as Anouilh and as Musset in *Fantasio*, use this mode of combination in a more strictly aesthetic manner: what they first present as comedy gradually reveals an underlying tragic quality, and in this way the modern dramatist manages to achieve the impact of tragedy in a world where, as Friedrich Duerrenmatt puts it, "the tragic is still possible even if pure tragedy is not." [12] This mode of combination has, moreover, an additional function which is lacking in the others, for from it arises the play's temporal dimension; unlike the *Oresteia* and *Hamlet*, in which the temporal dimension is a formal embodiment of the developing dramatic situation, in *Rosmersholm* and other plays that present a shifting view, the temporal dimension is established by the changes that occur in the spectators' increasing understanding.

Rosmersholm presents an extremely complicated use of this mode of combination, however, for when the shift in point of view has been completed, something more than a mere reversal has occurred. Not even Rebecca's second confession is entirely negative in effect. Despite Rosmer's conviction that he has failed in his life's purpose, Rebecca's confession proves that in one way at least he has been triumphant, and therefore so has she; in contrast to what she admits and to its effect on Rosmer is the fact

[12] "Problems of the Theatre," trans. Gerhard Nellhaus, in *Playwrights on Playwriting*, ed. Toby Cole (New York: Hill and Wang, 1961), p. 136.

that she can now confess only because living together with him has tamed her, has destroyed her capacity to act without regard to moral implications. As Rebecca herself puts it more positively, Rosmer "has ennobled [her] mind" (IV, p. 203). Her confession demonstrates, therefore, that the hope he had once embraced so eagerly was not a fantasy. Rosmer cannot believe that she is telling the truth, but he does believe that she now suffers in feeling guilt for her past, and consequently he tries to assure her that her "past is dead." Although he is fully convinced of his own powerlessness, he here adopts the role that had been characteristic of Rebecca in her earlier strength.

This aspect of Rebecca's confession shows that the original attitudes have not been completely superseded. Ibsen uses the shift in perspective in order to deepen rather than negate the original view. The primary result of the shift is that the final view becomes superimposed on the original so that the two merge in a single complex perspective. The audience must now accept a "truth" similar in its multiplicity to that of *Hamlet*, and Ibsen's treatment of the whole context in which Rebecca's confession occurs makes this complex perspective the only adequate means of viewing the action. Rebecca had conceived her earlier confession as the bringing of light; this one, she says, will give "light and shade to all the rest" (p. 199). And so it does. The spectators discover how evil she was only in discovering that she has been transformed to a state in which she regards her past behavior as a pattern of guilt demanding confession. The two impressions of her nature are inseparable; only through declaration of the old truth is the new truth completely rendered; but, simultaneously, the old truth undercuts the impact of the new. Nor does Ibsen allow the "transformation" itself to remain free of irony, for when Brendel also uses this word (p. 205), he is describing his own total collapse. Moreover, through Rebecca's confession Ibsen elaborates the play's nature symbols, which in the first act had helped define both the spirit of the new and Rebecca's allegiance to it. Her desire for Rosmer, she says, "came over me like a storm on the sea. It was like one of the storms we have up north in the winter time" (p. 201). This comparison establishes Rebecca's earlier self as an embodiment of wild nature—unfettered, powerful, inspiring, but wholly amoral. Now, in contrast, with her wings clipped, she has been tamed both literally and figuratively. Acclimatization to Rosmersholm has deprived her of freedom and vitality, but she has gained a moral sense. Life with Rosmer has replaced the storm with "stillness" (p. 202). He has endowed her soul with a new quality that calls up an entirely different image of nature: "There fell over me a peace of mind— a stillness, as on a fowling cliff under the midnight sun up at home." Increasing the complexity resulting from these contrasting images of nature is the juxtaposition of what Rebecca was to what she now is: half natural and half civilized, she conveys an impression only partially articulated by Brendel's denomination of her as a "mermaid" (p. 207). But the most fully rendered expression of this final complexity comes in Rebecca's ultimate realization of the significance of both her own experience and the action it helps to define: "The Rosmer view of life ennobles . . . but it kills happiness" (p. 203).

The complexity of their situation creates an impasse for Rosmer and Rebecca. He longs to believe that he has actually succeeded in ennobling her, but he cannot do so without evidence. She longs to convince him, for he will then be strong and free, but she does not know how. Here Brendel enters. He provides the suggestion that inspires their double suicide and thereby occasions the most emphatic instance of multiplicity in the entire play.

Some of the significance of their suicide arises from the meaning that Ibsen has assigned Beata's similar act. Through the play's various references to her death and particularly to the millrace where she drowned herself, this meaning, too, undergoes a rich development. When first mentioned by Madam Helseth as a place "where a thing like that's happened" (I, p. 122), the mill-race connotes unpleasantness, death, and finality. Kroll's later allusion to the "enigma of the millrace" (II, p. 159) indicates, however, that as symbol it defies easy formulation, and Rosmer perceives its inherent complexity when he refers to Beata's death there as a "poignant, accusing victory" (p. 169). Later references add a variety of particular significations. By threatening to go the way Beata went (p. 173), Rebecca alters Madam Helseth's place of unpleasantness into a haven. In the third act Rosmer equates the millrace with guilt (p. 180), and when he concludes that Beata drowned herself "for love of me—in *her* manner" (p. 181), he associates it with the kind of passion that disgusted him in Beata and that, as he will soon learn, motivated Rebecca. At the end of the act, when leaving with Kroll, Rosmer still fails to cross the footbridge (p. 194), and thus he once more establishes the millrace as a symbol of his inability to escape the past. Most of these individual significations are combined and transformed at the end of the play in Rebecca's final conception of the millrace as a place to expiate sin (IV, p. 211).

The symbolic richness of the millrace further validates the complex perspective established by the events of Act IV, and therefore the suicide of Rosmer and Rebecca is many things at one and the same time. From one point of view their suicide represents their final defeat. It is a logical outcome of their hopelessness and despair, and Brendel's exemplification of the futility of attempting to introduce ideals into the liberal movement adds one more proof of the bleakness of their future. The suggestions that they are driven to the millrace by the stifling house (p. 207) and that the white horse of Rosmersholm accompanies them on the bridge (p. 212) define their suicide as a victory for the past and its traditions over those who would seek to free themselves. Rosmer fears that suicide might mean acceptance of Beata's "perverted view of life" (p. 210), and when they have died, Madam Helseth announces that "the dead wife took them" (p.

THE IDIOM OF DRAMA

212). Nevertheless, other points of view are also relevant. If the suicide signifies their defeat, it also signifies triumph for them and for the spirit of the new; in death they will escape forever the forces that seek their defeat, and, moreover, by associating Brendel with Christ as he suggests this sacrifice, Ibsen implies that their death is some kind of salvation. But even the act itself indicates their triumph. Rebecca's willingness constitutes the play's most conclusive sign of her strength, courage, and desire to help Rosmer. Rosmer, now convinced of his success by this proof, not only regains faith in himself but also finally achieves full emancipation. His decision to join her changes him from a passive dreamer to a moral agent, and in committing suicide, he goes on the bridge for the first time since Beata's death. Both Rebecca and Rosmer have become strong and free. No longer does either lean for support on the other. When Rebecca asks, "Is it you who follow me? Or is it I who follow you?" his reply is unequivocal: "We two follow each other. I you and you me" (p. 212). A third view of the suicide, Rebecca's conception of it as expiation, tends to combine both the defeat and the victory. She feels that she must expiate her sins because she is now subject to "the Rosmersholm view of life." Rosmer, agreeing with her purpose, claims instead that it is their own "emancipated view of life" which makes expiation necessary and that though they will be paying for their sins, "there is no judgment over us. And therefore we must see to it that we judge ourselves" (pp. 210–211).

In its most important signification, however, their suicide represents the consummation of their marriage. Before going to the millrace, Rosmer lays his hand on Rebecca's head and marries her "as my true wife" (p. 211). While introducing the idea of suicide he had first requested that she perform an unspecified act for his *skyld*, which means both "sake" and "guilt" (p. 209). When she asked what he meant, he replied that he wanted her "to go the same way—that Beata went," and he added that it was necessary because of the one question he could never be rid of.

These speeches, which repeat crucial words, phrases, and ideas from the end of Act II, re-establish its central concern. There Ibsen had shown that in its ideal form their marriage promised victory and salvation, but that in becoming an actuality it would merely compound the guilt and evil that by implication characterized their current relationship. Now, however, by consummating their marriage in death, they can attain the ideal without fear of the destructive effects that its incarnation necessarily entails. In Act II, Rebecca had rejected Rosmer's offer by insisting that "never in this world" could she become his wife (p. 173). She was right: their marriage is not of this world.

In several instances the dialogue that ends the play articulates the multiple significance of their suicide. Rosmer anticipates it as a "fascinating horror" (IV, p. 210). Five consecutive speeches link it with three different views of life—those associated with Beata, Rosmersholm, and emancipation (pp. 210–211). It is, however, Madam Helseth's concluding speech that contains the richest expression of ambiguity. She sees something white, which is probably Rebecca's shawl but which also suggests the white horse. She calls on God to *forlade* "the sinful creatures," and her word, which means both "forgive" and "forsake," makes her sentence at once both a prayer for their salvation and a curse. The religious tone continues in the archaism of her final line—*Salig fruen tog dem*—and this statement is equally ambiguous, for it is not clear whether they were taken by the "dead wife" or the "blessed wife."

Madam Helseth's mention of "that white thing there" is especially instructive. Her words have an unusually rich impact, yet, like most details in drama, they signify almost nothing in themselves. Their impact is a result not of inherent meaning but of the context in which they are set. They refer, first of all, to a visual object, the shawl that Rebecca has draped about her before leaving the house. Since the shawl has already been emphatically associated with the white horse of Rosmersholm, and since Ibsen has already established Madam Helseth's superstitious nature, her words also suggest that the white horse—an important symbol of the power and influence of the past—confronts Rosmer and Rebecca on the bridge. This implication in turn derives further significance from the import that the metaphor of the white horse has acquired throughout the play as it is gradually reinterpreted by Rebecca's growing awareness. All in all, the various reverberations that Madam Helseth's inherently insignificant words awaken in the spectators' consciousness suggest that Rosmer and Rebecca have been destroyed by the forces of tradition that they had endeavored to escape. But this implication is itself fully meaningful only in relation to the complex perspective that has been established at the end of the play by Ibsen's manipulation of the entire action. It is, therefore, the mode of combination— whether it produces a single view as in *The Libation Bearers*, a double view as in *The Eumenides*, a multiple view as in *Hamlet*, or a shifting view as in *Rosmersholm*—through which the dramatist ultimately compels his spectators to see the dramatized experience in a perspective corresponding to his own.

Index

Action of depth, 64-67, 116
Aeschylus, 19-20
—*Agamemnon*, 78; characterization of Agamemnon, 91-98, 111; characterization of Clytaemestra, 74-75; chorus, 20-22, 36, 41; equivocality of universe in, 326-327; *see also* Aeschylus, *Oresteia*
   ll. 1-1068, 130-139; ll. 1-39 (Prologue), 15-16; ll. 160-183 (prayer to Zeus), 120-123; ll. 1069-1330 (Cassandra episode), 263-265
—*The Eumenides:* Apollo's argument, 73; chorus, 41, 337-338; full-scope analysis, 335-340; *see also* Aeschylus, *Oresteia*
   ll. 566-753 (trial scene), 235-237; conclusion, 271-273
—*The Libation Bearers*, 119; chorus, 41, 328-330; full-scope analysis, 327-335; *see also* Aeschylus, *Oresteia*
—*Oresteia*, 11; action of depth in, 66; audience foreknowledge and, 116-117; as example of explicit style of drama, 40; imagery, 176-192, 208, 339; parallel between

the murders of Agamemnon and Clytaemestra, 246-247; supernatural in, 302-305; temporal dimension, 299-305, 314, 362; "wisdom through suffering," 167-168, 179, 181-182
Agamemnon, see Aeschylus
Allusions, 168-174
Anouilh, Jean, 76, 362
Aristophanes, 76
Aristotle: *Poetics*, 3, 5, 280
Audience foreknowledge, 72-76, 116-120

Barish, Jonas A., 255 n
Bentley, Eric: on *Mourning Becomes Electra*, 119
Bentley, Gerald E., *see* Millett, Fred B.
Bergson, Henri: on farce, 203-204
Bethell, S. L.: on *Hamlet*, 30 n
"Bios Aischylou," 338 n
Bodkin, Maud, 315 n
Bowra, C. M., 337 n; on chorus of Greek tragedy, 19
Bradbrook, M. C., 22 n; on Elizabethan dramatic characters, 30; on Ibsen, 77; on ironic rever-

DATE DUE